PSYCHOEDUCATIONAL
FOUNDATIONS
OF
LEARNING DISABILITIES

PRENTICE-HALL SERIES IN SPECIAL EDUCATION
William M. Cruickshank, Editor

PSYCHOEDUCATIONAL
FOUNDATIONS
OF
LEARNING DISABILITIES

DANIEL P. HALLAHAN
University of Virginia

WILLIAM M. CRUICKSHANK
University of Michigan

Prentice-Hall, Inc., Englewood Cliffs, New Jersey

Library of Congress Cataloging in Publication Data

HALLAHAN, DANIEL P.
    Psychoeducational foundations of learning
disabilities

    (Prentice-Hall series in special education)
    Bibliography: p.
    1. Slow learning children.   2. Learning,
Psychology of.   3. Perceptual-motor learning.
I. Cruickshank, William M., joint author.   II. Title.
LC4661.H26   371.9′2   72-10543

ISBN 0-13-734285-3

10   9   8   7   6   5   4   3   2   1

PRINTED IN THE UNITED STATES OF AMERICA

Prentice-Hall International, Inc., London
Prentice-Hall of Australia Pty. Ltd., Sydney
Prentice-Hall of Canada, Ltd., Toronto
Prentice-Hall of India Private Limited, New Delhi
Prentice-Hall of Japan, Inc., Tokyo

Contents

Preface

This book is intended for those readers who wish to gain a comprehensive understanding of the problems and issues which face teachers and researchers in the field of learning disabilities today. The many and varied psychological and educational problems related to methods and research facing this ever-expanding field are presented within an historical, research, and practical perspective.

In the histories of special education and of the psychology of disability no issue has so suddenly captured the interest of parents, educators, pediatricians, psychologists, and the representatives of many other disciplines as has that generally termed "learning disabilities." Poor as the term is, still illusive of any meaningful definition, it has caught the imagination of those who serve children and of those who want children served. In the short period of a decade the term has attracted not only the attention of thousands of professional people and tens of thousands of parents, but it also has developed a mystique of its own. In many circles it is no longer the issue of learning disabilities, but the profession of Learning Disabilities.

Inherent in the rapid growth of this area of child development are problems which the unitiated often do not perceive. All is not well in the learning disability fraternity. It is an arena in education and psychology which can be characterized, as Winston Churchill once did in speaking of a colleague, as "profoundly superficial."

This book has been prepared in an effort to provide a perspective for both the researcher and the classroom teacher to the growth which has been experienced in this young field of professional effort. The book addresses itself essentially to two aspects of child growth and development which are related to specific learning disability, namely, psychological and educational factors. We have endeavored to organize the research, often limited in scope and depth, in a meaningful manner which will indicate, not only what the status of current knowledge is, but what the areas are which require much further elaboration and investigation. If the field of psychoeducational study in specific learning disability is put into an organized and historical order, the present and future generations of practitioners and researchers should move more easily to confront issues that are pressing for solution.

The issue of specific learning disabilities is often a matter of human neurology and of those things which contribute to a faulty neurological system. In this connection we have devoted some attention (Chapter 2) to the issues of environmental and nutritional deprivation as possible factors (in addition to accidents, injuries, and illnesses) which, at a prenatal, perinatal, or early postnatal period, may affect perception, intelligence or learning.

At the same time that further research into possible etiological factors is needed, we have strongly stressed in this book that the *behavior* of the learning disabled child must be foremost in the minds of researchers, and especially teachers. The teacher must deal with the everyday behavior of the child with little consideration of etiology. At the present time, the behavior of the child, *not* the cause of the behavior, must be what dictates the teacher's methods and materials.

Another implicit theme of the book is that the educational and psychological issues of the field of learning disabilities are not of sole concern to the learning disabilities theorist or practitioner. The breadth of learning problems of the learning disabled child warrant, in fact demand, that specialists in other areas of exceptionality become involved in these crucial issues. The teacher and researcher can learn much from the professionals in other areas of exceptionality. If strides are to be taken forward, ultimately we must consider the specific learning problems of children and not categorical labels.

This book points up the fact that Act One of the drama of specific learning disabilities is over. The time of the instant specialist and the dilettante must be brought to an early demise. What is illustrated in this volume is that much hard work involving research in both the basic and the applied fields related to psychological development and specific learning disability is needed—research that will stand the tests of appropriate design, implementation, and report. Careers in research in these fields exist for both the young person entering the profession and for those who have had longer experience with it. Children with specific learning disabilities do not need more untested educational recipes, theories, or assumptions. At both state and national levels energies must be harnessed that will bring the unsolved problems of these children to the point of basic understanding and subsequently permit the organization of service programs for them at all governmental levels in the nation.

D.P.H.
W.M.C.

Acknowledgments

We are indebted to many individuals for their direct and indirect assistance in the development of this book. Several persons around whom themes of this book are woven have not only made a direct input into the contents of the manuscript, but have also later read what we have written and provided critical comments to make these sections even more accurate. Among these persons are Arthur Benton, Marianne Frostig, William Gaddes, Gerald Getman, Katrina de Hirsch, Newell Kephart, and Ralph Reitan. To them we express a great deal of appreciation, for they have devoted considerable time to our manuscript in the interests of accuracy and historical fact. Mrs. Marie Strauss has also provided us with very helpful information on some matters relating to the writings of her late husband, Alfred A. Strauss. Samuel A. Kirk graciously provided us with information leading to the organization of the Association for Children with Learning Disabilities and added his recollections to those of one of the authors of the initial meeting of the Professional Advisory Board of ACLD.

At the University of Michigan several faculty members have contributed much by way of advice, reading, and critique of portions of the manuscript. We are indebted in particular to Professors John Hagen, William C. Morse, William C. Rhodes, and Percy Bates.

James Whitney, an undergraduate student at the University of Michigan, has played a particularly significant role as a research assistant in collecting and tabulating abstracts, in summarizing and in preparing some of the manuscript in its initial drafts. His important contribution has been of great assistance.

Rick McNelly also made significant contributions to the preparation of the manuscript in its early stages. Walter Kwik, Wallace Long, and John Schommer have performed important support services and functions along the way. We also thank Joan G. Kodner for her contribution in abstracting articles and typing during the early months of the project. Our thanks are owing also to Miss Edith Klein and to Mrs. Patricia Borden for their typing of the manuscript and for editorial suggestions.

Particular gratitude is extended to Mrs. Judy Hallahan for her major contributions to the manuscript through careful editing, writing, and rewriting, and helping us say what we really wanted to say.

PSYCHOEDUCATIONAL
FOUNDATIONS
OF
LEARNING DISABILITIES

CHAPTER 1

Introduction

With the advent and growth of the study of learning disabilities during the 1960s, a totally new area of exceptionality was suddenly created and began its astonishing expansion. Such growth never has been experienced by any other discipline within special education in such a short period of time. A cursory glance at the university training programs around the United States, at the public school special education classes, and at the most recent educational publications attests to the fact that learning disabilities has become established as a predominant area of concern. In terms of popularity, in fact, it has become a chief contender for first place.

A merely superficial look at this phenomenal growth rate might lead one to the erroneous conclusion that learning disabilities was solely a child of the decade of the 1960s. Although the field undoubtedly enjoyed its greatest growth during that decade, it is a major hypothesis of this book that its origins sprang from work done in the 1930s by individuals within the area of mental retardation.

The astounding growth of this field of childhood education has not been without its problems, nor has it yet resulted to any significant degree in either national or local programs of quality. In contradistinction, confusion and misconception too often appear to characterize the education of children with learning disabilities. An examination of the development of the education of the mentally retarded child will help to bring into focus some of the problems we perceive in the area of learning disabilities.

While the education of mentally retarded children has not always been of the highest quality, in the United States the field has been organized and accountable since the middle of the nineteenth century. Although the program, nationally, was oriented more toward service than toward training of personnel, it *was* organized. It has developed professional parameters, and in 1918 the first formalized teacher education was begun. Between 1920 and 1945 some concepts of curriculum were developed, and a limited amount of basic research was undertaken. Most significant, however, was the development of a small cadre of knowledgeable college professors who were actively employed in teacher education in colleges and universities. Thus, precedents regarding education of the retarded existed, a point of view on which there was general agreement had evolved, and some qualified college professors with a good base of experience were preparing small numbers of teachers.

Against this background of readiness, the parent movement began in the early part of the decade of 1940. Parents acting through state and federal governments were exceedingly effective in creating legislation and in causing it to be implemented on behalf of their children. This legislation, with related new state and federal funds, was superimposed on precedent and enabled a small but significant reservoir of qualified university professors to carry out teacher training. When the factors related to professional growth finally became available, the base already existed which permitted forward movement to exploit the new supports. The subsequent stimulation through Public Law 85–924 as later amended by Public Law 88–164 solidified the parental efforts of the preceding decade and resulted in a strong and vital national program.

There are important differences, however, between developments in the field of mental retardation and those in the area of learning disabilities. In subsequent chapters we will trace this history in detail. Here it will suffice to say that in contrast to mental retardation no precedents for program development existed in learning disabilities.

A few professional leaders were concerned with children who demonstrated unique learning characteristics as early as the late 1920s and early 1930s. They were working in isolation from one another and the impact of their efforts was to be felt only very modestly, thirty years later. Even these early efforts came more than seventy-five years after the beginning of similar work for the mentally retarded. During the late 1930s and the 1940s the number of persons concerned with children with specific learning disabilities was still very small, and the focus of these individuals was directed to clinical research rather than education.

In the face of the paucity of research, very limited personnel, and no teacher education, parents of children later defined as those with learning disabilities, taking their cue from the successes of parents of the mentally retarded and cerebral palsy children, undertook efforts to become an important national and local force. These lay people moved into a field characterized by vacuums, by a lack of knowledge, and by almost no personnel. Parents were ahead of the professionals. In large measure the cart was before the horse.

In 1960 when the parent program began to pick up momentum, there existed an absolute minimum of educational research regarding these children. Considerable exploratory research had been done in the area of psychopathology, but this had not been well corroborated, nor had it been translated into educational research or programs. The universities were not in a position to respond to the growing pressure for service programs. Few if any qualified college professors had had any experience with these children through direct contact, clinical programs, or research. Consequently, no teachers were available, nor were any being prepared to respond to the parental pressure for community programs. The parent movement was mounted, however, and it increased rapidly. From a state of practically no visibility in 1960, the annual national conventions of the parent group drew registrations of several thousands before 1970.

Parental pressure at the state and particularly at the local levels on superintendents of schools and school board members resulted in activity which, lamentably, was not accompanied by administrative understanding or by a supply of adequately prepared personnel. Neither existed. School administrators nevertheless began organizing classes. Any teacher who expressed interest in the problem was immediately appointed as the learning disability specialist, often with no more than three weeks of informal, summer-workshop training. School psychologists likewise found a whole new arena for the application of their tests, in spite of their lack of a fundamental understanding of the problem. Such developments were unequaled in professional education in the United States.

Local educators began to exert pressure on colleges and universities for qualified teachers, psychologists, and other professional personnel. None were available, but universities responded in the best way they could. Frequently, professors with an *interest,* but without experience or formal preparation, were appointed as specialist professors and as directors of programs for learning disabilities. Indeed it was the decade of the dilettante and the instant specialist in the university, as well as in the public school.

LEARNING DISABILITY AS A CATEGORY

As we will demonstrate in later chapters, the earliest formal research interests related to this field were centered in the area of the mentally retarded, specifically with exogeneous retarded children. The subsequent confusion regarding terminology has been discussed elsewhere, and need not be elaborated upon here (Cruickshank and Paul, 1971). Numerous terms began to appear in the literature, i.e., brain injury, perceptual handicap, exogeneous, *ad infinitum,* as a growing number of authors tried to describe the problem. Multiple terminology further confused the conceptualization of the field.

Some lay organizations had already formed. Chief among them were the associations which utilized the terms *"brain injured children"* and *"perceptually handicapped."* A common tie existed to bring these separate groups together logically, but allegiance to preferred terminologies prevented a merger for several years.

A conference to explore the problems of the perceptually handicapped was held by parents in Chicago on April 6, 1963. Dr. Samuel A. Kirk, then of the University of Illinois, addressed the meeting. His remarks are important in considering the matter historically. The issue of what to call these children was uppermost in the minds of many of the conference participants, who not only wanted better labels for their own children but also sought a term which would draw the various small organizations together into a large and politically powerful group (Kirk, 1963). Kirk was truly eloquent as he sought to provide counsel to parents in their search for a common base on which to organize efforts for their children.

> I know that one of your problems at this meeting is to find a term that applies to every child. Last night, a friend of mine accosted me with the statement, "We're going to ask you to give us a term." I didn't know how to answer his question, and I still do not believe I can answer it because the term you select should be dependent on your specific aims. Is your purpose a research one, or is it a management and training problem [Kirk, 1963]?

Then, by excluding children with certain sensory impairments, Kirk simultaneouly tried to call attention to a group of children who were then only vaguely understood.

> Any group that meets to discuss the problems of children with developmental deficits of one kind or another is facing a formidable task. I say a formidable task because no one yet has been able to present us with a solution to the management and training of these children. If we had a fool-proof solution to the management and training of deviations in children, this meeting would not be necessary. And the fact that there are so many diverse opinions and partial solutions should make this meeting highly interesting and hopefully challenging.
>
> As I understand it, this meeting is not concerned with children who have sensory handicaps, such as the deaf or the blind, or with children who are mentally retarded, or with delinquent or emotionally disturbed children caused by environmental factors. It is concerned primarily with children who can see and hear and who do not have marked general intellectual deficits, but who show deviations in behavior and in psychological development to

such an extent that they are unable to adjust in the home or to learn by ordinary methods in school. The causes of these behavior deviations have been postulated as some sort of cerebral dysfunction.

Kirk expanded this theme when he remarked:

There are two kinds of terms that have been applied to these children, either alone or in combination.

The first group of terms refer to causation or etiology. We try to label the child with a term that has biological significance. These terms are brain injury, minimal brain damage, cerebral palsy, cerebral dysfunction, organic driven-ness, organic behavior disorders, psychoneurological disorders, and a host of other terms. All of these terms refer to a disability of the brain in one form or another as an explanation of the deviant behavior of the child.

The second group of terms refers to the behavior manifestations of the child, and include a wide variety of deviant behavior. Terms such as hyperkinetic behavior, perceptual disorders, conceptual disorders, Strauss syndrome, social dyspraxia, catastrophic behavior, disinhibition, learning disorders, and the various forms of aphasia, agnosia, dyslexia and a host of other terms which describe the specific behavior deficit of the child.

He further stated:

Research workers have attempted to correlate the biological malfunctions with behavior manifestations. Actually the job of the neurophysiologists and the physiological psychologist is to explain deviations of the brain and their effect on emotional, perceptual, and cognitive behavior, or vice versa, to explain the behavior manifestations by finding the correlated brain dysfunction. This is a research task and of particular concern to the research neurophysiologist and physiological psychologist.

As I understand it, the task of the group meeting today, however, is not to conduct research on behavior and the brain, but to find effective methods of diagnosis, management, and training of the children. From this point of view, you will not be so concerned with the first category of concepts relating to etiology of brain injury or cerebral dysfunction, but with the behavior manifestations themselves and with the methods of management and training of the deviations in children. . . . I have felt for some time that labels we give children are satisfying to us but of little help to the child himself. We seem to be satisfied we can give a technical name to a condition. This gives us the satisfaction of closure. We think we know the answer if we can give the child a name or a label—brain injured, schizophrenic, autistic, mentally retarded, asphasic, etc. As indicated before, the term "brain injury" has little meaning to me from a management or training point of view. It does not tell me whether the child is smart or dull, hyperactive or under-active. It does not give me any clues to management or training. The terms cerebral palsy, brain injured, mentally retarded, aphasic etc., are actually classification terms. In a sense they are not diagnostic if by diagnostic we mean an assessment of a child in such a way that leads to some form of treatment, management, or remediation. In addition, it is not a basic cause, since the designation of a child as brain injured does not really tell us why the child is brain injured or how it got that way.

Kirk's comments were indeed the predecessors of the movement discussed since by numerous authors concerned with noncategorical labeling of children (e.g. Herbert Quay, T. Ernest Newland) and with the development of educational models based on psychoeducational characteristics of children (Cruickshank, 1967). His position was also fundamental to his development of the Illinois Test of Psycholinguistic Abilities, a significant diagnostic tool directed away from medical categories and toward psychological functions of a child. With some further preliminary remarks, Kirk presented to the parents for the first time the term "learning disabilities."

> I often wonder why we tend to use technical and complex labels, when it is more accurate and meaningful to describe behavior. If we find a child who has not learned to talk, the most scientific description is that he has not yet learned to talk. The labels of aphasia or mentally retarded or emotionally disturbed are not as helpful as a description and may, in many instances, tend to confuse the issue. Instead of using the term hyperkinetic we would understand the child better if the observer states that he continually climbs walls or hangs on chandeliers.
>
> I should like to caution you about being compulsively concerned about names and classification labels. Sometimes names block our thinking. I would prefer that people inform me that they have a child that does not talk instead of saying to me their child is dysphasic. People apparently like to use technical terms. I have received letters from doctors and psychologists telling me that "we are referring a child to you who has strephosymobila." I would prefer that they tell me that "the boy has been in school two years, and he hasn't yet learned to read even though his intelligence is above average." This description of the problem is more scientific than the label "strephosymbolia," since the latter term itself has a specific meaning. It actually means the child has twisted symbols because of lack of cerebral dominance. But it is used by some people to designate a child who is retarded in reading, regardless of the cause.
>
> Recently, I have used the term "learning disabilities" to describe a group of children who have disorders in development in language, speech, reading, and associated communication skills needed for social interaction. In this group I do not include children who have sensory handicaps such as blindness or deafness, because we have methods of managing and training the deaf and the blind. I also exclude from this group children who have generalized mental retardation. This approach has led me and my colleagues to develop methods of assessing children, or describing their communication skills in objective terms. . . .

A responsive chord was struck. Kirk's logical thinking challenged his listeners. His suggestion of a term essentially positive in nature produced a positive response from many who were anxious to place their child in the most favorable light. During a meeting on the evening following Kirk's address, after lengthy and frequently heated discussion, the convention voted to organize itself as the Association for Children with Learning Disabilities.

In February 1964, Kirk was asked by members representing the Association (Ms. Dolly Holstrom and Dr. Esther Burbridge) to suggest names of persons for a Professional Advisory Board. The committee was appointed that month but did not hold its first meeting until the annual convention of the Council for Exceptional Children in Chicago in the spring of 1965. Attending that first meeting were Raymond Barsch, Ross Beall, William Cruickshank, Marianne Frostig, William Gellman, Newell Kephart, Laura Lehtinen, and Helmer Myklebust, with Kirk acting as chairman. Many of these individuals have served on the Board for several years.

While numerous topics were examined during the first meeting, it is recalled that the term *learning disabilities* was a topic of considerable discussion. It was a term not heretofore used by any members of the Professional Advisory Board, and it was unfamiliar to several. As the definition of the term became apparent to the members (who were practically surrounded by parents intent on seeing how these professionals operated), there developed a general agreement that the term was one with which the professionals could live. In a large sense, this confirmation by a small group of professional persons of an action taken by the parents several months earlier, assured that the term *learning disabilities* would shortly be found in general use. Indeed, contrary to the hopes of Kirk, another category was born!

A PANDORA'S BOX IS OPENED

The nine members of the Professional Advisory Board, together with the parents themselves, failed to appreciate what had been created through the recognition of the term *learning disability*. Whereas Kirk had cautioned against the use of "technical terms" and had urged his listeners to describe the behavior of children, the professionals and the parents were not ready for such a sophisticated approach. Learning disabilities, with all its positive connotations, quickly became a focal point for superintendents, psychologists, teachers, legislators, parents, college professors, and many others. In some cases, it was accepted with religious fervor. Few observers recognized that in the creation of a new term the undergirding of research, competent professionals, and appropriate conceptualization of intervention processes were almost completely lacking. Members of the Professional Advisory Board to the Association, as detailed later, all had a relatively common understanding of the nature of the children to whom the new term was being applied. Kephart, Lehtinen, and Cruickshank had developed their concepts from the same sources. Barsch had received a similar orientation a few years afterward. The positions of these four early leaders were not far removed from those of Frostig and Myklebust. Although influenced early in his career by Ruth Monroe, Kirk had also had an exposure to the problem similar to that of the original Michigan group of Kephart, Lehtinen, and Cruickshank. Once a member of the Michigan professional group himself, Kirk also had continuing close contact with Alfred Strauss after the latter had moved to Racine, Wisconsin.

Because each knew essentially what the other members meant as the new term was applied and used, the Board members of ACLD quickly were able to accept the term learning disabilities. Common backgrounds of experience, frequent personal and professional contacts, and the writings of each provided a mutal base of operation. It would have been strange indeed if these men and women could not have agreed quickly on a new term. On the other hand, while it was recognized that non-categorical terms were advantageous and that parents needed a term reflecting essentially positive characteristics, in that first meeting some expressed the feeling that the term learning disability did not exactly express the crux of the problem. This feeling was widespread and has proven to be the case in subsequent years. Nevertheless, the term was adopted by the Advisory Board.

If everyone using the term learning disabilities had read and accepted its limitations by Kirk, some of the ensuing problems would not have arisen. Idyllic situations, of course, are rare. The term learning disabilities quickly took on meanings never anticipated by the newly-formed Professional Advisory Board to the Association. Before long, confusion became compounded. Despite the lack of a large reservoir of trained professionals in this field and the dearth of research and writing to provide a common definition, children with all sorts of problems, related or unrelated, were placed into classes for the "learning disabled" under the guidance of inadequately trained teachers. Personnel conducting diagnosis and placement often had no adequate concept of the problem. In his original presentation, Kirk had specifically excluded children with "sensory handicaps, delinquent or emotionally disturbed children caused by environmental factors," and other categories. Nevertheless, practicing educators and administrators, failing to see the core of the problem, quickly assumed that, since all of these children had learning problems from one point of view, they were logical candidates for a class of learning disabled children. Nothing could have been farther from the truth as the term was originally discussed by members of the Professional Advisory Board of the ACLD.

Classes for mentally retarded children have often been criticized as being "dumping grounds" for the benefit of school personnel who could not solve certain problems in children. This criticism could apply a hundred fold to the typical public school program for learning disabilities.

Reading problems, emotional problems, management problems, intellectual problems, speech problems, handwriting problems, and others, irrespective of their etiology or symptomatology are found grouped together on the premise that each is a learning problem. While the latter point may be valid, the administrative decision regarding placement does not result in a positive intervention program when heterogeneity within a class exhausts the capacity of a teacher to encompass individual differences, particularly when the teacher lacks training in some very complex aspects of teaching. Thus, the practical result of the new term quickly went far beyond its original conceptualization and understanding by some members of the Professional Advisory Board. Indeed, the popularization and misuse of the term could easily undermine its usefulness. The conversations of parents, legislators, young college instructors, physicians, psychologists, social workers, or school administrators make us realize that there is little consensus regarding learning disability. Confusion is everywhere.

AN ERROR IS MADE

The most significant early work fundamental to the issue of learning disabilities was undertaken with a subtype of mentally retarded children knows as exogenous. Existing research regarding the psychopathology of intellectually normal children in large meausre stems from the earlier studies with exogenous children, who constitute a major segment of the total population of the mentally retarded.

In his 1963 speech to the parent group, Kirk specifically ruled out the mentally retarded from his original conceptualization of learning disability. He did so not so much to urge parents to ignore the significant work which had been undertaken with exogenous mentally retarded children as to clarify an issue for a group of lay people. The parents, however, were all too ready to focus their attention on children of normal intelligence. Many of them already had sufficient problems with their children and were glad to be told that retardation need not be another. Some competition from other parent groups concerned with categorization further prompted ACLD to exclude retardation from its purview.

With such action, however, ACLD failed to recognize the historical fact that much of what is known about specific learning disabilities was derived from research into mental retardation. More important, it ruled out of the ACLD concern (at least psychologically) thousands of parents of mentally retarded "learning disabled" children of an exogenous type. This was unfortunate, for an opportunity was missed to diversify the education of mentally retarded children whose problems are clinically different from those of endogenous children. Also lost was the reciprocal benefit that could have been realized for both retarded and intellectually normal children whose learning disabilities stemmed from exogenous factors. Educators in particular continue to ignore the logical programmatic interrelations with subsequent losses to both groups of children.

While of the utmost importance, what Kirk and some others sought to do in describing children rather than in speaking of categories, has not been effective for these reasons. On the contrary, in large measure, their suggestions unwittingly excluded many children from the focus of those concerned with learning disabilities. The emphasis on description of behavior may have been suggested by Kirk before his listening audience and the great practitioner group of professionals were ready to receive and use it appropriately. No matter how significant the concept, the confusion and lack of logic observed in the field of learning disabilities make one realize that the profession was unready and unable to meet the challenge of a new idea.

THIS BOOK

Amidst programmatic confusion, a vast amount of recent literature has been concentrated on the child with learning disabilities. We feel that this literature should be organized, both to provide an orientation for the student and to assist in the refinement of the omnibus term, "learning disability." We feel also that etiological concepts may help to clarify definition of terminology. Therefore, while *issues of etiology are essentially assumptions insofar as human beings are concerned,* space has been allocated to this issue. No attempt has been made here, however, to deal with etiological problems of a neurological nature. While it is our thesis that much of the behavior of many children described as "learning disabled" must ultimately be considered within a neurological framework, this book will not treat specific neurological conditions giving rise to learning dysfunction.

Chapter 2, devoted essentially to the impact of nutritional and environmental deprivation on the developing organism, hypothesizes a relationship among these factors, neurological disturbance, and subsequent perceptual and learning problems.

Chapter 3 follows the history of learning disabilities by focusing on the figures and issues that were the prime movers in its genesis and development.

Chapter 4, through a systematic analysis of the literature, places within an historical framework the concerns and issues germane to the development of the concepts of learning disabilities.

Chapters 5, 6, and 7 are concerned primarily with some major psychological and psychoeducational issues which have arisen from the work of key historical figures in the field. Chapter 5 deals with the relationship between perceptual-motor and cognitive development; chapter 6 presents an analysis of research studies concerned with the efficacy of perceptual-motor training; and chapter 7 discusses the problems of attention and motor control.

The final chapter includes our thinking regarding directions to be taken by the field in the years immediately ahead.

CHAPTER 2

Etiological Factors

The problems of the great majority of children described as "learning disabled," in our opinion, are fundamentally based in neurological function or dysfunction. In large part, the confusion characteristic of the field of education for children with learning disabilities is due to the failure of professional persons to circumscribe the problem and relate it to the neurological system.

Neither the disciplines of neurology nor those of psychology yet have the techniques available always to be able to determine the precise nature of the neurological disturbance or its parameters. This disciplinary immaturity, however, does not obviate the fact that learning is physical and is related to cellular activities of the organism. Perception, memory, reasoning, comprehension, and motivation are all dependent upon the operation of a complex neurophysiological system.

There is no doubt that some children's learning problems are caused by environmental factors. Poor teaching and poor learning situations, for instance, can cause learning disorders of a type. Emotional and also physical tensions may result in measurable school maladjustment problems and may affect learning, but may not be a matter caused by neurological dysfunction or damage. Parental antagonisms, poor home environments, imperfect adult-child relationships also may play a part in the production of poor learning habits. Careful differential diagnosis, however, should isolate children with these experiences from those whose learning disorders are based on perceptual psychopathology, which in turn is embedded in neuorological dysfunction. A complicating factor in this regard, however, is the common observation that many children possess all or most of the behavioral characteristics of psychopathology recognized as being related to neurological dysfunction, even though neurological findings are negative. One of the great frustrations experienced by neurologists and clinical psychologists is their inability to ascertain specifically the nature of the neurological disorder in all cases, particularly when observable subject behavior indicates the presence of a nonidentifiable disturbance of a physical nature. Until more refined diagnostic techniques are available, however, we readily include these *suspect* cases among those where positive findings are available. These are the children toward whom Strauss, Werner, Cruickshank, Frostig, Kephart, Orton, and others writing in the same general view have addressed a concern.

We feel strongly that functional causes may bring about the abnormal development of certain learning patterns in the child without necessarily causing cellular disturbances. For example, it may be that a child can learn to be hyperactive or may, through lack of experiences, not learn or develop appropriate perceptual-motor behaviors. Educational programming for the learning disabled child with demonstrable neurological impairment and for the learning disabled child without brain injury should be virtually the same if the *behaviors* of the two are alike.

Confusion abounds today, however, since professional persons in almost every discipline, without adequately specifying exhibited behaviors, frequently place the child who is failing in school into a class for the learning disabled (or for the mentally retarded) simply because he comes from an economically deprived environment. Unfortunately, current definitions of learning disabilities exclude children with learning difficulties due to environmental influences. While they ensure that poor children will not be misplaced in classes for the learning disabled, they ignore those economically disadvantaged children who display behaviors identical to those of middle class children appropriately placed in learning disabilities classes. The consequence of all this is that many children of culturally different backgrounds are assigned to classes for the mentally retarded, while middle class children exhibiting the same behavioral characteristics are placed in classes for the learning disabled. It is, thus, our opinion that children who have learning problems due to environmental conditions should *not* be excluded from learning disability programs.

In addition to the neurological and nonphysical conditions which gave rise to problems of learning, it is necessary to deal with another causative factor, inadequate nutrition. Thus, three major aspects of human development, either separately or in combination with one another, may be influential in producing neurological damage and a resulting perceptual dysfunction related to specific learning disorders. These include (1) specific neuroclinical issues, (2) nutritional deprivation, and (3) factors of environmental deprivation.

NEUROCLINICAL FACTORS

Because the etiological factors of a neurological nature which are related to learning disabilities and neurology have been delineated in the literature frequently, we will not include them in this volume. Some data are included so that the relation between neurological dysfunction and psychopathology in children will be viewed from our perspective.

Cerebral palsy is a recognized neurological problem characterized essentially by its variety of gross- and fine-motor manifestations. In earlier work by one of the authors, Cruickshank and his associates (Cruickshank, Bice, Wallen and Lynch, 1965), intensively examined 325 children of the athetoid and spastic types of cerebral palsy, all of whom were relatively homogeneous regarding a variety of variables. Subjects included in the study were between the ages of 6 years and 15 years, 11 months. A group of 110 normal children was included as a control.

On a test requiring visual differentation of figure from background, both spastic and athetoid children showed distinct psychopathology as compared to the normal children, although the athetoids were more comparable to normals than were those diagnosed as spastic. Chronological age differences were noticeable when comparisons were made between athetoid and normal groups *versus* the spastic group. Similar findings were produced by additional tests involving more gross visual-motor skills, tactual perception in relation to fine-motor movement, and the capacity of cerebral palsy children to perceive accurately in relation to increased time for perception.

In these studies, the existence of perceptual dysfunctions, upon which learning to read is directly based, was obvious and identifiable in a population of children with specific and diagnosible neurological dysfunction. Neurological damage as a neuroclinical entity is seen here as being directly related to perceptual and learning malfunction. The literature contains so many examples of this relationship that it would be redundant to include them. This is not true, however, of the other two etiological factors mentioned.

In relation to the role of nutritional and environmental deprivation as etiological factors in the production of cellular dysfunction and the resulting specific perceptual disorders, the literature is not nearly so definitive as with regard to cerebral palsy, epilepsy, dyslexia, or other clinical categories. It is hypothesized, however, that severe nutritional or environmental deprivation continued over a sufficient length of time during crucial human growth stages may result in neurological malfunction, cellular atrophy, or in other types of cellular change, the end result of which may be the psychomotor characteristics associated with specific learning disorders.

NUTRITIONAL FACTORS, MENTAL RETARDATION, AND LEARNING PROBLEMS

Scope of the Problem

It has been known for a long time that malnutrition can result in limited physical growth. Only in relatively recent years has the question of a possible connection between nutrient deficiency and learning impairment come under serious scrutiny. Furthermore, most of the available literature considers nutritional deprivation in relation to mental retardation. In some cases mental retardation is both physical and neurological, and if nutritional deprivation can have an impact on intellectual level, it is suggested that it may also have an impact on cellular activities related to perception, attention and other learning-related phenomena. Specifically, protein-calorie malnutrition, the most common form of nutritional disease, is believed by many investigators to cause neural tissue disturbances resulting in mental retardation. It is hypothesized that if mental retardation can develop from protein-caloric malnutrition, as a result of neural tissue disturbances, deprivation may also have an impact on cellular activities related to perception, attention, and other learning-related phenomena, which constitute the bases for specific learning disabilities considered in this book. It is further believed by some observers that such disabilities are often irreversible in nature, except through training or as a result of changes which may be a product of maturation, the nature of which is not yet fully understood. This connection would seem wholly logical, for the organism's intake of nutrients is, of course, a primary determinant of growth and development. Also, the brain and its functions would seem to be as much subject to biochemical and metabolic forces as any other organ (Pearson, 1968). The gathering of experimental evidence to support these hypotheses has proven to be a task of great complexity, and at present the available knowledge is much more *suggested* than *conclusive* (Johnson, 1968). At this point, the surface has been barely scratched regarding an understanding of the vital physiological and biochemical questions about the relationship of nutrition to central nervous system development, metabolic processes, and the molecular components of learning, to say nothing of the intricate network of sociocultural factors which enmeshes research based on human populations.

Some comparatively complete knowledge concerning the prevalence of the problem of malnutrition throughout the world is available. It is known, for instance, that the incidence of early malnutrition in most areas of the world has reached such proportions that the disease is responsible, directly or indirectly, for more deaths during childhood than all other causes combined (Eichenwald and Fry, 1969). Further it is known that malnutrition is primarily confined to economically deprived populations, as illustrated here in Figure 1 (Béhar, 1968). Incidence studies indicate that the average height and weight (a common indicator of malnutrition in large populations) of low social economic status children from under-developed countries is consistently below the sixteenth percentile for children of the United States and Western Europe, while the heights and weights of their more well-to-do counterparts are comparable to those of children in the industrialized nations (Scrimshaw, 1967). In raw numbers, this means that at least 75 percent of preschool children in developing countries, or 60 percent of the world's total preschool population (approximately 350 million children), suffer from mild to severe protein-

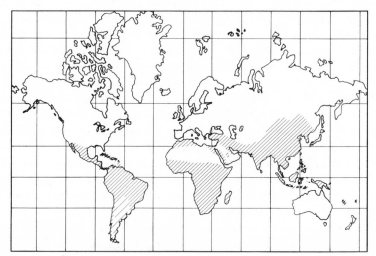

FIGURE 1   Geographic distribution of protein-calorie malnutrition (PCM).

Source: Béhar, M., Prevalence of malnutrition among preschool children of developing countries. In *Malnutrition, learning, and behavior,* N. S. Scrimshaw and J. E. Gordon (eds.). Cambridge, Mass.: M.I.T. Press, 1968, p. 40. Reprinted by permission.

caloric malnutrition and the apathy which often accompanies it (Béhar, 1968). Malnutrition is not confined to emerging nations, however, as revealed in such projects as the Department of Health, Education, and Welfare's National Nutrition Survey, which found alarming prevalence rates of malnutrition within the urban and rural poverty pockets of the United States. (1971)

On a humanitarian basis alone, these figures are staggering. When we add the distinct possibility of related learning disabilities and their implications for the world's future, the figures assume catastrophic proportions. Clearly, malnutrition is a truly international, interdisciplinary problem demanding the attention of nearly all fields of the natural and social sciences.

Theory and Research Designs and Problems

Essentially, all research in this field is aimed toward increasing present understanding of certain very basic questions concerning the interrelationships among malnutrition per se, sociocultural conditions known to be conducive to nutritional disease, and the often-observed consequent physical and mental retardation. Cravioto, DeLicardie, and Birch (1966) have pondered these problems within the framework of two theoretical schemes (Figure 2). While their work is somewhat arbitrary and oversimplified, it may help us to think more clearly about the problem under consideration (see also Collis, and Margaret, 1968).

As shown in both plans, and generally agreed upon by nearly all researchers, malnutrition arises from a common group of adverse social conditions, including poverty, ignorance, poor hygiene, overcrowding, parasitic and communicable diseases, superstition, and other factors that collectively and individually limit the availability and/or proper utilization of nutrients by the organism. It is also commonly known, as previously stated, that this malnutrition is in turn capable of limiting physical

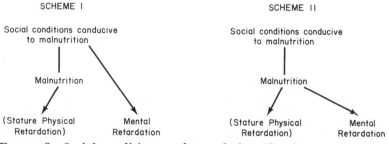

FIGURE 2 Social conditions and retardation (Cravioto et al.)

growth. The crucial problem, therefore, involves the ordering of the chain of causality of the neurological and general intellectual retardation so commonly observed in both clinical and research work with malnourished subjects. While Cravioto has found some limited evidence in support of his second scheme (see pp. 31-32) there is not yet *conclusive* evidence for either hypothesis.

For the present, the most rational tentative position is the combination theory of Scrimshaw and Gordon (1968), who believe that "both social and nutritional factors can affect mental development independently, yet also interact strongly (Figure 3). The end result, then, is additive, the effects of each of the two factors working alone plus further contribution from interaction of the two (Figure 3)." We extend their hypothesis to include learning disability as a manifestation of affected "mental development." Obviously, the clarification of this theoretical and practical problem must be the objective of future research.

So far, studies have thus far been largely ambiguous and indeterminate, because some of the most challenging problems in this area revolve around the resolution of the uniquely perplexing obstacles to objective field research in this area. In the past, numerically deficient and inadequately controlled sampling techniques, grossly varied criteria of malnutrition, and lack of sufficient follow-up have been significant problems. Other very severe limitations have resulted from inadequate measurement techniques which lead to highly inaccurate determinations of the presence of nutritional disease. Clinical signs of malnutrition are often not present at all in mild to moderate cases, further complicating the difficulties of precise diagnosis (Dayton, 1969). Also, poor psychometric performance may be more a function of cultural test bias than a reflection of an individual's true abilities. Tests are difficult to administer prior to middle childhood, whereas the nutritional insult usually occurs in infancy, leaving open the question of permanent developmental deficits (Read, 1969). The head circumference measurement, which roughly approximates brain size but not intelligence (Scrimshaw, 1967) can give only very superficial kinds of information, since skull size is affected not only by malnutrition,

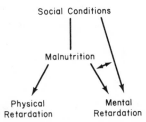

FIGURE 3 Nutrition and retardation from (Scrimshaw and Gordon, (1968).

but also by such factors as scalp size, temporal muscle, bony skull, and body weight and height (Garn, 1966, Frisch, 1970), as well as by disease processes (Robinow, 1968). The most common technique of the past for determining nutritional deprivation in large populations, the measurement of height and weight for age, has also received heavy criticism, as it is strongly affected not only by possible nutritional deficiencies, but also by genetic factors, diseases other than malnutrition, and normal maturational lag (Cravioto and DeLicardie, 1968). For these reasons, biochemical determinations of malnutrition will undoubtedly achieve more widespread use in the future. Possibly the most difficult experimental problems researchers face, however, involve control of the multitude of sociocultural and biological elements associated with malnutrition. Infection, psychological and social deprivation, parental education, lack of motivation, and a host of other factors within the poverty complex may be entirely capable of impeding learning, as well as precipitating specific learning disabilities and mental retardation (Dayton, 1969). It is obvious that if the role of nutrition in mental development is ever to be determined, these factors must be untangled and held constant by tightly controlled research designs.

For both ethical and methodological reasons, a great deal of the research concerning the effects of malnutrition on mental development has been performed with experimental animals. These studies have contributed a great deal to our knowledge, particularly concerning the physiological and biochemical processes of protein-caloric deficiency. Furthermore, results obtained in these studies have generally been consistent with clinical observations (Pearson, 1968). However, the classic problem of generalizability of laboratory results with lower species to complex human behavior within a sociocultural framework cannot be overstated.

It is extremely unfortunate that most studies with human populations have been narrow in scope, dealing usually with only one or two of the factors involved, and that often they have fallen prey to the research problems discussed above. Today there is general agreement that studies of a long-term, ecologically based nature must be given highest priority. At least two such investigations are currently underway in Guatemala and Mexico which promise to deliver some more definite answers within the next few years. Scrimshaw (1967) is quite explicit in defining the needs and purposes of such projects.

The subject is of such overwhelming importance to the future of the world that definitive research is imperative in order to determine the circumstances and manner in which malnutrition influences both intellectual and physical development. It must be research that distinguishes, in the preschool child, between the temporary effects of an acute disease process on test performance and behavior and the long-term consequences of chronic malnutrition.

Such research must take fully into account the influence of variations in the social or cultural environment, including the education, intelligence, and behavior patterns of parents and others with whom the child interacts. It must consider differences in the physical environment of housing, sanitation, and water supply, and the influence of the biological through exposure to the causative agents of parasitic and infectuous diseases. It must also distinguish between genetic factors and environmental ones.

Such research is multidisciplinary, demands the highest professional competence and dedication, is costly, and is exceedingly difficult; but it must be done. Unfortunately, it is so demanding of funds and talent that it can only be done in a very few localities a very few times. Superficial and poorly controlled or single-factor studies will serve only to confuse the issue further [pp. 499-500].

Normal and Abnormal CNS Development

Research on a possible link between nutrition and mental development has been centered on the growth of the foetus, the infant, and the young child, as these are the periods of life within which nearly all central nervous system development takes place. While studies indicate that during starvation the adult shows little cerebral weight loss (Dobbing, 1968) or decline of intelligence (Keyo, Brozek, Henschel, Mickelsen, and Taylor, 1950), such findings have not held true for children. Winick and Rosso (1969), for instance, found that Chilean infants who died of marasmus (extreme emaciation), the most severe form of protein-caloric deficiency, which occurs usually during the first year of life, possessed as few as 40 percent of the normal complement of brain cells.

Generally speaking, the foetus of an undernourished woman is quite well protected from malnutrition by metabolic priorities enabling it to obtain proteins at the mother's expense. Furthermore, the brain and other early-developing organs receive adequate protein in preference to such tissue as fat or muscle. Thus, if the nutritional status of the mother is sufficient to permit gestation, the foetus will probably grow normally, with the exception of some size stunting due to the fact that fat and water depositions are restricted during the last trimester (Coursin, 1965). Studies of such infants in developing countries have found their neuromuscular and central nervous system development to be within normal ranges (Geber and Dean, 1957).

Growth of all organs has been found to proceed in three stages: (1) hyperplasia, increase in the number of human brain cells, occurring during fetal growth and the first six months after birth, (2) hyperplasia and hyperthophy, the increase in size and number of the cells; and (3) hyperthophy, growth in size only (Dayton, 1969). It has been suggested that malnutrition during the hyperplasia periods may result in a retardation of cell division and a permanent reduction in the quantity of brain cells, while later protein deficiency leads to small cell size, an effect that seems to be reversible with the substitution of an adequate diet (Winick, 1969).

At birth, the brain gains in weight at a rate of 1 to 2 milligrams per minute. Within the next thirty-six months, it will reach 80 percent of its adult size (Scrimshaw, 1967). Because the brain is incapable of later regenerating tissue that is damaged or perhaps not even formed during this period, normal development in the first 3 years, and especially in the first six months, is crucial. If, indeed, nutritional deprivation and specific learning disabilities are coupled in some children, this is one critical point where problems may arise. While breast milk, even that of quite undernourished mothers, seems to provide adequate nutrition for at least the first three to four months (Thomson, 1968), this supply must soon be supplemented, usually by high-caloric, low-protein cereal gruels and starchy roots (Frisch, 1970). Thus, it is not surprising that growth of children in developing countries shows progressive retardation beginning no later than six months after birth and that the rate of mortality in these countries are ten to thirty times greater than those of industrialized nations for children between the ages of 1 and 4 years, while only three to five times greater during the first twelve months after birth (Frisch, 1970). Similar nutritional problems following the age of weaning appear to affect poverty-stricken children in the United States, as well (Dayton, 1969).

Experiments with Animals

As early as 1920, researchers found that in the rat, malnutrition during the first few weeks after weaning results in a reduction of brain weight which persists even after an adequate diet is substituted (Jackson and Stewart, 1920). These effects have since been found to be even more severe when the malnourishment occurs between birth and weaning (Widdowson and McCance, 1960). On the other hand, nutrient deficiency after the age of 3 weeks in the rat results in milder effects upon brain weight, with possible reversibility following implementation of proper nutrition (Winick, 1969). Thus it would appear that a critical period of brain development does exist, and that the earlier the deprivation, the greater the resulting damage.

Platt and his associates have described changes in the neurons and glia of both the spinal cord and medulla of rats, pigs, and dogs malnourished since weaning. These changes were evident even after 3 months of dietary rehabilitation (Platt, Heard, and Steward, 1964). Similarly Lowry and his co-workers, observing the cortical cells of pigs, discovered numerically reduced and swollen neurons (Lowry, Pond, Barnes, Krook, and Loosli, 1962). In both the Platt et al. and Lowry et al. experiments, the degree of degeneration varied specifically with the timing of the nutrient restriction.

In a study into the effects of malnutrition on cell division according to timing, Winick and Noble found that "early restriction interfered with cell division and that the animal was left with a deficit in the number of cells in all organs, even after adequate refeeding" (Winick, 1969, p. 669). As expected, later malnutrition during the hypotrophic phase reduced the size of individual cells but proved to be reversible. Furthermore, it was theorized that "as with ultimate cell number, total myelin content should be severely reduced only if under-nutrition is imposed during that period when myelin is most rapidly being laid down" (Winick, 1969, p. 671). This hypothesis has been supported by Dobbing and Widdowson, who found that early malnutrition produced seemingly permanent deficits in the amount and concentration of brain cholesterol which is strongly indicative of impaired myelin formation (Dobbing and Widdowson, 1965). Several other types of biochemical and anatomical alterations have also been explored (Winick, 1969), but at present our knowledge of these areas remains extremely limited, with a great deal of further research badly needed. Nevertheless, studies of animals strongly suggest rather global and pervasive deficits of the central nervous system resulting from inadequate nutrition during critical periods of development.

Of even greater significance for the educator are the reports concerning more clinical aspects of malnutrition. A classic experiment undertaken in Great Britain by Platt et al. placed rats and pigs upon severely protein-deficient diets at weaning (Platt et al., 1964). Clinical symptoms of central nervous system damage, including spasmodic trembling of head and forepaws, walking on tiptoes, incoordination of hind legs, and hyperirritability appeared within four days. Electroencephalograms were abnormal for all the animals. Again, severity of the symptoms varied with the timing and duration as well as with the protein value of the diet.

In another British experiment, Widdowson and his associates, using both rats and pigs, discriminated between simple malnutrition and protein deprivation (Widdowson, 1966). While the undernourished group became extremely nervous and hunger-driven, the protein-deficient animals exhibited tremendous apathy and loss of appetite. These symptoms bear a strong resemblance to kwashiorkor, an extreme form of protein-caloric malnutrition commonly found among humans in developing countries. If untreated, this condition results in death. The observation of reduced food intake and exploratory behavior has been confirmed by Lat, Widdowson, and McCance (1961).

In order to investigate the effects of maternal malnutrition upon offspring, Caldwell and Churchill (1967) fed a protein-deficient diet to a group of ten pregnant rats during the last half of gestation. Their offspring had lower birth and weaning weights and higher mortality rate prior to weaning than did a control group. In addition, the experimental progeny were found to be significantly inferior to the controls in two tests of learning ability. These results have been substantiated by Simonson, Sherwin, Hanson, and Chow (1968), who found that the offspring of pregnant rats placed on 50 percent dietary restriction during gestation and lactation were inferior to controls in running time, numbers of errors, and trials to criterion in a maze-learning task. Furthermore, Cowly and Griesel (1966) have produced evidence of an increasingly severe problem-solving defect as successive generations of rats are fed low-protein diets. Obviously, such experimental results have strong implications with regard to human populations living in extreme poverty.

Studies on the perceptual and learning process effects of infant malnutrition apart from maternal dietary deprivation are somewhat contradictory. For example, Collier and Squibb (1968) found normal motivation and learning responses in chickens that had been malnourished during the first two weeks after birth, but placed on adequate diets and tested after six weeks. On the other hand, Rajalakshmi, Govindarajan, and Ramakrishnan (1965) observed inferior visual discrimination learning in albino rats placed on protein-deficient diets for periods of four to six weeks.

At the Czechoslovakian Academy of Science, experimenters weaned two groups of rats at twenty-one and thirty days (Novakova, Faltin, Flandera, Hahn and Koldovsky, 1962). Learning and behavioral responses to an electric bell were significantly slower in the early weaning group, provided that an adequate diet was not submitted. When the animals were fed simulated rat milk, no differences appeared.

During extensive interdisciplinary research at Cornell University, Barnes and his associates (Barnes, Moore, Reid and Pond, 1967) produced a simulated kwashiorkor by depriving piglets of protein for eight weeks after weaning. Following six months of dietary rehabilitation, the animals were compared to normal controls in tests of both classical and operant conditioning. Interestingly, in neither type of learning was there any significant difference in the speed of acquisition. When the experimenters attempted extinction of the learning, however, "it was found that the control animals extinguished quite rapidly, but the pigs that had been malnourished had a greatly prolonged period of trials before the conditioned response disappeared. Some of the experimental animals did not extinguish at all during the test period" (Barnes, 1967, p. 146). While Barnes realized the somewhat confusing nature of these results, he observed that "it is evident . . . that there is a long-lasting behavioral abnormality that has been induced as a result of feeding the severely imbalanced diet to very young pigs" (Barnes, 1967). Also, it was found in another experiment by the Cornell group that male rats that were nutritionally deprived during nursing, and especially those that were continued on deficient diets after weaning, made significantly more errors than did a control group on a test of visual discrimination (Barnes, Cunnold, and Zimmerman, 1966).

Once again, it must be pointed out that present evidence relating dietary deficiencies to retardation and learning disability is highly suggestive, though inconclusive. Certainly, however, available results do warrant a great deal of further investigation, particularly in the area of well-controlled learning studies with higher-order animals.

Studies with Humans

Nearly every technologically underdeveloped country in the world has reported a significant number of preschool children with severe growth and maturation deficits due to malnutrition, leading to smaller adult stature (Scrimshaw, 1967). Béhar has four excellent graphs of weight for age for children of Guatemala, South India, Thailand and New Guinea which illustrate this point well (see Figures 4, 5, 6, 7). Generally, the pat-

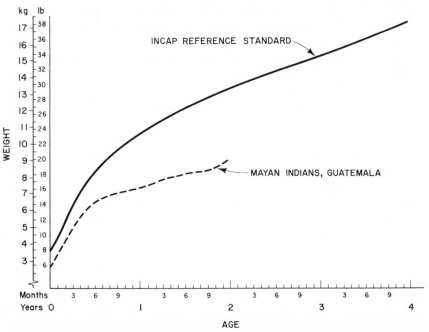

FIGURE 4   Average weight-for-age (kilograms and pounds) of 45 Mayan Indian children in Guatemala and corresponding values of the INCAP reference standard.

Source: Béhar, M., Prevalence of malnutrition among preschool children of developing countries. In *Malnutrition, learning, and behavior,* N. S. Scrimshaw and J. E. Gordon (eds.). Cambridge, Mass.: M.I.T. Press, 1968, p. 38. Reprinted by permission.

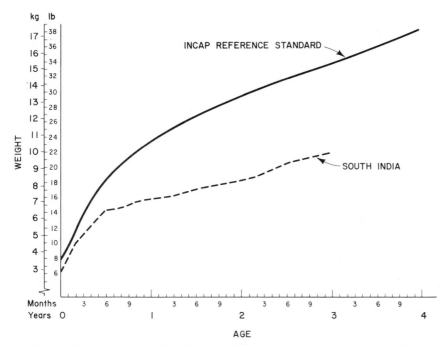

FIGURE 5   Average weight-for-age (kilograms and pounds) of children in southern India, by age, and corresponding values of INCAP reference standard.

Source: Béhar, M., Prevalence of malnutrition among preschool children of developing countries. In *Malnutrition, learning, and behavior,* N. S. Scrimshaw and J. E. Gordon (eds.). Cambridge, Mass.: M.I.T. Press, 1968, p. 38. Reprinted by permission.

tern is the same, with relatively normal growth during the first few months, followed by progressive physical retardation as the nutrition provided by breast feeding becomes more and more inadequate and as infectious diseases consequently become more prevalent (Béhar, 1968). Similar results have been obtained with measurements of height and weight for age (Béhar, 1968), bone maturation (Rohmann, Garn, Guzman, Flores, Béhar, and Pao, 1964), head circumference (Stoch, and Smythe, 1967), and various biochemical indices (Winick and Rosso, 1969). Scrimshaw (1967) cites the case history of one such child.

The febrile illnesses in the first two years . . . totaled 151 days and included, sometimes concurrently, eight episodes of diarrhea, five of severe upper respiratory infections, four bouts of tonsillitis, two of impetigo, and one each of broncho-pneumonia, unknown viral infection with rash, cellulitis, con-

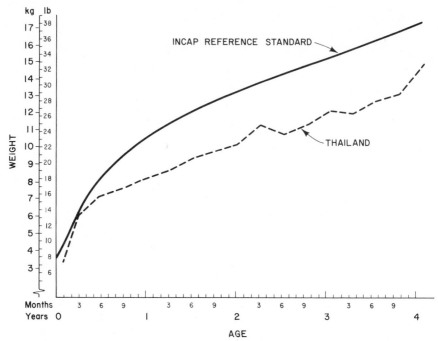

FIGURE 6 Average weight-for-age (kilograms and pounds) of children in Thailand, and corresponding values of INCAP reference standard.

Source: Béhar, M., Prevalence of malnutrition among preschool children of developing countries. In *Malnutrition, learning, and behavior,* N. S. Scrimshaw and J. E. Gordon (eds.). Cambridge, Mass.: M.I.T. Press, 1968, p. 39. Reprinted by permission.

junctivitis, stomatitis, bronchitis, and chicken pox. In addition, there was laboratory evidence of at least 60 days of enterovirus excretion, 56 days of three different bacterial species responsible for dysentery, 108 days of various intestinal protozoan infections, plus seven episodes in which staphylococci or streptococci were identified. During all of this the child was also harboring several species of intestinal worms.

It is scarcely surprising that this child and millions like her . . . fail to grow during this period, and that many of them die of either malnutrition or infection in the second year of life. The psycho-motor development of children such as the one described has been retarded by more than 6 months at one year of age [p. 497].

A number of investigators have explored the actual biochemical changes caused by protein-calorie malnutrition. While it has been suggested that there are consequent alterations in enzyme formation (Cravioto, 1958) in transport of cellular elements across the neuronal membrane

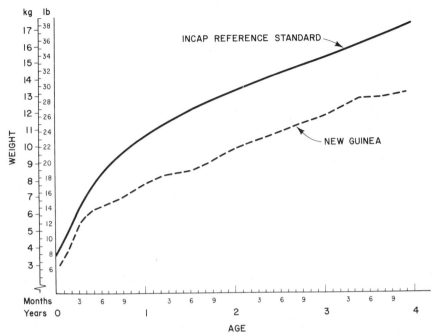

FIGURE 7 Average weight-for-age (kilograms and pounds) of children in New Guinea, and corresponding values of INCAP reference standard.

Source: Béhar, M., Prevalence of malnutrition among preschool children of developing countries. In *Malnutrition, learning, and behavior,* N. S. Scrimshaw and J. E. Gordon (eds.). Cambridge, Mass.: M.I.T. Press, 1968, p. 39. Reprinted by permission.

(Udenfriend, 1963), in synapse function (Gordon and Deanin, 1968), and in the formation of RNA (ribonucleic acid) and DNA (deoxyribonucleic acid) (Waterlow and Mendes, 1957), these remain to be clearly established. Furthermore, it must be remembered that physical and chemical changes, even when demonstrable, are extremely difficult to correlate with functional results. At present, knowledge of these changes in the developing CNS (central nervous system) is severely restricted and of only the grossest nature, as seen in Figure 8 (Winick, 1969).

Perhaps the most important area of research concerning the relationship between malnutrition and learning involves the learning behavior of human populations. While available studies are few and greatly flawed, they may lead to some tentative conclusions. The first such study (Kugelmass, Poull, and Samuel, 1944) was performed in New York City in 1944 with fifty malnourished school children, ages 2 through 9, and with

PHYSICAL OR CHEMICAL

Measurement	Animal	Human
Weight	Decreased	Decreased
Histology	Degeneration of neurones and glia	——
Cell number	Decreased in total brain, earliest effect on cerebellum	Decreased in total brain
Cell migration	Delayed in hippocampus	——
Myelin synthesis	Decreased	——
Norepinephrine and serotonin concentration	Transiently decreased	——
RNA content per cell RNA / DNA	Transiently increased	——
Head circumference	——	Decreased

FIGURE 8 Physical and chemical changes in the developing brain (Winick, 1969)

matched, well-nourished controls. After receiving nutritional supplements for periods of from one to three-and-a-half years, the experimental group demonstrated an increase of intelligence quotient averaging 18 points, compared to no significant change in the control group. While this study recently has been challenged by other research (Rajalakshmi, 1968) and has been criticized on the ground that the increase may have been effected by the mere attention given the malnourished children (Scrimshaw, 1967), it nonetheless remains one of the most convincing reports to date.

In another classic study, carried out between 1955 and 1967, Stoch and Smythe (1968) of South Africa recorded the height, weight, head circumference, electroencephalograms, and intelligence and other psychological test scores of twenty "Cape Coloured" infants who were "grossly malnourished in infancy." There were twenty matched controls. Even after ten years, the malnourished group was significantly smaller in height, weight, and head circumference. While only two of the malnourished group's EEGs were classifiable as abnormal, many showed marked instability under stress, and twelve displayed poorly formed low-voltage alpha waves, with poor response to eye opening. Only three examples of the latter condition were noticed in the control group. Other EEG variations have been observed by Baraitser (1959). On the New South African Individual Scale, a test of intelligence, an undernourished group achieved a mean full-scale quotient of 61.15, while the mean for the controls was 76.70. Furthermore, the undernourished children displayed deficits of visual-motor functioning and pattern perception resembling those of encephalopathic children. They also performed significantly poorer on tests of cognition, motivation, and personality variables. Another particularly interesting finding was that the experimental subjects demonstrated significantly less fantasy-affection behavior but more fantasy aggression.

It is extremely unfortunate that such thorough research as that of Stoch and Smythe should suffer from a glaring methodological error. While it is true that both groups of children came from a broadly defined "lower socioeconomic level," there are great disparities between their backgrounds. As Stoch and Smythe (1968) themselves admit, "Alcoholism, illegitimacy, and broken homes were the rule in the undernourished group, whereas the control group lived under more stable conditions. Only six of the parents of the undernourished children were gainfully employed, and the feeding of all children in this group was wholly inadequate" (p. 280). Thus we are forced to treat with caution their conclusion that "severe under-nutrition, during the first two years of life . . . results in a permanent reduction of brain size and a restricted intellectual development" (p. 287).

Working with previously marasmic Serbian children, Cabat and Najdanvic (1965) found a wide discrepancy in IQ between experimental and control groups. These results were supported by work done in Colorado by Chase and Martin (1970), as well as by Botha-Antoun, Babayan, and Harfouche (1968) in Lebanon. However, all these studies suffer from the same basic error, namely, a poor control over important socioeconomic variables which may have exerted considerable influence on the results. Read's evaluation (1969) of the Chase research, for example, is typical:

> Examination of the family records showed that the mothers of the malnourished infants were under particular emotional and economic stress at the time of their infants' malnutrition, and that home conditions were especially bad. Furthermore, a primary cause of the poor nutritional condition of these infants was family disorganization, probably influenced by poverty and lack of education. . . . Since these social problems also may influence intellectual development, the effects of malnutrition alone are somewhat clouded in this study [p. 14].

In Chile, a great recent decrease in breast feeding has combined with poor cultural and sanitary factors to produce large incidence rates of marasmus at very early ages. Mönckeberg (1968) has administered postrecovery physical and psychological tests to fourteen children between the ages of 3 and 6. All appeared clinically normal, with the exception of extreme shortness and small head circumferences. All had been given free milk supplements since treatment. Due to the fact that the mean IQ of this group was 62, with no individual scoring above 75, the author concluded that "brain damage in infancy is permanent at least up to the sixth year of life, despite improving nutritional conditions" (p. 270–272). To a very significant degree these figures are lower than those for the average low SES preschool Chilean (p < .001).

Mönckeberg also reported a study in which 153 preschool children were divided into three groups in order to determine the relative effects of social versus nutritional forces. As noted in Figure 9, Group A included

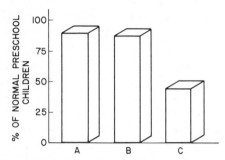

FIGURE 9 Preschool children of normal psychological development, by social groups. A: Chilean middle-class. B: low socioeconomic group with no malnutrition. C: low socioeconomic with much malnutrition.

Source: Mönckeberg, F., Effect of early madasmic malnutrition on subsequent physical and psychological development. In *Malnutrition, learning, and behavior,* N. S. Scrimshaw and J. E. Gordon (eds.). Cambridge, Mass.: M.I.T. Press, 1968, p. 276. Reprinted by permission.

middle-class children; Group B, lower-class children adequately nourished because of free milk and medical care; and Group C, lower-class malnourished children. The percentage of children exhibiting normal psychological development within each group is seen in Figure 9. While groups A and B were at a high and essentially equal level developmentally, only 50 percent of the children in group C were considered within normal limits. However, as Mönckeberg pointed out, the supplemental feeding program may have influenced environmental factors, such as maternal motivation, thus introducing further variables into the experimental framework.

Champaham, and his associates (Champaham, Srikantia, and Gopalan, 1968) recently reported an excellent study of nineteen 18- to 36-month old Indian children who were unsuccessfully treated for kwashiorkor. When they were between 8 and 11 years old, the children were compared to three carefully selected controls, matched for age, sex, religion, caste, socioeconomic status, family size, birth order, parental education, school attended, and general pattern of child care. Significant reductions in intelligence and intersensory integration were found, particularly within the areas of perceptual and abstract thinking. The discrepancy between experimental subjects and controls was notably wider within the 8-year-old group than it was for the 11-year-olds, suggesting that such defects as may be caused by early malnutrition gradually diminish with age. Cravioto and Robles (1965) also observed this phenomenon in their work with kwashiorkor patients, except that for those children admitted before the age of 6 months, adaptive, motor, language, and personal-social behavior appeared to be permanently impaired.

In one of the more well-known studies conducted to date, Cravioto and DeLicardie (1968) examined all school-age children living in Magdelina Milpas Altos, a rural village of central Guatemala. As it was assumed that for children shorter than their age mates there was a high probability of early nutrient deficiency, those within the lower quartile of height for age were compared for intersensory integration, a basic developmental building block of learning, with the children of the upper quartile, who were presumed least likely to have been malnourished. In order to control genetic, social, and maturational factors, the experimenters gathered anthropometic information on the parents; evaluated individual subjects for social, economic, educational, and sanitary status; and selected a control group of urban children of the same ages and range of heights, but with little likelihood of previous nutritional disease.

The researchers employed Birch and Lefford's technique for evaluating equivalences between haptic (tactile), visual, and kinesthetic modalities (Birch and Lefford, 1964). This procedure requires that a geometric form presented to the subject through one sensory system be compared to another form presented in another system. Thus, the subject may feel a hexagon in his hand (haptic), and then have to compare it with the shape described by his arm as it was moved by the examiner (kinesthetic).

For both groups, urban and rural, all equivalences improved logarithmically with age. For the rural children, the taller quartile performed significantly better than the shorter, especially at the younger ages, whereas for the urban children, intersensory integration did not vary with height. Furthermore, later examination showed that while the height of the urban children was correlated with the height of their parents, no such relationship existed for the rural subjects. A strong positive association was found, however, between the height of the rural children and the educational level of thir mothers, i.e., short children tended to have poorly educated mothers. This implies the "strong possibility that the better-educated woman will rely less on traditional methods of feeding and child care, which are among direct causes of reduced food intake in health and disease, particularly in early life" (Cravioto and DeLicardie, 1968, p. 265).

Having thus established a link between malnutrition, adverse social conditions, and poor intersensory development, Cravioto and DeLicardie turned their attention to the implications of their results, specifically with reference to the two theoretical schemes discussed above (see Figures 2 and 3):

> The primary inference of Scheme I is that social impoverishment, presumably including inadequate opportunities for learning, contributes independently to poor intersensory development. If this is indeed the case, a significant association would be expected between low stature and a variety of social factors implicated in poor psychological growth, such as family income, housing con-

ditions, proportion of income spent on food, personal hygiene conditions, and similar factors. It was therefore most striking to find from data of the present study (1) no significant association of neurointegrative function with financial status, with housing facilities, with proportion of total income, or with the total expenditure on food; (2) a weak inverse correlation with father's education; and (3) no correlation with conditions of personal cleanliness [p. 265].

These rather unexpected findings are strongly suggestive of a direct causal link between early nutrient deprivation and later impaired learning function. Like so many research findings, however, they must be replicated before they can be accepted as fact.

Cravioto (1972) has more recently presented some additional data which are important in this discussion. Speaking about the interrelation of nutritional deprivation and intellectual development, Cravioto discusses

. . . the results of the study carried out on a group of school-age children who had suffered severe malnutrition before their thirtieth month of age. The children were selected from the records of those who had been admitted for severe malnutrition with edema and skin lesions (kwashiorkor) to the Department of Pediatrics, Army Central Hospital in Mexico City between the years of 1952 and 1963. Their ages at the time of admission to the ward were between 4 and 30 months. At this time, they had weights 40 percent or more below the mean expected weight for age. Children suffering from chronic disease, either infectious or not infectious, as well as children affected with diseases of the central nervous system, were eliminated. Due to limitations of staff and financial resources, only children living in Mexico City were considered as candidates for the investigation. With these restrictions, it was possible to locate thirty-nine children.

Since it is a well-known fact that the environment in which these children live is so grossly inadequate, it was decided to include as a comparison group a sample of the living siblings in an attempt to diminish the effect of this variable on the results. Accordingly, in each family the sibling closest in age to the previously malnourished child was selected for inclusion in the comparison group.

The level of intelligence was assessed by a trained psychologist by means of the Weschler Intelligence Scale for Children (WISC) in both the verbal and the performance aspects. Auditory-Visual Integration was evaluated by the technique of Birch and Belmont and the level of Visual-Kinesthetic competence was explored by the technique of equivalence in the perception of geometric forms, as devised by Birch and Lefford.

As can be seen in Figure 10, the distribution of intelligence scores is markedly skewed with a large number of subjects scoring in the lower range of values. When the respective performance of the siblings and the malnourished groups are compared, it becomes evident that the children who were severely malnourished are significantly overrepresented in the lower extreme of the distribution.

If the verbal and performance scales of the intelligence test are analyzed separately (Figures 11 and 12), it may be noticed that significantly lower scores

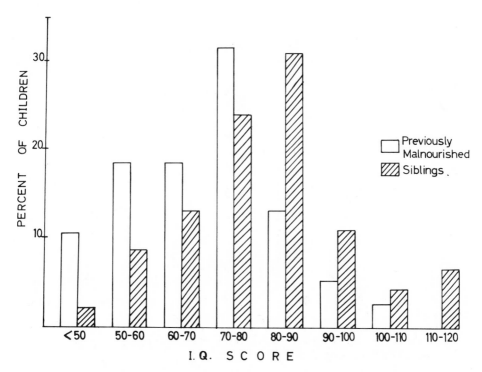

FIGURE 10   Distribution of IQ WISC-total Scores in previously Malnourished children and their siblings.

Source: J. Cravioto, "Nutrition and Learning in Children," in Nutrition and Learning in Children," in *Nutrition and mental retardation,* N. S. Springer, ed. Ann Arbor: Institute for the Study of Mental Retardation and Related Disabilities, 1972, p. 37. Reprinted by permission.

are attained by the previously malnourished children in tasks requiring verbal elements as well as in tasks demanding non-verbal responses. The difference of mean scores calculated by the "t" test is significant at the 0.01 level of confidence.

Figure 13 shows the mean performance of previously malnourished children and their siblings in a test which requires the child to identify visual dot patterns corresponding to rhythmic auditory ones. As may be seen, the children's ability to equate a temporally structured set of auditory stimuli with a spatially distributed set of visual ones is frankly inferior age by age in the group who had suffered severe malnutrition in infancy. To illustrate that this difference in performance is not due to a few extreme cases affecting the mean value, Figure 14 presents the cumulative percentage of seven year old children in the two groups. The data clearly indicate a lag in development of auditory-visual competence in children recovered from severe malnutrition.

The visual-kinesthetic intersensory integration, and ability closely related

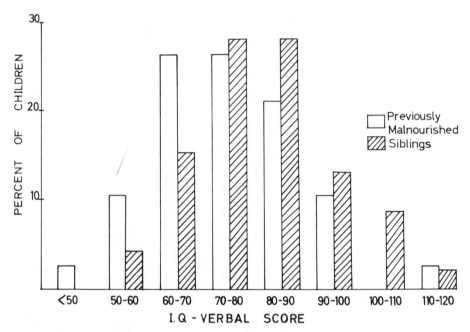

FIGURE 11   Distribution of IQ WISC-verbal scores in previously mal-nourished children and their siblings.

Source: J. Cravioto, "Nutrition and Learning in Children," in *Nutrition and mental retardation,* N. S. Springer, ed. Ann Arbor: Institute for the Study of Mental Retardation and Related Disabilities, 1972, p. 37. Reprinted by permission.

to learning to write, was explored by the method of equivalence in the per-ception of geometric forms. The kinesthetic sense, in this context, refers to the sensory input from the wrists, elbow and shoulder joints and from the arm and shoulder musculature as its principle components. In the test situ-ation, kinesthetic information was provided by placing the subject's preferred arm behind a screen, and with the arm out of sight, passively moving it through a path describing a geometric form.

Figures 15, 16, and 17 show the proportions of previously malnourished children and their siblings making errors in the identification of identical or non-identical forms at ages 5 to 7. It is evident that significant differences in accuracy of judgment exist always in favor of the siblings [pp. 35-40].

If one recalls the types of items contained in the Wechsler Intelligence Scale for Children which was administered to the children in Cravioto's study and reported in Figures 10, 11, and 12, the importance of the data presented in his later figures stands out. Lower intelligence-test scores

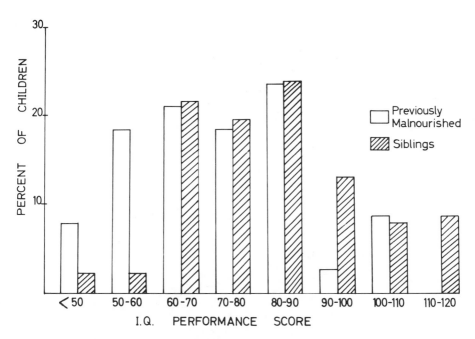

FIGURE 12   Distribution of IQ WISC-performance scores in previously malnourished children and their siblings.

Source: J. Cravioto, "Nutrition and Learning in Children," in *Nutrition and mental retardation,* N. S. Springer, ed. Ann Arbor: Institute for the Study of Mental Retardation and Related Disabilities, 1972, p. 38. Reprinted by permission.

are closely related to the deficits which his child subjects demonstrated in visual-kinesthetic sensory integration and in auditory-visual integration. Visual-kinesthetic integration and auditory-visual integration are inherent aspects of the deficit behavior of children with learning disabilities. The higher incidence of learning disabilities based on the deficiencies in integrative function in some children in lower socioeconomic strata may be related to severe nutritional deprivation as is being suggested in this chapter. These integrative deficiencies are probably not related solely to the lower intelligence levels as a characteristic unique to mental retardation. They appear certainly as an aspect of exogenous mental retardation, but are probably in varying degrees unique to the total intelligence spectrum. In this connection Cravioto states that the results of his studies suggest

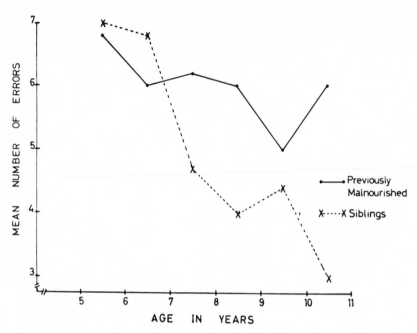

FIGURE 13 Auditory-visual integration in previously malnourished children and their siblings.

Source: J. Cravioto, "Nutrition and Learning in Children," in *Nutrition and mental retardation,* N. S. Springer, ed. Ann Arbor: Institute for the Study of Mental Retardation and Related Disabilities, 1972, p. 38.

. . . that an episode of chronic severe malnutrition in early life would increase the risk of scoring, both in intelligence tests and in the level of neuro-integrative development, quite below the expected values of the specific socioeconomic class of children under study [p. 40].

What, then, are the conclusions which we may justifiably draw from presently available research? Certainly it can be agreed that early malnutrition impairs growth, both of the body in general and of the central nervous system in particular, and that a deficit is likely to vary in severity with the age at which the insult occurs, with the degree of malnutrition, and with the duration of nutrient deficiency. Many investigators agree that the first six months of life represent a critical nutritional period for the human infant, as this is the period of maximal postnatal brain cell division. They also believe that damage incurred during this period is probably permanent. Beyond this point, any conclusions are tentative. Some animal studies demonstrate a direct causality between malnutrition

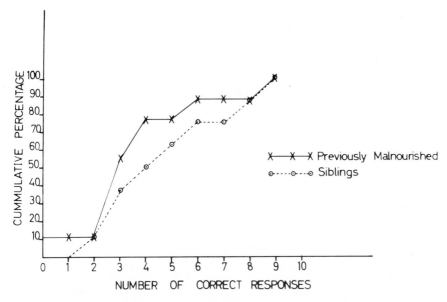

FIGURE 14   Auditory-visual integration at age seven years of severely malnourished infants and their siblings.

Source: J. Cravioto, "Nutrition and Learning in Children," in *Nutrition and mental retardation,* N. S. Springer, ed. Ann Arbor: Institute for the Study of Mental Retardation and Related Disabilities, 1972, p. 39. Reprinted by permission.

and learning disabilities, while others find no relationship at all. In humans, the most one can say is that the two conditions *seem* to be related and that research often suggests such a link. Firmer statements must await more conclusive evidence, which hopefully will be forthcoming in the not-too-distant future.

Considerations for Future Planning

Despite the present lack of an established causal connection between malnutrition and learning, it remains obvious that with vast masses of the earth's population suffering in various degrees from nutritional disease, dramatic and widespread measures are in order. However, such plans must reach far beyond simple provision of food supplies and must involve a thorough understanding of the cultural and ecological variables operating in each individual environment (Dayton, 1969). In addition to accurate determinations of the prevalence and severity of malnutrition within given populations, both quantitative and qualita-

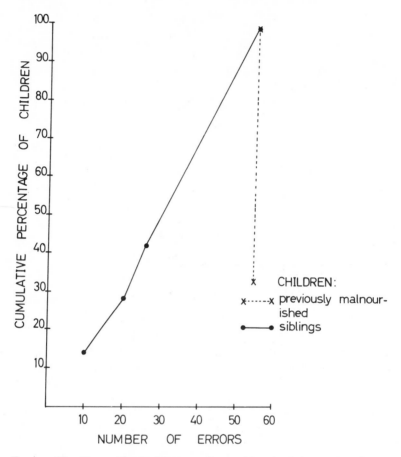

FIGURE 15   Errors in judgment of non-identical forms in the visual-kinesthetic modalities at 5 years of age.

Source: J. Cravioto, "Nutrition and Learning in Children," in *Nutrition and mental retardation,* N. S. Springer, ed. Ann Arbor: Institute for the Study of Mental Retardation and Related Disabilities, 1972, p. 41). Reprinted by permission.

tive determination of food distribution patterns must be made. Cultural food preferences and prohibitions need to be carefully examined, along with other factors ranging from breast-feeding habits to political implications. The thread between nutritional deficiency and learning difficulties is tightly woven into the intricate fabric of the broader social complex. Thus, the problem of malnutrition cannot be eradicated if it is not considered within its typical environmental setting of poverty, disease, and ignorance.

In spite of the need, however, there is a serious shortage of animal

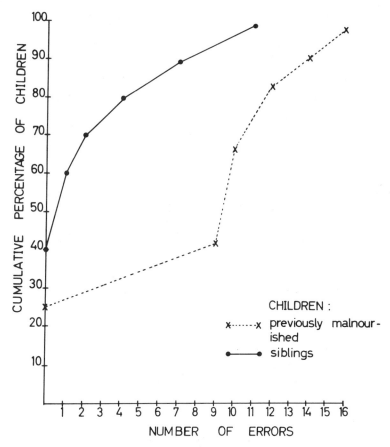

FIGURE 16   Errors of judgment of identical forms in the visual-kines-thetic modalities at 6 years of age.

Source: J. Cravioto, "Nutrition and Learning in Children," in *Nutrition and mental retardation*, N. S. Springer, ed. Ann Arbor: Institute for the Study of Mental Retardation and Related Disabilities, 1972, p. 42. Reprinted by permission.

protein in many developing nations. For this reason, plant and seafood proteins currently are being investigated and evaluated for their nutritional adequacy (Dayton, 1969). Other problems of food production, transportation, storage, and distribution must also be resolved if nations are to become capable of fulfilling the minimal nutritional requirements of their inhabitants. This holds true even for industrialized countries such as the United States which still have a significant incidence of nutritional deficiency in spite of their vast food surpluses. Moreover, along with a need for technological change is a need for education of

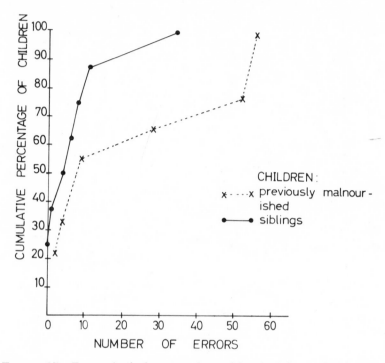

FIGURE 17 Errors in judgment of non-identical forms in the Haptic-Kinesthetic modalities at 7 years of age.

Source: J. Cravioto, "Nutrition and Learning in Children," in *Nutrition and mental retardation,* N. S. Springer, ed. Ann Arbor: Institute for the Study of Mental Retardation and Related Disabilities, 1972, p. 43. Reprinted by permission.

the masses with regard to food requirements of infancy and childhood. The alleviation of early deprivation must assume a major role in any future attempts to subdue the ravages of protein-caloric deficiency, the disease which may quite possibly emerge as a major determinant of learning abilities and indeed of man's future on earth.

CULTURAL DEPRIVATION

While nutritional disease afflicts broad segments of the earth's population, another type of "deprivation"—even more ambiguous in its effects and just as crippling—is working simultaneously and synergistically to inhibit the development of intellectual potential in millions of children or to modify it in the direction of specific learning disabilities. Whether it goes under the label of "psychosocial deprivation," "cultural disadvantagement," or any of a number of other euphemisms, the reality in question is the same—poverty. The fact is that the majority of children living in the world today are subjected to an array of pathological environmental conditions, nearly incredible in the complexity of their interaction, which serve to deny the individual of whatever chance he may otherwise have of escaping the devastating cycle of poverty, ignorance, and human waste. Despite its glaring and appalling presence, however, there is, as the Department of Health, Education, and Welfare (1968) has pointed out,

> . . . neither a broadly shared conceptual perspective on the meaning and nature of psychosocial deprivation, nor a well-established and comprehensive base of empirical knowledge concerning its consequences. However, psychosocial deprivation appears to involve a complex set of physiological-genetic, cognitive-learning, social-emotional, and social-structural causes and consequences. . . . For the individual, the result may be a modification of physical structure and function, as well as behavioral patterns which may affect the individual's social and/or intellectual functioning [p. v].

Though the mass destruction arising from inadequate nutrition remains at present on the periphery of American consciousness, the causes and effects of poverty and its resultant waste of human resources loom as the primary social and political issues of the twentieth century. This is doubtless due to the fact that in this country deficits imposed by purely environmental factors such as overcrowding, maternal and paternal deprivation, undifferentiated noise, inferior health and educational services, and maladaptive, if not utterly pathological, patterns of child-rearing probably far outweigh the losses resulting from malnutrition per se (Naeye, 1970). This by no means, of course, implies that nutrition is not a significant problem in the United States; on the contrary, it remains one of the key members of the family of poverty. Indeed, if any one thing distinguishes this horrible social complex, it is its syndrome-like quality, which, as we have seen in our consideration of malnutrition, has the effect of stifling desperately needed research and action programs. "Where one type of deprivation, e.g., social, is implicated, other types, biological or psychological, seem to be associated with it. . . . In short, although research may try to separate out specific aspects of deprivation for study, these aspects seem to be interwined [sic] with each other in nature" (HEW p. 64, 1968).

How widespread is the culture of poverty? In raw economic terms, as of 1968, 27 million children, or 40 percent of the nation's youth below the age of 18, lived in families with an annual income of less than $6,000. Of these, 9 million were under the general subsistence level of $3,000 (Children's Bureau Publication #46, 1968). However, as Wortis (1970) noted, the Poverty Index of the Social Security Administration, which considers family size, has estimated that 15 million American children, fewer than one half of whom receive public assistance, live below the subsistence level. Of these, some 9 million are white, with 6 million nonwhite. In relative terms, however, this means that 15 percent of the Caucasian population is severely economically deprived, as compared to a figure of 59 percent for our various racial minorities (Wortis, 1970). For what value gross figures have, an additional set of figures relating poverty to the national scene in the United States is worth reporting. Based on the recent report (1970) of the Bureau of the Census, 25.4 millions of persons were reported below the accepted poverty level in the U.S.A. (12.8 percent). Of this group 10.7 million persons were under 18 years of age. White persons accounted for 17.4 million with 6.4 million of these being under 18 years of age. Eight million were nonwhites (4.4 million persons under 18 years of age). Ten percent of the white population was found to be below the poverty level; 33.5 percent of the nonwhite population were at a similar level economically (U.S. Department of Commerce, 1970). With this shameful condition manifest in the "Land of Plenty," we can only surmise the extent of its seriousness across the globe, in countries where demographic and epidemiological data were lacking.

THEORETICAL MODELS

Throughout much of this country's history, poverty has been widely regarded as the natural gravitation of inferior individuals to the lower strata of society, with "hereditary" factors frequently called upon to explain the familial transmission of poverty from generation to generation. With only a few thinkers perceptive enough to point out the pervasive limitations which the entire culture of poverty imposes upon its subjects, the general public policy was to ignore the problem. It cannot be denied that the traditional view, with its roots deeply imbedded in prejudice and rationalization, is still a powerful national force to be reckoned. Rodger Hurley (1969), in his incisive book, *Poverty and Mental Retardation: A Causal Relationship,* sums up this philosophy in the words of a New Jersey grower discussing his migrant workers: "Nothing. . . . They never were nothing, they never will be nothing, and you and me and God Almighty ain't going to change them."

With the demise of the Horatio Alger myth, however, and especially with the Civil Rights Movement of the 1960s, the attention of the educated American public has been focused upon the problem in all its true complexity, and the "inherent inferiority" theory is falling into general disrepute. California psychologist Arthur Jensen's (1968) controversial speculations upon a racial-genetic factor are a notable exception. When, in 1968, the National Institute of Child Health and Human Development (H.E.W.) established four interdisciplinary teams to investigate the full scope of sociocultural deprivation, the result was the publication of the landmark *Perspectives on Human Deprivation: Biological, Psychological, and Sociological* (1968). Within this document is contained the most comprehensive overview to date of theoretical approaches to "deprivation and its impact upon behavior," which are outlined briefly below as follows (from pp. 106–11):

I. *Malnutrition Model:* This view, perhaps the most popular, holds that the child is deprived of the economic and psychological "nutrients" needed for healthy growth and development.
   A. *Economic deprivation:* "The heart of the problem of the disadvantaged is their inability to purchase goods and services of various kinds. . . . This view tends to emphasize the issue of available resources rather than of values, culture, and life style."
   B. *Deprivation as a lack of exposure to beneficial stimulation:* The deprived child "has not learned at home the concepts he will need in school or the vocabulary that is required for effective functioning in contemporary society. . . . His store of information about the world and the way it works is inadequate."
   C. *Deprivation as a lack of pattern in the experiential world:* "The experience of the child has not included an adequate array of patterns, sequences, and associations between events to allow him to develop an understanding of the relation of elements of the experiential world to one another. . . . The stimulation and the stimuli to which a child is exposed are not presented in a context which will permit him to use them or generalize them for some future situation or experience."
   D. *Deprivation as an absence of contingencies in the environment:* "The environment of the disadvantaged child is arranged . . . in such a way that the desired behavior is not adequately encouraged by appropriate reinforcement schedules."
   E. *Deprivation as interaction between developmental maturational needs and lack of stimulation:* "A common point of view in the discussion of the malnutrition model is that certain cognitive activities play a biologically stimulating role in the maturation of neural structures that are important for later cognitive development and learning. There is evidence from animal studies that stimulation of various kinds may affect the growth of neural structures, and it seems plausible that this interaction between biological structure and environment may be involved in the impact of psychosocial deprivation upon cognitive development and learning in humans."
II. *Cultural Disparity Model:* "These views emphasize structural features, seeing the difficulty as residing in disparities and conflict of values and goals between subculture and the large sociocultural system."
   A. *Deprivation as an outcome of cultural pluralism:* Deprivation lies

"not so much in absolute level of capability as in the differential evaluation of ethnic characteristics, [e.g., language patterns] by the dominant society."

B. *Deprivation as learning of behavior not rewarded by middle-class society:* Deprived children "learn behavior which is appropriate and useful for their home environment but which is not useful for subsequent experiences in the school."

C. *Deprivation due to the inadequacy of social institutions:* The belief that "the difficulty resides in the institutions of middle-class society whose representatives in the school, the police force, and other parts of the social structure fail to understand the child or the adult, to be sympathetic with his problems, to be able to communicate with him, or in other ways to permit him to learn about and relate to the central components of society."

III. *Social Structural Model:* "Disadvantage is an inherent feature of a complex, highly differentiated, hierarchical social system."

A. *Deprivation as an outcome of competition for scarce resources in the society:* "Dominant groups may for their own economic or social interest attempt to maintain the dependence of other segments . . . and to exclude them from competition in the labor market and other areas."

B. *Deprivation as a lack of alternatives for action in the society:* "The lack of power, prestige, and other resources for action places the individual in situations which require little thought or comparison and, therefore, stimulate relatively few of the cognitive operations that are needed for success in the middle-class society [Hess, 1964]."

It must be pointed out that by no means do these various approaches to deprivation necessarily conflict with one another; rather, they serve to underscore the multi-leveled nature of the problem, as reflected in the work of professionals drawn from a variety of fields. Thus, while the present writers will address themselves directly to only a few of these views, we fully recognize the existence of a multitude of components operating within the complex of environmental deprivation. Indeed, it is doubtful that the phenomenon can be comprehended in depth at all without a basic understanding of each level of variables—sociological, psychological, and biological—which act upon the disadvantaged individual.

INTELLECTUAL DEVELOPMENT AND ACADEMIC ACHIEVEMENT

That significant differences in cognitive and academic development exist between social classes is by now so well established as to be beyond dispute. The oldest and perhaps least informative method of assessing these differences involves the administration of intelligence tests to samples broken down by socioeconomic status and/or ethnic membership. Most investigators have failed to go beyond such broad correlates of class membership as race. In a survey of 240 studies of Negro-Caucasian IQ differences, Shuey (1958) found that only 17 considered the social status of their subjects in drawing conclusions. As Gottesman (1968) remarked,

> Intelligent behavior, as with every response, is multiply determined, and unless all the *relevant* variables are matched except race, no valid explanations can be made. Even a cursory glance at the literature about changes in IQ (for example, Anastasi, 1958; Tyler, 1965) reveals a vast number of statistically significant correlates of IQ. Among them are basal metabolism rate, EEG alpha frequency, height, weight, anxiety level, race and warmth of examiner, father's occupation and years of schooling, mother's attitude toward achievement, home cultural level, mother's concern with language development, degree of anoxia at birth, the desire to master intellectual skills, and others too numerous to mention. It should be obvious that IQ tests do not directly measure innate gene-determined intellectual capacity but do measure current intellectual performance as defined by a particular culture or at least by its psychologists [p. 25].

Reacting against such evident cultural bias, a strong and well-founded movement within the past decade has attempted to minimize the significance of the 10-20 point deficit of deprived subjects on IQ tests (Higgins and Sivers, 1958; Kennedy et al., 1963). A substantial contribution to this view has been made by researchers who have effectively revealed the nonfixed nature of IQ in deprived children (Dennis, 1960; Klineberg, 1935). Of particular importance is the longitudinal study of Skeels and Dye (1939) and Skeels and Skodak (1966), who placed thirteen nonorganically retarded orphans (age 7-30 months, mean IQ 64) in the care of institutionalized adult retarded women who then served as surrogate mothers. These were compared to a control group of twelve low-normal functioning orphans (mean IQ 87) who continued to live a routine existence at the orphanage. The experimental group remained at the institution for

> . . . the mentally retarded for periods which ranged from 5½ to 52 months. All gained in IQ by the end of their stay there from 7 to 45 points with a mean gain of 28 points. The individual IQ's now ranged from 79 to 113 with a mean of 92. . . . The youngest child was 7 months with an IQ of 89 when he was transferred to the institution from the orphanage, and returned in 5½ months with an IQ of 113. The oldest was 30 months with an IQ of 36 when he was transferred, and was 89 months with an IQ of 81 when he was returned to the orphange [Skeels and Skodak, 1965, p. 6].

Meanwhile, the control group in the deprived orphanage environment displayed a steady decrease in intellectual functioning. All but one lost between 8 and 45 points, and at the mean age of 48 months, their average IQ had dropped from 87 to 51. Thus, at the end of the experiment, the "retarded" experimental group was functioning normally, while their formerly normal peers were retarded. Furthermore, Skeels and Skodak, in a follow up report on the original subjects twenty-one years after the experiment found that the average experimental child had graduated from high school. One-third (including a girl with an original IQ of 35) had gone on to attend college, and one was a college graduate. On the other hand, half of the control group was unemployed, and all but one of those working were unskilled laborers. Obviously, this study reveals a great deal, not only of the nature of intelligence tests, but also of human deprivation.

In recent years, researchers have tended to focus their attention upon the academic deficits of the deprived individual and the personal characteristics which produce both low IQ scores and difficulty in school. HEW (1968) has listed several of the most commonly observed traits:

1. Restricted and limited knowledge of their environment;
2. Concretistic in their thought rather than conceptualistic (Sigel and Olmstead, 1967);
3. Using language for communication but not as a tool for reflective and introspective thought (John, 1963);
4. Reading and learning disability in terms of school tasks (Deutsch, 1963);
5. Presenting a high potential of school failure;
6. Time orientation in the present with short term perspective for planning (Miller et al., 1965);
7. Difficulty in dealing with representational material, imagery, etc. [p. 116].

Other characteristics frequently noted are difficulties in accepting delayed gratification (Miller et al., 1965), hyperactivity (Ausubel, 1963), higher performance than verbal ability as revealed by tests (Eells et al., 1951), difficulty with stimulus inhibition (M. Deutsch, 1963), and perceptual deficits (C. Deutsch, 1968). For example, McArdle (1965) found lower-class children do less well than middle-class children on an auditory discrimination task, while Covington (1967) obtained similar results with visual discrimination. Significantly, it was also found that the deprived children showed excellent posttest gains after being exposed to relevant stimulation. Children with such cognitive, perceptual, and behavioral handicaps almost invariably are unable to cope with the school's curriculum. This fact is well documented in research, and is corroborated by the reports of classroom teachers. All the characteristics noted by the aforementioned writers are found in varying relationships in children with specific learning disabilities.

Havighurst (1964) ranked the twenty-one school districts according to their median socioeconomic status. While sixth-grade children in the top seven districts had achievement scores between grade level and one year ahead of grade level, those in all but one of the lower seven were approximately one year behind. This pattern also held true for first graders, of whom only 40 percent in the lower SES districts were able to reach reading-readiness norms. Furthermore, Martin Deutsch (1960) found that while both black and white students of low SES performed significantly below national norms on the Stanford Achievement Test, the whites were considerably higher than blacks. Academic retardation increased with age for both racial groups, a commonly observed phenomenon known as the "cumulative deficit." Deutsch also found the low SES children to be inferior to middle-class subjects in tasks requiring concentration and persistence.

In its now-famous *Youth in the Ghetto* (1964), Harlem Youth Opportunities Unlimited (Haryou) reported an appalling cumulative deficit for Harlem school children, with third graders already a full year behind in reading comprehension, word knowledge, and arithmetic, and eighth graders at least two-and-a-half years below national norms. Haryou also found that well over half of Harlem high school students dropped out before receiving a diploma.

That minority group members suffer disproportionately the academic difficulties associated with socioeconomic deprivation was made abundantly clear by Coleman's report for the U.S. Office of Education in 1966. Following a nationwide testing program, Coleman concluded that Negro, Indian, Puerto Rican, and Mexican-American first graders are approximately one standard deviation below their white counterparts on standard achievement tests, and that they continue to fall further behind as they progress through school. This sustains the pattern noted by other researchers and summed up by Bond (1961) who observed that 3,581,370 children of laborers, as compared to 12,672 children of professionals and technicians, are needed to produce one National Merit Scholar!

ENVIRONMENTAL FACTORS IN DEPRIVATION

Confronted with substantial evidence of the underachievement of the poor, the obvious task becomes that of searching for the environmental causal factors, which must, of course, be identified before they can be remedied. While fine differentiations and measurements are sadly lacking here, there exists a common base of possible pathology influencing the cognitive growth of the deprived child. These phenomena have been described by a number of writers (O. Lewis, 1966; Riessman, 1962) and provide the basis for most of our speculations on the mediation of environmental stress to the individual.

Pavenstedt (1965) drew the important distinction between "upper-lower class" and "very low-lower class families." He found that while the former group had no books in the home (as noted also by M. Deutsch, 1964), lived amid constant noise, and took no interest in outside events, their families evidenced relative stability, clean living quarters, and little actual neglect of children. In the lowest group, however, the families were highly unstable, existing on a day-to-day basis, in a constant state of crisis within a chaotic world. These children often were extremely neglected. As babies, they were frequently isolated in cribs without toys in dark rooms, their cries ignored, with virtually no social stimulation other than the ever present blare of the television. They had very little opportunity for manipulating their environment, and their occasional efforts seldom resulted in a positive response; for in the overcrowded clutter of the slum home, the toddler's essential explorations are likely to be regarded as disruptive behavior by his overwhelmed parents. Indeed, Pavenstedt found, the role of the children in such homes was often that of a scapegoat for paternal frustrations. That such a life style is, undoubtedly, at least partially responsible for the apathy so frequently observed in such children has been pointed out by Taba (1964), who noted their motivational set of "getting by" rather than "getting ahead."

Other investigators have elaborated upon such conditions. H. Wortis et al. (1963), in a survey of child-rearing practices among low SES families, found that a third of the homes in their sample had over one-and-a-half occupants per room, and more than half of the chlidren did not have their own beds. Such crowding is naturally accompanied by a pervasive disorganization, as noted by Klaus and Gray (1968). Still others have commented upon the cultural alienation resulting from the absence of material goods in the home and slum or rural surroundings. Describing a typical home, Bagdikian (1964) wrote:

> This is the world of the vacuum cleaner, the dial telephone; the younger children would regard the circular arrangement of numbers and letters as a mystery. . . . Yet such mechanical fixtures are part of the vocabulary and concepts of the young, and school books and intelligence tests. The . . . children have never seen a movie and since a donated television set broke some time ago have lost even that touch with the outer world [p. 50].

Much of the early research on cultural disadvantagement grew out of the framework provided by studies on the effects of sensory deprivation upon animals. Consequently, a number of writers view the lack of sensory stimuli as a serious problem in the poverty complex (Berlin, 1966). While there can be little doubt that this is an important factor, especially in institutional environments (Dennis, 1960). some current investigators believe the problem to be one either of excessive, disorganized stimulation

(Wachs, 1967), or of lack of stimulus *variety,* which is actually a variant of absolute stimulus deprivation. There is certainly a *qualitative* difference between the stimulus world of middle-class children, with their toys, rides, pictures, games, and music, and that of some of their lower-class peers. Uzgiris (1970, p. 43) observed that:

> In a disadvantaged family, the visual surrounding is likely to be drab, but unless the infant is kept in some back room, the movements of others in the family are likely to produce changing visual inputs. There may be less variety in auditory stimulation, with the TV set constantly on. Against a noisy background, speech sounds may lose their distinctiveness and the child may learn to pay little attention to inputs through the auditory channel (C. Deutsch, 1964).

Another approach to the question of stimulation and experience is through the framework of cognitive schemata—configurations of symbols and images defined by their distinctive features—which are condensations of the individual's experiences. As Hunt (1961) stated, "Change in circumstances is required to force the accommodative modifications of schemata that constitute development. Thus, the greater the variety of situations to which the child must accommodate his behavioral structures, the more differentiated and mobile they become" (p. 258). In other words, the more a child experiences, the more he is capable of experiencing, provided that new situations are not radically discrepant in their essential features from the schemata which he already possesses. A number of writers (Hunt, 1965; Kagan, 1968; Sigel, 1968) have expressed the view that much of the lower-class child's school difficulty results from a mismatch between the structure of the middle-class curriculum and his own cognitive structures.

Another area in which a good deal of interest has developed concerns the effects of deprivation on personality development. Because emotional and behavioral problems are a recognized cause of learning difficulties, a brief glance is in order here.

Imaginative capacity is enhanced by frequent and meaningful contacts with adults, by privacy, and by opportunities to experience a wide variety of toys and materials (Singer, 1968). Dependence drive, which provides the basis for interpersonal relations and has long been thought to be distorted by early neglect, develops from "the infant's participation in progressively more complex patterns of reciprocal interaction with the mother" (Bronfenbrenner, 1968b, p. 251). Anxiety is also reduced by satisfaction of these security and affection needs, which Kami (1965) and Hess et al. (1965) have found to be much more capably handled in middle-class socialization. This is supported by Feld and Lewis (1967), who found black second graders significantly more anxious than their white classmates. With regard to task orientation HEW (1968) reported that "a very early child rearing climate marked by (1) recognition and prompt support of the infant's needs, and (2) the presentation of a rich variety of sensory inputs appears conducive to . . . the cultivation of a disposition to manipulate the environment" (p. 22). Finally, the conditions which generate self-esteem—acceptance, success, social and vocational skills, absence of stigmata—are as conspicuously absent in the culture of poverty as are the other desirable characteristics mentioned above. It certainly comes as no surprise that mental illness rates repeatedly have been found higher in the lower social strata of the population (Hollingshead and Redlich, 1958; Strole et al., 1962).

An aspect of economic deprivation receiving increased attention from educators, psychologists, and linguists during the past decade is that of language development, which, because it is the basis for reading, becomes the most important skill of all for school success. Unfortunately, nearly every force in the environment of the lower-class child acts to inhibit his use of the language. While a strong argument can be made for the view that, linguistically, lower-class nonstandard and particularly Black English dialects are highly complex and sophisticated (Labor, 1970), this provides little consolation; for the fact remains that speakers of nonstandard English do not have at their command the most essential tool for dealing with powerful social institutions on their own terms. The authors fully recognize that the ideal solution to this dilemma might be to change the attitudes of the power bases within society toward "different" modes of expression or to redistribute the power. Despite the immediate desirability of these alternatives, however, such a restructuring of society represents a long-range goal.

Perhaps the problem originates with the poor auditory discrimination resulting from high noise levels, as considered above in the work of Cynthia Deutsch, Covington, and McArdle. In *Crisis in Black and White* (1964), Charles Silberman gave an example of the classroom effect of this handicap on the child:

> He fails to develop an ability to distinguish between relevant and irrelevant sounds, and to screen out the irrelevant. If, for example, a truck rumbles by while the teacher is talking, the lower-class youngster hears only one big jumble of sound; the middle-class child has the ability to screen out the irrelevant noise of the truck and listen only to the teacher [pp. 270-1].

Other language difficulties of some poor children may evolve from the total absence of reading material in the home, often resulting in a complete ignorance of the existence of books and the concept of reading upon entering school. Compare this with the experience of the wealthier child, who has been read to, has played with letters and numbers, and has owned picture and story books since he was two. Furthermore, consider the vast gap in vocabulary between the two peers merely on the basis of their experiences in the home and out in the world. Whereas the middle-class student has been responded to, rewarded, and given feedback for his verbalizations since the babbling stage, the child of poverty probably has been ignored, if not stifled, in his attempts (Cahill, 1967). One of the most common observations concerning child-rearing practices among the poor is the dearth of verbal interaction between mother and child (Hess et al., 1965; John and Goldstein, 1964).

Even if the mother and child did interact extensively, as Hurley indicated, the child would benefit little, due to the model provided by the mother's own abbreviated syntactical structure. Bernstein (1961) has called attention to the "restricted" language style of the lower class, which depends upon the common background of speaker and listener to convey meaning. As Hurley (1969) has observed, "In the middle-class family a mother may say to her child, 'Joseph, go to the shelf and bring me the blue bottle of ink.' The lower-class mother in the same situation probably says 'get that,' or 'bring it here,' or even just points to the article she wants and by use of sign language, communicates her desires to the child" (p. 80).

Because the deprived student is not equipped with the basic tools he needs to cope with school, he starts out at a disadvantage and falls further behind year after year. It is likely that language difficulties constitute the one most significant cause of these children's failure to learn. There also exist other forces which simultaneously impair their abilities immeasurably. One of these factors, unfortunately, is all too often the school structure itself; another is the possible brain damage which may develop as a result of living in extreme poverty.

BIONEURAL RESULTS OF DEPRIVATION

In recent years a considerable body of research has demonstrated that central nervous system disorders may not be randomly distributed throughout the population; and it is now generally thought that brain damage, in some degree, is far more prevalent among deprived children than has traditionally been believed. Many of the learning, perceptual, and motor characteristics commonly ascribed to these children are in fact identical to the classic symptoms of cerebral dysfunction. This is illustrated by the work of Cawley (1966), who found Head Start children to be severely lagging on tests of eye-motor coordination, form constancy, position in space, spacial relations, motor speed, auditory attention, visual attention, language output, and stimulus organization and sequencing—disabilities which he attributed to "developmental lag." The reader should keep in mind, however, that there are only *behavioral* indications of cerebral dysfunction, and these are not proof-positive of brain injury.

In Muskegon, Michigan, Amante and his co-workers (1970) divided 219 school children into five socioeconomic groups and attempted to determine the distribution of CNS disorders in each group. While they found evidence of brain damage in 10 percent of the subjects from the upper three classes, the figure for the lower two classes was 24 percent. Furthermore, when the subjects in the lower strata group were analyzed by race, the rate for black subjects was found to be an extraordinary 58 percent, which supports the conclusion of Bronfenbrenner (1968a) and of Birch and Gussow (1970) that lower-class Blacks are even more susceptible to the pathogenic elements in their environment than are whites. Thus, though they recognized that their sample is quite small and the diagnostic tool (the Bender-Gestalt) exceedingly crude, Amante et al. concluded that "cases of brain damage in children are highly concentrated in the poor white and black segments of the community" (p. 106). Again, the conclusion is based upon behavioral measures.

At Baltimore's Sinai-Druid Comprehensive Health Center, which services an extremely disadvantaged area of the city, Kappelman, Kaplan, and Ganter (1969) obtained similar and more convincing results. Of 306 children referred for learning disabilities and evaluated by medical, psychological, hearing, language, and educational specialists, 55 percent were found to have *confirmed* organic damage. In light of their findings, these investigators suggested that "a reevaluation of rehabilitative and remedial programs designed for the disadvantaged child appears necessary in view of the major role of neurologically based disabilities in this population group. It is simply not adequate to label the poor achiever in the inner-city classroom as culturally deprived and to allow this all-inclusive term to explain his poor approach and response to the learning experience" (p. 32).

Two basic approaches have been taken in attempting to determine the etiology of possible organic damage. The first, derived from biomedical research on stimulus-organism interaction, is directly concerned with the neurological results of differing kinds and amounts of stimuli. The second generally consists of sociological-statistical attempts to correlate environmental variables known to be associated with CNS disorders with socioeconomic class membership. Since both approaches are valid and productive, Amante et al. (1970) have combined them into a comprehensive and highly useful theoretical paradigm, in which "the induction of CNS dysfunction and associated effects" are viewed as forming a self-perpetuating chain of causality (Fig. 18):

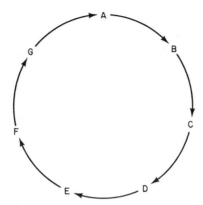

FIGURE 18 The self-perpetual chain of interrelated events (Amante et al., 1970, p. 110)

A. Interclass and interracial value, attitudinal, behavioral, and experiential differentials on the part of the parental generation conducive to the induction of CNS dysfunction relative to the filial generation (A Sociocultural Variable).
B. The consequent induction of CNS dysfunction (A Biological Variable).
C. The emergence of perceptual-motor problems and/or intellectual deficits symptomatic of the underlying CNS dysfunction (A Psychological Variable).
D. The eventual onset of various kinds of academic "learning disabilities," such as reading problems, related to the perceptual-motor difficulties and/or the intellectual deficits (An Educational Variable).
E. Consequent academic underachievement (An Educational Variable).
F. The determination of reduced socioeconomic status consequent upon academic underachievement—largely by means of occupational determination in the case of the male, and by means of marital selection, in the case of the female (A Sociological Variable).
G. The final induction of an emotional-motivational set, state, or "frame of mind"—consequent upon progressive, continuous, or ongoing socialization in a given region or sector of the social (class) structure—conducive to the development of the values, the attitudes, the behavior, and the experiences associated with factor "A" (A Social-Psychological Variable) [pp. 109-10].

STUDIES OF DIFFERENTIAL STIMULATION

As early as 1924, Child (1924) and Herrick (1924) hypothesized that the growth of the brain depends essentially upon the amount and type of stimulation received and the resultant motor reflex activities. Since then, a substantial amount of research has supported this view, and it is now universally agreed that sensory deprivation in sufficient quantity and properly timed results either in permanent organic impairment or in nondevelopment of neural structures. Furthermore, as Grotberg (1970) concluded, "a nondeveloping nervous system may indeed produce the same learning disability symptoms as a damaged nervous system" (p. 325).

Working with dark-reared mice, Valverde (1967) has reported a 20 percent reduction in the number of dendritic spines of the visual cortex, while Globus and Scheibel (1967) have obtained similar results with mice, as have Coleman and Riesen (1968) with cats. Cragg (1967) has also found the synapses of the visual cortex to be reduced in diameter in rats reared in darkness during the first three weeks after birth. In another recent experiment, Bell et al. (1971) found that, in mice, crowded living conditions resulted in slowed neuronal development, with reduced concentrations of brain protein and nucleic acids and decreased rate of intercellular synthesis of RNA and protein by DNA.

In a very important experiment, Rosenzweig (1966) raised one group of rats in an enriched environment replete with ladders, wheels, boxes, platforms, group exploratory opportunities, and maze training. The other group was raised in individual cages with opaque walls in a quiet, dimly lit room. After 105 days, Rosenzweig found "the cortex of the enriched rats weighs 4 percent more than that of the restricted rats (p. < .001)" (p. 323). Increases were noted both in cortical thickness and in glial cells, globules which apparently provide structural and nutritional support to the neurons. A significant rise also occurred in the total activity of acetycholine, the chemical which conveys electrical impulses across the synapse. Krech et al. (1966) have demonstrated that organic tissue retardation accompanies social deprivation in rats.

On a more theoretical level, Prescott (1967), after reviewing the literature on maternal and social deprivation, has argued that these are actually cases of somatosensory deprivation, and that the "behavioral pathologies associated with maternal-social deprivation, which include hyperexcitability, increased violence and aggression, impaired socialization, . . . movement stereotypes and apathy, . . . can be attributed specifically to neurostructural, neurochemical, and neuroelectrical deficits in the somatosensory system nad allied central nervous system structures" (Riesen, 1968, p. 297). While such an hypothesis would certainly appear plausible, it has yet to be supported by conclusive empirical research. At was seen in the analysis of malnutrition, the techniques of neurology and biochemistry are not yet developed to the point where they can confirm many of our suspicions; and the problems of transferring such knowledge from one species to another and of relating overt behavior to neurological phenomena present formidable methodological barriers. Great care must be taken in attempting to apply these results to human populations.

STUDIES OF SOCIOLOGICAL VARIABLES

On the sociological level, a large number of factors have been suggested as possible agents in causing brain damage. A number of researchers have implicated sensory bombardment, crowding, and high noise levels (Bell et al., 1971; Ferreira, 1969; Kincaid, 1965; Riesen, 1968). It is suspected that some congenital malformations may be the result of the pregnant mother's emotional state (Ferreira, 1969). Rosengren (1964) has noted that the lower-class mother frequently perceives her pregnancy (not without reason) as "sickness" and as "crisis." Also, because of poor lighting, fire hazards, and the absence of playgrounds in the city slum, the possibility of accidental brain damage is greatly increased (Clark, 1965).

The incidence of a great many diseases and physical disabilities varies inversely with socioeconomic status, and their presence may result in organic impairment if left untreated. Hurley (1969) divided these into two groups: those affecting the child through the mother during pregnancy, and those occurring after birth. As for the first group of diseases, pregnant lower-class women have been found to have a higher incidence of syphilis, toxoplasmosis, rubella, anemia, malnutrition, chronic vascular disease, and various reproductive malfunctions, each of which may affect the developing neurological system of the foetus (Hardy 1965; Masland et al., 1958; Thompson, 1963). Hurley continues (p. 65):

The second group—the diseases of infancy and childhood—likewise put the poor children at greater risk of suffering organic damage. Nonwhites have death rates, for example, up to more than twice those of whites for the following diseases: meningitis, measles, encephalitis, diphtheria, whooping cough, scarlet fever, nephritis, influenza, and pneumonia (Pettigrew, 1964).

That the life style of the poor is conducive to poor health is exceedingly well documented. Since the poor are unable to afford proper medical care, many pathological conditions must go untreated. Public treatment facilities are notoriously understaffed and complicated by bureaucracy, which only increases the suspiciousness of the poor with regard to medical treatment. Unquestionably a cultural conflict exists between the poor and the medical profession (Birch and Gussow, 1970; Hurley, 1969; Roth, 1969), and the conflict by no means is one-sided:

The general run of the research in this area has revealed a most interesting paradox: the poor in general are characterized by the more severe forms of physical and mental pathology and receive inferior treatment, while the more affluent segments of the population are characterized by less serious forms of physical and mental pathology and receive superior treatment. There is certainly sufficient evidence available to suggest that there is a good deal more to consider than simply the "resistance" of the lower class patient population to the reception of adequate medical services. Perhaps, in fact, the major component of the problem involves the "resistance" of middle or upper class medical specialists to extend adequate medical treatment to the lower class patient population [Amante et al., 1970, p. 118].

There is no more tragic aspect of sociocultural deprivation than the unnecessary loss of human potential which inevitably results from inadequate medical attention. The poor woman is likely to present a high pregnancy risk from the start, for she has her first child at a younger age, has more children, and goes on having them longer (despite the likelihood of her poor physical and emotional condition) than does her middle-class counterpart (Birch and Gussow, 1970; Rider et al., 1955). She probably will not receive competent and early obstetrical care. As many as 70 percent of poor mothers have been reported to receive little or no prenatal medical attention (Thompson, 1963), which, of course, leads to greatly increased chances of complications and prematurity. It is not surprising, then, that prematurity rates consistently have been found to be much higher in the lower classes. For example, while the prematurity rate for the entire population is usually around 7 percent, for the poor in Newark in 1965 it was 16.5 percent (Mayer, 1965). In Baltimore, Pasamanick and Knoblock (1961) found prematurity rates of 5.0 percent for upper class whites, 7.6 percent for lower class whites, and 11.4 percent for blacks. Furthermore, the incidence of complications was 5.0 percent and 14.6 percent for the two white groups, as compared to an astounding 50.6 percent for blacks. Similar results have also been obtained by other investigators (Donnelly et al., 1964; R. A. Ross, 1964). As Birch and Gussow (1970) have written, "No single condition is more clearly associated with a wide range of insult to the nervous system than the too early expulsion into the world of a child scarcely able to function as an independent organism" (p. 51). Thus the child begins his journey through poverty, against nearly hopeless odds, frequently doomed from conception.

The recognition of the deplorable psychological, sociological, and biological conditions resulting from poverty is obviously only a beginning. The true challenge now lies in the eradication of these ills. Unfortunately, the intervention measures applied in this country to date have been too narrow in scope, too few, too late, often incompetently administered, and almost invariably backed by inadequate funding. With the problem originating in widely and deeply held misconceptions of the nature of man and society, it is doubtful that anything short of radical reevaluations of national priorities and of social structure can have much effect. Hopefully, with ever increasing public awareness of the deprived populations, the decades ahead will see a corresponding increase in emphasis on human resources. Until such a philosophical change occurs, however, millions of children and adults will continue to be thwarted in their attempts to realize their birthright.

SUMMARY

In this chapter the authors have focused on nutritional and environmental deprivations as being, among other things, fundamental etiological factors in the production of specific learning disorders. Woven into these discussions the reader will recall mention of such things as rubella, toxemias, and others which are also related to ensuing specific learning disorders and to psychopathology in children. While poverty and environmental factors may be more specifically related to lower socioeconomic groups in the society, upper-class groups are not in any sense able to escape the impact of problems which result in learning disorders. Rubella, for example, is as much a factor of upper-class women as it is for other social groups. Accidents, injuries, and unsuccessful attempts at self-abortion are other factors reported as being related to CNS dysfunction in children from this latter group of mothers. Injuries to the foetus experienced during the birth process itself are reported in 35 percent of 1105 children with cerebral palsy (Hopkins, Bice, Colton, 1954). The issue of specific learning disorders is a matter for all social groups, although the relation of etiological factors among social-class groups may vary.

The focus here is on the interrelationship of neurological dysfunction, perception, and learning disorders in any social-class group. Two factors of major significance, nutrition and environmental deprivation, have been isolated for special attention as causative. Since all learning is neurologically based, any dysfunction of the neurological system, whether diagnosed, specified, and isolated or not, is of vital importance to the understanding and planning by psychologists and educators who must implement community-based programs for children. Research of a multidisciplinary nature is now essential to the further understanding of the problem. Educators, psychologists, neurologists, sociologists, and clinical psychopharmacologists in particular must combine their efforts in this direction.

In the chapters which follow we will examine the efforts which have been made by two of these disciplines, psychology and education, in the search for a fuller understanding of the problem.

CHAPTER 3

Investigators in the Historical Development of Learning Disabilities

A comprehensive discourse on any field of endeavor cannot ignore the people, ideas, and events which have influenced the development of that particular field. In this chapter we attempt to place in historical perspective the landmark research and literature of individuals who have been instrumental to the generation and growth of major concepts in the exploration of learning disabilities. Some of these concepts and the issues surrounding them are more fully explored in later chapters. They are grouped here to underscore their interrelatedness and their significance to the evolution of learning disability theory and research.

Astute historical analysis, whether political, scientific, or other, inevitably points to the relevance of incidents both within the same realm of study and from one diverse area of interest to another. In fact, the history scholar, recognizing the saliency of perceived relationships, expends the better part of his energy in striving to discover and decipher the interassociations of various persons and events. Seldom are there more manifest signs of the ramifications that particular historical occurrences can have for other seemingly unrelated events than in the field of mental retardation, profoundly affected as it was by the global conflict of this century. Even the unborn field of learning disabilities was notably influenced as it evolved from a particular series of studies within the field of mental retardation in general.

Heinz Werner

Samuel A. Kirk

Alfred A. Strauss

NEWELL C. KEPHART

MARIANNE FROSTIG

KATRINA DE HIRSCH

GERALD N. GETMAN

ALFRED STRAUSS AND HEINZ WERNER, INVESTIGATIVE PIONEERS

In the 1930s, the rise to power of Hitler's regime precipitated the emigration of many German scientists, including two men of singular importance to the eventual field of learning disabilities—Alfred A. Strauss, an associate professor of psychiatry at the University of Heidelberg, and Heinz Werner, an associate professor of psychology at the University of Hamburg.

Settling first in Spain, Strauss became guest lecturer at the University of Barcelona from 1933 to 1936 and during that lectureship cofounded both the first governmental and the first private child guidance centers in that country. National strife and the threat of civil war, however, prompted Strauss to leave the country in 1936. The next year, acting upon an invitation from Superintendent R. H. Haskell, Strauss accepted an appointment as research psychiatrist at Wayne County Training School in Northville, Michigan. Werner, too, following a brief stay in the Netherlands, emigrated to the United States where he accepted appointments for short periods of time at Harvard University and at the University of Michigan. He and Strauss soon found themselves together in the research department of the Training School. Thus it was that the imminent dangers accompanying Hitler's ascendancy brought these two men into close contact in the United States. It is doubtful that the theorization of either Strauss or Werner working separately on the psychological characteristics of brain injured, mentally retarded children would have achieved the impact of their collaborative efforts.

Curiously, not only the circumstances that provoked World War II, but also certain incidents related to World War I, had a bearing upon the work of Werner and Strauss. It was the research of Head (1926a, 1926b), and especially of Goldstein (1927, 1936, 1939), with soldiers who had suffered head wounds in World War I, that to a great extent determined the course of Werner and Strauss's research and conceptualizations.

Goldstein had found in his patients, whom he called "traumatic dements," the psychological characteristics of concrete behavior, meticulosity, perseveration, figure-background confusion, forced responsiveness to stimuli, and catastrophic reaction. The latter behavior, certainly the most unusual, is identified as an extreme emotional lability in which the brain injured individual reacts violently and becomes disorganized and disoriented. In what was diagnosed as an attempt to combat the feeling of catastrophe, Goldstein's patients frequently engaged in other behaviors which, while less threatening, were nevertheless abnormal. Excessive orderliness or meticulosity, for instance, usually replaced the disorganized behavior to which the men were prone. The extreme tidiness and concern for placing objects in a prescribed place were thought to exemplify the brain injured patients' rigid cautiousness in avoiding a catastrophic reaction. In addition, Goldstein clinically observed that his patients often exhibited perseveration, a tendency to repeat the same actions over and over again. This repetition of behaviors which could adequately be performed in an organized way appeared to be the organism's method of rescuing itself from disorganization.

Concrete behavior was also found to be a prevailing symptom of the brain-injured subjects. Goldstein observed (1939) that in numerous intellectual endeavors, whenever one of the subjects

> must transcend concrete (immediate) experience in order to act—whenever he must refer to things in an imaginery way—he then fails. . . . Each problem which forces him beyond the sphere of immediate reality to that of the 'possible,' to the sphere of representation, insures his failure [p. 29].

Abstract behaviors, for example, such as those involved in arithmetic operations, could only be performed with objects that could be touched and held. Like Sherrington, Goldstein postulated that the disintegration of abstracting or categorizing ability was, because of its primary place in the hierarchy of complex behaviors, the first intellectual sphere to be affected by injury to the central nervous system.

Additional symptoms recorded and thought to be interrelated were figure-ground confusion and forced responsiveness to stimuli. His patients' difficulties in paying attention to the figure while ignoring the ground convinced Goldstein of their pervasive inability to refrain from responding to inessential stimuli.

For Werner and Strauss it became a major concern to learn whether the psychological manifestations of brain injury found in adults by Goldstein would also be observable in children. Evidence of this concern is abundantly palpable in their writings. Marie Strauss has recently noted that, among others, Kurt Goldstein was one of those who most directly contributed to her husband's thinking.[1]

Soon after their arrival at Wayne County Training School, Werner and Strauss, working from an earlier study (1933) by Strauss, launched a series of investigations of brain injured, mentally retarded children. While the 1933 study had dealt with severely retarded children, the collaborative efforts of Werner and Strauss centered primarily upon retarded children who exhibited less profound intellectual impairment and other than gross neurological disturbances.

Werner and Strauss, both struggling with their newly acquired English

[1] Personal communication from Marie Strauss, February 26, 1971.

language, groped for appropriate terminology to characterize the children they were investigating. For the most part, they referred to them either as *exogenous,* indicating mental retardation due to neurological defects, or as *endogenous,* indicating mental retardation due to familial factors. It appears that commitment to exclusive use of these terms was not complete, however, since as late as 1943 Strauss employed the unintentionally offensive term "cripple-brained" as a synonym for exogenous (Strauss, 1943). Nevertheless, the endogenous versus exogenous distinction enjoyed most frequent usage and eventually came to be associated with both men. Actually, in a brief footnote, Strauss (Strauss and Lehtinen, 1947) credited the origin of the dichotomy to Larsen (1931). The terms were first applied by Strauss in the 1933 German study and then became popularized by both Werner and Strauss in the United States.

In their experimentation, Werner and Strauss considered a child exogenous if there were no evidence of mental retardation in his immediate family and if his case history indicated a prenatal, natal, or postnatal disease or injury to the brain. In addition, a child might be diagnosed as brain injured on the basis of behavioral traits, which, as Sarason (1949) has aptly pointed out, results in the possibility of circularity when one attempts to attribute the cause of certain behaviors to brain injury. Nevertheless, the evidence of Werner and Strauss does indicate that within the mentally retarded population there does exist a subgroup which displays certain kinds of behaviors. Whether or not the behaviors are a consequence of insult to the brain, as Werner and Strauss have claimed, their presence in some retarded children is no less real. In this sense, it is logical to make the exogenous versus endogenous differentiation in the identification of distinctions based upon behavior, regardless of whether the behavior has an etiological base.

Early Perceptual-Motor Studies of Werner and Strauss

A number of the experiments conducted by Werner, Strauss, and their colleagues dealt with perceptual and perceptual-motor functions. Werner and Strauss (1939b), for example, analyzed the visual-motor performance of exogenous and endogenous children on a marble-board task in which the subject first was asked to copy on another board a design made by the experimenter and then was instructed to draw on paper the experimenter's design. Performing better than their exogenous peers, the endogenous children performed similarly to normal children of comparable mental age. On the other hand, the exogenous children went about their constructions in an entirely different and quite extraordinary manner. Whereas the endogenous youngsters were apparently guided by a sense of form, the exogenous subjects capriciously moved from one part of the board to another. On the basis of this behavior, Werner and Strauss maintained that the disorganized patterns of the exogenous child reflected visual-motor impairment.

In order to ascertain whether the exogenous versus endogenous distinction was observable in sensory modalities other than the visual-motor system, an experiment (Werner and Bowers, 1941) was conducted to assess performance on an auditory-motor task. After each of seventeen melodic patterns of varying difficulty was played on the piano, the experimenter requested that the child reproduce the pattern vocally. As was found on the visual-motor task, the auditory-motor experiment revealed that the vocalization of exogenous children lacked melodic-harmonic synthesis and satisfactory endings, whereas the responses of endogenous subjects resembled normal children's more global, homogeneous responses. This experimental evidence ostensibly indicated the existence in exogenous children of a rather general impairment across sensory modalities.

Without de-emphasizing the historical value of the Werner and Bowers study, it should be noted that the investigation, in keeping with the quality of educational and psychological research produced in the early 1940s, was of a very crude nature. The mechanical refinements for reproducing and recording musical melodies and sophisticated research designs were not at their disposal as they would be today. Naturally, this criticism is also appropriate for the early research of Werner and Strauss. Yet while their work by today's standards would be considered imperfect, its historical and theoretical value is beyond calculation.

In an effort to explain the singular behavior of the exogenous children they tested, Werner and Strauss employed Goldstein's concept of "forced responsiveness" to stimuli. The exogenous children, like Goldstein's adults, were perceived as unable to direct attention to the task at hand because of the interference of inessential stimuli. Supporting this conclusion were the results of an experiment in which groups of exogenous and endogenous children viewed a tachistoscopic presentation of common objects, each of which was embedded in a clearly structured background (Werner and Strauss, 1941). When asked what they had just been shown, the exogenous subjects were more likely than the endogenous controls to evidence an over-attraction to stimuli by reporting that they had seen the background rather than the figure.

At a more abstract level, too, evidence was accumulating that exogenous children could be differentiated from endogenous children. Strauss and Werner (1942) developed tests of concept formation based upon the earlier studies of Cotton (1941) and Halstead (1940) with brain-injured adults. In one testing situation, when the child was asked to group simple objects that went together, Werner and Strauss found the exogenous children to be easily distracted by the vividness, intensity, and/or extensity of inessential elements. On a task requiring the child to place objects before one of two pictures of real-life situations (e.g., a picture of a house on fire and a picture of a boy drowning), it was found that the exogenous children chose objects rarely picked by the endogenous subjects. When asked the rationale for their selections, the exogenous children were much more likely than their endogenous peers to report inessential details as the basis of their choices.

With regard to personality characteristics, Strauss and Kephart (1940), using a behavior-rating scale, found that exogenous children could be differentiated from endogenous children on a number of behaviors, the former being more disinhibited, erratic, impulsive, socially unaccepted, uncontrolled, and uncoordinated. In studies of the exogenous child, these behaviors eventually became synonymous with hyperactivity (Strauss and Lehtinen, 1947).

Thus it was that Werner and Strauss and their colleagues, with a variety of experimental tasks, offered substantiating evidence that the psychological characteristics of Goldstein's brain-injured adults were shared by children classified as exogenous. Furthermore, in two studies (Werner and Thuma, 1942a, 1942b) of an experimental-physiological nature, the authors corroborated Goldstein's theoretical position with regard to the isolation of neural events as a consequence of brain injury. Werner and Thuma borrowed Goldstein's theoretical construct of neural isolation to explain why exogenous children, more than endogenous children, exhibited, among other things, defective perception of apparent movement and lower critical flicker frequencies.

Werner and Strauss and their colleagues also were interested in the implications of such findings with regard to the learning and education of exogenous children. In a survey of the first 500 admissions to the Wayne County Training School, Strauss and Kephart (1939) had found that exogenous children as a group declined 2.5 IQ points during residence in the institution over four to five years. The endogenous children, on the other hand, had increased 4.0 points during institutionalization. In a further investigation of this difference in the direction of IQ trend, Kephart and Strauss (1940) looked at those subjects whose intelligence test scores could be traced from a period of time prior to admission at the school to a period of time afterward. Whereas the exogenous children showed a steady decline in IQ over the years, the endogenous children experienced decline only until the time of institutionalization, whereupon the trend was reversed and IQ scores increased. Apparently, the exogenous children were not benefitting from an educational program intended for both them and the endogenous children. It was hypothesized by the Wayne County group that the reason for this discrepancy was the inability of the exogenous children to profit from a highly stimulating environment and curriculum.

Recognizing the need for educational methods geared to the particular psychological nature of the exogenous child, Werner and Strauss (1940) recommended without elaboration the attenuation of inessential stimuli and the accentuation of essential stimuli in the environment of such a child. This strategy, as explained by Strauss (1943) in more detail, formed the backbone for the classic volume authored by Strauss and Lehtinen (1947), but actually derived from the culmination of more than a decade of research and clinical work by Werner and Strauss at Wayne County Training School. Unfortunately the significant contribution of Werner was not recognized in the authorship of this book, which is based in a very major way on his research efforts of a decade.

What the Strauss and Lehtinen publication advocated was a comprehensive psychological and educational program for exogenous children. Their basic educational attitude is evident in the following statement from the volume:

> Since the organic lesion is medically untreatable, our efforts may extend in two directions: in manipulating and controlling the external, overstimulating environment and in educating the child to the exercise of voluntary control [p. 131].

In conjunction with these objectives, Strauss and Lehtinen designated specific tasks for alleviating the particular problem or problems of the individual child. Included among these tasks were a number of perceptual-motor training activities.

A Bequest to the Field of Learning Disabilities

Before exploring the ways in which various investigators, Cruickshank, Kephart, and other learning disabilities proponents, relied upon the early concepts of Werner and Strauss, it is worthwhile to note the general tenor that the work of the early pioneers established for the field of mental retardation as a whole, because without it the eventual development of the study of learning disabilities would have been impeded.

A basic tenet borrowed by the field of learning disabilities from the work of Werner and Strauss was first presented by Werner (1937) in a paper wherein, as a developmental psychologist, he contended that in order to more fully understand normal child psychology, as well as mental deficiency, one must go beyond mere standardized achievement test scores.

An analysis must be made, he maintained, of the mental processes underlying the achievements.

In a more thorough exposition, Werner and Strauss (1939a) advocated functional analysis, an approach to the education and psychology of mentally retarded children which is strikingly similar to that of present-day learning disabilities theorists. In functional analysis, one is concerned not with a particular test score, but with how the child achieved that score. As stated by Werner and Strauss, the general method of functional analysis was "the examination of an individual in critical situations which elicit the impaired functions" [p. 61]. Along with this analysis of functions of the mentally retarded went the insistence that each child must be assessed in terms of his particular abilities and disabilities.

> It is clear that the results of functional analysis, rather than the data from achievement tests, should serve as a guide for remedial work. The methods, techniques and materials for training must be chosen for their adequacy in relation to the functional impairment [p. 62].

The conceptual posture of Werner and Strauss, coupled with their research into the differentiation between exogenous and endogenous mental retardation, did much to destroy the then-popular notion that mental retardation was a homogeneous state. Concern for the diagnosis of particular disabilities and educational procedures based upon the Werner and Strauss recommendations became an intrinsic element of the basic principles upon which the field of learning disabilities was constructed.

PERCEPTUAL-MOTOR THEORISTS WITHIN THE FIELD OF LEARNING DISABILITIES

Having established the presence of a relationship between the domain of mental retardation and that of learning disabilities, we will now trace the ideational development of particular learning disabilities theorists back to the work of Werner and Strauss. Some of the major concepts of the latter two which inspired learning disabilities theorists embraced and expanded have already been mentioned. In essence, the bequest of Werner and Strauss to the fundamental principles of learning disability theory includes maximum concern for: (a) specific individual disabilities and techniques to deal with them; (b) perceptual-motor difficulties and training to modify them; and (c) the psychological characteristics of hyperactivity and distractibility and educational procedures to minimize them.

William Cruickshank

Before the above-mentioned tripartite contribution of Werner and Strauss could be said to provide a germinal core for the field of learning disabilities, there had to be an historical transition from their work with the mentally retarded to a concern for the intellectually normal. The first attempt to apply Werner's and Strauss's conceptions of exogenous mental retardation to children of normal intelligence, and thus a major step in the formation of the needed link, was the doctoral dissertation of Jane Dolphin (1950), written under the supervision of William Cruickshank. It was no accident that the work of Cruickshank took this direction, since close contact with both Werner and Strauss at Wayne County Training School in the early years of his career had profoundly affected the development of his own philosophy (Cruickshank, 1971).

Essentially, the Dolphin dissertation and also the Dolphin and Cruickshank studies that took root from it substantiated the Werner and Strauss discoveries regarding exogenous children. Dolphin and Cruickshank worked with an experimental population of cerebral palsied children of near-average, average, and above-average IQ. These children, when compared to their nonhandicapped peers, demonstrated deficiencies in the discrimination of figure from background (Dolphin and Cruickshank, 1951a), in concept formation ability (Dolphin and Cruickshank, 1951b), in visual-motor performance (Dolphin and Cruickshank, 1951c), and in tactual-motor performance (Dolphin and Cruickshank, 1952). In a study under the direction of Cruickshank (Cruickshank, Bice, and Wallen, 1957), the Dolphin-Cruickshank investigations were expanded to a full-scale exploration of the perceptual and figure-ground abilities of cerebral palsied children. The latter was expanded still further, and in-depth studies of figure-ground relationships were undertaken with different two- and three-dimensional presentations of colored and black-and-white stimuli (Cruickshank, Bice, Wallen, and Lynch, 1965). Once again, the results attested to the hypothesis that cerebral palsied children displayed the same psychological characteristics found by Werner and Strauss in their exogenous, mentally retarded subjects. Additionally, the investigations lent substantive support to the educational recommendations earlier forwarded by Cruickshank and Dolphin (1951). Noting the similarity in psychological characteristics manifested by cerebral palsied children and by Werner and Strauss's exogenous children and criticizing the use of traditional teaching methods with them, Cruickshank and Dolphin called for a reassessment of the education of the cerebral palsied. This reassessment would entail adoption of and elaboration upon the recommendations forwarded by Strauss and Lehtinen (1947) for exogenous children.

In the late 1950s, Cruickshank was responsible for a number of dissertations dealing with various aspects of cerebral palsy, exogenous mental retardation, and epilepsy. For example, D. Y. Miller (1958) found that a group of exogenous children did not differ from an endogenous control group on a number of variables associated with the reading process. Trippe (1958) presented data to indicate the absence of a relationship between certain aspects of performance on a test of visual figure-background ability and scores on a number of projective tests. Neely (1958) found no significant relationships between reading or arithmetic achievement and visual figure-ground ability *unrelated* to learned experience in school; however, his research did reveal significant relationships between reading or arithmetic achievement and visual figure-ground ability *related* to learned experience in school. Norris (1958) reported evidence that extraneous sound interfered with the constructive task performance of cerebral palsied children. Shaw (1955; see also Shaw and Cruickshank, 1956a, 1956b), using the marble-board test, was unable to differentiate the visual-motor performance of epileptic and nonconvulsive children. Using the Bender-Gestalt, he also found no difference between the two groups on their total scores, although he did learn that epileptic children had more difficulty in placing the figures on the paper, in spacing them, and in making them the proper size. Consequently, Shaw suggested that while epileptic children can perform a simple visual-motor task, they have problems in integrating subparts in a harmonious manner.

Thus, studies and conceptualizations by Cruickshank, and the work he encouraged, provided the impetus for extending the ideas of Werner and Strauss to the study of intellectually normal children, i.e., cerebral palsied children of varying intellectual abilities. Nevertheless, since cerebral palsied children are brain injured, there remained the need for a conceptual transition to the assessment of children of normal or near-normal intelligence who, while displaying behavioral characteristics often associated with brain damage, could not assuredly be assumed to have suffered central nervous system impairment. Such children, frequently referred to at that time as "minimally brain injured," would today be considered "learning disabled."

Cruickshank again was one of the instrumental figures in establishing the requisite link. Noting the accumulation of clinical evidence that some non-mentally retarded and non-cerebral palsied children showed perceptual-motor problems, distractibility, hyperactivity, and perseveration (the earmarks of Werner and Strauss's exogenous group and Cruickshank's cerebral palsied), Cruickshank and his colleagues in the late 1950s performed a demonstration-pilot study which adopted and refined the educational methods proposed by Strauss and Lehtinen (1947). While some children in the project had been diagnosed as brain injured, the primary bases for inclusion were normal or near-normal intelligence and the existence of the behavioral characteristics highlighted by Werner and Strauss. The resultant publication following termination of the project (Cruickshank, Bentzen, Ratzeburg, and Tannhauser, 1961), in addition to reporting the experiment's effectiveness, also provided numerous suggestions regarding teaching materials and the reduction of stimuli in the classroom.

A former student of Cruickshank, Norris G. Haring, later extended the former's concept of environmental structure with the use of behavior modification principles. Haring and his associates at the University of Washington, where he is director of the Experimental Education Unit at the Child Development and Mental Retardation Center, have reported success in applying behavior modification techniques to learning disabled children (Nolen, Kunzelmann, and Haring, 1967) and to a variety of other populations (Haring and Nolen, 1967; Haring and Whalen, 1965). Haring and Phillips (1972), stating their rationale for a behavior modification approach, have noted the importance of the environmental variables that confront the child. In providing many stimuli that affect his behavior, the environment may actually exert control over the highly distractible child. Although Haring, like Cruickshank and Strauss and Lehtinen, would advocate the use of a cubicle for the exceedingly distractible child, he also maintained that the environment could be structured by establishing contingency reinforcement procedures. Noting that the Skinnerian paradigm of "stimulus-response-reinforcement" is a highly structured concept, Haring and Phillips submitted behavior modification as a means of providing a structured environment for the distractible child.

Seminar on Brain-Injured Children. Another historically important endeavor by Cruickshank was his mobilization in October, 1965, of twenty-seven experts from a variety of disciplines, for the purpose of grappling with some of the burgeoning issues in the rapidly expanding investigation of brain injury. The common core around which discussion was to be centered consisted of papers submitted to Cruickshank for publication in a volume later edited by him, *The teacher of brain injured children* (1966).

The active participants and their affiliations at the time were William Adamson, Pathway School, Norristown, Pennsylvania; Ray Barsch, University of Wisconsin, Madison, Wisconsin; William Cruickshank, Syracuse University, Syracuse, New York; Marianne Frostig, the Frostig School, Los Angeles, California; Elizabeth Friedus, Teachers College, Columbia University, New York, New York; William Gaddes, University of Victoria, British Columbia, Canada; James Gallagher, University of Illinois, Urbana, Illinois; Riley Gardner, the Menninger Foundation, Topeka,

Kansas; Herbert Grossman, University of Illinois Medical Center, Chicago, Illinois; Miriam P. Hardy, Johns Hopkins University Medical Center, Baltimore, Maryland; Homer Hendricksen, Temple City, California (substituting for Gerald Getman, Luverne, Minnesota); Newell Kephart, Purdue University, Lafayette, Indiana; Peter Knoblock, Syracuse University; William Morse, University of Michigan, Ann Arbor, Michigan; Sheldon Rappaport, Pathway School; Ralph Reitan, University of Indiana Medical Center, Indianapolis, Indiana; Charles Strother, University of Washington, Seattle, Washington; and Miriam Tannhauser, Montgomery County Board of Education, Rockville, Maryland. The observer-participants included: Samuel Clements, University of Arkansas Medical Center, Little Rock, Arkansas (representing National Association for Children with Learning Disabilities); Sue Davis, Martinsville, Virginia (representing Council for Administrators of Special Education, Council for Exceptional Children); Louis Fliegler, University of Denver, Denver, Colorado (representing Division of Teachers' Education, Council for Exceptional Children); John Garrett, graduate student, Syracuse University; June Jordan, staff member of Council for Exceptional Children, National Education Association; William Meyers, Department of Psychology, Syracuse University; Geraldine Scholl, Handicapped Children and Youth, Washington, D.C. (representing United States Office of Education); Ray Simches, State Department of Education, Albany, New York (representing National Association of State Directors of Special Education); and Eva Wolfolk, Syracuse University.

The meeting was unlike any before or since in this field. A stenotypist, constantly occupied during the two days of conversational interaction, submitted an 850-page typewritten account of the proceedings.[2] While a multitude of concerns were examined, the major portion of the first day was devoted to the most pressing problem encountered during the entire seminar—definition. This topic, more than any other, revealed differences of opinion and provoked considerable controversy.

As the opening speaker, Gallagher set the stage for debate with his insistence that the children whom he and his colleagues had gathered to discuss should be identified with terminology that was educational in its orientation. The term "brain injured," he maintained, was too ill-defined and not educationally useful. He pointed out that the label "brain injured" often created discouragement for parents and teachers who might feel that the affliction was untreatable. Such negative reaction might even arise when the child evidenced no conclusive signs of brain damage.

---

2 Two copies of this document exist that are available for research purposes: one is in the Curriculum Library, Division of Special Education and Rehabilitation, Syracuse University; the other, in the personal library of William M. Cruickshank, University of Michigan.

Asserting that any definition should serve a purpose, Gallagher argued the need for a definition with a distinctly *educational* purpose. "Developmental imbalance" was the term which, he felt, best connoted the possibility of educational prescription and remediation. Because children labeled as brain injured often develop irregularly, with some abilities lagging behind others, he proposed that his own description was more educationally relevant than an appellation based on etiology. In Gallagher's view, a child who is markedly lower in visual-motor ability than in language ability would be developmentally imbalanced. Once cognizant of this imbalance, the educator could focus remediation on the specific areas of deficiency.

Gallagher additionally opined that such a new approach necessitated new psychological test instruments to coincide with the concept of imbalances. Whereas psychological measures previously had been used to classify children, this new definition called for instruments capable of measuring intra-individual differences. According to Gallagher, the Illinois Test of Psycholinguistic Abilities (Kirk, McCarthy, and Kirk, 1961) was designed for such a purpose.

What differentiates the term "developmental imbalance" from the more traditional label of "brain injury" is that, like the description "learning disabled" or "perceptually disabled," it reflects a *behavioral* emphasis. Children with no known brain injury could still be classified as developmentally imbalanced. Thus, individuals who are often referred to as "emotionally disturbed" or "culturally disadvantaged" would, along with truly brain injured children, be considered developmentally imbalanced.

Debate followed the presentation of Gallagher's paper. Sheldon Rappaport, the main advocate for continued use of the term "brain injured," argued emphatically that without a concern for etiology, one might overlook a possible intracranial pathology, which could result in death. He further suggested that rather than fear the consequences of labeling, one ought to explain to children that they are brain injured and help them to accept their differences.

Elizabeth Friedus, perhaps the most vehement supporter of the need for a behavioral definition, reminded the group of the teacher's role in dealing with the child and his behavior. Thus, while a neurological examination may be recommended to ascertain whether the child's very existence is jeopardized, it is essentially irrelevant to the educator whether the child is truly brain injured or not.

Samuel Clements related the conclusions reached by the National Institute for Neurological Diseases and Blindness, which had recently ratified the term "minimal brain injury" for referring to children whose near-average, average, or above-average general intelligence was accompanied by learning and/or behavioral abnormalities associated with subtle deviant functions of the central nervous system. These deviancies might be characterized by various combinations of deficits in perception, conceptualization, language, memory, and control of impulse or motor function. Objecting to the medical bias of the latter designation, Cruickshank advised the common acceptance of a term that would be truly meaningful for educators, since the problem of engaging the child in successful experiences is essentially educational.

Unfortunately, participants in the seminar reached no specific conclusion on this most critical issue of nomenclature. The discussions and the failure to achieve agreement regarding terminology did, however, highlight the fact that the term, learning disability, did not meet the needs of the key professionals who were working in the field. The points of view of Ralph Reitan and Miriam Tannhauser perhaps reflect the ambivalence of many of the discussants. While Reitan postulated the need for definitions on many levels, he recognized the inadequacies of any particular level's definition when viewed from another level. No one definition, he concluded, should result from the conference. Tannhauser believed that a definition was needed for each of three levels: (a) etiology, (b) classification and administration, and (c) education. But she did not specify what terms or definitions might be suitable.

All told, the results of this discussion on terminology and definition were both promising and discouraging. While the general concensus, especially among educators, pointed to the need for an educationally relevant definition, no such definition was adopted. Nor has any consistent terminology been agreed upon to date. A child in Michigan would be called perceptually handicapped; in New York, brain injured; in California, neurologically impaired or educationally handicapped. In Florida or Maryland, he would be said to have special learning disabilities. Unfortunately, these terms carry with them a wide assortment of implications, and although there is increasing emphasis on the need for an educational definition, none has yet emerged to the exclusion of others. "Learning disabled" is probably the most popular term; but it still is far from being unanimously accepted, since many think it contains numerous possibilities for serious misunderstanding and error.

While other topics ocupied the attention of the seminar participants, only the extensively debated subject of terminology holds such importance for the present historical analysis. From an historical perspective, it is interesting to note the conferees' general disposition toward an exclusively behavioral definition which would prove educationally relevant. A survey of the literature between 1960 and 1965 undeniably discloses a downward trend in the concern with etiology. Had the conference occurred as few as five years earlier, it is questionable whether the same participants would have defended so adamantly the necessity for a term and definition of a nonetiological nature.

Newell C. Kephart

Another key figure in the evolution of the field of learning disabilities was Newell Kephart, who, like Cruickshank, was initiated into this area of concern through his association with Werner and Strauss at Wayne County Training School. In addition to coauthoring with Strauss several early studies of the exogenous mentally retarded (Kephart and Strauss, 1940; Strauss and Kephart, 1939, 1940), Kephart collaborated with Strauss on the second volume of *Psychopathology and education of the brain-injured child* (Strauss and Kephart, 1955), an updating of the first volume by Strauss and Lehtinen (1947). This second volume yielded an important contribution in terms of the eventual development of the field of learning disabilities in that it included discussion of the brain injured child of normal intelligence. An even more significant contribution to the field of learning disabilities per se, however, was Kephart's *The slow learner in the classroom* (1960), a theoretical discourse on children with perceptual-motor problems, with suggestions for remediational teaching techniques.

Essential to an understanding of Kephart's particular orientation is a knowledge of his basic philosophy as outlined in the 1960 publication. To Kephart's way of thinking, the primary challenge to the living organism involves learning to adapt to the environment. Owing to the extreme variability of the environment surrounding the human organism, the learning required of the child is considerably more complex than for any other living organism. Lower organisms, because of the greater constancy of their environment, need not rely as much on learning as do higher organisms. Animals living at certain depths below sea level, for example, have a small repertoire of inflexible behaviors that coincide with the steady and unvaried kind of environment in which they live.

Actually, neither Kephart's hypothesis of a positive correlation between complex behavior and rank on the phylogenetic scale, nor his suggestion of an association between the latter and the importance of learning, was a new insight. Numerous investigators preceding Kephart had provided supportive evidence for both these concepts.

Hebb (1949) was an early proponent of the idea that higher-level species are capable of more complex learning, though less rapid "first learning," than is possible in lower-level species. As an explanation for these hypotheses, Hebb set forth the A/S ratio (A = Associative Cortex, S = Sensory Cortex), a theoretical construct representing the difference between that proportion of the organism's brain that serves an associative function and that proportion involved exclusively with receptor input or motor output. "Cell assembly" was Hebb's neurophysiological explanation of the process by which the autonomous central processes become entrenched in the association areas of the cortex.

Observing a positive correlation between increase in the A/S ratio and ascension on the phylogenetic scale, Hebb posited that the larger association areas explain the potential for greater complexity of behaviors in the higher-level species. Furthermore, he conceived of early perceptual learning as the increasing control of the sensory projection areas over association-area activity. The larger the A/S ratio, the longer it takes for this sensory-area control to be established in early perceptual learning. According to Hebb, the human organism, because of its large A/S ratio, is capable of achieving some very complex behaviors, but only at the expense of slow advancement in the early stages of learning.

It is noteworthy that Hebb posited slowness in early perceptual learning, whereas Kephart referred to slowness in more complex learning, owing to the complicated nature of the behavior to be learned. In spite of appearances, these two viewpoints are not necessarily contradictory, since each one refers to a different level of learning. Hebb theorized that the more basic kinds of learning are also learned more slowly in man than in lower organisms.

More recently, Hunt (1961) elaborated upon the theoretical formulations of Hebb by updating the latter's neurophysiological conceptions. Borrowing Pribam's (1960) conception of the intrinsic and extrinsic cerebral systems, Hunt suggested that an I/E (I = Intrinsic, E = Extrinsic) might be substituted for the A/S ratio. In a discussion focused primarily on the effects of stimulus deprivation and enrichment, he presented evidence that as the A/S or I/E ratio increases up the phylogenetic scale, there is a corresponding increase in the importance of early stimulation for later intellectual development. Like Hebb and Kephart, Hunt asserted that higher-level organisms are more dependent upon early learning opportunities than are lower organisms.

In fact, the many studies which showed the influence of environment upon intellectual development (e.g., Brattgard, 1952; Riesen, 1947; Rosenzweig, 1966; Skeels and Dye, 1939; von Senden, 1932) are all in accord with the conclusion of Kephart: the living organism to some extent (the extent depending upon the organism's phylogenetic level) needs learning experiences. In other words, at a variety of levels, living organisms require opportunities for learning in order to develop to their fullest potential. In this sense, the theory of Kephart is essentially environmentalistic.

The Kendlers' work (Kendler and Kendler, 1962) with horizontal and vertical processes in problem-solving tasks also lends credence to the Kephart notion of more complex behavioral capabilities in higher-level organisms. Evidence from the Kendler research suggested that lower organisms and very young children perform problem-solving tasks on an S-R basis, whereas older children, being capable of mediation, are not limited to the constraints of S-R bonds. As part of the experimental design, humans and lower-level (rat) subjects were presented two squares varying in size (small or large) and brightness (black or white). Positively reinforced over a number of trials for choosing the large square, regardless of brightness, both the rat and the human child learned to make the correct choice consistently.

Reaction to reversal shifts and nonreversal shifts, however, differed markedly in the two organisms. In this experiment, the reversal shift consisted of a new set of trials for which response to the small square constituted a rewarded behavior. This is a reversal shift in the sense that the object's dimension is still that quality to which the subject is expected to react. In the nonreversal shift, on the other hand, the second task involved reinforcement for selecting the black square, regardless of size. Results indicated that the child learned the reversal faster than the nonreversal shift, while the rat (and other infrahuman organisms) more readily learned the latter. The Kendlers explained this difference in terms of the mediational capabilitity of the human child, who almost effortlessly learned an implicit response for an implicit cue along the relevant dimension. It was concluded that the lower organism's behavior could be explained by a single-unit S-R theory, whereas the behavior of the human child required a mediational theory which took into account language capabilities.

The point to be understood here is that, using language as the explanatory construct, the Kendlers provided further evidence for the correlation between phylogenetic level and the capability for complex behavior. In addition, their theory relates to the A/S or I/E ratio in two ways: the horizontal S-R chains are analogous to the "primary learning" referred to by Hebb; and the vertical, or mediational, chains can be likened to the later, more cognitive, kind of learning that is characterized for Hebb by fresh combinations of phase sequences. It is apparent, then, that the work of Hebb, Hunt, and Kendler and Kendler strongly corroborates some of Kephart's major theoretical formulations.

More directly significant to the field of learning disabilities is Kephart's emphasis upon the perceptual-motor development of the child. Having been exposed to the concepts of Werner and Strauss with regard to the perceptual-motor problems of children, Kephart has stressed this facet of child development. Largely on account of the numerous teaching techniques forwarded in his 1960 publication, Kephart, as much as any other individual, has been responsible for the upsurge in interest in children with problems of a perceptual-motor nature.

In approaching the study of perceptual-motor phenomena, Kephart relied heavily upon the Brown and Campbell (1948) servomechanistic model of perceptual development.

> When the output pattern has been generated, it is sent down the efferent nerves . . . and response results. On the way . . . a portion of the output pattern is . . . fed back into the system at the input end. The presence of feedback in the perceptual process makes the system a servomechanism [p. 60].

This model led Kephart to the most crucial aspect of his conceptualizations: the theory that input and output are inseparable. In other words, perception cannot be separated from motoric response. Kephart (1960) therefore postulated that ". . . we cannot think of perceptual activities and motor activities as two different items; we must think of the hyphenated term perceptual-motor" [p. 63].

In terms of early perceptual development, it can be seen that Kephart was influenced by Werner and Strauss (1939a, 1939b), Gesell (1940), Werner (1948), Hebb (1949), Harlow (1951), and the Gibsons (Gibson, 1953; Gibson and Gibson, 1955), whose combined formulations represent the historical bases for Kephart's writings. Kephart believed, as did Harlow and Werner, that the infant sees only undifferentiated masses of brightness, referred to by Werner as "syncretic form." Werner's theory that the child picks out a "signal quality" or "signal qualities" in order to identify and differentiate objects, as Kephart noted, is similar to the Gibsons' perceptual development theory, which emphasizes the differentiation of elements from undifferentiated forms.[3]

Kephart's view of perception thus was both heavily influenced and given support by other theorists. In particular, he relied upon the work of Werner, whose global, analytic, and synthetic perceptual stages (1957) were cited by Kephart as being in accord with his own thoughts on the subject. These three stages refer to the hypothesis that the perceptual development of the child progresses from undifferentiated perception to the breakdown into parts to the integration and reconstruction of the parts into a whole figure.

An important aspect of Kephart's formulations on perception is his emphasis upon the belief that laterality, the ability to distinguish the left from the right side of the body and to control these individually or simultaneously, is required before the child is able to differentiate left from right (i.e., directionality) out in space. In Kephart's view, the child without laterality will not develop directionality and therefore will not, for example, recognize the difference between "b" and "d." Confusion

---

3 It should be noted that Kephart referred to the mid-1950s work of the Gibsons, who have since elaborated upon their theory and have accumulated empirical support.

of these letters would stem not from reversal, but from the absence of any basis upon which to differentiate them. The supposition of a transition from a bodily awareness of left and right to such an awareness in objective space is also evident in the theoretical formulations of Werner (1948) and Piaget (Piaget and Inhelder, 1956). Kephart's adherence to the concepts of both men no doubt contributed to the development of his own thoughts on the subject.

Also intimately linked to Kephart's laterality-directionality relationship is the idea that motor and kinesthetic development precede visual development. With regard to a child's perception of a square, he wrote:

> In a square, for example, he is presented with the horizontal line which forms one side of the figure. The directionality of this line, the right- and left-hand aspect of the visual stimulus, is the result of his matching a visual pattern to a kinesthetic pattern [1960, p. 25].

Kephart based the rationale of his training activities upon this most basic concept, the perceptual-motor match. Believing that in the child motor development comes before perceptual development, Kephart maintained that in an educational program perceptual information must be matched to motor information.

Gerald Getman

It is inconceivable to speak of Kephart and his contributions to the field of learning disabilities without also considering the optometrist, Gerald Getman, with whom Kephart collaborated for a number of years. Getman alone, and through mutual efforts with Kephart, provided basic clinical data concerning retarded, brain-injured, and perceptual-motor disabled children. The collaboration of these two men proved especially beneficial to the development of numerous concepts regarding the informal assessment of perceptual-motor abilities (primarily visual-motor) and training techniques designed to remediate them.

In the 1940s, two totally different experiences profoundly influenced Getman's thinking, enabling him to further his optometric skills and also to blend this knowledge with that from other professional orientations. In the first instance, Getman, along with some twenty-five to thirty other optometrists, attended summer workshops under the direction of Samuel Renshaw, then head of the Department of Experimental Psychology at Ohio State University. There Getman benefitted from Renshaw's experimental orientation to the problems of intermodal processes and his investigations into the effects of visual performance upon total performance.

The second experience involved Getman's close contact with the famed developmental psychologist, Arnold Gesell, from whom he received a strong developmental orientation. In the early 1940s, Getman and Glenna Bullis, then a member of the staff of Gesell's Child Development Clinic at Yale University, had discovered their mutually similar research interests. Introduced to Gesell through Bullis, Getman spent as much time as possible away from his private practice in Luverne, Minnesota, in order to consult with Gesell and to use the facilities at Yale University for investigating with Bullis the role of vision in infant and child development. Culminating this massive research effort was the publication of *Vision: Its development in infant and child* (Gesell, Ilg, Bullis, Getman, and Ilg, 1949). Thus, the unusual contacts, especially for an optometrist, with Renshaw the experimentalist and Gesell the developmentalist, strongly influenced Getman in the 1940s and readied him for making important contributions to the field of learning disabilities over the next two decades.[4]

With the knowledge and insights gained through his attendance at Renshaw's summer sessions and through his research with Gesell, Getman in 1954, 1955, and 1956 offered his own summer programs for optometrists at his Luverne, Minnesota office. For these sessions, he prepared two manuals (Getman, 1954a, 1954b) which contained the germinal seeds for many of his later ideas concerning visual-motor development and training for children with perceptual-motor difficulties. At the invitation of Kephart, the classes were transferred in 1956 to the facilities of the Adult Education Department at Purdue University, with Kephart operating as faculty sponsor.

Thus began a long and fortuitous relationship between Getman and Kephart, who that summer coauthored *The perceptual development of retarded children* (1956). An extension of Getman's two previous manuals, this publication dealt with various aspects of perceptual-motor development and training in both the retarded and the brain injured child. The interchange of ideas between Getman and Kephart is evident when one notes the similarities between this joint effort and Kephart's *Slow learner in the classroom* (1960). Kephart's association and joint authorship with Strauss (1955) and with Getman (1956) undoubtedly provided meaningful contributions to the conceptualizations forwarded in his 1960 landmark publication.

Getman and Kephart also shared ideas in a sphere somewhat removed from writing endeavors, when, during the summers of 1957 and 1958, they organized a camp for brain-injured children and their parents, with Getman in charge of the clinical program. At the camp, many theoretical

4 Personal communication from Gerald Getman, October 27, 1970.

notions of the two men were put into practice and refined through application to individuals derived predominantly from Getman's private practice.

In addition to his role in the development of Kephart's position, Getman himself has emerged as a central figure in the field of learning disabilities. One of his most important contributions to the field was *The physiology of readiness* (Getman, Kane, Halgren, and McKee, 1964), which described basic perceptual-motor training activities. Along with an introduction of numerous training procedures, Getman et al. imparted several philosophical premises since adopted by many practitioners in the field of learning disabilities:

1. Academic performance in today's schools depends heavily upon form and symbol recognition and interpretation.
2. There are perceptual skills which can be developed and trained.
3. The development of perceptual skills is related to the levels of coordinations of the body systems, i.e., the better the coordinations of the body parts and body system the better the prospects are for developing perception of forms and symbols.
4. The child whose perceptual skills have been developed and extended is the child who is free to profit from instruction and to learn independently. The greater the development of the perceptual skills, the greater the capacity for making learning more effective [p. iii].

Getman et al. then suggested six complete programs for aiding the development of perceptual motor skills:

1. Practice in General Coordination,
2. Practice in Balance (Walking Beam),
3. Practice in Eye-Hand Coordination,
4. Practice in Eye Movements,
5. Practice in Form Recognition (Templates),
6. Practice in Visual Memory (Imagery).

The content of these programs points to the similarity between Getman's orientation and that of both Strauss and Kephart. Although the direction of this relationship is not readily perceivable, the striking similarities in the recommended training activities of these three individuals point to the obvious overlapping of concepts and ideas.

Also relevant to Getman's theoretical development was the exchange of knowledge between himself and Sheldon Rappaport, founder of Pathway School and president from 1961 to 1970, with whom Getman collaborated at Pathway School for brain-injured and learning-disabled children. Rappaport himself has attained considerable stature in this field, having done work in aphasia (Rappaport, 1964, 1965) and, working in the same vein as Strauss, Cruickshank, and Kephart, more recently being concerned with learning disabilities of a perceptual-motor origin (Rappaport, 1969). While Rappaport brought ideas from ego psychology to Pathway, much of the program there was modeled from his collaboration with Cruickshank. In later years, other concepts were added; but Cruickshank's thinking was still of major import until Rappaport left Pathway in 1970.

In contrast to Getman et al.'s highly concrete *The physiology of readiness* is the more theoretical recent outline of Getman's position (1965). There Getman acknowledged his indebtedness to the optometrist, A. M. Skeffington, identified by Getman as one of the "greatest influences" upon his theorizations.[5] As Educational Director of the Optometric Extension Program in Duncan, Oklahoma, Skeffington in 1923 first presented his concepts of modern, functional visual care. Through his own work and through his constant professional associations with other disciplines, most notably education and psychology, Skeffington was instrumental in encouraging exploration of factors beyond the narrow performance measured by the Snellen Wall Chart (Getman, 1963).

Based upon nearly 40 years of papers and lectures (Skeffington, 1926–1965) delivered through the Optometric Extension Program (for which Getman also has written for better than 20 years), Skeffington presented a model of perceptual performance that would later be employed by Getman as the starting point of his own conceptualizations. The Venn diagram of Skeffington portrays four interrelated components, all of which merge to produce the emergent, vision. Included in this representation are (a) the Anti-Gravity Process, (b) the Centering Process, (c) the Identification Process, (d) the Speech-Audition Process, and (e) the Emergent-Vision.

According to the Venn diagram, the first process, Anti-Gravity, is the set of motor responses used by the organism for locomotion, exploration, and organization of itself within its environment (Getman, 1965). The Centering Process refers to the ability to orient oneself to one's surroundings. The Identification Process allows the individual to obtain a "whatness" of objects in the environment during the early stages of his development, first through mouthing explorations, then through eye-hand manipulations, and eventually through verbal labeling. The visual, tactual, and auditory sensory modalities and the information they come to provide are integrated at this third stage through the discrimination of likenesses and differences and through the labeling of objects in the environment. The Speech-Audition Process, which for Getman has strong visual components, refers to communication skills. The Emergent-Vision is that final process which is the resultant of all other interrelated pro-

[5] Personal communication from Gerald Getman, October 27, 1970.

cesses and performance modalities. As opposed to sight, which, in Getman's terminology, is merely the stimulation of the light receptors of the eyes, vision must achieve hierarchical dominance, in the opinion of Skeffington and Getman, before the human organism is capable of symbolic manipulations. In keeping with Skeffington and Getman's professional orientation, visual is thus considered the most important human sensory modality.

No doubt due in part to the strong developmental orientation he had gained from Gesell, Getman recognized that Skeffington's model limited what one could say about the development of the visual process in the infant and child. He therefore expanded Skeffington's theory when creating his own explanatory model of visual development. In the first level of Getman's model, the Innate Response Systems, are included the innate reflexes which the intact infant brings with him into the world (e.g., tonic neck reflex, startle reflex, light reflex, grasp reflex, and stato-kinetic reflex). At the second level, and connected to the first (in fact, all levels are interconnected in an endless feedback net), is the General Motor System, which encompasses the locomotor activities of creeping, walking, running, jumping, skipping, and hopping. The third level is composed of Special Motor Systems, a more extensive combination of the first two systems. Eye-hand relationships, bi-manual relationships, hand-foot relationships, voice, and gesture associations make up the elements of this level.

So far Getman's model differs little from those of most developmental psychologists, such as Piaget and especially Gesell. However, at the fourth level, Getman's optometric orientation induced him to stress the Ocular Motor Systems, in which movement and coordination of the eyes become essential to the steering of all movements. Included in this category are fixations, saccadics, pursuits, and rotations. Speech Motor Systems, the fifth and final level, is composed of babbling, imitative speech, and original speech skills.

While hardly creating as thorough or current a treatment of language as many of the developmental psychologists have advocated (indeed, many language theorists and developmental psychologists, including Chomsky [1965] and McNeil [1970] would take issue with Getman's emphasis upon vision, lamenting his model's devaluation of language), nevertheless, Getman constructed a framework which led him to maintain, "The significant aspect of the speech (auditory) motor systems to this author as an optometrist is the evidence that skill in visualization cannot really be attained without the interplay of vision-language processes" [p. 70].

The Visualization Systems, encompassing pictorial mental images, represent, according to Getman, an emergent, the result of all the systems of the model. With the development of the Visualization System, the child can progress to the culmination of what so far in the model has been a physiopsychological mode, Vision-Perception. Vision and perception are equated here by Getman to underscore his belief that the visual system is the most accurate human processing system and the one most basic to school learning tasks. When a single perceptual event is compared in a match-mismatch process (Glaser, 1962), with a construct loaded with different elements of input, the child has reached the psychophysiological stage of Cognition, or, in other words, has acquired new knowledge. Considering the physiopsychological systems that culminate in vision or perception more basic than the cognitive stage, Getman did not expand in any great detail cognition and its elaboration through further experience.

In addition to his reliance upon the work of Skeffington, Gesell, Renshaw, and Kephart, Getman also has been influenced by the work of Strauss and of Cruickshank, particularly with regard to the concept of stimulus reduction. Installation of cubicles at Pathway School, where Getman was employed, was recommended by Cruickshank in the early 1960s. In a series of papers released by the Optometric Extension Program (Getman, 1968–1969), Getman related his experiences in the use and modification of cubicles at Pathway. Remarking that Cruickshank had been "the first to assert that the cubicle was not a panacea" [p. 23], Getman injected his own optometric knowledge in order to refine the use of the cubicle.

In Getman's estimation, one of the first points to consider was the possibility that performance within an enclosed space (three walls at distances of fewer than eighteen inches from the child's eyes) might result in an increased physiological stress to the visual system. Such a near-point learning environment without opportunity to release attention to more distant objects, Getman felt, could cause visual problems for the child.

Another important question raised by Getman was the extent to which a homogeneous visual periphery would eliminate peripheral signals needed for orientation. Getman cited a study conducted during one of Renshaw's summer sessions at Ohio State University, where adults wore face-fitting, periphery-eliminating frames. On optometric tests and on tests of binocular functioning, all the subjects showed deterioration of visual functioning, including form and motion fields. In less than two weeks' time, these subjects experienced distortions which were not surmounted for nearly a year. On the strength of this evidence, although it was collected from experiments with adults under conditions somewhat different from those in which children would be placed, Getman cautioned against the indiscriminate overuse of cubicles.

Getman, as had Cruickshank previously, also noted the existence of numerous lighting problems connected with cubicle use at Pathway and elsewhere. Shadows frequently fell over the posterior halves of the desks; and, with overhead illumination, the intense brightness and dark shadows resulted in a most inadequate lighting arrangement.

Auditory distractions, too, were a consequence of the physical properties peculiar to a cubicle. In a sense, the booth acted as an echo chamber in which sounds from around the room were constantly reverberating. Getman further asserted that a spatial dislocation of voices occurred for the child seated in a booth. Still another problem by which the youngster in the cubicle was often confronted was whether to shift his attention to the noise from outside the cubicle, or whether to pay attention to the stimuli in front of him. If Getman's observations were correct, the way in which the cubicle was being used was resulting in an effect precisely opposite to that for which it was intended. Children in the cubicle, while shielded from visual stimuli, were prone to the distraction of auditory stimuli.

With the aforementioned questions and concerns regarding the cubicles, Getman might well have opted for their removal from the classrooms. On the contrary, though, he most emphatically stated that he had no desire to eliminate cubicles altogether. Instead, he modified both their construction and their use in an effort to make them "as functional and developmentally valid as possible within the needs and programs of each classroom" [p. 31]. With regard to the physical construction, the height of the cubicles was reduced from eight to four feet, and the lighting was carefully planned in order to eliminate distracting shadows. Reducing the size of the walls lessened the lighting inadequacies and also eliminated the problem of auditory reverberations.

While Getman recognized the appropriateness of and the child's preference for facing into the cubicle in order to concentrate on new or more difficult materials, for most work he recommended to teachers that they turn the child 90 degrees away from the cubicle front. In this position, the child was still impervious to most stimuli and was also able to talk to the teacher in a face-to-face manner when the occasion demanded. Echo effects, too, were reduced by this placement. The child, being easily disoriented and unintegrated, was better able to observe from what direction the teacher's voice was coming and to associate voices with facial expressions, thus garnering additional situational cues.

Getman's writings on the Pathway experience point to the obvious impact that the conceptualizations of Strauss and particularly of Cruickshank had on his work. In an exciting and refreshing way, Getman introduced new ideas to a situation that required modification in order to be in accord with the concepts of his own disciplinary focus, rather than rejecting that situation totally. In this theoretical and practical approach lies the real value of the intermingling of ideas within and between disciplines.

Ray Barsch

An interchange of concepts is also evident in the professional development of another key figure in the learning disabilities movement, Ray H. Barsch. Sent by the Brain Injured Society in Milwaukee to visit the summer camp staffed by Getman and Kephart, Barsch returned to the Jewish Vocational Center and the Easter Seal Center, where he was working as program director. In 1960, he and Getman, who acted as clinical director, instituted a summer camp program for both children and parents at Stevens Point, Wisconsin.[6] This mutual venture, offering ample opportunity for the sharing of ideas, no doubt contributed to both Getman and Barsch's understanding of children with learning problems. In fact, one of Barsch's first publications (Barsch, 1961), probably based on the knowledge derived from his experience at the Stevens Point Camp, dealt with parent counseling. As evidenced by an article he wrote for the Optometric Extension Program (1964), Barsch's association with Getman and with the optometric profession in general also had significant bearing on the creation of his theory of "Movigenics."

Prior to any discussion of the elements of Movigenics, it should be pointed out that with regard to historical antecedents, Barsch, like numerous other learning disabilities theorists, was influenced by Strauss. While Barsch was in Milwaukee, he collaborated with Strauss, who at that time was in charge of the Cove Schools in Racine, Wisconsin. The product of their combined work is evident in Barsch's concern for the management and reduction of stimuli in the environment (Barsch, 1965a).

Best described as the study of the development of spatial movement patterns that are the physiological bases of learning, the theory of Movigenics is rooted in eight major theoretical constructs, as noted in McCarthy and McCarthy (1969). All these postulates relate to Barsch's emphasis upon the evolutionary perspective of the human organism's quest for *survival*. Barsch posited that man, as well as all other living organisms, lives and must survive in an energy surround containing numerous types of stimuli with which he must deal. This first point apparently underlies Barsch's concern, which he shares with Strauss and Cruickshank, for control of the classroom environment.

Secondly, Barsch vehemently maintained that survival in this energy surround is dependent upon the organism's capability for efficient movement within the environment. Without such movement abilities, man would lose the struggle for survival.

The most important energy with which man must contend in order to move, and hence survive, is the force of gravity. Thus, according to

---

[6] Personal communication from Gerald Getman, April 9, 1971.

the third point of Movigenics, the organism must integrate its numerous movement patterns in an effort to overcome this basic element of nature.

As McCarthy and McCarthy pointed out, the theory's fourth point was a definition of the state of man:

> The human organism may be defined as a homeostatic, adapting, bilaterally equating, dynamic, multistable system designed as an open energy mechanism so as to promote its survival in an energy surround [p. 38].

A fifth major aspect of Barsch's theory is his position that the individual builds a set of axial coordinates relative to his body. These coordinates aid in man's struggle to maintain his balance while confronting gravitational forces.

The sixth core component of Movigenics includes the element of space, which, next to movement, receives the most emphasis from Barsch. Visual, auditory, tactual, and kinesthetic spatial volumes must all be dealt with as the organism attempts adequate movement. Without the ability to coordinate and integrate the spatial volumes of these sensory modalities, the organism again is left to the mercy of the environment.

The seventh postulate, a byproduct of Barsch's first six statements, asserts that movement affords man a better chance for survival. On this basis, an educational program designed to promote the ability to move and to integrate movements within a spatial world would be of significant value.

Relative to the final point of Barsch's construct, McCarthy and McCarthy noted that communication was the transfer from one person to another of one's own "space world."

> The manner in which the individual has been able to effectively process, organize, and integrate all previous visual, auditory, kinesthetic and tactual information represents his communicative potential [p. 39].

Such logic led Barsch to hypothesize the development of movement patterns as precursors of the ability to communicate.

Regarding Barsch's theoretical position, a number of concerns arise. For instance, it is probable that Barsch overrated man's need for survival by ascribing it to the central role of his theory. While current scientific thought certainly recognizes the evolutionary significance of man's survival needs, Barsch may have confused phylogentic with ontogenetic characteristics. It may well be that proper movement patterns are essential to more conceptual and intellectual kinds of activities, but the assumption that man in his current state needs movement in order to survive seems to ignore several hundred millennia of phylogenetic development. Although quick and efficient movement may have been imperative for survival at one time in man's history, it does not necessarily follow that modern man is so dependent. Moreover, the relative devaluation of language would elicit considerable censure from theorists and researchers of language development. In relegating language for the most part to the role of communicating one's locus in space, Barsch, even more than Getman, is vulnerable to criticism of the overly simplistic attitude implicit in his view of the function and place of language.

In the perceptual-motor training activities which he recommended, Barsch built a curriculum around the twelve elements that he considered important for learning (Barsch, 1967). These components, or dimensions, of the Movigenics Curriculum are muscular strength, dynamic balance, spatial awareness, body awareness, visual dynamics, auditory dynamics, kinesthesia, tactual dynamics, bilaterality, rhythm, flexibility, and motor planning. As was true of the theoretical constructs discussed above, Barsch's curriculum emphatically stressed the development of motor movement and spatial awareness. In spite of this emphasis, however, the specific recommended activities are similar to those advocated by Strauss, Kephart, and Getman.

Marianne Frostig

During the 1960s, yet another individual won prominence in the area of perceptual-motor development and training. Marianne Frostig, founder and director of the Marianne Frostig Center of Educational Therapy in Los Angeles, California, is recognized as a leading figure in the field of learning disabilities. It should be noted that Frostig herself would, if being categorized, prefer to be known as a "developmentalist" rather than a perceptual-motor theorist and practitioner (personal communication to the authors from Marianne Frostig, December 31, 1971). However, since Frostig's major national impact in the field of learning disabilities has been primarily within the scope of perceptual-motor training and theory, she has been placed within that framework. While her philosophical roots are less securely embedded in the Wayne County Training School program than are those of other persons discussed previously (i.e., Cruickshank, Kephart, Getman, and Barsch), Frostig nevertheless regards Werner, Strauss, and Lehtinen, as well as people such as Hebb, Schilder, Bender, Angyl, Freud, Vernon, and Karl and Charlotte Buhler, particularly important to her orientation.[7]

The Marianne Frostig Developmental Test of Visual Perception. Frostig's renown stems chiefly from her development of the Marianne

[7] Personal communication from Marianne Frostig, July 7, 1970.

Frostig Developmental Test of Visual Perception (Frostig, Lefever, and Whittlesey, 1961; Frostig, Maslow, Lefever, and Whittlesey, 1964) and from her design of a training program (Frostig and Horne, 1964) to develop or remediate visual and visual-motor abilities assessed by the test. The test is composed of five subtests, each of which purportedly measures a discrete area of visual perception which is relatively independent of the other four. These supposedly independent abilities are (a) eye-motor coordination, (b) visual figure-ground discrimination, (c) form constancy, (d) position in space, and (e) spatial relations.

1. Eye-Motor Coordination: The first subtest requires the child to coordinate the visual sensory modality with motor movements required in drawing with a pencil. The specific tasks involve drawing a continuous line between two boundaries which vary in direction and width.
2. Figure-Ground: The child must outline with a pencil one specific figure that is embedded in and intersects with the lines of other figures. That this ability is felt to be important enough and/or that inability in this area is considered pervasive enough to merit inclusion of a figure-ground subtest underscore the influence of Werner and Strauss, pioneers of the concern for figure-ground difficulties.
3. Form Constancy: The child is asked to discriminate various geometric shapes in a variety of orientations, shadings, and sizes. This skill is essentially analogous to recognition of a particular letter of the alphabet from one book to the next, regardless of shape or typescript inconsistencies.
4. Position in Space: On this subtest, the experimenter may, for example, ask the child to identify a particular figure from among a number of choices. Actually, all the choices represent identical figures, but all except the appropriate one have been rotated in space to various degrees. This subtest, it is purported, directly relates to the common characteristic of learning disabled children—tendency to reverse and rotate letters and numbers. Such a tendency obviously complicates the processes of learning to read and to perform arithmetic problems.
5. Spatial Relations: This subtest purports to assess the ability to detect the positions of objects in relation to one another and in relation to oneself. For example, after being shown a pattern composed of dots joined together by lines, the child must copy this figure by linking with a pencil his own set of dots.

Test results can be analyzed in terms of scaled scores, age equivalents, and perceptual quotients. The Perceptual Quotient (PQ), which unfortunately may be confused in derivation and in meaning with IQ, reports the child's visual-perceptual ability in relation to that of his age peers. A low PQ indicates that the child is in need of visual training.

By far the most damaging criticism of the Frostig test concerns the inadequate sample used for standardization. As Frostig, Maslow, Lefever, and Whittlesey (1964) have readily admitted, the experimental population was not a truly representative one. Since 1970 Frostig has begun testing economically disadvantaged children. In addition, normative samples for the Frostig test are now being collected in Mexico, Argentina, Germany, South Africa, Australia, and Poland.[8] Although the revised standardization sampled a large number (2,116) of children, the vast majority of these were white, middle-class youngsters. Since no attempt was made to include appropriate numbers of Spanish-speaking, black, or other minority group members, cultural bias inevitably affects any generalizations about the test performance of nonwhite, non-middle-class youngsters. Yet it is well known that these are the very children who frequently evidence learning problems (Hallahan, 1970; Pasamanick and Knoblock, 1961; Schwebel, 1966).

There also exists disagreement regarding the independence of the subtests, a most crucial aspect with regard to the differential diagnosis of particular visual-motor deficiencies. While Frostig, Lefever, and Whittlesey (1964), Olson (1966a), and Silverstein (1965) found intercorrelations indicating relative independence, factor analyses (Corah and Powell, 1963; Olson, 1968) have tended not to support the supposition of unrelatedness. Since the question of subtest independence has yet to be resolved, extreme caution should accompany use of the test to differentiate specific aspects of a child's perceptual functioning.

Myers and Hammill (1969), after summarizing a number of validity studies regarding application of the Frostig test to a variety of populations (e.g., Bryan, 1964; Frostig, Maslow, Lefever, and Whittlesey, 1964; Olson, 1966a, 1966b, 1966c; Sprague, 1964), arrived at the following conclusions:

> a. The DTVP [Developmental Test of Visual Perception] adequately predicts reading readiness at the first-grade level, but not the level of achievement attained at the first grade. . . .
> b. It is related to a 'small degree' with second- and third-grade reading [p. 246].

Reliability studies on the total scores have generally been high. Frostig et al. (1964) reported test-retest coefficients in the 80s and 90s, with split-half reliabilities in the high 70s and 80s. Low reliabilities of the subtests, both test-retest and split-half, however, militate against using individual subtests to diagnose specific visual-perceptual difficulties. Nevertheless, the generally high validity and reliability coefficients in terms of total scores render the test useful at least as a screening instrument to predict achievement at the early primary grades. While Anderson, in his review of the test for the authoritative Buros' *Mental measurements yearbook* (1965) may have been correct in judging that Frostig et al.

---

[8] Personal communication from Marianne Frostig, December 31, 1971.

"prematurely offered their test as a finished product" [p. 553], it is only fair to add that the test was an extraordinary first attempt to tease out the various components of visual perception. The fact that it may have failed to differentiate among the various aspects of visual perception, while unfortunate for the learning disabilities premise that differential abilities require assessment, does not preclude the possibility of refining this type of measuring device with further research.

It should be mentioned also that the test developed by Frostig, like the Illinois Test of Psycholinguistic Abilities (Kirk, McCarthy, and Kirk, 1961, 1968), to be discussed later, represents a departure from the usual type of test constructed to assess the psychological functioning of the child. In this sense, both instruments are truly pioneering efforts. Frostig's test was designed to assess perceptual-motor abilities rather than more conceptual, intellectual functioning. Nonetheless, historical events concerned with the measurement of mental functioning have had a profound influence not only upon the origin and development of tests for the learning disabled child (Frostig has noted, for example, that Vernon [1950] was influential in the development of her thinking), but also upon the development of the field of learning disabilities as a whole.

Relative to mental measurement, there has been an historical shift in the popularity of theories pertaining to the structure of the intellect. The primary figure in the initial stages of intelligence testing was Binet. Although theoretically conceiving of factors in intelligence, he promoted with his test a concept of general intelligence. Spearman (1904, 1927), through correlational and other statistical techniques, adopted a two-factor theory with "g" (general intelligence) as the dominant factor. In the 1930s Spearman revised his formulations to include group factors. Thurstone (1938) in the late 1930s posited thirteen factors comprising intelligence. In keeping with the trend, Guilford (1956) constructed a three-dimensional model of the intellect, allowing room for an even greater number of factors. Thus a change has been initiated among some theorists (most notably Spearman, Thurstone, and Guilford) from a theory of a unified general intelligence factor, "g," to more refined group factors, and finally to specific ability theories. The culmination of this theoretical evolution, occurring in the late 1950s with Guilford's formulations, but evident at least since the work of Spearman two decades earlier, helped to provide a ripe climate for the development of learning disability theory. Since the concept of specific abilities and disabilities can be considered a sine qua non of learning disability theory, the historical trend within mental measurement theory to concern for identification of specific abilities assumes tremendous importance.

As for the practical application of Frostig's training program, it can be used either remedially or developmentally (Myers and Hammill,

1969). The major components of the program follow the five subtests of Frostig's test. As with the Illinois Test of Psycholinguistic Abilities, a specific program was constructed to deal with the particular aspect measured by each of the subtests. Because of this purposeful correlation between the test and the program, the specifically recommended training activities are quite similar to the items contained on the test. Although Frostig places great emphasis on visual and visual-motor training via workbook excercisces, her program also has much in common with those of Barsch, Kephart, and especially of Getman.

The association between test and program creates a tendency for the teacher to administer the complete package to a child. However, as noted above, it is as yet undetermined whether one should assume unrelatedness for the subtests. For this reason, the teacher who administers only the Frostig test and then bases her remediation solely upon its results may inadvertently pave the way for error. Frostig herself recommends the administration of a battery of diagnostic tests before instituting a remedial program. McCarthy and McCarthy (1969) noted that besides her own test, Frostig uses Wepman's Auditory Discrimination Test (Wepman, 1958), the Wechsler Intelligence Scale for Children (1949), and the Illinois Test of Psycholinguistic Abilities (Kirk et al., 1961, 1968).

Kephart, Getman, Barsch, and Frostig—Points of Contact

It seems appropriate at this point, due to the many similarities among Kephart, Getman, Barsch, and Frostig, to note some of the commonalities and differences among them. With regard to their overall commonality, it should be remembered that Kephart, Getman, and Barsch, for significant aspects of their thinking, derived their ideas from the work of Werner and Strauss. Kephart had direct contact with Strauss at the Wayne County Training School and collaborated with him on numerous writings which can be considered forerunners of learning disabilities literature. Getman and Barsch were exposed to the concepts of Werner and Strauss more indirectly through Getman's association with Kephart and through Barsch's brief association with Strauss and his work with Getman. In addition, both Getman and Barsch have no doubt become familiar with the writing of Werner and Strauss. Frostig, while not directly involved with the work of Werner, Strauss, Kephart, Getman, or Barsch, has acknowledged that Werner and Strauss shaped her thinking.

Therefore, Kephart, Getman, Barsch, and, to a certain extent, Frostig all share the Werner and Strauss orientation. Most notably, the basic concern exhibited by all four theorists for the perceptual-motor aspects of development can be attributed to their association with Werner and Strauss, who were the first to investigate systematically a variety of perceptual-motor disabilities. Further, all four practitioners offered the same training techniques or variations of the techniques introduced by Strauss. But whereas Werner and Strauss were talking, for the most part, about the mentally retarded, Kephart, Getman, Barsch, and Frostig translated these concepts to the investigation of children with normal intelligence. The fact that all four assume perceptual development to be a forerunner of conceptual development and that without the proper development of the former the latter will be adversely affected reveals another link to Strauss and especially to Werner. In Myers and Hammill's (1969) schematic comparison based upon Osgood's communication model of various learning disabilities theorists, Kephart, Getman, Frostig, and Barsch were all seen to deal primarily with the "reception of nonmeaningful, although organized or patterned, stimuli" [p. 286]. This reception is the "integration level," as opposed to the representational level with which theorists such as Myklebust have been relatively more concerned.

Another concept of Werner and Strauss, regarding the reduction of environmental stimuli and the need for environmental structure (which has been furthered by the work of Cruickshank), has become a part of both Barsch's and Getman's conceptualizations. Kephart and Frostig, while they may share concern for the concept, have not addressed themselves strongly to this issue.

All four of these perceptual-motor theorists demonstrate similar thinking by agreeing that motor development precedes and is necessary for perceptual development. Even Getman, who is so emphatic about the central role of visual perception, has constructed a theoretical model which places the motor before the visual aspects of development. Kephart, more than any of the other three, emphasizes this sequence.

The theories of these four individuals can be differentiated from one another, however, in the relative emphasis each places upon either visual or motor development. Viewed on a continuum of motor to visual orientation, Barsch can be found toward the motor end, while Getman exhibits a decidedly visual orientation. Barsch, for example, calls his program the "Movigenic Curriculum." Getman, on the other hand, considers vision to be the primary inspection and appraisal system and the ultimately superior system for orientation and for all spatial judgments.[9] Kephart and Frostig appear toward the middle, with the latter leaning more than the former toward the visual extreme. Of course, this hypothetical continuum merely represents the relative *emphasis* of each of

[9] Personal communication from Gerald Getman, April 9, 1971.

the four. Getman does not ignore motor behavior but, compared to the other three, he places the most emphasis upon vision. Barsch, more than any of the others, stresses motor development, but simultaneously maintains: "Vision defines distance, color, relationships, textures—and becomes the true integrating agent for touch, kinesthesia and audition" [Barsch, 1965b, p. 7, quoted in Myers and Hammill, 1969, p. 124].

Although Kephart, Getman, Barsch, and Frostig all believe that one needs to diagnose a child's particular problem before applying specific educational techniques, Frostig, and to a certain extent Kephart, would be more inclined to emphasize the diagnostic aspect of learning disabilities, which accounts for their creation of diagnostic instruments. Frostig is more interested in testing than is Kephart, as can be seen from her writings and from the nature of her test. Roach and Kephart (1966), on the other hand, candidly admitted that their instrument was not intended to meet the rigid criteria of a test but rather was designed to play a surveying function, as the title (Purdue Perceptual-Motor Survey) indicates. Because of her confidence in the diagnostic process, Frostig has devoted much time and energy to the construction and refinement of her test. This perseverance has been rewarded by the fact that her instrument seems to be more widely used than Kephart's both in clinical and in research settings. With regard to testing in general, there is something upon which all four individual's agree: the test or tests, whether formal or informal, should be used only insofar as they provide information that can be translated into an educational program.

Finally, Kephart, Getman, Barsch, and Frostig as well as Cruickshank share common ground in their deemphasis of etiology, reflecting a trend that has been advancing within the entire field of learning disabilities. While the problem of central nervous system damage is the domain of some authors, many investigators, including these four, preferred to direct their attention to the construction of educational programs based upon the behavioral characteristics of children's perceptual-motor problems. At one time Kephart (Strauss and Kephart, 1955) and Barsch (1961), for example, wrote primarily about the brain injured child, but their later work reflects behavioral rather than etiological concerns.

Glen Doman and Carl Delacato

While nearly all the theorists considered thus far have engaged in devising educational curricula and training methods to deal primarily with the behaviors of learning disabled children, the next theorists to be discussed have focused on treating an assumed or diagnosed damage to the central nervous system.

In the late 1950s, Glen Doman, a physical therapist, and Carl Delacato, an educational psychologist, worked together on a theory of
"neurological organization." The first statement deriving from this collaboration was made in 1959 by Delacato in his exposition on *The
treatment and prevention of reading problems.* In the following year,
Doman, Spitz, Zucman, Delacato, and Doman (1960) also advanced the
theory of neurological organization and its central concept of patterning, which was a modification of the developmental patterns of Gesell
and especially of Temple Fay, a noted Philadelphia neurosurgeon who
had a profound influence upon the concepts of Doman and Delacato.
The five elements of their theory as outlined in the Doman et al. (1960)
article came primarily from Fay's theorizations (Wolf, 1968).[10] These
five elements are (a) placing the child on the floor for training activities
in order to remediate damaged areas of the brain, (b) externally manipulating the child into body patterns characteristic of the level of the
damaged brain, (c) imposing hemispheric dominance and unilaterality,
(d) administering carbon dioxide therapy (Fay [1953] hypothesized that
carbon dioxide increased the size of the small vessels of the brain and
resulted in better blood circulation to the brain), and (e) stimulating
the senses to improve body awareness.

Fay, the historical precursor of the Doman-Delacato treatment method,
was a pioneer in many different aspects of neurology. Within the medical field he was perhaps best known for his early work in human re-
frigeration. As his career progressed, however, he became more and more
interested in the treatment of brain injured patients. In 1943, Fay left his
position as head of the Department of Neurosurgery and Neurology at
Temple University to found the Neuro-Physical Rehabilitation Clinic
in Philadelphia, where he was director from 1946 to 1952. In the late
1940s and the 1950s he wrote extensively concerning pattern movements,
which formed the core of his treatment for various kinds of brain injuries in children and adults. In 1947 he became one of the six founding
fathers of the American Academy for Cerebral Palsy, attesting to the
degree to which he was involved in the treatment of the brain injured.

Doman and Delacato became acquainted with Fay at the Norwood
Rehabilitation Center in Philadelphia, where there was intimate exchange of ideas among the three men. Eventually, Doman and Delacato
adopted many of the ideas and concepts of Fay.

In 1955, Doman and others founded the Rehabilitation Center, where
Fay served as consultant until 1957, and saw his ideas carried even further. Meanwhile, Delacato concerned himself primarily with the reading

---

[10] For a more thorough discussion of Temple Fay and his influence on Doman
and Delcato, the reader is referred to *Temple Fay, M.D.—Progenitor of the Doman-
Delacato treatment procedures* (Wolf, 1968).

process, acting as director of the Reading Clinic at Chestnut Hill Academy in Philadelphia. Later, he became director of Psychological Services at the Rehabilitation Center, where the concepts of neurological organization were engendered. Publication of these concepts appeared in 1959 (Delacato, 1959) and in 1960 (Doman, et al., 1960).

Within a short time, the theoretical and especially the treatment procedures of Doman and Delacato gained widespread popularity and notoriety, no doubt because of their new methods, their reports of success, and their extensive press coverage. Reorganized in 1963, the Rehabilitation Center was incorporated into the Institutes for the Achievement of Human Potential, with Doman as director and Delacato as associate director. The Avery Postgraduate Institute was opened in 1966. Its main function was "the training of cybernetic developmentalists, neurological organization reading specialists, and directors who . . . . serve in this country and abroad as staff members of units which employ the concepts and procedures of neurological organization" [Wolf, 1968, p. 38]. Individuals from a variety of disciplines attended the Avery Postgraduate Institute, and within two years satellite affiliates of the Institutes had been established in sixteen states and in the countries of Brazil, Canada, and Mexico.

Critique of Doman and Delacato [11]

Although the neurological organization treatment procedures of Doman and Delacato have met with popularity and acceptance from the general public, they have also been the target of widespread criticism from members of the medical, psychological, educational, and other professions. In fact, the Doman-Delacato theory and treatment procedures have resulted in the most heated debate to date within the field of learning disabilities and probably also within the field of education in general. Like their progenitor, Fay, Doman and Delacato created a flood of controversy and argument. The dispute over the Doman-Delacato method led several prestigious professional organizations (American Academy for Cerebral Palsy, which, paradoxically, included Fay as one of its founders; American Academy of Physical Medicine and Rehabilitation; American Congress of Rehabilitation Medicine; Canadian Association for Children with Learning Disabilities; Canadian Association for Retarded Children; Canadian Rehabilitation Council for the Disabled; and National Association for Retarded Children) to adopt in 1968 the

[11] The following is a presentation of professional judgments with regard to the work of Doman and Delacato. These ideas are included for their historical relevance and in no way necessarily reflect the authors' position.

following official statement, quoted here in its entirety because of its historical significance:

Official Statement: THE DOMAN-DELACATO TREATMENT OF NEUROLOGICALLY HANDICAPPED CHILDREN

During the past decade the Institutes for the Achievement of Human Potential and their affiliates have made increasing claims for the efficacy of their methods of treatment for brain damage and other disorders . . . (Bird, 1967; Institutes for the Achievement of Human Potential, 1967b). A few organizations have issued cautionary statements . . . (American Academy for Cerebral Palsy, 1965; American Academy of Neurology, 1967; American Academy of Pediatrics, 1965; American Academy of Physical Medicine and Rehabilitation, 1967; Canadian Association for Retarded Children, 1965; United Cerebral Palsy Association of Texas, undated). Information has recently become available which makes it important to review the current status of the controversy and propose some recommendations.

The reasons for concern include the following:

1. Promotional methods (Beck, 1964; Linton, undated) appear to put parents in a position where they cannot refuse such treatment without calling into question their adequacy and motivation as parents;

2. The regimens prescribed are so demanding and inflexible (Beck, 1964; Linton, undated; Maisel, 1964), that they may lead to neglect of other family members' needs (Freeman, 1967a);

3. It is asserted that if therapy is not carried out as rigidly prescribed, the child's potential will be damaged, and that anything less than 100% effort is useless (Beck, 1964; Linton, undated);

4. Restrictions are often placed upon age-appropriate activities of which the child is capable, such as walking or listening to music (Institutes for the Achievement of Human Potential, 1963; Lewinn, Doman, G., Doman, R. J., Delacato, Spitz and Thomas, 1966), though unwarranted by any supportive data and knowledge of long-term results published to date;

5. Claims are made for rapid and conclusive diagnosis (Institutes for the Achievement of Human Potential, 1964) according to a "Developmental Profile" (Institutes for the Achievement of Human Potential, 1965) of no known validity. No data on which construction of the Profile has been based have ever been published, nor do we know of any attempt to cross-validate it against any accepted methods;

6. Undocumented claims are made for cures in a substantial number of cases (Bird, 1967; Institutes for the Achievement of Human Potential, 1967b), extending even beyond disease states to making normal children superior (Beck, 1964; Institutes for the Achievement of Human Potential, 1967a, 1967b); Institutes for the Achievement of Human Potential, undated), easing world tensions (Institutes for the Achievement of Human Potential, 1967b), and possibly "hastening the evolutionary process" (Delacato, 1959; Institutes for the Achievement of Human Potential, 1967b);

7. Without supporting data, Doman and Delacato have indicted many typical child-rearing practices as limiting a child's potential, increasing thereby the anxiety of already burdened and confused parents (Doman and Delacato, 1965; Freeman, 1967a).

The controversy over these claims and assertions has recently been reviewed in some detail (Freeman, 1967a).

The Theory

The theory is alleged to be of universal applicability (Institutes for the Achievement of Human Potential, 1967b); Institutes for the Achievement of Human Potential, undated), but is largely based upon questionable and over-simplified concepts of hemispheric dominance and the relation of individual sequential development to phylogenesis (Robbins and Glass, 1969). Further, it asserts that the great majority of cases of mental retardation, learning problems, and behavior disorders are caused by brain damage or "poor neurological organization" (Institutes for the Achievement of Human Potential, 1964), and that all these problems lie somewhere on a single continuum of brain damage, for which the treatment advocated by the Institutes is the only effective answer (Beck, 1964; Institutes for the Achievement of Human Potential, 1967b).

Presently available information does not support these contentions. In particular, the lack of uniform dominance or sidedness is probably not a significant factor in either the etiology or therapy of these conditions (Belmont and Birch, 1965; Bettman, Stern, Whitsell, and Gofman, 1967; Money, 1962, 1967; Robbins and Glass, 1969; Spitzer, Rabkin, and Kramer, 1959; Stephens, Cunningham, and Stigler, 1967).

Cultural and anthropological differences have also been "explained" by the theory. For example, the lack of a written language in some primitive tribes is attributed to restrictions upon crawling and creeping (Green, 1967), an exceedingly narrow and questionable view.

A careful review of the theory (Robbins and Glass, 1969) has led to the conclusion that "the tenets are either unsupported or overwhelmingly contradicted when tested by theoretical, experimental, or logical evidence from the relevant scientific literature. As a scientific hypothesis the theory of neurological organization seems to be without merit."

Current Status of Claimed Therapeutic Results

Results published by the Institutes or their supporters are inclusive (Doman, et al., 1960; Freeman, 1967b; Institutes for the Achievement of Human Potential, 1964). Many reports of improvement in reading ability have been heralded as support for the theory (Delacato, 1959, 1963, 1966), but statistical analysis has shown no demonstrable benefit (Glass, 1966; Robbins and Glass, 1969).

It has been pointed out repeatedly that some young handicapped children have been misdiagnosed or given an unduly pessimistic prognosis. The course of maturation in these children is quite varied and may result in an unwarranted claim that improvement was due to the specific form of treatment (Freeman, 1967a; Koch, Graliker, Bronston, and Fischler, 1965; Masland, 1966). Some of the cases dramatically publicized by the Institutes have been children with traumatic brain damage, who often make substantial gains without any special treatment.

Some controlled studies of the Doman-Delacato claims with respect to reading have been carried out and have shown no benefit (Robbins, 1965a, 1966a, 1966b, 1967).

Previous cautionary statements have emphasized the need for well-controlled studies. The theoretical and practical problems involved in carrying out a study of all aspects of the Institutes' claims present many difficulties (Rosner, 1967b). A well-designed, comprehensive study (supported by both federal and private agencies) was in the final planning stage when the Institutes withdrew their original agreement to the design (Rosner, 1967a). With the failure of this attempt, the burden of proof for claimed results lies with the Institutes.

At present there are no data available which contradict the likelihood that any improvement observed with this method of treatment can be accounted for on the basis of growth and development, the intensive practice of certain isolated skills, or the non-specific effects of intensive stimulation.

Summary

The Institutes for the Achievement of Human Potential appear to differ substantially from other groups treating developmental problems in (a) the excessive nature of their undocumented claims for cure and (b) the extreme demands placed upon parents in carrying out an unproven technique without fail.

Advice to parents and professional workers cannot await conclusive results of controlled studies of all aspects of the method. Physicians and therapists should acquaint themselves with the issues in the controversy and the available evidence. We have done this and concur with the conclusions of Robbins and Glass (1969):

> There is no empirical evidence to substantiate the value of either the theory or practice of the neurological organization. . . . If the theory is to be taken seriously . . . its advocates are under an obligation to provide reasonable support for the tenets of the theory and a series of experimental investigations, consistent with scientific standards, which test the efficacy of the rationale.

To date, we know of no attempt to fulfill this obligation.

While the preceding statement exemplifies in outline form the major objections forwarded with regard to the Doman-Delacato treatment theory and procedures, Robbins and Glass (1969) have provided the most thorough analysis, criticizing not only the theoretical concepts upon which Doman and Delacato based their treatment approach, but also the studies used by them to support the effectiveness of their training methods. (The latter criticism will be discussed in a later chapter.)

One of the core concepts found to be untenable by Robbins and Glass is that ontogeny, the development of the individual, recapitulates phylogeny, the development or history of the species. As noted by Robbins and Glass, this concept is currently discredited by a number of sources (DeBeer, 1958; Gardner, 1963; Kraus, 1964; Moody, 1962). For example, Gardner (1963) concluded that even though some areas of the human brain correlate with sections of the brains of some animals below man on the phylogenetic scale, the existence of gross structural and functional differences still remains (Robbins and Glass, 1969). Robbins and Glass note that another author has concluded that, in terms of anatomy, the relationship is only present in gross structural similarities (Hudspeth, 1964).

In addition, Robbins and Glass point out that, although the original biogenetic law (now discredited) dealt with human ontogeny only through the embryonic stages, Delacato extended it to include development beyond fetal growth. This extension of the recapitulation theory was not unique within the field of psychology. At the turn of this century, G. Stanley Hall had forwarded Recapitulationism, which was later empirically disproven (Grinder, 1967). Doman and Delacato were in strict keeping with Haeckel's law, however, in their conception of the various sequential stages of human brain development, each of which corresponds to a stage of lower-animal development. The medulla level of the human corresponds to that of the fish, the pons to the amphibian, the midbrain to the reptile, and the early cortex to the primate. The final stage in man, cerebral dominance, was, according to Doman and Delacato, unique to the human species.

Another Doman-Delacato assumption attacked by Robbins and Glass regards the localization of function within the brain. Citing the classic studies of Lashley (1929) and the more recent work of Halstead (Shure and Halstead, 1958), Robbins and Glass argue that current neurophysiological thinking refutes the attempt to posit specific brain areas for specific behaviors. In the light of literature testifying to the relative commonness of mixed laterality in a normal population (Cole, 1964; Hécaen and Ajuriaguerra, 1964), Doman and Delacato may be unjustified in their claim that the human organism, owing to cerebral dominance, is naturally one-sided. In the Doman-Delacato program, children who do not express consistent laterality are trained to do so by an individual who discourages and inhibits use of one of the sides of the body, a procedure also employed by Dr. Winthrop Morgan Philps, an orthopedist, in his treatment of children with cerebral palsy in the decade 1940–1950. The hypothesis which underlies a program of forced unilaterality as advocated by Doman and Delacato has to do with its supposed positive relationship to reading readiness, a relationship seriously questioned by Robbins and Glass on the basis of evidence to the contrary (e.g., Balow, 1963; Balow and Balow, 1964; Belmont and Birch, 1965; Capobianco, 1966, 1967; Coleman and Deutsch, 1964; Flescher, 1963; Hillerich 1964; Robbins, 1965a, 1965b; Silver and Hagin, 1960). The contention by Doman and Delacato that the right-sided person's expressive language functions are controlled by the left hemisphere of the brain and vice versa for the left-sided individual is also questioned. Robbins and Glass felt that studies of aphasia (Penfield and Roberts, 1959), of experimentally induced aphasia through intracarotid injection of Sodium Amytal (Wada and Rasmussen, 1960), of postneurosurgical aphasia (Penfield and Roberts, 1959), of electrocortical interference (Penfield and Roberts, 1959), and of cases of unilateral brain injury (Zangwill, 1960), led to the conclusion that speech functions are generally controlled in the left hemisphere, regardless of handedness.

Several minor aspects of neurological organization theory are also criticized by Robbins and Glass, but the ones presented above are the most crucial to the Doman-Delacato conceptualizations. Owing to the wide array of negative evidence, Robbins and Glass therefore conclude:

> Our examination of these assumptions indicates that the tenets are either unsupported or overwhelmingly contradicted when tested by theoretical, experimental, or logical evidence from the relevant scientific literature. As a scientific hypothesis, the theory of neurological organization seems to be without merit [p. 346].

Doman and Delacato Compared to Other Perceptual-Motor Theorists

Superficially, there appears to be a great deal of similarity between the approach of Doman and Delacato and those of the previously discussed perceptual-motor theorists, Kephart, Getman, Barsch, and Frostig. All assume a relationship between perceptual-motor abilities and academic achievement, which means that the training activities of all these practitioners often overlap. The similarities probably are not accidental. During some of his classes in the late 1950s, Skeffington introduced Delacato to many of his optometric acquaintances.[12] Apparently, Delacato's early work was of some interest to Getman and Skeffington, who devoted much time to the discussion of his concepts. Although this is hardly enough evidence to posit a large mutual exchange of ideas, there was no doubt some degree of interchange between Delacato and the others.

While some cursory similarities exist between Doman and Delacato and other perceptual-motor theorists, there are crucial theoretical and practical differences. The basic tenet of neurological organization theory, recapitulation, for example, is unique to Doman and Delacato. Neurological organization theory also maintains that one must train children in specific motor patterns in order to stimulate particular areas of the brain. In this way, Doman and Delacato assumed they could treat the functioning of the brain rather than the behavior. The other perceptual-motor theorists, on the other hand, made few assumptions regarding the correspondence between their educational training methods and activity within the brain. They might agree with the statement that ultimately

---

[12] Personal communication from Gerald Getman, April 9, 1971.

the training they advocate results in some neurophysiological change; but, unlike Doman and Delacato, they are more reluctant to assume what those changes are.

Kephart (1960) perhaps came closest to the position of Doman and Delacato in remarking, "We must develop patterns of neurological activity which will produce appropriate muscle movement patterns rather than simply dispensing a single neurological impulse to a single muscle" [p. 41]. Kephart did not elaborate upon the comment, however, and his position beyond this statement does not really stress the direct treatment of the brain as does the position of Doman and Delacato. In contrast to the latter individuals, who derived their neurological organization theory from the specific neurological theory of Fay, Kephart maintained that he himself had relied upon the neurological theories of Penfield and Sherrington. Due to his reliance upon these last two men, Kephart thus developed a program oriented toward developing generalizations rather than specific skills.[13]

The Doman-Delacato group, following their theory of the necessity for single-handedness, would recommend that a child with poor reading and without a well-defined handedness be given training which would promote use of a dominant hand and inhibit use of the subdominant hand. Kephart and Getman would be opposed to such training, as would Ayres (1964), who felt that both sides of the body should function as an harmonious unit before one should be concerned about engendering hand dominance.

Another important aspect of training which differentiates proponents of neurological-organization theory from the other perceptual-motor theorists pertains to the question of whether the child should be actively or passively engaged in training. Following a strict one-to-one correspondence between training and the alteration of brain structure, Doman and Delacato recommended procedures which often call for the external manipulation of the child's limbs, whereas Kephart, Getman, Barsch, Cruickshank and Frostig have all emphasized the active involvement of the child in the training process.

Within an historical context, the theory of neurological organization as advanced by Doman and Delacato, and particularly the controversy which has surrounded it, have attained paramount significance. Since the early writings of learning disabilities theorists were notable for their differences and lack of cohesiveness, the possibility of comparing authors or ideologies was practically precluded by the diversity of terminology and definition of terms. Yet, although they may not have realized it, many theorists tended to accept or to oppose violently some

[13] Personal communication from Newell C. Kephart, April 6, 1971.

of the very concepts which were popularized only when Doman and Delacato translated them into an educational program.

With the advent of a concisely stated theory of neurological organization, theorists within the field of learning disabilities were finally able to focus upon and respond to many critical issues. In effect, the theory and research of Doman and Delacato acted as a catalyst in prompting the examination of attitudes which heretofore had not been related to learning disability concerns. Learning disabilities theorists suddenly had to reevaluate their own philosophies in terms of differences from and similarities to that of Doman and Delacato. The major controversies precipitated by the theory of neurological organization within the early stages of the learning disability movement caused a near-crisis that resulted in the clarification and strengthening of the ideas of various theorists and of the field as a whole.

It may even be said that the Doman-Delacato controversy had some bearing upon the transition from the concern for etiology as evidenced by the labels "brain injured" and "minimally brain injured" to the consideration of behavioral characteristics as reflected by the term "learning disabled." Suspicious of enthusiastic claims regarding treatment of the brain of brain injured children, many individuals may have hesitated to posit the existence of damage to the central nervous system in children, either because they were concerned about the possible association with controversial figures or because they were cautious about these speculations. Too, many theorists had second thoughts about the popular assumption that diagnosis of brain injury necessarily had educational pertinence. The rejection of neurological-organization educational methods, owing to their proponents' claim of direct brain training, may well have motivated interest in the discovery of educational methods based strictly upon learning abilities and disabilities, in which case the term "learning disabled" would be more meaningful than would the label "minimally brain injured."

LANGUAGE DISABILITY THEORISTS WITHIN THE FIELD OF LEARNING DISABILITIES

Up to this point, in keeping with the trend within the field of learning disabilities, discussion has been confined to individuals interested in the educational and psychological implications of children with disablities of a perceptual-motor nature. Relatively little attention in learning disability theory and research has been given to one of the most critical areas of child development, language. That this should be so is puzzling, since language disabilities no doubt exist and since a deficiency in either the reception or the production of language would prove especially disabling because of the central role which language plays in psychological development. The deemphasis of communication skills by the majority of learning disability specialists is no doubt related to the fact that their progenitors, Werner and Strauss, paid relatively little attention to language problems in children. Language was not completely ignored, at least by Strauss. In his later years he must have come to recognize its importance, for before his death in 1957 he was working on a book of some magnitude dealing with aphasia.

Samuel Orton

Although the majority of investigators and literature within the field deal with perceptual-motor disabilities, there have been some significant contributions and contributors to the understanding of language disabilities. Operating concurrently with Werner and Strauss in the 1930s, Samuel Orton, a neuropathologist, first studied the effects on language of acquired brain damage in adults and then attempted to relate them to the case of brain injured children (Myers and Hammill, 1969). The most notable features of his theory involve speculation concerning events within the brain and postulation of an inherited base of reading disabilities.

Like the contemporary theorists Doman and Delacato, Orton (1937) believed that mixed dominance, or "motor integrading" as he called it, exerted strongly negative influence upon learning to read. In fact, he felt that nearly all dyslexic symptoms could be explained by mixed dominance. Reading reversals were attributed to the possibility that when words were stored in the dominant hemisphere, their mirrored counterparts were recorded in the subdominant one. An individual without a clearly established dominant hemisphere might be expected to experience strong confusion. Contemporary evaluation, as mentioned in the discussion of Doman and Delacato, tends to discredit the mixed-dominance theory.

A second important aspect of Orton's philosophy was his belief that reading disability—or, more specifically, the mixed dominant state of the brain—was transferred hereditarily. While a few individuals today echo this contention, there is a dearth of solid empirical support for the notion.

Orton's educational remediation techniques have attracted through the years less censure than was directed at his theoretical speculations, possibly because his theorizations, involving as they did postulates concerning brain functioning, were far removed from the practical teaching situation. Paradoxically, if Orton had nurtured his theoretical concepts in an educational setting, he might very well have recommended many Doman and Delacato training procedures (e.g., the forced establishment of dominance) some twenty to thirty years before they did. Opposed to the sight method of reading instruction, Orton felt that the auditory capabilities of reading disabled children should be exploited through a phonetic approach (Myers and Hammill, 1969). In addition, like Fernald (1943), Orton advocated required letter tracing as an additional kinesthetic cue.

While the theoretical conceptions of Orton have not lured a great number of followers, his ideas are historically relevant by virtue of the fact that they were among the first concerning children today diagnosed as learning disabled. Writing at about the same time as Werner and Strauss and concentrating more specifically than these two (who were concerned primarily with brain damaged, mentally retarded children) on children who fit today's description of learning disabilities, Orton did not attract as many disciples as Werner and Strauss. In spite of occasional references by Werner and Strauss to language disturbances, for the most part they were perceptual-motor theorists; and since they have been progenitors to a relatively great number of theorists, the field of learning disabilities, as a whole, has acquired a perceptual-motor slant. Why they and not Orton attracted so many followers is open to speculations that range from the belief by others of their constructs to the chance association at Wayne County Training School of future significant contributors.

Katrina de Hirsch

Orton's ideas nevertheless have been influential to the development of significant theorists. Katrina de Hirsch is a case in point. While certainly not an avid disciple of Orton's, she did adopt at least some aspects of his thinking as starting points for her own theoretical discussion of children with "specific dyslexia" (de Hirsch, 1952) or what Orton would have termed "strephosymbolia," a disorder of the child who "is theoretically, at least, bright and reasonably well adjusted . . . [but] runs into trouble when he is first exposed to the printed word" [p. 100].

After studying in Buenos Aires, de Hirsch attended the University of Frankfurt am Main, where she was exposed to the teaching of the well-known Gestaltists, Gelb, Goldstein, and Wertheim.[14] With her ac-

14 Personal communication from Katrina de Hirsch, July 21, 1970.

quired background in Gestalt psychology, de Hirsch then pursued a degree in speech pathology at London's Hospital for Nervous Diseases. There she had as a teacher Woster Drought, one of the first to write on childhood aphasia. Working with both adults and children in the In- and Out-Patient Departments of numerous hospitals for the neurologically impaired, de Hirsch gained intensive practical experience as well as a strong theoretical exposure to neurological dysfunctions.

Her own evolving theoretical framework at that time centered around the idea that disorders of speech in children can be placed on a continuum of language dysfunctions. When coming to the United States in 1941, therefore, she was delighted to learn that Orton espoused the point of view that speech defects in children represent but one aspect of a continuum of verbal symbolic disturbances embracing oral, printed, and written language deficits as well as occasional trouble with numerical symbols. (At that time the discipline of speech pathology was not concerned with children's linguistic disorders.)[15]

That same year, at Columbia-Presbyterian Medical Center, together with Portia Hamilton, de Hirsch started the first language-disorder clinic in this country, the Pediatric Language Disorder Clinic, which is functionally part of Pediatric Psychiatry, under the direction of Dr. William Langford. After a year, Hamilton resigned and de Hirsch became director of the clinic, which is oriented toward diagnosis and research. It was in this clinic that she found much of the raw material for the formulation of her concepts.

Like Orton and Myklebust, de Hirsch should be considered as a language pathology theorist. In 1952 she described the receptive and expressive language deficits of dyslexic children, including their difficulty with processing of complex linguistic verbalizations, their trouble with formulation, their dysnomia, their tendency to cluttering, their disorganized verbal output, and their frequent failure to cope with spatial and temporal categories. She also pointed out that because such children often are unable to form anticipatory schemata of what a sentence is going to say (de Hirsch, 1963) their reading comprehension is seriously limited.

Influenced by the work of Strauss and Werner, de Hirsch investigated the perceptual-motor dysfunctions of this group: their spatial disorientation, their visuo-motor and figure-ground problems, their hyperactivity, and their primitive motility patterning. As did Bender, she looked at these phenomena as manifestations of central nervous system dysfunction, or, more frequently, as developmental lags, sometimes so severe that they amount to a maturational defect.

---

[15] Personal communication from Katrina de Hirsch, July 21, 1970.

The first major publication in which de Hirsch outlined her concepts regarding specific dyslexia appeared in 1952 in the *Folia Phoniatrica* in Switzerland. Today, she feels that some of the statements made 20 years ago are still valid.[16] In the 1952 publication, de Hirsch referred to many disturbances of a nonlanguage nature associated with specific dyslexia. Attention to at least four major psychological characteristics broadened her thinking considerably with regard to reading disability:

1. First, she commented, "Comparable difficulties are sometimes encountered in visual perception or recall" [p. 102]. While possessing more than adequate visual acuity, children may still have problems in the recall of details or in the reproduction of spatial configurations.
2. Visual-motor problems were also mentioned for their frequent association with language deficiencies. Though it was Orton who had previously found dyspraxic characteristics in his strephosymbolic children, de Hirsch over the years expanded this consideration considerably to include various aspects of visual-motor functioning.
3. Relying upon the investigations of Werner and Strauss, de Hirsch recognized the common occurrence of figure-ground disturbance in children with language problems. She reasoned that perhaps the problems in visual and auditory sequences, first noted by Orton, might reflect a more basic figure-background confusion. The child who must reproduce a pattern of pencil taps, for instance, must distinguish the figure from the ground in order to reconstruct the specific configuration. (It is difficult to determine how de Hirsch considered this task to be one of figure-ground discrimination ability.) Rather than an auditory deficiency, the child exhibiting problems on such a task might have a more general problem in forming "Gestalten." In 1954, de Hirsch expanded this notion in an article entitled, "Gestalt psychology as applied to language disturbances."
4. De Hirsch lastly observed that most children with severe language disabilities, like Strauss and Lehtinen's (1947) brain injured subjects, were hyperactive, distractible, uninhibited, and disorganized.

Consistent with a more eclectic approach, and unlike Orton and his pupils, de Hirsch has recently indicated that she does not recommend one specific approach to remediation.[17] While she believes that many children benefit from phonics (this is essentially true for those who have trouble coping with Gestalten or whole words), her own remedial techniques are centered upon the child rather than the method. Thus, they are tailored to the individual child's specific needs.

De Hirsch agrees with Orton that familial constitutional factors are significant in a large number of children suffering from weakness in the language area. Having become interested in Zangwill's position that such familial language deficits may reflect underlying central nervous system

[16] Personal communication from Katrina de Hirsch, July 21, 1970.
[17] Personal communication from Katrina de Hirsch, December 29, 1971.

immaturity, which in turn may be genetically determined, she came to believe that something of the kind might hold true for ambiguous lateralization. As did Orton before her, she found that poorly defined lateralization frequently accompanies language disorders. Her investigations of ambilaterality at kindergarten age and reading difficulty two years later, however, showed a negative correlation. These findings and those of Birch led her to modify her stance.

Today, while de Hirsch feels that Kimura's work has confirmed the importance of uncertain cortical dominance for language pathology as originally stressed by Orton, she agrees with Silver that it is by no means certain that handedness reflects cerebral dominance. Sharing Bender's point of view, which had very considerable impact on her work, de Hirsch now believes that both delayed cerebral dominance and language disorders may reflect a maturational dysfunction.[18] The postulate of maturational lag was tested out by de Hirsch, Jansky, and Langford as part of a larger study in an investigation which followed the performance of prematurely born children between the ages of five and eight (1966). Deficits in academic functioning in general and reading in particular were found to be greater for these experimental subjects than for a group of controls.

Not to discount the impact of other aspects of her work, de Hirsch is probably best recognized for her studies of the prediction of reading failure. In the early 1950s, through her observation of normally intelligent 3-, 4-, and 5-year-old children who had been referred to her clinic because of a variety of oral language deficits, she found that she could identify those who subsequently exhibited difficulties in learning to read (de Hirsch, 1957).

Dissatisfied with predictions based only upon a clinical population, de Hirsch later headed a statistical investigation funded by the Health Research Council of the City of New York (de Hirsch, Jansky, and Langford, 1966). The sample comprised fifty-two children born at term, all from lower middle-class backgrounds and with IQs between 89 and 116. At kindergarten age the children took a battery of thirty-seven tests designed to assess perceptual-motor abilities, body image, and a large variety of linguistic performances. On the basis of the Predictive Index derived from scores on these tests, de Hirsch et al. were able to identify correctly ten out of eleven children who subsequently failed in reading at the end of second grade. Follow-up research carried out by Jansky consists of two batteries, one predictive and one diagnostic, and one contains a number of tests from the original Predictive Index. The prognostic battery is suitable for heterogeneous groups and for children with IQs ranging from high to low.

18 Personal communication from Katrina de Hirsch, December 29, 1971.

Perhaps the chief value of de Hirsch's work lies in its synthesizing effect. For thirty years she has been a member of a pediatric psychiatric team and a consultant in language pathology at the New York State Psychiatric Institute. Working in this capacity, and drawing upon her early neurological training, she has attempted to integrate a variety of theoretical positions relative to the study of language disabilities in children. Her concern with the complex interaction between linguistic disturbances and psychopathology is reflected in a paper describing two groups of adolescents, both manifesting severe learning disabilities. For one group, academic failure was but one aspect of severe ego impairment and a reflection of a schizoid disorder. For the other, scholastic difficulties were related to a residual language deficit which had resulted in damage to the child's self-image and a total rejection of academic goals (de Hirsch, 1963).

Nowhere is the overlapping of de Hirsch's thinking with that of the perceptual-motor theorists (e.g., Kephart, Getman, Barsch, and Frostig) more apparent than in her conclusion (1968) that for those reading disabled children who can be predicted to fail, formal reading instruction should be postponed until success has been achieved with "perceptuomotor" and oral language education.

Samuel A. Kirk

One of the significant figures in learning disabilities is Samuel A. Kirk, who became deeply involved in the language disabilities of children at a rather late date in his career.

Kirk (1970), a psychologist, has indicated that his first encounter with a child who today would be classified as learning disabled came in the early 1930s while he was a graduate student at the University of Chicago and a resident instructor in a school for delinquent, retarded boys. At that time, he became absorbed in the tutoring of a 10-year-old described as "word blind." After reading the work of Monroe, Hinshelwood, and Fernald on the subject, Kirk applied himself to the task of tutoring the boy in reading, and within seven months the program proved successful.

Not long afterward, Kirk was invited to confer with Marion Monroe about his successful venture. Obviously impressed with Kirk's effort, Monroe agreed to accept Kirk under her tutelage in a program involving the diagnosis and remediation of children evidencing severe reading problems.

Taking what he gained from the experience to the Wayne County Training School, where he preceded even Werner and Strauss, as well as Cruickshank and Kephart, he was employed as a psychologist at Wayne County and simultaneously enrolled in courses at the University of Michigan. Influenced by the stress in the early 1930s on brain functioning and nonfunctioning, Kirk combined his teaching and research at the training school with courses in neurology and in physiological and experimental psychology at the University. Following brief experimentation concerning the effects of brain lesions in rats, Kirk became disenchanted with research which he felt had little relevance to the learning problems of children. As he has stated (Kirk, 1970):

> . . . studying physiological psychology and neurology and my own research on the brains of rats, have had no relationship to what I did then, or·have done since, or what I do now for children with learning disabilities [pp. 106-7].

Perhaps most directly relevant to his eventually extensive involvement in language was Kirk's establishment in 1949 of the first experimental nursery school "for so-called 'mentally retarded children'" [Kirk, 1970, p. 107]. As Kirk stated, "To be able to analyze the communication problems of younger children at the outset or before remediation, it became necessary for us to develop tests to isolate some of these abilities and disabilities" [p. 108].

These early attempts, however, did not satisfy Kirk's desire to develop an instrument for testing discrete abilities. Believing the failure to be due, in part at least, to a lack of a solid theoretical framework, Kirk enrolled in a course taught by Professor Charles Osgood at the University of Illinois (Kirk, 1970). Simultaneously enrolled in that course was Dorothy Sievers, a student of Kirk's, who developed numerous tests based on the Osgood communication model and then incorporated them into her dissertation (Sievers, 1955). Two years later, James McCarthy submitted a dissertation (on cerebral palsied children) which represented another attempt to construct a test for measuring individual abilities (McCarthy, 1957). Following the completion of these two studies Kirk, although satisfied with the applicability of the Osgood model, decided that yet another test for tapping discrete abilities would have to be devised.[19]

Thus, after fifteen years of clinical experience, much graduate work by students, and a great deal of field testing, Kirk and his colleagues finally produced their landmark test, the Illinois Test of Psycholinguistic Abilities (Kirk, McCarthy, and Kirk, 1961). Seven years later they published the Revised Edition (Kirk, McCarthy, and Kirk, 1968). It is noteworthy that the ITPA, a primary if not *the* primary test identified with

[19] Personal communication from Samuel Kirk, January 17, 1972.

field of learning disabilities, was developed in its original conceptual state within the area of mental retardation.

The Illinois Test of Psycholinguistic Abilities. In general, the Illinois Test of Psycholinguistic Abilities, is used with children aged 2 to 10 years. Although some of the twelve subtests do not have norms which extend all the way down to 2 years or up to 10 years, 11 months, they all cover at least the ages from 2 years, 4 months to 8 years, 7 months. The 8-year, 7-month upper limit applies only for one subtest. All the others have an upper limit of at least 10 years.

According to Kirk et al., the test was to be used principally in the diagnosis of psycholinguistic abilities and disabilities of children. Because of the emphasis upon intraindividual assessment rather than upon classification suggesting remedial prescription, the test was recommended by the authors for pinpointing specifically what might be causing any number of academic problems. With the focus on discrete abilities, the authors declared that the test would be most useful for children who had been labeled "learning disabled," "minimally brain injured," or "perceptually handicapped," i.e., children who, while not retarded, are lacking in specific areas of ability.

The Illinois Test of Psycholinguistic Abilities, adapted from the communications model of Osgood (1957a, 1957b), is composed of a three-dimensional model containing. (a) channels of communication, (b) psycholinguistic processes, and (c) levels of organization. The channels of communication include the modalities through which sensory information is received and then expressed in a response. While numerous combintions of sensory input and response output are possible theoretically, only the more educationally relevant auditory-vocal and visual-motor channels have been included in the Illinois Test of Psycholinguistic Abilities. The second aspect of Osgood's model includes those major psycholinguistic processes involved in the use of language—reception, organization, and expression. Reception, the decoding process, is the act of obtaining meaning from stimuli, e.g., the understanding of words, pictures, or gestures. The organizing process refers to internal manipulation of concepts and linguistic skills. Expression, or the encoding process, represents the ability to express ideas vocally or with gestures.

Organizational levels in the Illinois Test of Psycholinguistic Abilities are the representational, comprised of mediating behaviors that grasp symbols that give meaning to an object or activity, and the automatic, which includes the responses of less organized but nevertheless highly regulated and integrated habit chains.

Six functions are ostensibly assessed at the representational level of the Illinois Test of Psycholinguistic Abilities. Two of these, involving the processes of auditory and visual reception, test the ability to derive meaning from spoken words and visual symbols. The organizing process is required for two of the subtests. Auditory and visual association, necessitating the relation of concepts given orally and visually, are the abilities supposedly tapped here. The remaining two subtests at the representational level test the child's ability for verbal and manual expression of concepts. Within the six functions assessed at the automatic level, where purely receptive and expressive abilities have been ignored, two main areas have been included—closure and short-term sequential memory, both of which are measured visually and auditorially. Grammatic closure, assessing the use of the redundancies of oral language in manipulating syntax and grammatic inflections, belongs at this automatic level. Included by the authors under closure ability is the subtest of sound blending, which assesses ability to synthesize separate parts of a word into a whole.

The revised edition of the Illinois Test of Psycholinguistic Abilities has been subjected to a validity study (Paraskevopoulos and Kirk, 1969) in which Illinois Test of Psycholinguistic Abilities' scores were correlated with scores on the Stanford-Binet Intelligence Scale. According to the authors, the correlations were suppressed due to the use of selective factors that tended to build a homogeneous group. Standard deviation of the IQ score for this group was only 8 points instead of the 16 points exhibited by the general population. Correlations between the composite and IQ (.38 to .64), the composite and MA (.42 to .70), the PLQ and IQ (.41 to .67), and the PLQ and MA (.33 to .55) were higher than the composite or PLQ correlated with any of the subtests. Auditory Association and Grammatic Closure showed the highest of subtest correlations with MA and IQ. Auditory Association correlated with MA from .34 to .58 and with IQ from .28 to .57. Grammatic Closure correlation with MA ranged from .18 to .50, and with IQ it ranged from .21 to .51. The Auditory and Visual Sequential Memory subtests, along with the two supplementary tests—Auditory Closure and Sound Blending—showed exceedingly low correlations with Stanford-Binet IQ and MA, most correlations being in the teens and twenties, with a few negative correlations. Subtests at the representational level tended to correlate higher with MA and IQ than did those at the automatic level. Auditory subtests at the representational level and Grammatic Closure, with correlations in the twenties and thirties, showed the highest relationships to the Vocabulary Test score of the Stanford-Binet.

The validity study of the revised edition of the Illinois Test of Psycholinguistic Abilities just mentioned is the only one to be found in the literature to date. The correlations, even if one keeps in mind their suppression by homogeneity factors, certainly are not overly impressive.

Although the two tests do not purport to measure precisely the same thing, the Stanford-Binet is a highly verbal test, so that higher correlations would be anticipated. Passing judgment on the basis of only one study is difficult, however, especially since it is not known exactly how much these correlations are, in fact, "suppressed."

Validity studies on the experimental edition, on the other hand, do lend themselves to evaluation. The two editions are so similar that a review of the validity studies dealing with the experimental edition can serve as an indicator in evaluation of the revised edition.

McCarthy and Olson (1964) performed a number of statistical operations in order to determine the concurrent and predictive validity of the 1961 Illinois Test of Psycholinguistic Abilities. The criterion measures were already-extant language tests and language-based portions of various achievement tests. Each subtest was correlated with a criterion test preselected on the basis of its apparent similarity to the particular subtest. A total of eighty-six subjects, ranging in age from 7 years, 4 months, to 8 years, 6 months, was comparable to the standardization sample in social class membership, sex, and mental age. Correlation coefficients for concurrent validity ranged from .03 to .65, with a median of .15, while predictive validity coefficients ranged from −.19 to .53, with a median coefficient of .23. For concurrent validity, less than half the correlations were significant. For predictive validity, just slightly more than half were significant. Although these correlations are hardly impressive, there is the very distinct possibility that the Illinois Test of Psycholinguistic Abilities' subtests are tapping skills which have not been measured by the criterion tests. It is safe to say, however, that the predictive and concurrent validity studies of McCarthy and Olson were inconclusive.

Construct validity of the experimental addition has also been assessed and questioned by the research of Weener, Barritt, and Semmel (1967). Examining the intercorrelations of the subtests, they criticized the Illinois Test of Psycholinguistic Abilities on the grounds that it does not really correspond to the theoretical model of Osgood, upon which it was purportedly built. In other words, subtests do not hang together within levels, channels, and processes. Weener et al. emphasized this lack of clarity in their reference to a factor analysis performed on the test. Like the Frostig subtests, individual Illinois Test of Psycholinguistic Abilities' subtests were found to contain only partial evidence of single-ability assessment. In addition, the largest factor after rotation was one of general linguistic ability.

In the unpublished research of Semmel and Mueller (1962), however, quartimax orthogonal rotation identified a simple structure in which each of the subtests appeared to be defined by a single factor. The subjects for this study were 118 mentally retarded (rather than normal) children from day and residential centers in Tennessee. Chronological ages ranged from 6 years, 5 months to 19 years, with a mean of 12 years, 7 months. Mental ages ranged from 3 years, 6 months to 9 years, 1 month, with a mean of 5 years, 10 months. IQs fell between 20 and 80, with a mean of 49. There were fifty-nine males and fifty-nine females of undetermined etiology, except for the inclusion of eighteen children known to have Down's Syndrome.

On the whole, results of the validity studies performed by the Illinois Test of Psycholinguistic Abilities' authors, their colleagues, and others are frequently contradictory and inconclusive. Moreover, most of the reported studies have been performed on the experimental edition rather than on the newer, revised edition. The Illinois Test of Psycholinguistic Abilities' merit, or lack thereof, therefore, has not yet been adequately assessed.

Taking the correlation matrices from numerous studies on the experimental edition, including a number of the above investigations, Ryckman and Wiegerink (1969) submitted them to a principal axis factor analysis. They found that as age level increased, the test was more discriminatory in terms of measuring single abilities. At the 3-year-level, there appeared a general factor with strong auditory-vocal channel emphasis and a factor heavily weighted on the visual-motor channel. Three factors appeared at the 5-year, 6-month age level. The first of these was the general factor evident at the 3-year level, while the other two were an apparently indefinable factor and a visual-motor factor. At the 8-year level were four factors not resembling any of those at the other two levels. These were a general language, an encoding, a memory, and a visual-decoding factor. When Ryckman and Wiegerink also analyzed the data to ascertain whether the factor loadings would reflect breakdown into channels, levels, and processes, results were consistent with the others in that at older age levels, the three components of Osgood's model emerged as reasonably separate entities.

In terms of reliability, both internal consistency and stability coefficients have been calculated (Paraskevopoulos and Kirk, 1969). Internal consistency was studied for each subtest and for the Illinois Test of Psycholinguistic Abilities' composite. The internal reliability coefficients were carried out on the original 962 children of the standardization sample. As the investigators stated, since the normative sample was homogeneous because of selection procedures, the reliability coefficients were likely to be lowered. Paraskevopoulos and Kirk therefore corrected for IQ but were unable to rectify many variables, e.g., achievement, age, and sensory-motor ability. For the most part, the coefficients were quite adequate, occurring predominantly in the high 80s or 90s.

Stability of the Illinois Test of Psycholinguistic Abilities was determined by retesting three age groups of children from the standardization sample. Some six months after the original assessment, 71 of the 4-year-olds, 55 of the 6-year-olds, and 72 of the 8-year-olds were relocated and tested. Those selected for this reliability study did not differ significantly from the larger group on their scores for the first testing. The coefficients obtained were generally of a moderately high nature for all three age groups, falling for the most part in the 60s and 70s. No age trend was discernible. Visual Sequential Memory and Sound Blending were the least stable subtests, the former having a coefficient of .38 at the 5-year level and .28 at the 6-year level, the latter showing coefficients of .42 and .54 at each of those respective age levels.

Kirk and Paraskevopoulos have also presented data on the interscorer reliability for the Verbal Expression subtest. Since this subtest is the most open-ended in terms of scoring, it is appropriate that its analysis should have been carried out. The coefficients were in the high 90s for both experienced and novice examiners.

Hopefully, the discussion presented above gives some indication of the vast amount of planning and research focused on the Illinois Test of Psycholinguistic Abilities, an undisputed milestone in the field of learning disabilities. Even more than Frostig's test, it has become an extraordinarily popular clinical and research tool. In fact, Kirk (1970) noted that it has provided the basis for over twenty dissertations alone since its conception.

As with any new instrument, particularly one that represents a departure from the traditional measurement test, there are some features that must be dealt with judiciously if the test is to be perfected. As was noted above, judgment of the Illinois Test of Psycholinguistic Abilities must await further studies on the revised edition. While the literature pertaining to the experimental edition is inconclusive or negative with regard to construct and to concurrent and predictive validity, the authors have demonstrated fairly adequate concurrent validity with the new edition. Also, the study of Ryckman and Wiegerink (1969) demonstrated that, while the test may not tap nine distinct abilities, it does tend to precipitate single factors as age level increases. For the upper ages, the levels, channels, and processes in the model emerge as fairly separate factors as well. It therefore appears that Kirk et al. have been more successful than Frostig et al. in building a series of subtests that assess independent functions.

Yet even if the Illinois Test of Psycholinguistic Abilities to some extent does measure discrete abilities, individual subtests still may not be assessing what they are purported to measure according to the model and their names. In fact, there are strong indications that some of the subtests have been misnamed or misplaced. This faulty labeling could easily have resulted from the attempt by Kirk and his colleagues to adhere to Osgood's model. On the Visual Reception subtest, for example, a memory disability for visual stimuli could contribute to a low score. When the subject is shown a picture and then asked to identify its likeness in another group, he must retain a visual image for a short period of time. On the Visual Closure subtest, the ability to identify partially hidden objects may involve more than mere visual-closure ability. Since the objects to be found vary in their positions and angles, this task may also require recognition of an object from a variety of angles. Furthermore, the array of stimuli in the picture invites failure for a child with figure-background problems. Since the Vocal Expression subtest necessitates vocal encoding of visual stimuli, its components are actually visual-vocal rather than auditory-vocal in nature. The Visual Association and Visual Reception subtests may have been considered appropriate to the visual-motor channel and the representational level, but it is hard to believe that the single pointing response required by these subtests is a symbolic representational gesture. Finally, although Grammatic Closure is classified under the automatic level, it has the second highest of subtest correlations with mental age as determined by the Stanford-Binet. Why this should be so is difficult to rationalize, since mental age supposedly is measured primarily by the ability to manipulate symbols and concepts.

On the basis of the preceding discussion and evaluation, it would seem that reliance on the Illinois Test of Psycholinguistic Abilities should be approached cautiously, particularly with children under the age of about 6 years. In the hands of a skilled clinician who is cognizant of its limitations and strengths, the test no doubt can be a useful addition to a battery of tests. As with all tests, however, it should not be used alone for assessment or remedial recommendations.

The user of the instrument also must be especially aware that the test as a whole does not entirely correspond to the model upon which it is supposedly built. Such a drawback is theoretical, of course, and does not necessarily eliminate the test's practical value. Particular subtests, while perhaps failing to measure the purported process, level, or channel, do create standardized situations in which a child must perform tasks that, at the very least, have much face validity in terms of their relevance to learning situations. More research is needed to determine the extent of the Illinois Test of Psycholinguistic Abilities' usefulness or, to be more specific, the ways in which and the conditions under which it would be most useful.

Like the Frostig test, the Illinois Test of Psycholinguistic Abilities is strengthened by the immediate educational applicability that renders it significant both for the field of learning disabilities and for the general area of test construction. In order to maximize the value of results, however, the examiner should also become familiar with a text prepared by the senior author (Kirk, 1966) and with a publication by Barbara Bateman (1968), a disciple of Kirk over seven years in the 1960s,[20] who made inestimable recommendations for the educational interpretation of Illinois Test of Psycholinguistic Abilities' results. In addition to the emphasis on language disabilities, it is this concern for the relationship between diagnosis and remediation which makes the work of Kirk and his colleagues so important to development of the field of learning disabilities.

With regard to attention to language, it is interesting to observe that while Kirk's test carries the name "Psycholinguistic Abilities," there are, within the model and within the subtests, a number of items concerned with visual-motor functioning. Thus, although Kirk emphasizes language a great deal more than do theorists in the perceptual-motor domain (e.g., Kephart, Getman, Barsch, Frostig, Doman, and Delacato), both his test and his remediation recommendations account for many different aspects of perceptual and perceptual-motor performance.

Helmer Myklebust

Whereas Kirk has combined a concern for language and perceptual-motor behavior, another major figure, Helmer Myklebust, has been more exclusively concerned with disabilities of a lingual nature. Along with Kirk, Myklebust has been one of the key figures drawing attention to the language disabilities of learning disabled children.

The involvement of Myklebust with language problems as learning disabilities appears to be a natural outgrowth of his early, extensive exploration of deafness and aphasia. For many years, he had wrestled with the relationship between deafness and language development. Recognizing within his own child study center a number of children who were able to hear but nevertheless were unable to develop auditory language (i.e., receptive language), Myklebust became interested in the diagnosis and remediation of auditory disorders (Myklebust, 1970). It was this interest which finally drew him into the orbit of learning disability theorization.

Besides identifying five major types of learning disabilities—auditory language, arithmetic, reading, writing, and nonverbal (Johnson and Myklebust, 1967)—and making recommendations for their diagnosis and remediation, Myklebust is perhaps best known for his development and

[20] Personal communication from Barbara Bateman, February 22, 1971.

popularization of the terms "psychoneurological learning disability" and "learning quotient."

"Psychoneurological learning disability" was reached as a compromise label when Myklebust became dissatisfied with other terms in popular use. Although the term consolidates concern for brain-injury etiology and behavioral characteristics, Myklebust is more occupied with etiology. Recently, in fact, he wrote that his "main interest for more than a decade now, has been the relationship between brain and behavior, particularly as these pertain to learning" [1970, p. 112]. Myklebust is not alone, of course, in postulating neurological dysfunction at the base of all learning disabilities, but his approach to the problem has not been congruent with the general trend. While workers such as Kephart, Getman, Barsch, Frostig, and especially Kirk have either shifted stress from etiology to behavior or have always thought it more educationally relevant to attend to behavioral characteristics rather than etiological diagnosis, Myklebust has continued to posit etiological bases.

Myklebust's development of the learning quotient marked a first attempt to quantify the extent of a child's learning disabilities by comparing his expected potential to his actualized performance. Creation of the quotient was an attempt to provide the diagnostician with a tool for gauging whether the child is mentally retarded or learning disabled. In fact, as will soon be seen, in Myklebust's learning-quotient concept, a mentally retarded child, as well as a child of superior intelligence, might still be diagnosed as learning disabled.

Actual calculation employs the following formula to derive first an Expectancy Age (Myklebust, 1968):

$$\frac{\text{Mental Age} + \text{Life Age} + \text{Grade Age}}{3} = \text{Expectancy Age}$$

After a child has taken both verbal and nonverbal tests, the higher of his two scores is used to estimate the Mental Age component. Observing that a child may exhibit what is a primarily verbal or a primarily nonverbal learning disability, Myklebust assesses both but relies on the better performance to indicate the child's potential. The Life Age indicates physiological maturity. Grade Age was incorporated as reflection of experience, particularly the opportunity for school learning. Once the Expectancy Age has been calculated, it is then divided into year level as obtained on achievement tests in order to establish the learning quotient. Thus, a child with an Expectancy Age of 10 years and a reading achievement age of only 8 years would have a learning quotient of 80 in reading. Aware of the arbitrary nature of determining the point at which the learning quotient of a child would indicate a learning difficulty, Myklebust decided to use a cutoff score of 89.

NEUROPSYCHOLOGICAL PIONEERS

Theorists discussed to this point share at least two significant characteristics. In the first place, whether primarily perceptual-motor or linguistic in orientation, all have been disposed toward the educational aspects of learning disabilities. Second, and most important to the dominant premise of this chapter, all of them share to some extent a professional debt to the pioneering efforts of Werner and Strauss—some through direct professional contact and others through familiarity with their writings.

While all of these theorists may occasionally have alluded to the psychological or neuropsychological aspects of learning disabilities or brain damage, for the most part they have been more involved in providing conceptualizations concerning educational methods. This statement excludes Doman and Delacato who, as noted, have made extensive speculations and hypotheses concerning brain functioning. This predominant emphasis upon remediation (even the diagnostic emphases of Frostig and Kirk are ultimately education based) possibly accounts for their turning away from a concern for etiology and concepts such as "brain injury" or "central nervous system impairment" to more educationally relevant terminology, such as "learning disability," "developmental imbalance," "perceptual handicap," or any similar behavioral description.

It is important to remember, however, that Werner and Strauss were studying children with what they considered to be brain injury. An historical analysis of the field of learning disabilities would thus be incomplete without a consideration of those individuals who pioneered the investigation of the psychological correlates of neurological dysfunction. Arthur Benton and Ralph Reitan are two such individuals.

Arthur Benton

Benton, while prepared to accept the thesis that learning disabilities in children are the result of multiple determinants, elected to pursue in his laboratory work a focus on the neurological (or neuropsychological) aspects of educational failure.[21] He acquired this neurological orientation only after first delving into experimental and clinical psychology (Birch, 1964). Following the completion of his master's thesis study of conditioned reflexes, Benton took an assistantship in psychology at the New York State Psychiatric Institute and Hospital, where his close association with the psychiatrists prompted him to shift his interest to clinical prac-

21 Personal communication from Arthur Benton, July 9, 1970.

tice and research. When his doctoral dissertation was completed at Columbia, Benton served for a period of time as an officer in the Navy Medical Service Corps. As a senior psychologist, working in conjunction with Morris B. Bender at the San Diego Naval Hospital, he became increasingly intrigued with clinical neuropsychology.

Benton has been recognized particularly for his experiments into the relationship between numerous kinds of behavioral characteristics and the locus of cerebral lesion. He is also noted for the elucidation of certain hypothesized psychoneurological syndromes. An example of this latter concern, and one that contains great import for the field of learning disabilities, is Benton's series of investigations springing from the Strauss and Werner (1938) study of Gerstmann's syndrome (Gerstmann, 1927). Gerstmann had identified a syndrome of disability in which pervasive finger agnosia and agraphia may or may not be accompanied by acalculia and right-left discrimination problems. In a test of this syndrome, Strauss and Werner (1938) reported a positive relationship between poor finger schema and arithmetic disability (acalculia) in mentally retarded children.

Benton, Hutcheon, and Seymour (1951) criticized the composition of Strauss and Werner's special arithmetic ability and disability groups, after finding that the arithmetic index (derived by comparing arithmetic achievement to mental age and reading achievement) for one "disabled" child was higher than those for two children in the ability group. Furthermore, Benton et al. pointed out that within the ability group was one subject whose arithmetic age was below both mental age and reading age, which made his assignment to the special arithmetic ability group highly questionable. Another child in the ability group possessed an arithmetic age merely two or three months superior to his mental age and, if anything, could only have been said to have special reading ability. The appropriateness of placing four of the fourteen subjects in the special arithmetic group was thus debatable. Regarding the disability group, Benton et al. discovered that the majority of cases had arithmetic ages either higher than, equal to, or insignificantly lower than their mental ages.

With these methodological weaknesses in mind, Benton et al. performed their own study, using a normal and a mentally retarded group of children. No support for the contention of Werner and Strauss was forthcoming. The experimenters did find, however, that for mentally retarded subjects there existed a significant association between finger localization ability and the ability to discriminate right from left on one's own body. Approaching significance was the relationship between finger localization and right-left discrimination of the parts of another person's body. For normal subjects, there was no significant correlation between finger schema and either aspect of right-left discrimination.

These results were explained by referring to the clinical observations of Gerstmann, who had discovered both the invariable relatedness of agnosia to agraphia and the irregular presence of acalculia and right-left discrimination. With this refutation of an earlier study by Strauss and Werner, Benton launched his investigation into right-left discrimination ability and various aspects of body schema, two topics which were to occupy a major portion of his research efforts over the next twenty years.

In 1957, Benton and Menefee explored the relationship between handedness (the degree of preference for one hand over the other) and right-left discrimination of one's own body parts. Using normal children, they found a small but positive significant association (in the low 20s) between the two variables. In previous studies (Benton, 1955; Benton et al., 1951) a relatively high correlation (about .40) had been discovered between right-left discrimination and finger localization ability in brain injured and mentally retarded children with chronological and mental age held constant, while low correlations (about .20) had been found between the two in normal subjects. Keeping in mind the cumulative results of Benton's research, Benton and Menefee hypothesized that organic factors might be important to the relatedness of various aspects of "body schema." The hypothesis was accompanied, however, by the statement that, according to what was known from existing studies, the relationship probably would be of only moderate magnitude. Benton et al. concluded:

> . . . the present findings suggest a considerable degree of specificity in the status of these behavioral skills that are often grouped together by the clinical observer under a single concept, such as "laterality" or the "body schema" [p. 24].

In another study, Benton (1958) found with normal children that subjects having a systematic tendency to reverse right and left on the right-left discrimination tasks were not deviant in finger localization, handedness, or arithmetic. These findings contradicted those reported earlier by Cénac and Hécaen (1943), whom Benton faulted for their numerous deficiencies during subject selection. Benton did find, however, that performance of the reversal group was inferior to that of the control group of nonreversers on tests of reading and language skills.

Again using normal subjects, Benton (1959b) investigated yet another aspect of the development of finger-localization ability in children. This time, he detected a significant relationship between finger localization and certain types of finger praxis (those tasks requiring finger movements in relation to one another). Furthermore, right-left discrimination appeared to be related to finger localization but not to finger praxis, indicating that the association between finger localization and finger praxis was a function of the specific nature of the finger schema construct.

However, with regard to the frequently observed correlation between right-left discrimination and finger localization, especially in mentally retarded and brain injured children, Benton suggested the need for a construct broader than that of finger schema to account for the relationship. The relevance of the above investigations to the study of learning disabilities becomes apparent when one considers that the behaviors discussed by Benton have often been attributed to children with learning disabilities.

Even more pertinent to the study of learning disabilities are Benton's recent considerations of the incidence of some of these behaviors among neurologically impaired children and his research into the relationship between these behaviors and reading disability. Discussing the importance of central nervous system dysfunction, Benton (1969b) reported a 20 percent frequency of defective finger recognition among brain damaged children with normal IQ. In addition, he referred to an investigation in which an even higher proportion was obtained (Clawson, 1962). Other indirect evidence for the association between finger agnosia and brain injury comes from Benton's (1959c) discovery of a higher incidence of defective finger localization ability in mentally retarded (25 percent) as compared to normal (5 percent) children equated for mental age. While adult studies have tended to find a higher frequency of finger localization impairment in patients with damage to the left hemisphere (Benton, 1961), no such consistent relationship has been found in children.

Virtually the same findings as those for finger agnosia have been reported with regard to right-left discrimination. Clawson (1962) found right-left discrimination impairment to be more frequently displayed in brain injured children of normal intelligence than in normal or emotionally disturbed subjects. Too, Benton (1955) uncovered a higher incidence of right-left discrimination problems for mentally retarded children when compared to normals. In contrast to what had been concluded on the basis of adult studies, Benton (1968) later referred to the lack of any such convincing evidence for the relatedness of right-left discrimination problems to damage of the left hemisphere.

Although Benton recognized that Reed (1967) had found certain patterns of finger localization ability to be related to reading skills, he concluded after reviewing the literature that right-left discrimination ability did not relate in an important way to reading ability (1968). This latter opinion refutes the theoretical formulations of Kephart (1960), who stated that the discrimination of right from left, whether in relation to one's own (laterality) or to another's (directionality) body, should affect academic achievement. This influence, Kephart argued, ought to be particularly manifest in reading, an ability purportedly requiring the constant discrimination of reversible letter and word pairs, e.g., "b"

and "d," "p" and "q," "saw" and "was." On the basis of his own conclusions, Benton would undoubtedly be averse to these views on the
relationship among laterality, directionality, and reading achievement.

Another area to which Benton devoted his energy is that of test construction. Benton (1963) devised a test for the diagnosis of brain damage
through a memory-for-designs format. Similar to the Bender-Gestalt in
requiring the subject to draw geometric designs, but providing the alternative of having him draw from memory, the Benton Visual Retention
Test has norms for 8 years of age and above.

Generally agreeing that Benton's test compares favorably with others
of its kind, reviewers (e.g., Hanawalt, 1959) nevertheless have noted its
inadequate reporting of the standardization population, numbers of subjects, sex differences, statistical methods, reliability, and correlation
among the three forms (Hanawalt, 1959). Too, as Benton admitted, it
has not been firmly established that the test is consistently valid for
diagnosing brain damage. Nor does it have unquestionable validity for
singling out individuals who, regardless of etiology, will have visual-
motor problems which may lead to learning problems, although the
notion contains more than a modicum of face validity. In this respect,
he has pointed out the various factors other than brain damage which
may lead to defective performance on a memory-for-designs test (Benton,
1963, p. 49). As noted in chapter 5, flaws of this type are by no means
unique. The diagnosis of brain injury through psychological testing
traditionally has been fraught with seemingly insurmountable methodological problems.

The efforts described here comprise but a small representation of the
contributions made by Benton, whose research and clinical experiences
led him to investigate neuropsychological aspects of a wide variety of
abilities, e.g., aphasia (Benton, 1959a, 1967b, 1969a), reaction time (Benton and Joynt, 1959; Benton Sutton, Kennedy and Brokaw, 1962), motor
impersistence (Benton, Garfield, and Chiorini, 1964), and apraxia (Benton, 1967a; Dee, Benton and VanAllen, 1970). These explorations into
the nature of brain damage have made Benton one of the foremost
figures in the neuropsychological field.

Ralph Reitan

While Benton has devised a test for the diagnosis of brain injury and
visual-motor problems Ralph Reitan over the past twenty years has developed batteries of tests of considerably broader scope. With test batteries
intended to measure a wide variety of abilities, it has been Reitan's purpose to explore as thoroughly as possible the psychological characteristics

of brain injured individuals rather than to construct a specific test for the diagnosis of brain injury. This tendency, reflected by the relative lack of concern for establishing normative information for his instruments, certainly differentiates Reitan from the researcher who has constructed a test "for" brain damage and pays close attention to norming procedures.

Reitan based his work upon that of Ward Halstead, who set up a full-time laboratory at the University of Chicago in 1935 for the purpose of studying the psychological effects of brain injury in adults. This landmark research by Halstead, it should be noted, was carried on concurrently with the work of Werner and Strauss. Unfortunately, except for a few reciprocal references, there was apparently no direct contact or collaboration between the two groups of researchers who, it may be said, were separated only by the age of their subjects and about 300 miles. Halstead's significant comments upon the effects of brain lesions appeared in the now-classic *Brain and intelligence: A quantitative study of the frontal lobes* (1947). For this volume Halstead used twenty-seven tests, ten of them eventually grouped as Halstead's Neuropsychological Test Battery, which is presently applied in the testing of individuals above the age of 14.

After performing preliminary research from 1951 to 1953 in his laboratory at Indiana University, Reitan modified Halstead's test battery to make it appropriate for use with children 9 to 14 years of age. Resulting from this revision was the Halstead Neuropsychological Test Battery for Children. In 1955, Reitan began work on a further adaptation for children under the age of 9. That battery came to be known as the Reitan-Indiana Neuropsychological Test Battery for Children.[22]

The format and intent of the latter battery have been well described by Reitan. The Category Test requires pictorial matching of objects on the basis of various cues, such as color, area, or oddity. The child is not advised of the cue to which he must attend but forms his own concept by being positively or negatively reinforced (with bell or buzzer) when he activates an answer lever.

For the Tactual Performance Test, the blindfolded child must fit blocks into a horizontally placed board, first with the preferred hand, then with the nonpreferred hand, and finally with both hands. Time required for completion of the task is recorded. Incidental memory and localization scores are obtained also, by removing the board and requiring the blindfolded subject to "reconstruct" it with the blocks in their appropriate slots.

The Rhythm Test presents pairs of rhythmic beats for which the child must discern whether they are different or the same.

[22] Personal communication from Ralph M. Reitan, July 7, 1970.

83063

The Speech-Sounds Perception Test involves the taped playing of variations on the "ee" sound. The subject selects one syllable from among three printed alternatives.

The Finger Oscillation Test measures tapping speed. With the index finger first of one hand and then of the other, the child must tap as rapidly as possible on five consecutive ten-second trials.

For the Time Sense Test, the child presses a key to start the rotation of a clock hand. After ten rotations, the hand is to be stopped as near to its starting point as possible. Following a number of trials, the clock face is then turned away from the subject, who must perform the same task while relying only upon his memory of the time span required for ten rotations.

On the Marching Test the subject is to proceed with a crayon from one figure to another on a page of vertically placed circles. He must perform the task with each hand separately and then with both hands together.

The Color Form Test, the Progressive Figures Test, and the Matching Pictures Test are designed to assess aspects of conceptual and abstract thinking ability, as well as visual-motor skills. The Color Form Test requires the child to draw a line from one figure to another as he alternates the basis for each move (i.e., color or form). On the Progressive Figures Test, the child is shown a page with numerous figures, each one composed of a shape enclosing a different, smaller shape. He proceeds from one to another, using the smaller inner shape as an indicator for movement to the outside shape of the next figure. For the Matching Pictures Test, the child matches pictures of items on the basis of common characteristics.

In the assessment of visual-spatial relationships, Reitan has included the Target Test and the various subtests of the Individual Performance Test. On the Target Test, the subject must duplicate a certain pattern by connecting the points in a square-shaped arrangement of nine dots.

On the Matching V's subtest of the Individual Performance Test, the child identifies figures whose angle sizes are the same. Other tasks require the child to reproduce a six-sided star, to copy concentric squares, and to match figures.

A number of other tests constructed by Reitan are purported to assess abilities related to aphasia and sensory-perceptual problems. For example, the child must name objects, copy geometric shapes, read, perform arithmetic, identify body parts, discriminate between the left and right hands, and respond to items of bilateral, tactual, auditory, and visual discrimination.

With the above battery and others designed for adults, Reitan and his colleagues have been involved since the early 1950s in the investigation of a wide variety of psychological abilities and their relation to brain damage. A significant proportion of these investigations involved the study of differential effects of damage to either the right or the left hemisphere. Experiments with adults, for instance, have consistently indicated that lesions of the left cerebral hemisphere are associated with verbal abilities and that lesions of the right hemisphere affect nonverbal abilities (Anderson, 1951; Fitzhugh, Fitzhugh, and Reitan, 1962; Kløve and Reitan, 1958; Matthews and Reitan, 1964; Reed and Reitan, 1963; Reitan, 1955).

As noted by Benton (1967a), the history of concern for lateralization was characterized by a dramatic shift. With regard to visual constructive tasks, it was originally thought (Kleist, 1934; Strauss, 1924) that the posterior parietal area of the left cerebral hemisphere was crucial. However, after a period of about fifteen years, a study by Anderson (1951), studies by Reitan and his associates (Fitzhugh, Fitzhugh, and Reitan, 1962; Kløve and Reitan, 1958; Matthews and Reitan, 1964; Reed and Reitan, 1963; Reitan, 1955), studies by Zangwill and his associates (McFie, Piercy, and Zangwill, 1950; Paterson and Zangwill, 1944), and studies by Hécaen and his associates (Hécaen, Ajuriaguerra, and Massonet, 1951; Hécaen, Penfield, Bertrand, and Malmo, 1956), the accumulated data contradicted the earlier findings.

To date research with adults, including the aforementioned work of Reitan and of Benton (Benton, 1962; Benton and Fogel, 1962), tends to support the lateralization of gross measures of verbal abilities with the left hemisphere and the association of nonverbal abilities with the right hemisphere. Other than providing this gross dichotomy, however, the research evidence is much less clear with respect to the localization of specific skills. The extensive work of Teuber (Teuber and Liebert, 1958; Teuber and Weinstein, 1954) referred to by Deutsch and Schumer (1967) indicated that some tasks may depend on localization of the lesion, whereas others may be affected by damage to either hemisphere.

The experiments with adults, taken as a whole, serve to underscore the inconclusiveness and confusion presently characterizing studies of localization. The situation is even more problematical with respect to studies of localization of function in children. Even the right- versus left-hemisphere dichotomy, which holds up reasonably well for adults, has not been found to be applicable with children.

Problems Impeding Neuropsychological Progress

At this early stage in the study of brain-behavior relationships, it seems clear that the greatest hindrances to theoretical breakthrough revolve around methodological problems. In particular, both neurological measures (EEG, for example, which is used merely for identification of brain damaged individuals) and the pinpointing of lesion location are still in the infancy stage of refinement. Whereas in studies of acquired brain injury in adults one can at times judge the location of an insult, the situation is more complex in the child who received the damage prenatally, paranatally, or postnatally some time before diagnosis.

Factors related to the developing child's brain and to his growing repertoire of behaviors further help to account for the greater inconsistency of results in child studies. Related to this methodological problem is the almost invariable heterogeneity of the brain damaged group under study with regard to the nature of the brain damage (e.g., extent, location, and age at onset of damage). As Deutsch and Schumer (1967) have pointed out, the term "brain injury" covers a multitude of conditions of damage to the central nervous system. The subject one investigator includes in his "brain damaged" group may differ on any number of crucial variables from the subject included on the basis of another experimenter's criteria.

Problems such as those listed here have impeded the progress of definitive research. For at least two decades, investigators such as Benton and Reitan have progressed only slightly beyond the groundbreaking state in their inquiries into the neuropsychological effects of brain lesions. Implications for the education of children identified as "brain injured" and/or "learning disabled," partly because of the necessitated immature quality of research, have been virtually nonexistent.

In addition to the methodological confusions and inconsistency of results, yet partially dependent upon them, are other explanations for the dearth of educationally applicable findings. Coincidental with the rapid growth of the learning disability orientation in the early 1960s was the lessening of faith and interest on the part of educators for research endeavors directed at brain-behavior relationships. This lack of interest unquestionably has affected production of neuropsychological research relevant to education. Until those individuals with both neuropsychological and educational preferences develop an active mutual interest in one another's work (e.g., in the form of collaborative research efforts), there is little hope for a productive exchange of information regarding the child identified as brain injured and/or learning disabled.

TOWARD INTEGRATION

William Gaddes

One of the few individuals to work at reducing this isolationist tendency is William H. Gaddes, a researcher in brain-behavior relationships who has drawn heavily on the work of Arthur Benton, Norman Geschwind, Ralph Reitan, and Hans-Lukas Teuber. In the Neuropsychology Laboratory at the University of Victoria in British Columbia, Gaddes in the past few years has been a vigorous proponent for the intermingling of neurological and educational concepts. At the previously mentioned brainstorming seminar initiated by Cruickshank in 1965, Gaddes enthusiastically argued for the addition of neurological concepts to teacher education. Without much strong opposition or support for this proposal, Gaddes decried what he felt to be an unfortunate void in teacher training.

Several years later, evidently feeling that the situation had not been improved, Gaddes published an article lamenting the ignorance of teachers with respect to neurological theory and diagnosis (Gaddes, 1968). Declaring that public schools are so arranged as to accommodate left-cerebral-hemisphere superiority, Gaddes even speculated that, according to what was neurologically known, special education classes might be more successful if divided into those children with left- and those with right-hemisphere damage. In a recent communication,[23] he spelled out his views on a neuropsychological approach to the diagnosis and education of children with learning disorders. While the ultimate choice of educational methods for the particular child would depend upon psychological and behavioral evidence, Gaddes maintained that neurological data would contribute meaningfully to a diagnostic understanding of the child and to better predictions about the possible level of his ultimate potential achievement.

Thus, as disillusionment and dissatisfaction with neuropsychological offerings have multiplied over the past decade, Gaddes has remained one of the lone defenders of their relevance, championing the currently unpopular notion that educators and neuropsychologists can work together as a team. Owing to continuous historical separation of the two fields, the opinions of Gaddes at this time have rarely been implemented although he himself works regularly with neurologists, neurosurgeons, and teachers to help children with learning problems. Until existing barriers are overturned and replaced by more widespread collaborative clinical and research endeavors, it is impossible to judge whether such integration might indeed be profitable.

Cynthia Deutsch and Florence Schumer

It has been mentioned previously that Reitan's work represented a break from the brain-behavior research tradition of disregard for diagnosis for its own sake. Exemplary of this rejection of convention was his building of tests to assess a variety of abilities that might be affected by

[23] Personal communication from William H. Gaddes, July 6, 1971.

brain damage. One comprehensive research investigation has carried the orientation of Reitan even further. Cynthia P. Deutsch and her associates at the Institute for Developmental Studies of New York University, attentive to the numerous methodological problems inherently involved in the diagnosis of brain injury, have purposely discarded the traditional approach to testing (Deutsch and Schumer, 1967).

Unconcerned about test validation, Deutsch and Schumer instead were interested in the construction of instruments which would competently measure those behaviors crucial to the particular hypothesis under investigation. Justification for their rationale came from the general conclusion that research studies using a number of specific tests proved superior to those employing single test scores in an effort to differentiate brain injured from normal subjects. Not preferring any one test or battery of tests, Deutsch and Schumer, even more than Halstead and Reitan, have had the freedom to investigate a number of hypotheses.

The particular inquiries to which Deutsch and Schumer have addressed themselves were largely derived from the work of Birch and his associates. As Deutsch and Schumer have explained, "Birch's viewpoints have entered into our own thinking" [p. 27]. Using the classic writings of Sherrington (1951) as a theoretical base, Birch, through research and theoretical investigations, had characterized both the phylogenetic and ontogenetic developmental trend in man by the ability to integrate and use sensory stimuli impinging on two different sensory modalities (Birch and Lefford, 1963, 1964). Most important to the discussion here is the research which also found that central nervous system damage delays intersensory integration. Birch and Belmont (1965a), for example, found brain injured (cerebral palsied) children to possess less ability than normals to integrate auditory with visual stimuli. Furthermore, they found a developmental trend in this ability. The specific task required matching an auditorially presented pattern of pencil taps with a visually presented pattern of dots.

More specifically related to the question of learning disabilities is the Birch and Belmont (1964) finding that retarded readers are characterized by poor auditory-visual integration. Other research by Birch includes collaboration with Joaquin Cravioto on a series of investigations into the effects of nutrition on brain functioning. As earlier stated, with experimental tasks requiring intersensory integration, they ascertained that undernourished children are apt to have problems in relating information from two different senses (Cravioto, Birch, and Gaona, 1967; Cravioto, DeLicardie, and Birch, 1966).

The study by Deutsch and Schumer involved thirty-nine children of normal or near-normal IQ. The youngsters had been diagnosed as brain injured on the basis of neurological examinations, medical histories, and electroencephalographic recordings matched to those of a normal group of comparable age (approximately 6 years to 12 years, 6 months), sex, and socioeconomic status. In order to evaluate the children in modality-input terms and to assess problems in intersensory information and unimodal performance in auditory, tactual, and visual areas, the experimenters devised a number of tests to sample behaviors corresponding to the above variables. Tests of a unimodal nature necessitated the separate processing of input from the visual, auditory, and tactual modalities. Multimodal tasks were a visual-motor memory-for-designs test and a visual-auditory, intersensory-bimodal, reaction-time test. Too, there were tests of modality preference, lateral dominance, right-left discrimination, and concept formation.

Among the major findings and conclusions of Deutsch and Schumer were the following:

1. Test intercorrelations and factor analysis revealed for the brain injured group specific perceptual disabilities rather than general perceptual impairment.
2. In unimodal procedures, the two groups tended to perform similarly; but on intersensory tasks, the brain damaged children performed more poorly than normal subjects.
3. Tasks for the tactual modality were especially difficult for brain injured children, suggesting that tactual training might best be subordinated to training in the other modalities.
4. The poorer concept formation performance of the brain injured group tended to originate with input and stimulus preferences rather than with conceptual ability per se.
5. Certain results pointed to the crucial role of motivational factors such as set and attention in the performance of brain injured children. Possible development of training procedures incorporating motivational factors therefore seemed to merit investigation.

As might be expected, Deutsch and Schumer's approach answers some of the criticisms from educationally oriented practitioners disillusioned with brain-behavior research. Although the heterogeneity of their brain injured subjects and its consequent effect on the possibility of generalization is one target of criticism, Deutsch and Schumer's advocacy of experimental measures designed to be useful in the testing of particular hypotheses certainly has merit. Such a philosophy encourages investigators to observe the child in a variety of ways instead of relying upon standardized tests already in existence. One complication, of course, is that the available assessment devices can tend to dictate the kinds of research questions which can be explored. Yet, on many occasions, surely it would be more advantageous to construct a measuring instrument which suits the particular behavior under study (e.g., Hagen and Hallahan, 1971).

Furthermore, the emphasis of Deutsch and Schumer upon analysis of the learning process in stimulus input terms makes their research uncommonly applicable to educational settings. In particular, learning disabilities theorists should find this aspect of Deutsch and Schumer's work especially encouraging. Consideration for the complexity of the abilities and disabilities of the brain injured child certainly is consistent with learning disability objectives. Not only does such consideration lend itself to the possibility of providing knowledge for diagnosis of specific disabilities, but it also conforms to the overriding concern of learning disability theory for the specific learning characteristics of children.

The attitude of Deutsch and Schumer, particularly as regards their methodological and philosophical orientation, would be of unquestionable worth if adopted by researchers in learning disabilities. This implies not that learning disabilities research should assume a neurological basis of learning disorders, but that the Deutsch and Schumer stance on test construction could provide a much-needed model in the investigation of children identified as learning disabled, regardless of etiological considerations.

Thus it can be seen that Deutsch and Schumer, and Birch also, working with the more refined research tools of the 1960s, have explored further some of the clinical and quasi-experimental observations conducted twenty-five to thirty years previously by their predecessors. Cognizant of their relationship with at least one of these forebears, Deutsch and Schumer have made reference to the fact that, like themselves, Strauss had viewed ". . . the behavioral deficits of brain injured individuals in the context of the integrations of different functional systems" [p. 226]. By looking at specific abilities and their interrelatedness rather than placing confidence in single-score intellectual and achievement measures, Deutsch and Schumer, like Werner and Strauss, have been absorbed in charting the ways in which the child designated as brain injured processes stimulus input.

Major theorists within the field of learning disabilities also inherited in large measure from Werner and Strauss the concepts which led them to attempt to specify particular psychological processes and their functioning in isolation and in interaction. In spite of their relative lack of interest in etiological factors, many learning disabilites theorists do share a common commitment with psychologists such as Deutsch and Schumer in their concern with analysis of psychological behavior.

The similarity of orientations for Deutsch and Schumer and many of the learning disabilities investigators provides fertile groundwork for the integration of information and approaches. It should be interesting to observe whether learning disability theorists will respond positively to this propitious opportunity.

INTERNATIONAL EXPANSION

The line of argument of the present chapter leads one to the conclusion that the early pioneers, Werner and Strauss, set the basic groundwork upon which the current field of learning disabilities lies. Their efforts provided the germinal impetus for a field of study which now encompasses a large portion of the globe. The investigations of many international researchers, only a few of whom can be mentioned here, into the problems of the learning disabled child, contributed substantially to the rapid and widespread growth of interest in the field.

In Britain, M. L. J. Abercrombie and his associates have long been concerned with disorders of eye movement, which they believe to be partially responsible for the perceptual deficits of brain damaged children. In one study (1963), they compared the performance of fifteen cerebral palsied children on simple saccadic and pursuit tasks with a group of twelve normals, age 6-15. Measurement by electro-oculography showed that the CP children were generally more erratic in their eye movements, and performed about 50 percent worse than the control group, thus strengthening the hypothesis that eye coordination is among those motor skills which are affected by this type of cerebral dysfunction. However, in addition to its use of extremely small sample, this study also fails to match the subjects by mental age, which was found to correlate with test performance, thus distorting the results. Nonetheless, the theory that some of the learning disabled child's perceptual problems result directly from faulty eye movements remains an interesting possibility.

Another British researcher in the field of perception, Klaus Wedell (1960) at the University of Birmingham, replicated and clarified Cruickshank, Bice, and Wallen's (1957) study of perceptual differences in cerebral palsy subtypes. Four groups of approximately twenty—spastics with right, left and bilateral motor defects, and athetoids—were matched with each other and a normal control group of forty for age (6-10 yrs) and IQ (with emphasis on representing a wide range of intelligence). All subjects were compared on tests of pattern matching, copying, and free construction, which involved a number of diverse perceptual tasks. Like Cruickshank et al., Wedell found the combined spastic group to be significantly inferior to the athetoids and normals. Interestingly, the spastics with right-sided defects were clearly superior to their left-sided and bilateral counterparts. In addition, Wedell also found that a manikin test, measuring the ability to integrate separate stimuli into a whole (a factor which had been suggested by Cruickshank as a major component of perceptual disorders in cerebral palsy), differentiated his groups more than any other test. He concludes:

The findings of this study would thus support Cruickshank's view. This ability to "organize" individual stimuli into a whole is, moreover, fundamental to the ability to discriminate figure from ground, if a figure is to be perceived at all. Strauss' findings on exogenous mental defectives could perhaps better be described as indicating an *inappropriate* "organization" of stimuli [p. 226].

This position is also given support by the Belgian investigator Francine Robaye-Geelen (1969), who reports a study in which a group of thirty spastics of normal intelligence were given Rorschachs and found to be extremely subject to impulse and deficient in integration of sensation.

In another very comprehensive study, Robaye-Geelen (1967) administered a battery of twenty-eight tests of intelligence, perceptual-motor skill, and personality to fifty minimally brain damaged and fifty normal children, who were matched for age and IQ. As predicted, the brain damaged group performed more poorly on every test, though, of course, not all individual children were deficient in all areas tested. Also, she found that while the differences between the groups decreased with age, they never completely disappeared. Next, using the mass of data obtained by the tests, Robaye-Geelen performed a factoral analysis in order to determine the primary sources of difficulty. She obtained four groups of components which coincide well with those identified by earlier investigators: deficiencies in figure-ground perception, closure, organization of stimuli into a whole, and sequencing of stimuli.

International authors have also made a sizeable contribution to our understanding of the neurological aspects of learning disabilities. For example, the British neurologist MacDonald Critchley (1953) has analyzed the effects of lesions of the parietal lobes. Employing many case histories and informal diagnostic devices, he has given an extremely comprehensive neurological account of the resultant disorders of tactile function, motility, body image, visual-spatial ability, and linguistic performance. The Russian neuropsychologist A. R. Luria (1966a, b) has undertaken much the same task in the light of more recent knowledge of cortical function. In addition to interpreting the major types of cerebral dysfunction, he also presents a thorough description of numerous tests of motor, kinesthetic, visual, linguistic, reading, writing, and arithmetic ability. Of particular relevance is his analysis of attention disorders (see chapter 7).

Important work in the learning disabilities field has also been performed by other international figures. Roy I. Brown, for instance, has performed several distractibility experiments in England (1964). In France, Mme. Stella Albetreccia was a pioneer in the area of perceptual-motor training (1958). Sweden's Helle H. Nielsen (1964) and Börje Cronholm and Daisy Schalling (1967) have been concerned, respectively, with personality and cognitive deficits of cerebral palsied children and adults.

The Canadian Sam Rabinovitch (1968) has written on the education of the learning disabled child, and the work of his countryman, William Gaddes, has been previously discussed in this chapter. In addition to these few, of course, many other workers all over the world have contributed to our knowledge of learning disabilities.

Two facts, however, are clear with regard to the internationality of the professional literature. The first is that, throughout the history of special education, there has been pitifully little international exchange of information. Wortis (1971), for example, notes that "among more than 1000 references to the literature" in his 1970 annual review, "only 16 are to foreign sources" (p. vii). This figure is certainly not atypical, and is also extremely unfortunate as the insights provided by researchers working within other cultural frames of reference have contributed so much to the advancement of other fields of study.

The second fact to be considered is that, due to the unique historical and cultural factors operating during the past forty years, the development of learning disabilities into a separate area of concern was primarily an American phenomenon, though, ironically, some of its foremost figures were of European origin. Only after the groundwork was laid in this country did widespread international interest occur. The next chapter documents this expansion within the United States through a systematic analysis of data from the literature.

CHAPTER 4

Historical Trends
Within
the Literature

METHODOLOGY

As theoretical and experimental inquiry into the nature of learning disabilities was generating a new and independent field of study, a distinct body of literature developed concurrently, embodying the unique attitudes and techniques of individuals within the field. Between 1936 and the present (the years of 1936–40 were chosen in order to include the early collaborative efforts of Werner and Strauss), this literature, despite its varying emphases in different eras, has reflected a number of major trends with regard to focus and philosophy.

In order to amass the data required for mapping out the general directions taken by learning disabilities writers, it was first necessary to consider the contents of article abstracts, either as they appeared with the articles or within *Psychological Abstracts*. It was then decided that the purposes of the present chapter would best be served by selecting a limited number of key publications to be searched for relevant information. The process of identifying representative journals was as follows. First, a preliminary random search of *Psychological Abstracts* was conducted for approximately every fifth year since 1936. For each period, every article dealing with brain injured children (whether of retarded, normal, or undesignated intelligence) and "learning disabled" (or any of the appropriate synonyms) children was recorded.

It became apparent that six journals had accounted for the majority of representative articles. These journals were *American Journal of Mental Deficiency, Cerebral Palsy Bulletin* (whose name was changed in 1962 to *Developmental Medicine and Child Neurology*), *Exceptional Children, Journal of Consulting Psychology* (whose name was modified in 1962 to *Journal of Consulting and Clinical Psychology*), *Journal of Learning Disabilities,* and *Perceptual and Motor Skills.* For the period between 1936 and 1950 references are cited from other than these six publications, since within that decade and a half so few relevant articles were printed that to limit their selection to a few journals seemed inappropriate.

For the selected journal articles appearing between 1951 and 1970, abstracts were obtained by one of three methods: (a) if the article itself was accompanied by an abstract, as was usually the case, this abstract was used; (b) if no abstract appeared with the article, *Psychological Abstracts* was consulted; (c) for those few articles for which no abstract could be found by one of the first two methods, the article was read in its entirety and then summarized. This selection procedure yielded a total of 449 abstracts, 35 from the period of 1936–50 and 414 from the years 1951–70.

Individual abstracts were classified into one or more different categories, each one promising potential relevancy for historical analysis but having a general enough definition so that articles could be assigned on the basis of information contained in brief resumes. As classification proceeded, categories were added or eliminated. By the end of this selection procedure, the articles had grouped themselves into twenty-nine categories representing six major content divisions: (a) Population Characteristics, (b) Experimental *versus* Non-Experimental Studies, (c) Psychological Behavior Characteristics, (d) Perceptual-Motor Behavior, (e) Educational Considerations, and (f) Testing and Diagnosis. Table 1 represents these groupings and the categories within them.

Population characteristics. Articles within the Population Characteristics division fell into four categories, depending upon whether they dealt with (a) brain damaged, mentally retarded children, (b) brain damaged children of normal intelligence, (c) brain damaged children of undesignated intelligence, or (d) children identified as learning disabled. The first category was specifically included for its representation of the amount and kind of work that has derived from the early efforts of Werner and Strauss. Articles which might be considered transitional in the move away from concern with mentally retarded, brain injured individuals went into the second category. Articles in the third category ordinarily represented a highly theoretical discussion of brain injured children, with no focus on a specified intelligence level. All articles from which abstracts in this category derived were read in their entirety in order to ensure that no article was so assigned simply because of in-

TABLE 1   A LISTING OF THE SIX DIVISIONS AND CATEGORIES WITHIN EACH

1. Population Characteristics
   1.1 Brain damaged, mentally retarded
   1.2 Brain damaged, normal intelligence
   1.3 Brain damaged, unspecified intelligence
   1.4 Learning disabled

2. Experimental *versus* Nonexperimental Studies
   2.1 Experimental
   2.2 Nonexperimental
   2.3 Case studies

3. Psychological Behavior Characteristics
   3.1 Cognition-language
   3.2 Perceptual-motor behavior
   3.3 Socioemotional behavior and adjustment
   3.4 Hyperactivity-distraction
   3.5 Figure-ground confusion
   3.6 Perseveration
   3.7 Memory

4. Perceptual-Motor Behavior
   4.1 Vision
   4.2 Audition
   4.3 Tactual-kinesthetic processes
   4.4 Visual-motor ability
   4.5 Intersensory integration

5. Educational Considerations
   5.1 Reading
   5.2 Spelling
   5.3 Arithmetic
   5.4 Perceptual-motor training
   5.5 Behavior modification
   5.6 Education in general

6. Testing and Diagnosis
   6.1 Tests for brain injury
   6.2 Tests for learning disabilities

sufficient information on intelligence in its resume. The fourth category included those articles that designated the population under discussion as being learning disabled, perceptually handicapped, learning disordered, and so on.

Of the six divisions, Population Characteristics was the most general. Any article not fitting into one of its four categories is not considered in the present investigation.

Experimental versus nonexperimental studies. Articles were assigned to this division on the basis of their experimental or nonexperimental (mostly theoretical) orientations. Furthermore, an additional category had to be retained for case studies, since these differ from the theoretical articles but are not truly experimental.

Psychological behavior characteristics. The division of Psychological Behavior Characteristics included those behaviors most frequently studied or discussed. In addition to the three general categories of cognition-language, perceptual-motor behavior, and socioemotional behavior and adjustment, there are four broader categories which include hyperactivity-distraction, figure-background confusion, perseveration, and memory.

Perceptual-motor behavior. Owing to the great number of articles treating perceptual-motor aspects of behavior, this group formed a separate division. Its categories were vision, audition, tactual-kinesthetic processes, visual-motor ability, and intensensory integration.

Educational considerations. Articles dealing with the academic subjects of reading, spelling, and arithmetic were placed in the Education Division. Two additional categories embraced those articles dealing with the educational methods of perceptual-motor training and behavior modification. The final category was a general one encompassing articles on education or remediation. Every article assigned to the Education grouping by definition fell within this "education in general" category. Those articles which did not qualify for any of the more specific categories but nevertheless had educational orientations were also included in this category.

Testing and diagnosis.   This final grouping included two categories, one for the testing and diagnosis of brain injury, the other for the testing and diagnosis of learning disabilities.

It should be apparent that except for the Experimental versus Non-experimental grouping, any one article could be classified under any number of categories. For example, a particular article could be concerned with perceptual-motor aspects as well as with the exploration of cognitive development and hyperactivity. In this case, the article would fall into the three categories of perceptual-motor behavior, cognition-language, and hyperactivity-distraction.

RESULTS OF THE ABSTRACT ANALYSIS

Article Frequency

Figures 19 and 20 depict the total number of articles collected for each year from 1936 through 1970. The use of two graphs is justified by the differential methods of data collection, as mentioned above, for those articles up to and after 1950. An erratic frequency pattern was obvious between 1936 and 1950, the largest number of articles per year being seven. Figure 20 reveals a gradual increase in the appearance of relevant articles after 1950. By 1968 the growth in sheer numbers was indeed dramatic. As indicated by the hashed portion of the 1968–70 bars, one journal, the *Journal of Learning Disabilities,* accounted for the tremendous increases from 1968 to 1970. Despite the fact that the first volume of this journal appeared in 1968, it is more accurate to consider it a result rather than a cause of the sharp rise. The very establishment of a single journal devoted primarily to the study of learning disabilities attests to the great upsurge of interest in this area.

Looking generally at each of the journals, we note that the pattern of representation for the *American Journal of Mental Deficiency* roughly shows a bell-shaped curve, with the greatest frequencies occurring around 1959 and 1960. Whereas the *Journal of Consulting Psychology (Journal of Consulting and Clinical Psychology)* and *Cerebral Palsy Bulletin (Developmental Medicine and Child Neurology)* both show an irregular pattern of incidence, *Perceptual and Motor Skills* and especially *Excep-*

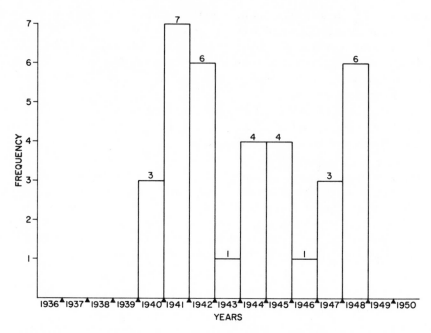

FIGURE 19   Incidence of articles from *Psychological Abstracts* dealing with brain damaged or learning disabled children.

tional Children, which may be viewed as a broad indicator of the field of special education, have steadily increased the publication of related articles since about 1959. *The Journal of Learning Disabilities,* in its short, three-year history, shows a consistent increase in such articles. The data of Figures 19 and 20 illustrate a steadily increasing preoccupation with the study and discussion of brain injured and learning disabled children, with a marked rise occurring in the late 1960s.

Population Characteristics

Although it is helpful for quick reference, a graphic representation of the incidence by year for all the articles collected for this chapter gives no indication of the types of children studied. Figures 21, 22, 23, and 24 reflect the relative concern for each of four kinds of populations: brain damaged, mentally retarded (BD-MR); brain damaged with normal intelligence (BD-N); brain damaged with unspecified intelligence level (BD-U); and learning disabled (LD). Information for the graphs in Figures 21, 22, 23, and 24 dates back only to 1941, since the period of 1936–40 provided too small an *N* (3) for meaningful calculations.

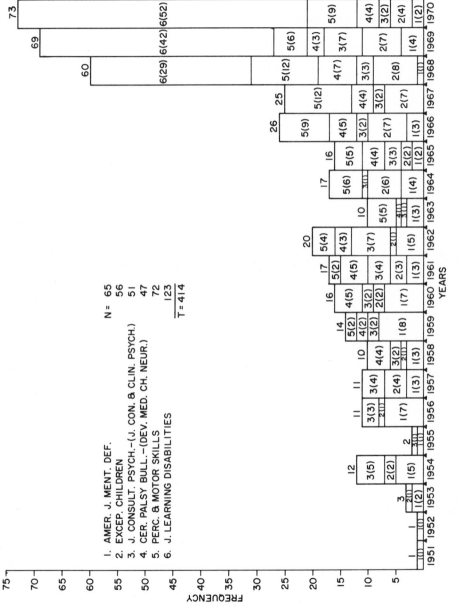

FIGURE 20 Incidence of articles dealing with brain damaged or learning disabled children.

137

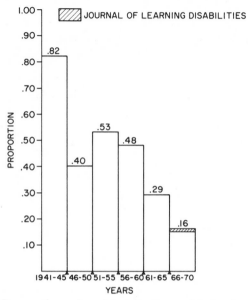

FIGURE 21 Proportion of articles dealing with brain damaged, mentally retarded children.

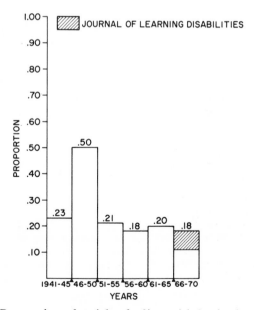

FIGURE 22 Proportion of articles dealing with brain damaged children of normal intelligence.

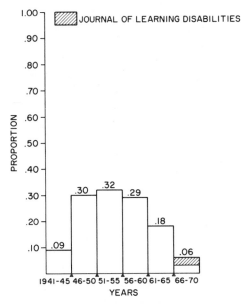

FIGURE 23 Proportion of articles dealing with brain damaged children of undesignated intelligence.

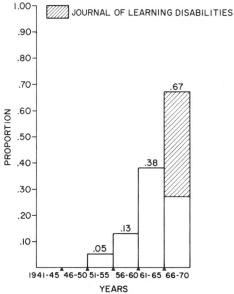

FIGURE 24 Proportion of articles dealing with learning disabled children.

While Figure 21 reveals a steady decline in the proportion of articles on BD-MR children (down from 82 percent in 1941–45 to 16 percent in 1966–70), Figure 22 indicates a relatively stable interest (approximately 20 percent of the articles) in BD-N children for the same time period. Figure 23 shows that while a large percentage of articles never did discuss BD-U populations, there was a marked decline from 31 percent in 1946–55 to 6 percent in 1966–70. Figure 24 documents the rapid increase in the proportion of articles dealing with children designated as LD. During the last five-year period, 1966–70, 67 percent of the publications sampled addressed themselves to learning disabilities.

Comparing Figures 21, 23, and 24, we can readily see that with increased attention to learning disabilities there has been a proportionate decline in emphasis on brain damaged, mentally retarded children and brain damaged children with unspecified intelligence. It is likely that this change represents a shift from the original focus of Werner and Strauss to the translation of their concepts by their followers, who developed the field of learning disabilities.

Articles concerned with BD-N children have maintained a constant proportion, but because of the decline in articles dealing with BD-MR and BD-U populations, the former have come to account for a greater proportion of articles dealing with brain damage (see Figure 25). This relative increase in focus on brain damaged children with normal intelligence, coupled with the rapid proportional increase in interest in learning disabilities, can be used to document the shift away from the retarded to children who would be labeled "minimally brain injured" and especially to children referred to as "learning disabled," with little or no reference to etiology.

In addition to the relative increase in the proportion of articles on BD-N subjects, there was a distinctly reduced concern for BD-MR groups as the number of studies for LD populations rose. Also, as the proportion of LD articles became greater, articles dealing with brain injury as a whole, regardless of intelligence level, declined (see Figure 26). Soon after the introduction into the sample of a learning disability orientation in 1954, there simultaneously appeared a rapid increase in learning disability articles and a steady decline of writing on brain injury. The greatest shift occurred during the 1961–65 period. In 1956–60, 95 percent of the articles were concerned with brain injured children, and 13 percent dealt with children who would meet the current definition of learning disabled.[24] However, from 1961–65, the brain injury articles had dropped to 66 percent, while the learning disability articles had almost tripled to 38 percent. These opposing trends continued in 1966–70, with articles

[24] The total exceeds 100 percent since some articles met the requirements in more than one category.

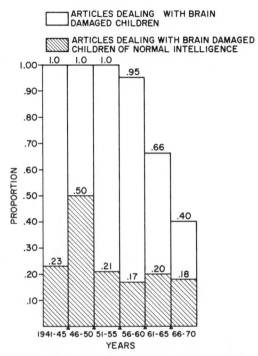

FIGURE 25 Proportion of articles dealing with brain damaged children versus proportion of articles dealing with brain damaged children of normal intelligence.

on learning disabilities exceeding the number on brain injury, 67 percent to 40 percent.

Experimental versus Nonexperimental Studies

In order to gain a better understanding of the focus of the specified categories, BD-MR, BD-N, and LD, these were analyzed to determine the frequency with which each was experimental or research in nature rather than theoretical. Since the analysis was concerned with specified populations, BD-U was eliminated. Furthermore, due to the low percentage of BD-U articles (13 percent) in general, and due to their questionable meaningfulness to the other concerns of this chapter, they have not been included in the rest of the graphs. Owing to the low *N*s for BD-MR and BD-N before 1951, the years 1936–50 have been combined. Also, because only one learning disability article appeared in 1951–55, the LD bar on the graphs starts at the 1956–60 period. Case studies, since they are

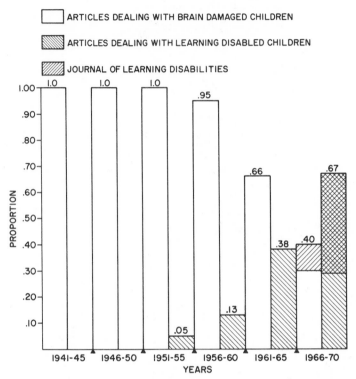

FIGURE 26 Proportion of articles dealing with brain damaged children versus proportion of articles dealing with learning disabled children.

neither experimental nor nonexperimental, were not considered in the analysis. Their low representation, approximately three percent, would have rendered them meaningless anyway.

The experimental versus nonexperimental dichotomy reveals a rather consistent ordering over the years, with the BD-MR literature being highly experimental, the BD-N less so, and the LD having the smallest proportion of articles with research orientations (see Figure 27). The hypotheses that BD-N found its origins in BD-MR and that LD grew out of both BD-MR and BD-N are congruent with the above ordering if it can be assumed that the earliest work in these particular areas tended to establish a clinical and theoretical base upon which research then followed. In other words, the proportionate ranking of BD-MR, BD-N, and LD, with regard to experimental orientation, may possibly indicate the relatively new, immature state of BD-N and especially of LD in comparison to BD-MR. That research interests developed gradually for these fields is borne out by the general increase over the years for all three kinds of populations, with the height of experimentation occurring be-

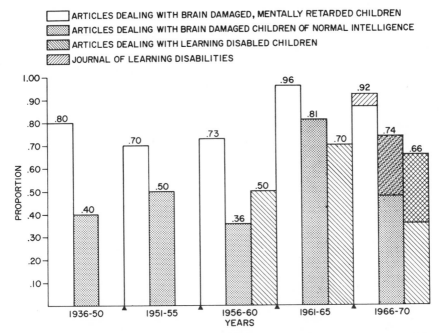

FIGURE 27 Proportion of experimental studies for articles dealing with brain damaged, mentally retarded children, brain damaged children of normal intelligence, and learning disabled children.

tween 1961 and 1965 for all three. Because of the slight decrease in experimentation studies from 1961–65 to 1966–70, there also appears to be a leveling off of experimental activity for all three populations. There is a possibility, speculative though it may be, that the data for 1966–70 indicate a tendency toward integration of the rapidly growing body of research for each of the three fields.

Psychological Behavior Characteristics

The behavior characteristics of figure-ground discrimination ability and particularly of perseveration and memory were found to be of relatively little concern in the literature dealing with any of the three populations. Figure 28, depicting the proportion of studies concerned with figure-ground discrimination, demonstrates a relatively minor interest in this ability, except for the 1961–65 time period. This trend is of particular interest, of course, since the subject was one with which Werner and Strauss dealt in a number of their studies.

Superficially, it would seem that interest in figure-ground ability has

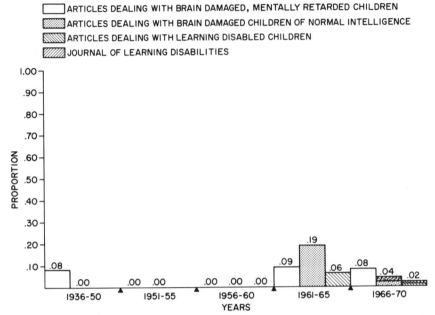

FIGURE 28. Proportion of articles concerned with figure-ground discrimination for articles dealing with brain damaged, mentally retarded children, brain damaged children of normal intelligence, and learning disabled children.

been sporadic and minimal. Keeping in mind, however, that figure-ground studies tend to be highly experimental and restricted in scope, it would be erroneous to assume insignificant concern for figure-ground problems in children. This becomes more evident when we note that even fewer studies in the sample gave attention to such a basic psychological process as memory.

Another major topic of concern to Werner and Strauss has aroused considerably more interest than figure-ground disabilities. Hyperactivity-distractibility, which subsumes figure-ground discrimination, has precipitated a relatively important amount of research and theoretical activity (see Figure 29). Through the years, articles on BD-MR and BD-N subjects have maintained a noticeably high percentage of emphasis on distractibility and/or hyperactivity. Other than a curious dip around the 1951–55 period, the BD-MR grouping shows a consistent upward trend which coincides with the BD-N articles. (The dip for BD-MR may be the byproduct of different data-gathering methods used for obtaining articles before 1951.) Curiously, however, while interest in distractibility-hyperactivity for BD-MR and BD-N populations has increased from about

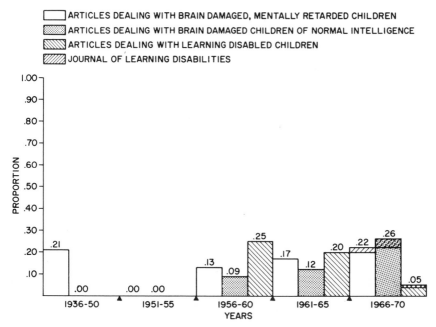

FIGURE 29 Proportion of articles concerned with distractibility-hyperactivity for articles dealing with brain damaged, mentally retarded children, brain damaged children of normal intelligence, and learning disabled children.

10 percent in 1956–60 to about 25 percent in 1966–70, there has been an almost one-to-one reversal for LD articles over the same time period. Whereas at the introduction of publications dealing with learning disabilities one out of every four sampled articles concerned itself with attention and/or hyperactivity, only one out of twenty articles sampled between 1966 and 1970 was similarly oriented. These trends suggest a constant waning of interest in a psychological process that, from all indications, should be of vital concern (see chapter 7) to learning disabilities theorists and researchers.

The influence of Werner and Strauss is evidenced by the increase in perceptual-motor research in the literature dealing with the brain injured and mentally retarded, the brain injured of normal intelligence, and particularly the learning disabled. It is interesting to compare this vital preoccupation with perceptual-motor behavior with the relatively meager concern for the more abstract, higher-level characteristics of cognition and language (see Figures 30, 31, and 32). Socioemotional behavior and adjustment are included in Figures 30, 31, and 32 in order to indicate the concern for affective behavior.

While the sampled articles dealing with BD-MR and BD-N have con-

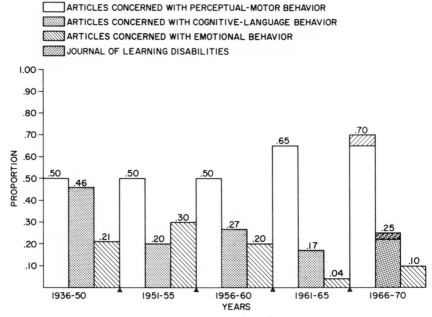

FIGURE 30 Proportion of articles on brain damaged, mentally retarded children concerned with perceptual-motor, cognitive-language, and emotional aspects of behavior.

sistently shown a fair amount of proportionate concern for perceptual-motor aspects of behavior, the most dramatic increases occurred in the late 1950s for the BD-N and in the early 1960s for the BD-MR groupings. Whereas the BD-MR studies continued to rise to a peak of 70 percent for perceptual-motor articles during 1966–70, the frequency of BD-N publications has declined from 81 percent during 1956–60, to 69 percent during 1961–65, to 63 percent during 1966–70. The fifteen-year history of LD articles (1956–70) showed a consistent proportion of articles with a perceptual-motor orientation (62 percent for 1956–60, 60 percent for 1961–65, and 65 percent for 1966–70).

At the same time that the vast majority of BD-MR, BD-N, and LD articles were attending to perceptual-motor development and maldevelopment, a much smaller proportion was concerned with more abstract cognitive and language processes. For the BD-MR and BD-N articles, cognition-language subject matter has fluctuated between 17 percent and 35 percent from 1936 to 1970. For the LD sample, there was a steady decline from 50 percent during 1956–60 to 33 percent during 1961–65, to 21 percent during 1966–70. Attention to socioemotional behavior and adjustment for each of the three populations formed approximately the

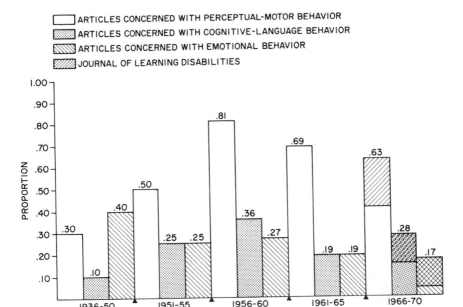

FIGURE 31 Proportion of articles on brain damaged children of normal intelligence concerned with perceptual-motor, cognitive-language, and emotional aspects of behavior.

same pattern as that for cognition-language but fell about 10 percentage points below it.

According to the general psychological behaviors under investigation, then, historical analysis reveals the BD-MR, BD-N, and LD articles have been largely concerned with perceptual-motor aspects of behavior to the relative exclusion of cognition and language, and especially of affective behavior. Referring again to Figures 30, 31, and 32, and it can be seen that in BD-MR and BD-N there appears to be a relatively consistent breadth of percentage points over the years between perceptual-motor behavior on the one hand, and cognition-language and socioemotional behavior on the other. For the LD articles, however, Figure 32 reveals an apparent historical trend wherein perceptual-motor articles have remained at about the same level, but cognition-language and socioemotional articles have clearly declined.[25]

25 It should be remembered that this decline refers only to proportional concerns. Looking at absolute numbers of articles, one would find an increase over the years in learning disability articles dealing with socioemotional and cognition-language content. However, since the proportions of articles in these two areas have declined, the increase in absolute numbers may be viewed as a function of the large increase in numbers of articles dealing with learning disabilities.

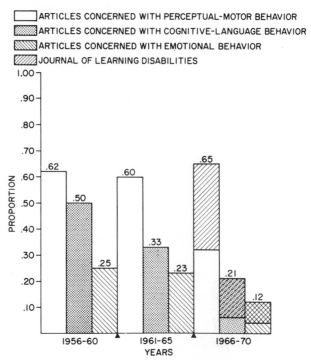

FIGURE 32 Proportion of articles on learning disabled children concerned with perceptual-motor, cognitive-language, and emotional aspects of behavior.

Thus, writers within the field of learning disabilities, even more than those writing about brain damaged children, have seemingly become less and less concerned about cognitive and language abilities and socio-emotional behavior of children with learning disabilities. As a result of the fact that Werner, Strauss, and others closely associated with them were its historical precursors, the study of learning disabilities is almost by definition a study of perceptual-motor development. Yet it seems that a research direction ripe for exploration would involve the cognitive and language processes of children unable to learn. This holds true for children labeled brain injured (regardless of tested intelligence) and learning disabled.

Aspects of Perceptual-Motor Behavior

Looking more closely at proportional breakdowns of those articles concerned with perceptual-motor behavior, we can see that the major sensory modalities under study have been vision and audition for BD-MR,

BD-N, and LD (see Figures 33, 34, and 35). Because of low *N*s prior to 1956, these graphs include only the time periods 1956–60, 1961–65, and 1966–70. Though the auditory and tactual-kinesthetic modalities traditionally have received far less attention than visual perception, there does appear to be a growing trend within BD-N and LD for consideration of audition. Visual-motor development, like visual processing, has accounted for a large percentage of the perceptual-motor studies. Within BD-MR, visual-motor articles have increased slowly but steadily. Visual studies, while remaining high in comparison to audition and tactual-kinesthetic processes, have decreased almost to the same degree. Within BD-N and LD, the pattern has been fairly consistent, possibly because articles on BD-N and LD frequently are talking about the same type of child. While the number of visual studies was declining, visual-motor studies were even fewer in proportion during 1956–60 and 1966–70, although the latter did reach a peak in 1961–65 and exceeded the number of visual studies.

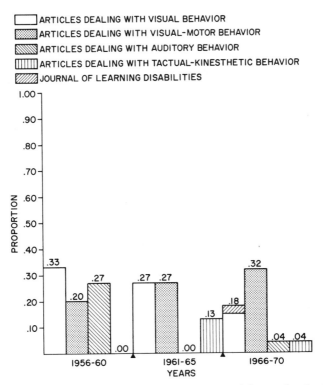

FIGURE 33 Proportion of perceptual-motor articles on brain damaged, mentally retarded children dealing with visual, visual-motor, auditory, and tactual-kinesthetic behavior.

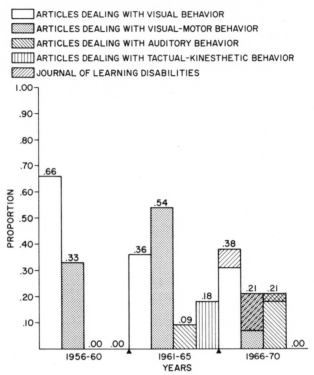

FIGURE 34 Proportion of perceptual-motor articles on brain damaged children of normal intelligence dealing with visual, visual-motor, auditory, and tactual-kinesthetic behavior.

For the same fifteen-year period, Figure 36 shows indications of a simultaneous concern for intersensory integration. This interest, primarily denoting the integration of the auditory and visual senses, is more than a casual one, especially within the field of learning disabilities, where it accounted for 17 percent of the perceptual-motor articles during 1961–65 and 12 percent during 1966–70.

Educational Considerations

Looking at academic subject matter, we can see that an insignificant proportion of articles was directed to arithmetic and spelling, whereas nearly 100 percent of all abstracts mentioning academic subjects made reference to reading. Figure 37 shows that reading disabilities have experienced an irregular pattern of interest for BD-MR and BD-N groups,

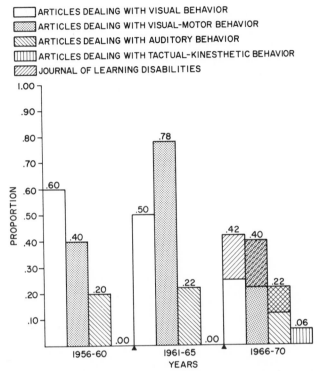

FIGURE 35 Proportion of perceptual-motor articles on learning disabled children dealing with visual, visual-motor, auditory, and tactualkinesthetic behavior.

while a greater proportion and more consistent pattern developed for the LD studies.

With regard to particular educational methods employed, there is little question that, in keeping with the perceptual-motor theoretical orientation of BD-MR, BD-N, and LD, the perceptual-motor training techniques have taken precedence over any other educational method (see Figure 38). In fact, behavior modification, the only other specific method receiving notable attention, generally accounted for only 3 percent or less of the articles on all three populations during all time periods. Behavior modification as a training technique thus did not warrant placement on a graph.

Education and Remediation versus Testing and Diagnosis

Over the past few years, much discussion has been devoted to the relative merits of diagnostic versus remediational aspects of learning

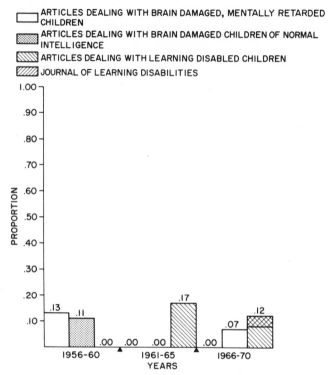

FIGURE 36 Intersensory integration studies as a proportion of perceptual-motor studies for brain damaged, mentally retarded children, brain damaged children of normal intelligence, and learning disabled children.

problems. In particular, a growing number of voices within the field of learning disabilities have called for a reversal of attention in order to halt usual predominance of diagnostic research and theory over educational aspects. These critics contend that undue attention to testing and diagnosis has obscured the implications for remediation. Because of these objections, many have advocated a moratorium on diagnostic testing unless the results are directly applicable to remediation.

Looking at Figures 39, 40, and 41, it appears that adversaries of a diagnostic orientation have achieved conspicuous success in their encouragement of literature that is educationally relevant. Each of these three graphs depicts the proportionate concern for educational or diagnostic elements. Within the older and more traditional grouping of BD-MR (Figure 39), there has been an irregular but noticeable trend toward lessened concern with diagnostic testing. This downward trend, coupled with an irregular fluctuation in the proportion of articles dealing with

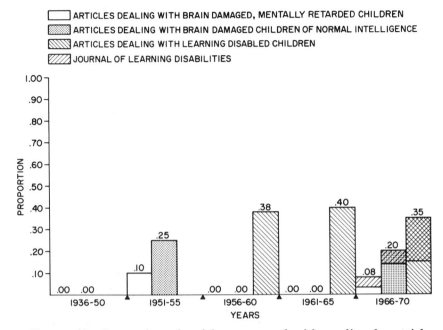

FIGURE 37 Proportion of articles concerned with reading for articles dealing with brain damaged, mentally retarded children, brain damaged children of normal intelligence, and learning disabled children.

education or with educational implications, has resulted in a general growth of preoccupation with education relative to testing, so that during 1966–70, 35 percent of the articles were educational in nature, as opposed to the 32 percent that were diagnostic.

As Figure 40 indicates, the relative increase in concern for education over diagnosis has been even more marked for articles dealing with the BD-N group of children. In fact, by the 1966–70 period, 52 percent of the articles sampled were educationally oriented, whereas only 26 percent were oriented toward testing. This marked trend for BD-N comes as no surprise. Owing to the similarity of the populations studied within BD-N and LD, it would be expected that the two areas would overlap with respect to relative emphasis on education and diagnosis.

For the LD articles (Figure 41), the educational orientation is quite noticeable. From the earliest years of 1956–60 and onward, the focus has been outstandingly educational. Furthermore, the gap between education and diagnosis has widened through the years. By the 1966–70 period, 72 percent of the LD articles were categorized as educational, while only 23 percent presented diagnostic subject matter.

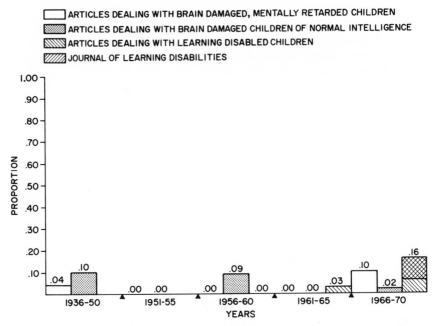

FIGURE 38 Proportion of perceptual-motor training studies for articles dealing with brain damaged, mentally retarded children, brain damaged children of normal intelligence, and learning disabled children.

Comparing the three kinds of populations under consideration, then, we can see a hierarchy of concern for education over diagnosis, with LD articles evidencing the greatest educational emphasis. BD-N is a distant second, and BD-MR is decidedly lowest but is beginning to move in the educational direction. This hierarchical arrangement applies not only with respect to interest in education as opposed to diagnosis, but also with regard to the sheer proportion of educational articles for each of the three types of populations. Since 1956, approximately 70 percent to 80 percent of the LD articles have been geared toward education. At the same time, BD-N articles were educationally relevant in 54 percent of the examples for 1956–60, 19 percent for 1961–65, and 52 percent for 1966–70. The BD-MR articles found to be specifically educational in nature reached 27 percent during 1956–60, dipped to 17 percent in 1961–65, and rose again to 35 percent in 1966–70.

An additional point deserving notice is that a great many of the diagnostic instruments used for LD populations (e.g., the Illinois Test of Psycholinguistic Abilities and the Frostig Developmental Test of Visual Perception) simultaneously became educational rather than etiological in orientation as the scope of educational concerns was widening. Thus,

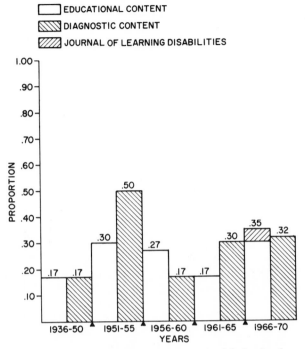

FIGURE 39   Proportion of articles concerned with brain damaged, mentally retarded children dealing with education versus those dealing with diagnosis.

the dichotomy of education versus diagnosis for the LD population actually becomes less rigid than it is for the BD-MR and BD-N groups. This point again underscores the preponderance of educational articles within the LD as compared to BD-MR and BD-N groups. It also strengthens the hypothesis that learning disability theorists and researchers for the most part have rejected the etiological orientation favored by the fields of BD-MR and BD-N, from which learning disability study evolved. Too, the trend toward educational as opposed to diagnostic concerns in the investigation of BD-MR and BD-N children may point to the influence of the newer field of learning disabilities, or it may represent the combined effect of LD and BD-MR on BD-N.

SUMMARY

By the method delineated early in this chapter, 449 articles broadly representing the educational, psychological, and medical disciplines were classified into one or more categories providing relevant information

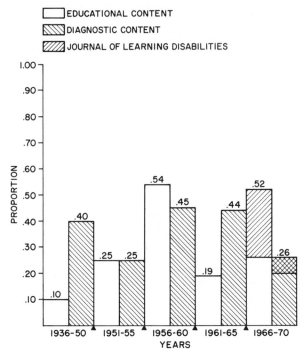

FIGURE 40 Proportion of articles concerned with brain damaged children of normal intelligence dealing with education versus those dealing with diagnosis.

about the history and development of learning disability theory and research. When information deriving from this categorization procedure was graphed, the following findings emerged:

1. Over the thirty-four years from 1936 to 1970 there was a large and consistent increase in the total number of published articles concerned with children identified as brain injured or learning disabled. The sharpest increase took place between 1968 and 1970.
2. For the particular populations under study through the years, a proportionate decrease in articles written about brain injured, mentally retarded children has been accompanied by an increase in concern for brain injured children of normal intelligence. A still greater interest in learning disabled children, without regard to possible organic factors, was also manifest. These findings are congruent with the hypothesis that the early work of Strauss and Werner with so-called exogenous, mentally retarded children has been replaced by theoretical and research study of children identified as learning disabled.
3. With regard to whether articles were experimental (research) or nonexperimental (theoretical) in orientation, the articles dealing with brain injured,

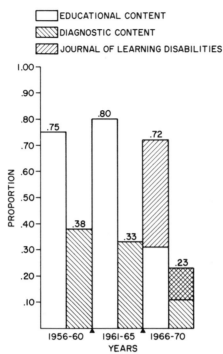

FIGURE 41   Proportion of articles concerned with learning disabled children dealing with education versus those dealing with diagnosis.

mentally retarded populations consistently pertained to the former category. Writings dealing with brain injured children of normal intelligence were less experimental in nature, and articles on learning disabled children tended to be least experimental of all.

4. There was an increasing proportion of attention to distractibility-hyperactivity behaviors in the examples using brain injured populations, but the trend was just the reverse for the field of learning disabilities.

5. Both the articles concerned with brain injured children and those dealing with learning disabled children have reflected a continuous predominance of interest in perceptual-motor behaviors as compared to cognitive-language behaviors and especially to socioemotional aspects of behavior. The field of learning disabilities, in particular, has been primarily attentive to perceptual-motor development and maldevelopment. The preponderance of perceptual-motor articles may be interpreted as denoting the influence of Strauss and Werner and their followers.

6. Observation of perceptual-motor articles reveals that for all populations studied, the majority of articles have been concerned with visual and visual-motor aspects of perceptual-motor behavior. The auditory and especially the tactual-kinesthetic modalities have been relatively ignored in comparison to the visual sense.

7. With regard to academic subject matter, the research and theorization on

reading have predominated over arithmetic and spelling for all populations considered.

8. Between 1936 and 1970, only two distinct methods of education have prevailed—perceptual-motor training and behavior modification. Perceptual-motor training has unquestionably become the most popular method of education, especially for the learning disabled population.

9. With regard to the proportion of articles emphasizing educational rather than diagnostic aspects, the examples for all populations have become increasingly educational. This trend toward educational relevancy is most apparent for articles written about learning disabilities when they are compared to those concerned with brain injured children of normal intelligence and especially when they are matched with articles on mentally retarded children. It therefore appears that the field of learning disabilities is devoted primarily to educational and remediational rather than to diagnostic considerations.

CHAPTER 5

Perceptual-Motor Development and Its Relation to Cognition and Academic Achievement

Theoreticians and researchers in learning disabilities traditionally have tended to highlight the significance of perceptual and perceptual-motor development or maldevelopment in children. In fact, problems of a perceptual-motor nature have come to achieve first priority among workers within the domain of learning disabilities.

Domination of the literature by perceptual-motor theorists does not merely indicate concern for perceptual disability per se, however. What individuals such as Kephart, Getman, Barsch, Ayres, and Frostig are most attentive to are the deleterious effects of such impairment upon children's learning and academic achievement. In fact, one hypothesis almost universally shared by members of the perceptual-motor school is that adequate conceptual development is dependent upon accurate perception. Kephart (1960), for example, has stated that concepts essentially are categorizations based on similarities and differences. It follows, therefore, that concepts built upon inaccurate perceptions are bound to be inaccurate as well.

STRAUSS AND WERNER RELATE PERCEPTUAL AND CONCEPTUAL DEVELOPMENT

As with so many other aspects of learning disability research, current thinking pertaining to the integral role of perceptual development in later cognitive growth seems to have originated in the formulations of the pioneers, Werner and Strauss. Particularly Werner, who was one of the foremost theoreticians of child development and comparative psychology in his era, was intrigued by the relationship between perceptual and conceptual development in the child. Both men, in an article (1939a) cited previously for its relevance to the evolution of learning disabilities because of its emphasis upon specific abilities, posited a course of child development in which early perceptual-motor activities were considered crucial to conceptual development.

With specific reference to the concept of number, Werner and Strauss outlined a progression which included first a number concept linked with body activity, motor rhythm, and counting by fingers; then an understanding of numbers as perceptually organized units, "concrete number forms;" and finally, abstract conceptualization of numbers independent of their "picture-like properties" [p. 38]. For a child to be capable of performing arithmetic operations, Werner and Strauss maintained, he must be able to organize them perceptually.[26]

A later publication by Werner (1948) extended the observation of thought processes to a more primitive stage than that at which abstraction becomes possible. In his "thing of action" concept (Langer, 1970), Werner hypothesized that the very young child's thought was constructed on the basis of sensory-motor factors. According to this hypothesis, how a young child perceives an object is largely determined by the kinds of things he can actively do with it. It was the opinion of both Werner and Strauss that damage to the central nervous system resulted in lack of advancement beyond this primitive, perceptual-motor-based thought stage. Consequently, they contended that the bizarre perceptual abnormalities experienced by their exogenous children were at the root of inferior concept formation.

THEORETICAL AND EMPIRICAL SUPPORT FOR A PERCEPTION-COGNITION RELATIONSHIP

Perceptual-motor-oriented theorists in learning disabilities will also find that the formulations of contemporary developmental theorists are replete with support for their views on the relationship between perception and conception. Perhaps the foremost developmental theorist, at least in terms of popularity, addressing himself specifically to the issue of perceptual and cognitive development, is Jean Piaget.

In a relatively recent work, Inhelder and Piaget (1964) noted that since children perceive similarities and differences between objects long

---

[26] On the strength of this observation, Cruickshank, Marshall, and Hurley (1971) have organized a complete educational approach to mathematics for children.

before learning to classify or to order them, it would be worthwhile to explore the possibility that classification and seriation find their origins in perceptual activities. Believing, as does Kephart, that visual-perceptual development follows and is subordinated to haptic (or tactual-kinesthetic) perception, Inhelder and Piaget posited, in language reminiscent of Werner's "thing of action" theory, that the child perceives objects in terms of the actions that can be performed upon them. Confidence in this developmental sequence led Inhelder and Piaget to the hypothesis "that the origins of classification and seriation are to be found in sensori-motor schemata as a whole (which include perceptual schemata as integral parts)" [p. 13].

Inhelder and Piaget emphasized, however, that in concept formation it is not class per se which is perceived when one asserts, "This is an orange." Such a judgment requires the ability to abstract and to generalize. What one perceives is "a certain spatial configuration of elements which compose it" [p. 10]. The orange thus is beheld with regard to its several stimulus attributes and is associated with numerous sensori-motor schemata, such as peeling, cutting, eating, and so forth. It is apparent, therefore, that Inhelder and Piaget consider perceptual, and especially perceptual-motor, development essential to conceptual development. Using Piaget's logic, a disability in perceptual-motor skills would result in cognitive problems.

Another leading theorist of cognition, Jerome Bruner (Bruner, 1957; Bruner, Goodnow, and Austin, 1956; Bruner, Olver, and Greenfield, 1966), has also theorized that there is an intimate link between perception, which itself involves categorization and inference, and cognition. While Bruner did not claim that all perception can be explained in his theoretical account (Wohlwill, 1962), he has attacked what he considers to be the unjustified assumption that different sets of laws for perception and conception can be applied in a wide variety of situations. Despite criticism from Piaget and Morph (1958) and Wohlwill (1962) with regard to the difficulty of adapting Bruner's position to conceptual development in children, Bruner's argument about perception as a form of conceptualization would readily support the hypothesis that problems in the perceptual sphere will interfere with concept formation.

The views of Joachim Wohlwill (1962), too, confirm the perception-conception relationship espoused by Kephart, Getman, Barsch, Frostig, and other perceptual-motor learning disability theorists. Wohlwill has asserted that as the child proceeds developmentally from perception to conception, he needs relatively less stimulus information. For perception, the young child requires a great amount of stimulus redundancy, whereas for conception this requirement is substantially reduced. In addition, as the child becomes increasingly capable of conceptual thought, he simultaneously becomes better equipped to ignore irrelevant information. Wohlwill considered this ability to differentiate relevant from irrelevant information the sine qua non of concept formation. In this sense, then, he pictured the concomitant growth of attention and conceptual abilities.

A natural outgrowth of Wohlwill's thinking is the postulate that in the transformation from perception to conception, the need for spatial and temporal contiguity decreases markedly. While not explicitly saying so, Wohlwill's formulations imply that proper conceptual development is at least partially dependent upon proper perceptual development. Emphasis on the interdependence of perception and cognition renders this view consonant with those of Kephart, Getman, Barsch, and Frostig with regard to the effect of perceptual disabilities on higher-level abstract thinking.

Whereas Piaget, Bruner, and Wohlwill all view the child as progressing from a greater to a lesser need for perceptual stimulus information, Eleanor Gibson (1969) has proposed a model which contradicts this assumption. Relying upon Gollin's (1960, 1961) findings that children as they grow older increase in their ability to fill in incomplete figures, Wohlwill, for instance, had concluded that with an increase in age, the subject relies less upon stimulus information. But Gibson said the young child is actually far less adept at using stimulus redundancy than are older children or adults who become better able to use stimulus information by learning the distinctive features needed for recognition of an object.

For Gibson, it seemed more probable that the growing child does not stop needing and using stimulus information but instead learns more efficient ways of processing the stimuli presented to him. The child might actually respond to additional aspects and subtle nuances and cues of the stimuli as he develops. In Gibson's analysis, although concept formation develops markedly over the years,

> it does not follow that our percepts become more and more reflections of our concepts. We do not perceive less because we conceive more. If we did, it would be maladaptive for getting information about what is going on in the world around us [p. 449].

Gibson appropriately recognized that many highly abstract and generalized class concepts are of a more advanced nature than is perceptual learning. While the concept of a tree, for example, is very general, the image of a particular tree in a certain location is quite specific. Regardless of the level at which it is apprehended, however, recognition of a concept is always dependent upon prior learning of certain distinctive and invariant features. In spite of Gibson's theoretical disagreements with other developmentalists, therefore, her contention that perception remains a critical ability for conceptual thought throughout a lifetime also provides theoretical justification for postulating the dependence of conceptual skills on the efficiency and accuracy of perceptual ability.

Thus, the formulations of Piaget, Bruner, Wohlwill, and Gibson, all leading theorists in perceptual and cognitive development, furnish a solid theoretical base for the thesis that perceptual and perceptual-motor problems will result in conceptual difficulties. Such support for perceptual-motor-oriented theorists of learning disabilities becomes still more impressive when one considers that even though the concepts of Piaget, Bruner, Wohlwill, and Gibson differ in many crucial aspects, any one of them could be used to corroborate the posited relation of perception to conception as held by major investigators of learning disabilities.

Some empirical evidence, too, fortifies the notion of a perception-cognition relationship. In an experiment of concept learning in preschool and second-grade children, McConnell (1964) found indications that perceptual processes sometimes take the place of verbal, symbolic processes as mediators. Studying the differential effects of perceptual and verbal pretraining on later concept-formation ability, he found that for both the preschoolers and the second graders, positive transfer resulted when perceptual training stressed a dimension relevant to the conceptual task, while negative transfer resulted if the dimension was not relevant. Furthermore, when the perceptual arrangement was irrelevant but verbal cues were apropos, the older subjects exhibited a positive transfer, whereas the younger ones showed a negative one.

The implication of this study for the present discussion is that erroneous perceptual information can impede concept attainment at different age levels. By extension, this experimental finding lends credence to the assumption that the learning disabled child, whose perceptions are frequently faulty, will meet with difficulty in attempting to form concepts. It should be pointed out, however, that McConnell's experimental tasks in both perceptual pretraining and concept formation covered a time span of only one experimental session in which perceptual information or misinformation was "induced" upon the children. We can only infer what the results mean for perceptually disabled children who experience difficulties over a number of years.

Another report attesting to the integral role of perception and perceptual-motor skills in conceptual development was made by Ireton, Thwing, and Gravem (1970) on a longitudinal study performed at the University of Minnesota in connection with the Collaborative Study of Cerebral Palsy, Mental Retardation, and Other Neurological and Sensory Disorders of Infancy and Childhood (supported by the National Institute of Neurological Diseases and Blindness). Investigators found significant correlations between performance at the 8-month age level on the Bayley Mental Scale (containing primarily perceptual and motor items) and IQ at the age of 4 as measured by the Stanford-Binet. Categorical analysis further revealed that a low mental score on the Bayley device was a better predictor of low 4-year IQ than high mental score was a predictor of high 4-year IQ. The latter finding, in particular, may indicate that an infant with poor perceptual-motor performance tends to exhibit poor conceptual, abstract performance at a later age. Despite the correlational nature of some of the data, which makes it impossible to prove causal relationships, the results generally supported the hypothesized connection between perception and cognition.

Deutsch and Schumer (1967) have found even more explicit evidence that the perceptually disabled child will, in certain situations, experience conceptual problems. Those brain injured children identified as exhibiting a deficit in the visual processing modality, when compared to brain injured children without such an impairment, were more apt to perform poorly on concept formation tasks designed similarly to those of the Kendlers (Kendler and Kendler, 1959, 1962). Only partial evidence of the perception-cognition association was forthcoming from this experiment, however, since subjects with visual assets were no more likely than subjects with visual deficits to display mediational skills on other tasks. Nevertheless, it is significant that the data do suggest the existence of such an association.

Taken as a whole, then, the theories of Piaget, Bruner, Wohlwill, and Gibson and the few published empirical studies on the relationship between perceptual or perceptual-motor factors and concept formation tend to support the positions of many learning disability theorists.

THEORETICAL AND EMPIRICAL SUPPORT FOR A PERCEPTION-ACADEMIC ACHIEVEMENT RELATIONSHIP

Because of their educational orientation, theorists in learning disabilities have naturally moved in their concern about the relatedness of perception to cognition to a consideration of the possible effects of perceptual factors upon academic achievement in general and reading ability in particular. Thus, although there is evidence to the effect that conceptual ability correlates with reading ability even more highly than does IQ (Braun, 1963), the perceptual-motor-oriented learning disability theorists traditionally have ascribed reading difficulties to the misperception of letters and words rather than to faulty abstraction and conceptualization abilities.

Kephart (1960) was one of the first to posit a cause-and-effect relationship between perceptual-motor abilities and academic achievement. Citing several empirical investigations (Lowder, 1956; Potter, 1949; Robinson, Letton, Mozzi, and Rosenbloom, 1958), and the clinical evidence of Strauss and Lehtinen (1947) and Strauss and Kephart (1955), Kephart asserted that perceptual-motor skills, such as drawing and copying, do have a bearing upon academic achievement.

The empirical studies to which Kephart referred, besides having been based on correlational data, showed relationships tending to account for only about 15 percent to 40 percent of the variance, depending upon the variables studied. In fact, one of the studies (Potter, 1949), can be interpreted as negative evidence, since the *r* between copying forms and reading achievement was only .18 when mental age was controlled. Because of the limitations inherent in Kephart's early arguments, therefore, it seems advisable to investigate subsequent studies in order to ascertain the extent of experimental support for the supposed relationship between perceptual and perceptual-motor abilities and academic achievement.

As noted previously, literature pertaining to the relationship between perception and school success has focused on the reading aspects of academic achievement. In addition, much of the theoretical and research emphasis for reading disabilities has been centered upon visual perceptual and visual-motor processes and their development in children (see chapter 4). For this experimentation, researchers have used a wide variety of instruments and tests designed to assess visual and visual-motor development to determine what differences exist between poor and normal readers. Standardized tests of intelligence and school achievement tests have also been administered in the effort to relate perceptual development to learning ability.

It is appropriate to point out that a number of studies on perception and achievement have suffered from such basic, methodological limitations as poorly designed and/or poorly defined measurements, weak controls for subject intelligence, and arbitrary criteria for identifying the poor reader. With regard to this last point, for example, a child might be classified as reading disabled if he were anywhere from six months (Erickson, 1969) to five years (Coleman, 1959) behind grade level. The existence of innumerable methodological inconsistencies such as these no doubt has had much to do with the creation of conflicting results that have plagued this area of research.

Yet in spite of these limitations, many researchers with varying degrees of success and reliability have been able to relate visual-perceptual handicaps to learning problems and especially to reading difficulties. It has been consistently observed, for instance, not only that more boys than girls experience difficulty in learning to read, but also that boys more frequently than girls display problems of a visual nature (Davol and Hastings, 1967; Katz and Deutsch, 1963; Leton, 1962). This finding comes as no great surprise, since boys are overrepresented in the learning disability population as a whole. Because of this preponderance of problems among boys, in fact, most studies in the literature have used only male subjects in their experimental and control populations.

Keogh and Smith (1967), who performed a well designed longitudinal study in which the Bender-Gestalt test was administered to seventy-three subjects at the kindergarten, third-, and sixth-grade end-of-year levels, discovered that female superiority in visual-motor performance at the kindergarten level was completely supplanted by male superiority by the end of third grade. By the sixth-grade level, all significant sex differences on Bender-Gestalt performance had been obliterated. Both sexes were observed to improve with age in visual-motor ability, with the girls starting earlier and the boys improving at a faster rate that compensated for their late start.

With regard to the relationship between visual-motor ability and academic performance, Keogh and Smith found that a good predictor of school achievement, as measured by the reading and spelling subtests of the California Achievement Test in the third grade and the Iowa Test of Basic Skills in the sixth grade, was the kindergarten score on the Bender-Gestalt. In other words, children performing poorly in visual-motor ability in kindergarten tended to do less well academically in later grades. In their conclusion, however, the authors made no attempt to hypothesize a possible cause-and-effect relationship between perceptual-motor performance and later school achievement. They were merely concerned with the applicability of the Bender-Gestalt as a predictor of academic achievement.

In another experment, Snyder and Freud (1967) administered several visual-perceptual measures, including the Bender-Gestalt, Spiral Aftereffect (Spivack and Levine, 1957), and Necker Cube (Levine and Spivack, 1962) tests to 667 first graders, then compared the results with those on the Lee-Clark Reading Readiness Test (California Test Bureau, 1962). Finding sizable correlations between scores on the battery of visual and visual-motor tests, on the one hand, and reading-readiness test performance on the other, the authors concluded that perceptual immaturity at the first-grade level is a major contributor to later reading difficulty, even for children of normal IQ.

Further evidence for a relationship between perceptual-motor ability and academic achievement comes from the Skubic and Anderson study (1970) involving eighty-six fourth graders of normal intelligence. Following their classification on the basis of the Stanford Achievement

Test, forty-five high and forty-one low achievers were asked to perform eleven perceptual-motor tasks devised by the authors to assess abilities involving both gross and fine, static and transport types of motor movement. The high achievers were significantly superior to low achievers on six of the eleven perceptual-motor tests. Performance on the perceptual-motor battery was positively and significantly correlated (around .50) to the performance on the Stanford Achievement Test and the California Test of Mental Maturity. Once again, correlational data for a relationship between perceptual-motor ability and academic achievement was obtained.

Using fifty-four retarded readers and fifty-four matched controls from grades one through six, Lyle (1969) investigated through factor analysis the relationships among the Wechsler Intelligence Scale for Children, several standard educational achievement tests, and tests of finger agnosia, lateral dominance, and reversals in reading and writing. Two orthogonal factors relating to reading problems were identified by Lyle. One was a factor of perceptual and perceptual-motor distortions, the other a weakness in formal verbal learning. Finger agnosia, lateral dominance, and mixed hand-eye dominance were not found to be related to reading ability.

Coleman (1968) assessed eighty-seven first- through sixth-grade subjects showing severe language deficits and reading difficulties on unspecified tests, guidance evaluations, and teachers' ratings. As measured by tests of Kephart (1960) and Barsch (1965a), half the children had visual or visual-motor dysfunctions judged severe enough to impede learning. Failure to mention his criteria for identifying the reading disabled child, however, renders Coleman's results relatively uninterpretable.

Erickson (1969) tested the ability of seventh-grade boys to integrate successive partial impressions of abstract stimuli into a whole (Gibson, 1947) and compared this skill to reading ability as assessed by the Iowa Test of Basic Skills. Results of the comparison indicated that low performance on the perception test was likely to be associated with reading deficits of one-half to one full grade level. In other words, the visually oriented subjects did significantly better than nonvisually oriented subjects on reading tests, even as late as the seventh grade.

Singer and Brunk (1967), however, failed to find a relationship between performance on a rather specific perceptual-motor task and overall academic achievement. The task was one which required the child to reproduce a geometric figure presented on a screen with rubber bands and a board filled with pegs. Stretching the rubber bands around the appropriate pegs, the child was to copy a total of fourteen patterns ranging in difficulty from easy to complex. Especially because of its unconventional measure of visual-motor ability, however, this study by no means disproved the existence of a relationship between perceptual-motor and academic ability.

Besides exploring the connections of visual, auditory, and visual-auditory processes to reading, some research has been able to relate similar, miscellaneous perceptual factors to reading disability. For example, Davol and Hastings (1967) administered a modification of Fleishman's (1957) response orientation device to 192 children in kindergarten and the first three grades. Studying these youngsters, evaluated by their teachers as either normal or poor readers, the authors discovered that poor readers of low socioeconomic backgrounds were significantly retarded in comparison to normal readers in the development of spatial orientation, which includes responses to right-left, up-down, and anterior-exterior perceptual cues. Davol and Hastings felt that the inability to respond correctly to such spatial orientation cues could cause difficulty in processing printed materials. In another experiment yielding related findings, Elkind, Larson, and VanDoorninck (1965) observed sixty third through sixth graders, half rated slow readers and half rated average by unnamed tests. The poor readers were found to be significantly inferior on a set of hidden-figure tests developed by the authors. This ability to ignore the inessential but respond to the relevant cues in the printed materials might, as the authors concluded, be related to the absence of requisite skills for proficient reading.

Since the presently available results from studies like those just discussed represent diverse findings and varying degrees of accuracy, it is probably wisest to concur with Coleman (1959), who had concluded that although "marked retardation in visual perceptual development is characteristic of reading disability cases as a group, there are exceptions" [p. 117]. Furthermore, while researchers struggle with the difficulty of determining whether impaired perceptual-motor development precedes reading disability or vice versa, we should also consider the possibility that the problem is a circular one, wherein visual-perceptual disabilities may be seen to impair early reading acquisition, and poor reading subsequently may be viewed as restricting experiences that would enhance visual-perceptual development.

THE RELATIVE IMPORTANCE OF DIFFERENT SENSORY MODES AT DIFFERENT AGE LEVELS

Besides investigating the nature of the connection between visual and visual-motor development and academic success, numerous researchers have also tried to determine whether visual-perceptual ability may be related to achievement at all age levels or only at the earliest ones. Because of the initial problem in discriminating between letters and words at a perceptually immature age, it is not illogical to assume that visual skills should be important in beginning reading. Some evidence even suggests that such skills continue to be crucial for reading success at higher levels. Erickson (1969), for example, found visual-motor deficiency to be related to reading disability in higher primary grades. Data from Coleman's (1968) study, too, indicated that many fifth and sixth graders of retarded reading ability were impaired on visual-perceptual skills. The Coleman study, however, has three distinct limitations. First, the criteria for inclusion in the retarded-reader population were unspecified. Second, only 50 percent of this population was found to have visual-perceptual problems. And finally, since Coleman was looking specifically for visual-perceptual handicaps, he may well have missed the presence of some other perceptual deficiency in his subjects.

Yet, evidence of the relatedness of perceptual difficulties to reading disability has continued to accrue. Exemplary of the recent experiments yielding such findings are those by Lyle (1969) and Whipple and Kodman (1969). Lyle found visual deficits in his fifth- and sixth-grade retarded readers, although he did observe that such problems tended to decline in importance with increasing age through the primary-grade years. Whipple and Kodman compared 120 fourth and fifth graders, half of whom had been identified as poor readers by the Bijou Wide-Range Achievement Test, while the other half demonstrated normal reading ability. According to these investigators, the poor readers were functioning at the level of normal 6- to 8-year-old children in their ability to perform a Gibson and Gibson (1955) perceptual learning task involving the matching of nonsense drawings from memory.

In contrast to this evidence of the sustained association between visual-perceptual deficit and reading disability through the primary grades, several other investigations have generated data indicating that with increasing age, visual and visual-motor deficits decline in importance as others (e.g., auditory deficiencies and/or interactions among visual and other perceptual modes) reflect growing relevance to reading disability. Golden and Steiner (1969), for example, found in a study with second graders that even by 8 years of age, deficiencies in auditory rather than visual functions seem to be more related to reading difficulties. The authors felt that such evidence mainly served to emphasize the need for careful individual diagnosis in reading disability. Evidently the case can be made that some poor readers may need more training in such skills as auditory memory, sound blending, and auditory closure, while others may require a program aimed at improving visual and visual-motor skills. This is the only study discussed here, however, that found evidence for this sensory-modal shift among poor readers below the fourth-grade level.

A wealth of research within the last decade, on the other hand, has shown an intersensory interaction of the visual and auditory modalities to be closely related to reading proficiency in later primary-grade years. The logic behind hypothesizing a reliance upon auditory-visual integration appears to be sound, since the reading process would seem to involve the association of visual stimuli with their appropriate auditory counterparts.

Although Leton (1962) did not himself offer specific data bearing on visual-auditory interaction, he was one of the first investigators to suggest the need for broader experimentation into the underlying processes of learning and reading disabilities. Leton felt that visual and visual-motor tests alone were inadequate diagnostic tools, since they cannot pinpoint the sources of perceived problems. Further, despite their emphasis on the visual mode of perception, these tests cannot really render clues as to whether reading difficulties may be visual, motor, or visual-motor in origin. Such tools are also of little value if the origin of difficulty is in other than the visual mode. As Leton noted, too many investigators jump to cause-and-effect conclusions concerning visual impairment and reading difficulty without taking into consideration other possible factors. Leton therefore advocated more complete diagnosis of each reading disabled child through the application of a wide battery of tests, including the Bender-Gestalt, the Wide-Range Achievement Tests, an IQ test, and both visual and auditory examinations.

In his own study, Leton seems to have ignored his own good advice. Evaluating thirteen poor readers, drawn from remedial reading classes, and thirteen normal readers, he did obtain trends in the expected direction, i.e., the poor readers exhibited greater perceptual deficiencies and also scored lower on both achievement and IQ tests. Yet the results are virtually meaningless, for Leton not only neglected to define the tests by means of which his poor readers were selected, but also failed to mention the specific tools used to assess auditory ability. Thus, the main value of Leton's study lay in its philosophical emphasis on more complete diagnostic evaluation of reading disability.

Having circumvented many of the methodological weaknesses inherent in Leton's format, many researchers have subsequently been successful in demonstrating the occurrence of a shift at about the fourth-grade level in emphasis from the visual to the auditory mode with regard to reading disabilities. In later years, poor readers appear to have more difficulty with auditory or with intersensory auditory-visual tasks than with purely visual tasks. Tests such as that developed by Berry (1967), based on refined versions of a task originally designed by Birch and Belmont (1965a, 1965b), required the subject to pick up cues from stimuli involving one sensory mode (e.g., a visually perceived pattern of dots) and then to respond by matching stimuli from another sensory mode (e.g., an auditory series of tones, one pattern of which matched the visual dot pattern). This presentation of a visual followed by an auditory pattern reversed the presentation of Birch and Belmont, and, in Berry's estimation, was more congruent with the order of intersensory integration required in the reading process. Berry administered her test to fifteen normal and fifteen slow readers, aged 8 to 13, whose reading ability had been assessed by the reading subtest of the Iowa Test of Basic Skills. As expected, she found that slow readers were noticeably more deficient in visual-auditory integration.

Other studies such as Berry's have consistently produced correlational data showing that a developmental lag in ability to perform intersensory tasks is related to reading disability. Katz and Deutsch (1963), using first-, third-, and fifth-grade Black subjects of low socioeconomic status, assessed reading ability with the Gates Advanced Primary Reading Test for the third and fifth graders and the Reading Prognosis Test (Weiner and Feldmann, 1963) for the first graders. They also administered several perceptual tests involving bimodal, visual-auditory, and stimulation and response patterns. These latter tests included a Bimodal Reaction Time Apparatus (Sutton, Hakerem, Zubin, and Portnoy, 1961); the Continuous Performance Test (Rosvold, Mirksy, Sarason, Bransome, and Beck, 1956); and a modality preference test, concept formation test, memory span test, and several discrimination tasks, all designed by the authors.

From their results, Katz and Deutsch determined that poor reading was associated with difficulty in shifting from one sensory mode to another. Moreover, the poor readers were observed to have greater difficulty in differentiating between qualitatively similar visual and auditory stimuli. They also performed less well on learning and memory tasks involving such stimuli. On simpler tasks, the poor readers had their greatest problems with visual stimuli, but on more complex tasks they performed poorest when dealing with auditory stimuli. Although perceptual ability was found to improve with age for poor as well as for average readers, this ability was a slow-going process for the reading disabled children. As they grow older, therefore, poor readers faced with tasks of increasing complexity apparently do least well on items for which they must deal with auditory stimuli. This point may indeed reflect a shift in the relative importance of visual and auditory impairment with regard to reading disability.

Birch and Belmont (1965a, 1965b, 1966) and Sterritt and Rudnick (1966a, 1966b; Rudnick, Sterritt, and Flax, 1967) have engaged in a lively dialogue concerning the relationship between visual-auditory impairment and reading disability. Birch and Belmont (1965b) had originally designed a test intended to assess the ability to perform within a cross-modal pattern of stimulation and response. First, the experimenter tapped out a rhythmic pattern on a table edge while the subject watched. Afterward, the subject was to match a set of dots with the pattern he had just heard. On the basis of their results, the authors concluded that the ability to perform such a task is highly related to reading ability in the early primary grades but that the importance of such skills declines in the later grades, i.e., by the fourth grade.

As Sterritt and Rudnick aptly remarked, the task designed by Birch and Belmont is more appropriately deemed visual rather than auditory-visual, since the subject could see as well as hear the tapping. In order to conduct what they felt would be a truly auditory-visual experiment, Sterritt and Rudnick performed the tapping sequence outside the child's range of vision so that only the auditory cue would be received. They also administered a purely visual task in which a blinking light delivered the stimulation. Findings demonstrated that the significance of achievement on the purely visual task declined with age in relation to reading disability, while performance on the refined cross-modal task took on increased importance along with, but independent of, IQ. In a follow-up study employing the same performance tasks with third graders and measuring reading ability with the reading subtest of the Iowa Test of Basic Skills, Rudnick, Sterritt, and Flax (1967) substantiated the original conclusions and pinpointed the occurrence of the shift at the fourth-grade level.

THEORETICAL SPECULATIONS CONCERNING AN AGE-RELATED, SENSORY-MODAL SHIFT

Rudnick et al. proposed a plausible theory to account for the significance of the sensory-modal shift in reading disabled children. It was their hypothesis that in beginning reading the visual mode functions predominantly, and through it the child learns of the things or ideas for which words stand. Impairment in the visual mode of perception therefore should relate highly to reading ability in the early primary grade. As the reading material becomes most difficult, visual-auditory connections essential to comprehension ought to become more crucial. The authors felt that clinical, neurological support for their theory could be derived from observations by the neurologist Geschwind, who had stated (1964):

> While one learns in speaking to name objects with which one has had both tactile and visual experience, learning to read is almost exclusively de-

pendent on pure visual-auditory connections (particularly after the earliest stages). When these pure connections are cut off the patient can no longer read [p. 167].

If auditory functions and visual-auditory connections do become increasingly salient to reading in the third and fourth grades, Rudnick et al. pointed out, then deaf children could be expected to experience tremendous difficulty in trying to advance beyond this level in reading ability. Indeed, Myklebust (1960) had already confirmed this prediction with data which showed that deaf children suffered progressively severe reading disabilities from ages 9 to 15. In fact, as Myklebust had observed, the deaf student completing high school frequently possessed reading skills inferior to those of a third grader.

Still another theoretical model, that of Neisser, weighs the relative contributions of visual and visual-auditory processes for reading. Neisser, whose work (1967) dealt with iconic storage in tachistoscopic experiments, believed that visual stimuli such as letters or words caused the subject to construct an "icon," or image, lasting for approximately one second. Drawing upon the work of Sperling (1963), Neisser maintained that if the individual is to store this information more permanently, he must be aided by the important factor of verbal coding. In effect, Neisser contended that one must translate the fleeting visual image into a verbal code if the image is to be retained over a period of time.

Neisser's conceptual framework might well be applied in the effort to determine whether reading problems are the result of visual-processing problems or whether they stem from deficiencies in auditory-visual integration. The translation or coding process spoken of by Neisser can be likened to the process of integrating visual and auditory information. Applying his tachistoscopic procedures to children with reading problems, we could explore whether a particular child's problems lay in the formation of icons, in their translation into a verbal code, or in both. If the child were experiencing difficulty in the construction of icons, he would be said to exhibit a visual problem. If, on the other hand, he were unable to verbally code the iconic image, we might conclude that his difficulty was one of visual-auditory integration.

PERCEPTUAL AND PERCEPTUAL-MOTOR PROBLEMS AS POSSIBLE CAUSES OF DIFFICULTIES IN COGNITION AND ACADEMIC ACHIEVEMENT

As mentioned in chapter 4 and discussed at length in chapter 6, numerous learning disabilities theorists have advocated a variety of perceptual and perceptual-motor training activities for children who appear to have perceptual or perceptual-motor-based learning difficulties. The rationale for such procedures has derived from the hypothesis that perceptual and perceptual-motor problems hinder conceptual ability and academic achievement, especially reading achievement. Certainly the efforts considered in this chapter provide a rich theoretical base and considerable empirical support for the notion that perceptual problems can result in later difficulties in conceptual, abstract, intellectual operations. Too, numerous studies of a correlational nature suggest that visual-perceptual disabilities in the early grades and visual-auditory integration disabilities in the later grades may be at the root of reading disabilities. Yet despite the intuitive appeal of this last possibility, the correlative data regarding perception and reading do not justify unqualified endorsement of the proposition that perceptual disabilities *cause* reading disabilities. After all, correlation between the two problems may be the result of a causal effect proceeding in *either* direction, or they may both be associated with a third, unknown causative agent.

For just such reasons, current research efforts into the causes of reading disabilities have attracted a great deal of criticism. Cohen (1969a, 1969b, 1970) has been one persistently vociferous critic. Although in his first article he oversimplified the problems of and solutions to reading disabilities by urging educators to be less concerned with underlying processes than with teaching letters and words, his adversaries (C. D. Benton, 1969; Frostig and Maslow, 1969; Getman, 1969; Schiffman, 1969; Solan, 1969) also missed the mark by reacting primarily to his oversimplification without addressing themselves to the argument itself. In 1970, Cohen published a more realistic argument which favored fewer investigations into the underlying causes of reading problems and more research aimed at developing effective means of teaching reading disabled children to read. If he was thereby advocating a halt to correlative studies, his argument definitely had both common sense and logic on its side. Sufficiently high correlations have already been demonstrated among perceptual factors and reading disabilities. Yet the surface has scarcely been scratched with regard to exploration which might result in definitive conclusions about causes. There is an almost inexcusable dearth of investigations into the psychological processes involved in reading and the particular psychological malfunctions in the disabled reader.

Considered as a whole, the theoretical and empirical evidence so far accumulated on perception and its relation to cognition and achievement surely warrants the exploration of perceptual and perceptual-motor training techniques and their efficacy for learning disabled children. In terms of the education of individual children, the research evidence, even though correlative, does indicate that *as a group* reading disabled children experience perceptual disturbances. An important point to keep in mind, though, is that considerable overlap occurs between groups of normal and retarded readers. Thus, there exists a strong possibility that multivariate causal factors are involved. Although referring more specifically to the child who has been diagnosed as brain injured, Reitan's (1964) comments about reading disabilities appears valid here:

> . . . the significant causal factors probably are . . . complex in the instance of each person affected. . . . Among the consequences of brain lesions that may be important are a loss in general adaptive abilities manifested by learning deficits and inability to sustain concentrated attention and motivation, a loss in the ability to appreciate the symbolic significance of language symbols, impairment in the ability to form and generalize rational concepts, and deficits in the perception and manipulation of visuo-spatial configurations [p. 20].

With reference to the philosophy and practices upon which perceptual-motor programs are built, Reitan's analysis is clearly applicable. To foist perceptual-motor training indiscriminately upon children simply because they are behind grade level in reading ability is to disregard its *raison d'être,* to overstep the boundaries of its appropriateness, and to abuse its possible potential. If it is to be at all meaningful, perceptual-motor training must be administered only to those children who explicitly manifest perceptual-motor problems.

CHAPTER 6

The Efficacy
of Perceptual-Motor
Training

With the considerations of chapter 5 kept in mind, we now focus our attention on studies appraising the effectiveness of perceptual, motor, and perceptual-motor training. Based upon many years of clinical and classroom experience with children manifesting a variety of learning problems, the techniques and programs of Barsch, Frostig, Getman, Kephart, and others have gained widespread popularity and acceptance on the educational scene, as evidenced by their success on the educational materials market. If it is true that the work of each of the above theorists and practitioners finds its roots at least partially in the pioneering efforts of Werner and Strauss, and, to a certain extent, in the methods of such pioneers as Montessori, then the use of perceptual-motor exercises reflects a lengthy history of success as determined by clinical judgment.

While clinical, subjective support of these methods has a long tradition, controlled experimental investigation has lagged behind the work of clinicians by a number of years. Only in the past decade have there been attempts to use well-defined research strategies in order to determine the efficacy of perceptual-motor training. This is no doubt partially explained by the fact that systematic, statistical treatment of problems confronted by education, in general, does not have a long history. In fact, the slow accumulation of research investigations is not even unique to education. The history of the behavioral sciences and of specific problems within each of them often manifests a timetable similar to the one regarding perceptual-motor training (Campbell, 1959). New ideas, concepts, theories, and practices, more often than not, are adopted before they have been put to rigorous test. As a rule, informal, and thus subjective, investigation of a particular concept or practice precedes a more formal, controlled investigation.

The delay in undertaking research strategies in order to test the value of perceptual-motor training may also be explained partially by the orientations of perceptual-motor theorists themselves. Major theorists and practitioners in this area have been individuals whose expertise and interests have been along clinical rather than research lines. Getman, for instance, readily states that he is a clinician rather than a rigorous experimentalist.[27] Yet his and others' theoretical and clinical contributions certainly are not to be questioned. Nor does their disinclination to use controlled research necessarily imply disregard for precision. Their particular skills and talents have led them to provide invaluable, albeit informal, evidence concerning the appropriateness and refinement of particular teaching methods.

With the wide publicity and acceptance of perceptual-motor training methods, more and more professionals have become interested in them. In the past few years, therefore, a large number of studies have been designed to test experimentally the validity of perceptual-motor training techniques. The vast majority of these investigations have led perceptual-motor advocates to conclude that their methods have positive results. In terms of the particular perceptual, motor, or perceptual-motor methods used and the characteristics of the populations under investigation, however, the studies vary greatly. Subjects, for example, have ranged not only in age but also in classification, from normal to severely mentally retarded.

Before this rapidly increasing amount of information becomes unmanageably bulky, some organization of the studies is sorely needed. The major objective of this chapter, therefore, is to investigate and to bring some order to the findings of these diverse studies. The research will be discussed with respect to the particular approach investigated, population, duration of study, and results.

Each of the studies is also analyzed with regard to adequacy of research design used. Three factors led to the decision that such a critique is necessary. First, experimentation in perceptual-motor training is rife with sources of error. Second, the previously mentioned, relatively short history of research in this area increases the likelihood that studies conducted to date may not meet very rigorous research standards. Third, a recent critique (Robbins and Glass, 1969) enumerating many methodological flaws in evidence purporting to show positive effects of one particular

[27] Personal communication from Gerald Getman, April 9, 1971.

178 PSYCHOEDUCATIONAL FOUNDATIONS OF LEARNING DISABILITIES

approach (Doman-Delacato) helped draw our attention the lack of similar critiques on other studies concerning techniques and programs of perceptual-motor training.

With reference to the latter point, the critique by Robbins and Glass of the Doman and Delacato program was based upon sources of invalidity that have been identified by Campbell and Stanley (1963). The present critique, for the most part, includes a search for these same sources of error. If anything, the present analysis is a more lenient one in that, recognizing the difficulties of field experimentation, we decided to overlook certain problems which arise in almost any study performed in an educational setting.

Since the school or classroom does not lend itself well to the strict controls that can be enforced in the laboratory, it is probable that some sources of error are almost always inherent in educational experiments. The limitations of time, money, and the structure of the educational system are formidable barriers to perfectly controlled research. For example, the existing school schedule and structure often make it necessary to violate the random assignment of subjects to experimental and control groups. We must usually be satisfied with the random assignment of whole classes. Differential teaching abilities and how to measure them also present difficulties. Superficially, it might seem that the problem of differential teaching ability would be circumvented if one teacher were to use all the different methods to be compared; but in addition to the physical and logistic problems, this procedure creates the methodological dilemma of assuring that the teacher will devote equitable amounts of time, energy, and talent to the employment of each method under investigation.

In the critique to follow, the above considerations are kept in mind. Picayune problems in experimental design are not mentioned unless they are so numerous as to render a study questionable. Some design problems are more easily controlled and more crucial to a sound experimental design than are others. It is a greater problem, for instance, if no control group is employed than if the teaching ability of the teachers used is not mentioned as a control variable. To discount entirely the findings of a study that meets all the requirements of well-controlled research except for the absence of distinctions between the teachers' abilities borders on the pedantic.

The thirty-one articles, not including the eleven cited by Robbins and Glass (1969), in this critical review were chosen primarily from the literature of 1965 through 1970. They were taken from the following major journals: *American Journal of Mental Deficiency, Exceptional Children, Journal of Learning Disabilities,* and *Perceptual and Motor Skills.* This chapter encompasses virtually all the studies which, over the past decade in these four major journals, have dealt with the effectiveness of perceptual-motor training. In addition, some studies contained in other well-known journals have been included. In no way, however, were any articles selected on the basis of prior knowledge of their results or methodology. A few other individual studies not included might differ slightly from the ones herein, but generalizations may be made about the research findings of the entire field from the numerous articles considered. This selection procedure is intended to insure as accurate as possible a representation of the most recent literature concerning the subject matter.

The studies discussed are arranged in five sections. The first section, the only one devoted to a particular program, deals with studies concerning the effectiveness of Doman and Delacato's training procedures on various populations. Because of the usual methods of and controversy surrounding Doman and Delacato's techniques, a discussion of the empirical evidence concerning their approach warrants special consideration. The other four sections, constructed according to characteristics of the population under study regardless of the particular approach employed, deal with studies using the following subjects: (a) children who are mentally retarded; (b) children who display learning disabilities; (c) children who have been identified as "culturally or economically disadvantaged"; and (d) children in regular classes who have not been differentiated in any way and are thus assumed to fall, for the most part, in a normal distribution with regard to measured IQ, learning disabilities, and socioeconomic status. Each of these four groupings is further subdivided and discussed on the basis of the particular approach tested.

At this point, it may be helpful to refer to Tables 2–6, in which the above organization is presented in schematic form. Each of the tables presents additional information on the studies, including a breakdown of the time spent administering the experimental treatment; the total number of hours the experimental techniques were applied; the dependent variables under study; the results for each of the dependent variables (whether or not there was a positive experimental effect); and the existence of any sources, or possible sources, of error in the methodology of the study.

THE DOMAN-DELACATO APPROACH

Robbins and Glass (1969) presented a critique of eleven experimental studies, two performed by Delacato himself, which have been cited in Delacato's three major books (Delacato, 1959, 1963, 1966) as evidence to support his training techniques. Using the sources of experimental invalidity noted by Campbell and Stanley (1966), (sources similar, by the way, to those used here), Robbins and Glass subjected these eleven empirical studies to close examination. Robbins and Glass offer a complete discussion of the multitude of sources of invalidity they claimed to have found in these studies. Suffice it to say here that Robbins and Glass commented that these experiments purporting to show the efficacy of the Doman-Delacato training techniques "are exemplary for their faults" [p. 347].

Additional studies not included in the Robbins and Glass critique also demand keen appraisal. The following paragraphs evaluate the critical findings of four Doman-Delacato training studies, authored respectively by Robbins (1966b), Stone and Pielstick (1969), Kershner (1968), and O'Donnell and Eisenson (1969).

Robbins (1966b) carried out an empirical test of the theory of neurological organization, comparing three separate second-grade classes that had been conducted in three distinct ways. While one class received a traditional second-grade curriculum, the second experimental group engaged in Doman-Delacato-advocated activities for periods ranging from one to three months, and the third received a program of general activities not consistent with the Doman-Delacato theory of neurological organization.

Robbins's major conclusions from this study all rejected basic tenets of neurological organization theory:

1. Creeping is not significantly related to reading.
2. When measured by the California Achievement Tests (Tiegs & Clark, 1957), mean reading differences between children who are lateralized and those who are not, as determined by Harris Tests of Lateral Dominance (Harris, 1958), are not significant.
3. When the ability to creep is controlled, there are no significant differences in reading between lateralized and nonlateralized subjects.
4. Compared to both of the two control groups, the experimental subjects did not significantly increase their reading ability following exposure to the experimental training program.
5. The experimental program did not affect the amount of lateralization.

Robbins candidly admitted the possible sources of error in his own study: (a) he could not randomly assign subjects to each of the three groups; (b) as a result of nonrandom selection, the experimental group exhibited initially significant superiority in reading and arithmetic; and (c) there could be no control over differential teaching skills. Nevertheless, although these three sources of invalidity cannot be overlooked, they are not necessarily the sine qua non of a sound experimental design. As stated earlier, in educational research of this nature, the opportunity for perfect random assignment of subjects and for the equation of teaching ability for teachers of different classes is a rarity. If there are no observable dif-

TABLE 2 A Summary of Studies Using the Doman-Delacato Method

Study	Population	Theory or Approach Tested	Length of Treatment	Total Hours (approx.)	Dependent Variables	Results	Sources or Possible Sources of Error
Robbins & Glass (1969), review of 11 studies purporting to show positive evidence for Delacato's treatment program		Doman-Delacato				+ · · ·	Yes (11 times)
Robbins (1966b)	second-grade (undifferentiated)	Doman-Delacato	30 mins. per day/ 3 months	30	creeping, achievement tests, laterality	− − −	No
Stone & Pielstick (1969)	kindergarten (undifferentiated)	Doman-Delacato	30 mins. per per day/ 5 days a week/ 18 weeks	45	visual-motor development, reading achievement, language development	+ − −	Yes
Kershner (1968)	TMR children, 8–18 yrs. old	Doman-Delacato	235 mins. per day/ 74 days	290	creeping and crawling, language development, motor development	+ + −	Yes
O'Donnell & Eisenson (1969)	reading disabled, 7–10 yrs. old	Doman-Delacato	30 mins. per day/ 5 days a week/ 20 weeks	50	visual-motor integration, reading achievement,	− −	No

TABLE 3 A SUMMARY OF THE STUDIES ON MENTALLY RETARDED POPULATIONS

Study	Population	Theory or Approach Tested	Length of Treatment	Total Hours (approx.)	Dependent Variables	Results	Sources or Possible Sources of Error
Hill, McCullum, & Sceau (1967)	MR, IQ below 70, about 12 yrs. old	Frostig & variety of visual-motor activities	20 mins. per day/ 5 days a week/ 4 mos.	27	directional awareness	+	Yes
Allen, Dykman, & Haupt (1966)	EMR children	Frostig	1 hr. per day/ 1 semester	80	visual-motor ability	+	Yes
Talkington (1968)	severely and profoundly retarded, 7–18 yrs. old	Frostig	1 hr. per day/ 5 days a week/ 3 months	60	visual-motor ability	+	Yes
Alley (1968)	EMR, 7–10 yrs. old	Frostig	30 mins. per day/ 5 days a week/ 2 months	20	motor, perceptual-motor, visual-motor, visual-motor retention, psycholinguistic abilities	− − − − −	No
Alley & Carr (1968)	EMR, 7–10 yrs. old	Kephart	30 mins. per day/ 5 days a week/ 2 months	20	motor, perceptual-motor, visual-motor, visual-motor retention, psycholinguistic abilities	− − − − −	No

Study	Subjects	Method	Duration	N	Abilities measured	Results	Significant
Edgar, Ball, McIntyre, & Shotwell (1969)	MR, $\overline{X}$ IQ = 34, CA = 3–8 yrs.	Kephart	20 mins. per day/ 3 days a week/ 8 months	32	motor development, language development, social development, adaptive behavior	+ + + −	No
Maloney, Ball, & Edgar (1970)	MR, $\overline{X}$ IQ = 42, $\overline{X}$ CA = 14 yrs.	Kephart	40 mins. per day/ 3 days a week/ 2 months	16	perceptual-motor development, body image, finger localization	+ + −	No
Maloney & Payne (1970)	MR, $\overline{X}$ IQ = 42, $\overline{X}$ CA = 14 yrs.	Kephart	8-month follow-up of above	16	body image	+	Yes
Painter (1968)	one slow learner with IQ of 85	Barsch & Kephart	21 30-min. training sessions over 2 months	10	IQ, verbal & psycholinguistic abilities	− +	Yes
Painter (1966)	lower half in MA of kindergarten	Barsch & Kephart	21 30-min. training sessions over 7 weeks	10	ability to draw human figures, body image, visual-motor ability, sensory-motor spatial performance, psycholinguistic abilities	+ + + + +	Yes

TABLE 3 (continued)

Study	Population	Theory or Approach Tested	Length of Treatment	Total Hours (approx.)	Dependent Variables	Results	Sources or Possible Sources of Error
Watkins (1957)	MR, X̄ IQ = 45	Strauss & Lehtinen	10 months	?	staff ratings of progress	+	Yes
Lillie (1968)	MR, X̄ IQ = 77, low SES, X̄ CA = 61 mos.	variety of motor training	5 months	?	motor development	+	Yes
Ross (1969)	EMR, early elementary	variety of motor training	25 mins. per day/ 3 days a week/ 6 months	30	sports skills, motor skills	+ +	Yes
Chanksky & Taylor (1964)	EMR, ages 8–11 yrs.	perceptual training with block design construction	1 hr. per week/ 10 weeks	10	IQ, visual-motor retention, achievement test	+ + +	Yes
Webb (1970)	Profoundly retarded, 2.5–17.5 yrs. old	variety of sensory-motor training techniques	5.5–10.5 months	?	social maturity, sensory-motor development	+[28] +	Yes

[28] Although statistical results were negative, the author implied that, based on clinical judgment, the results were positive.

184

TABLE 4 A SUMMARY OF THE STUDIES ON LEARNING DISABLED POPULATIONS

Study	Population	Theory or Approach Tested	Length of Treatment	Total Hours (approx.)	Dependent Variables	Results	Sources or Possible Sources of Error
Lewis (1968)	reading disabled, second grade	Frostig	3 hrs. per week/ 10 weeks	30	visual-motor ability, reading achievement	− +	Yes
Cohen (1966)	reading & perceptually disabled, first grade	Frostig	20 mins. per day/ 10 weeks	17	perceptual development, reading achievement	+ −	Yes
Halgren (1961)	slow learners, ninth grade	Getman, & variety of visual training	5 days a week/ 10 weeks	?	IQ, reading achievement	+ +	Yes
Keim (1970)	low visual-motor ability, 5–6 yrs. old	Winter Haven Program	not reported	?	IQ, language, visual-motor ability, reading achievement	− − − −	Yes
Khan (1968)	emotionally disturbed with visual-motor problems	variety of visual-motor training	1 hr. per day/ 5 days a week/ 10 weeks	50	reading achievement	+	Yes
McCormick, Schnobrick, & Footlik (1969)	underachievers, first grade	variety of perceptual, motor, and perceptual-motor training	1 hr. per day/ 2 days a week/ 9 weeks	18	reading achievement	+	Yes

TABLE 5   A SUMMARY OF THE STUDIES ON "DISADVANTAGED" POPULATIONS

Study	Population	Theory or Approach Tested	Length of Treatment	Total Hours (approx.)	Dependent Variables	Results	Sources or Possible Sources of Error
Alley, Snider, Spencer, & Angell (1968)	economically disadvantaged, kindergarten	Frostig	25 mins. per day/ 8 months	67	visual-motor development, reading achievement,	+ +	Yes
Elkind & Deblinger (1969)	economically disadvantaged, second grade	Elkind	30 mins. per day/ 3 days a week/ 15 weeks	22	perceptual tests, achievement test	+ +	Yes

TABLE 6 A SUMMARY OF THE STUDIES ON UNDIFFERENTIATED (NORMAL) POPULATIONS

Study	Population	Theory or Approach Tested	Length of Treatment	Total Hours (approx.)	Dependent Variables	Results	Sources or Possible Sources of Error
Ball & Edgar (1967)	kindergarten (undifferentiated)	Kephart	20 mins. per day / 5 days a week / 3.5 months	23	right-left discrimination (nonverbal), right-left discrimination (verbal), finger localization, IQ	+ − − −	No
O'Connor (1969)	first grade (undifferentiated)	Kephart	6 months	?	motor ability, drawing geometric figures, lateral preference, lateral dominance, external lateral awareness, internal lateral awareness, achievement test	+ − − − − + −	Yes
Jensen & King (1970)	kindergarten (undifferentiated)	variety of perceptual, motor, and perceptual-motor activities	20 mins.	.5	reading	−	Yes
Gill, Herdtner, & Lough (1968)	nursery-school (undifferentiated)	variety	20 mins. per day	?	perceptual-motor ability, field independence	+ +	Yes

ferences in teaching ability, we may be less concerned about this problem. If covariance analysis procedures are used to control for any pretest differences, these lessen the chances of a possible source of error. Still, though chances for error may have been lessened in the above study, we cannot conclude that Robbins's work was perfectly controlled. But, considering that in applied educational research, certain limitations are almost intrinsic to any educational setting, it is possible to conclude that Robbins's study is methodologically sound. A criticism of Robbins's investigation nevertheless arises. Since Robbins used undifferentiated second graders, his subjects reflected a normal distribution of abilities, whereas Delacato's theory purports to be applicable to children experiencing academic difficulties. Taking Delacato's viewpoint, then, the Robbins's population was not altogether appropriate.

More in line with Delacato's criteria for subject selection was an investigation conducted by Stone and Pielstick (1969), who studied a group of kindergarteners for reading readiness, a skill which Delacato contends would benefit from his procedures, as Stone and Pielstick noted. For thirty minutes a day, five days a week, over eighteen weeks, Stone and Pielstick's subjects were exposed to Delacato training. Comparing pre- to posttest gains on the Peabody Picture Vocabulary Test (Dunn, 1959), the Lee-Clark Reading Readiness Test (Lee and Clark, 1962), and the Developmental Test of Visual Perception (Maslow, Frostig, Lefever, and Whittlesey, 1964) for the experimental group and a control group designed to eliminate the possibility of Hawthorne Effect, the investigators identified a significant effect of treatment for the experimental group on the Frostig test, but no significant differences on the Peabody Picture Vocabulary Test or the Lee-Clark Test.

Stone and Pielstick pointed out that Dunn did not report long-term reliabilities for the Peabody Picture Vocabulary Test and that their own test-retest on a sample independent of the one under investigation resulted in a nonsignificant r of .187. They also stated that this r threw doubt on the usefulness of their results based on the Peabody Picture Vocabulary Test. In addition, the authors admitted that the ceiling of the Lee-Clark Test could invalidate both its use and the resultant findings in this study.

Since the authors noted the possible sources of error on the two measures that showed the Doman-Delacato treatment to have no effect, and since they also acknowledged that on the only other measure, the Frostig test, the results significantly favored the Doman-Delacato training, it is puzzling that they concluded, "It would appear that whatever effects the Doman-Delacato treatment may have, there is little support for the notion of its benefit to reading readiness in kindergarten children" [p. 67]. A more appropriate statement would be that, because of this study's methodological limitations, it reached no definite conclusion. We could even say that, based on a limited amount of valid and reliable data, the results tended to favor the Doman-Delacato treatment.

In an investigation into the effects of the Doman-Delacato program of neurological organization on the development of trainable, mentally retarded children, Kershner (1968) compared an experimental group receiving seventy-four teaching days of neurological training and a Hawthorne control group receiving nonspecific activities designed to achieve better coordination, balance, rhythm, and body image. Kershner reported that his findings supported Doman and Delacato's position that creeping and crawling are improved through creeping and crawling exercises and that IQ as measured by the Peabody Picture Vocabulary Test is improved significantly more for the experimental than for the control group. Yet, no important difference was found between the groups with regard to the improvement of their motor proficiency on the Kershner-Dusewicz-Kershner Adaptation of the Vineland-Oseretsky Motor Development Tests (K. Kershner, Dusewicz, and J. Kershner, 1967).

As pointed out by Kershner, any conclusions indicating that the Delacato training produced crucial gains in IQ on the Peabody Picture Vocabulary Test must be accompanied by a concern about the large pretest differences between the two groups (the mean was 39.77 for the experimental group and 61.94 for the control group). Although an analysis of covariance procedure was used, the extreme differences between the two groups may mean that two different populations actually were represented. In addition, although not noted by Kershner, the fact that the experimental group had the drastically lower mean Peabody Picture Vocabulary Test IQ indicates the possibility that on the posttesting, the phenomenon of regression toward the mean was more pronounced in this group. Thus, because we must be wary of accepting the results on the Peabody Picture Vocabulary Test, all that can be said with any assurance is that practice in creeping and crawling increases the ability to creep and crawl.

Even this latter conclusion, as well as the results of the entire study, may be brought into question if differential treatment of the two groups is critically examined. Not only did the amount of structured activity favor the experimental group, but also the organization of the experiment jeopardized the control for Hawthorne Effect. It should be noted that a recent systematic investigation has been made (Cook, 1967) which calls into question the existence of the Hawthorne Effect. While not refuting the results of this study nor its widespread implications, for the sake of experimental rigor we chose to include lack of control for the Hawthorne Effect as a possible source of error. As will be noted later in the chapter, a very limited number of studies were judged to be inadequate *solely* on this basis. Kershner's schedule for the experimental and control groups showed that the control group's teacher daily spent about an hour on what the experimenter considered an experimental and innovative program. The rest of the day was devoted to rather traditional kinds of free-play activities which could hardly have convinced a knowledgeable teacher that they were designed experimentally to help children achieve better rhythm, balance, coordination, and body image. The experimental group, on the other hand, spent a total of 235 minutes per day on a structured program of Doman-Delacato activities. Additionally, Kershner implied that there was a certain amount of individual instruction in the experimental classroom, but he made no mention of this variable with regard to the control group. The above differences, or possible differences, relative to treatment of the two groups, may seriously limit the validity of the findings.

In a better designed and more conclusive study, O'Donnell and Eisenson (1969) found that, after thirty minutes a day for twenty weeks, two experimental groups subjected to various aspects of Doman-Delacato procedures did not differ significantly from a Hawthorne control group on pre- versus posttest gains for a number of variables. Children 7 to 10 years of age who scored below the twenty-fifth percentile on the Stanford Diagnostic Reading Test were screened for: (a) IQs of 90 or above on the Peabody Picture Vocabulary Test, (b) reading abilities below a certain grade level on the Gray Oral Reading Test (Gray, 1963), (c) uncertain lateral expression or crossed lateral dominance on the Harris Tests of Lateral Dominance (Harris, 1958), and (d) normal visual and auditory acuity. The sixty disabled readers thereby selected were randomly assigned to one of three groups, with teachers who were rotated weekly to provide equal teacher exposure. Pretest scores did not differ significantly.

For all pre- and postmeasures taken, including the Gray Oral Reading Test, the Stanford Diagnostic Reading Test, and the Developmental Test of Visual-Motor Integration (Beery and Buktenica, 1967), the three groups did not differ significantly on their mean gain scores. Thus, this study, with a population apparently selected to represent one for which the Delacato approach is supposed to be beneficial, did not indicate that the Delacato training program produced results better than those evident when selected physical education activities were employed.

STUDIES ON MENTALLY RETARDED POPULATIONS

While the previous section dealt with the one particular approach (Doman-Delacato), this section considers studies that used a variety of techniques with children identified as mentally retarded. Investigators cited have attempted to evaluate procedures from the programs of Frostig, Kephart, Barsch, Strauss and Lehtinen, and others.

Studies Using Frostig's Program

In a study (Hill, McCullum, and Sceau, 1967) of children from 8 to 15 years of age, with IQs below 70, a program using some of Frostig's training procedures and the authors' own techniques was initiated for twenty minutes a day, five days a week, for four months. Hill et al. designed this study to investigate whether right-left directionality could be induced in mentally retarded children. The fourteen members of a special-education class were randomly assigned either to an experimental group or to a control group. Children in the latter group received the same treatment as did the experimental subjects except for the omission of verbal directional labels. For example, instead of being told, "The ball is in your *right* hand," as the children in the experimental group were instructed, the children in the control group were informed, "The ball is in *this* hand."

Using a test of right-level awareness developed by Belmont and Birch (1965) as a pre- and posttest measure, the investigators found no significant differences between the two groups before or after four months of training. When both groups were combined, however, further statistical treatment revealed a significant decrease in errors for the total group after training. Thus, investigators concluded that verbal labeling was not necessary to promote directional awareness, since sensory-motor training alone resulted in positive effects.

Hill et al. appear to have made post hoc data manipulations in order to find significant results. By combining what were originally an experimental and a control group, they produced one experimental group with, it should be added, an increased *N*, and then drew conclusions from statistically significant differences found in this group as a whole. They also left themselves open to an even stronger criticism that, by creating one "experimental" group, they did not provide for any control group. Thus, the significant differences found could have been due to maturation, practice on the test, or a number of other uncontrolled variables.

Using the Frostig-Horne (1964) training program alone, Allen, Dykman, and Haupt (1966) investigated its effects on educable retarded children. After one semester of training, Allen et al. reported significant improvement for the ten experimental subjects over the six control subjects on pre- and posttest administrations of the Developmental Test of Visual Perception when three of the five subtests (II—Figure-Ground Discrimination, III—Figure Constancy, and V—Spatial Relations) were combined.

Methodological limitations, however, are apparent in this study. Since the control group participated in the usual school activities, there remains the possibility that Hawthorne Effect was present. Too, although children were supposedly assigned randomly to the two groups, there remained large enough differences between the two groups on the subtests of the pretest to demand an analysis of covariance procedure. Such large pretest differences also indicate that variables such as age and IQ (which were not even reported) should have been looked at to determine if the groups differed on these characteristics. Even though the authors claimed that children were assigned randomly, it is suspicious that the groups were formed inequitably, with ten subjects in one and six in the other. Were the groups originally composed of ten subjects each? If so, then the control group suffered an extremely high mortality rate of 40 percent. Also to be regarded with caution is the grouping of the three subtests for the analysis of variance according to the authors' own opinion that those subtests were similar because in all three the "testee is shown a model figure to be used in performing the required tasks" [p. 41]. A rationale supported by more solid empirical evidence, e.g., factor analysis, would have lent more legitimacy to this regrouping for statistical analysis.

With severely and profoundly retarded children (IQ ranging from 17 to 48, CA ranging from 84 to 220 months), Talkington (1968) studied the effects of three months of Frostig-type training, five days per week, for one hour daily. Frostig's Developmental Test of Visual Perception was the dependent variable under study in a pre- versus posttest paradigm. Significantly greater gains in favor of the experimental group were found for each of the five Frostig subtests.

It remains unclear, however, whether or not Talkington took into account and controlled for the Hawthorne Effect. Without mentioning its control, he claimed that the control group "participated an equal amount of time in preschool classroom activities such as coloring, stories, music, puzzles, and games" [p. 505]. Nevertheless, whether both groups really received an equal amount of extra attention is certainly debatable. In the same vein, to what extent the two groups had an equal amount of structured programming also remains unanswered.

Furthermore, even though both groups were randomly selected, it would have been helpful if the author had reported the pretest means of the two groups. This omission, as well as the above-mentioned questions concerning Hawthorne Effect, may represent a problem of inadequate data reporting rather than a real source of invalidity. In either case, it does complicate the process of drawing conclusions from the study.

Alley (1968) studied the efficacy of two months of Frostig-type visual-perceptual training with regard to sensory-motor, visual-perception, and concept-formation abilities of educable, mentally retarded children between the ages of 7 years, 5 months and 9 years, 10 months. No significant treatment effects were found between the experimental and control groups for: (a) motor abilities, using the Lincoln-Oseretsky Motor Development Scale (Sloan, 1955) and selected areas of the Purdue Perceptual-Motor Survey (Roach and Kephart, 1966); (b) visual perceptual abilities, using the Benton Visual Retention Test (Benton, 1963), the Developmental Test of Visual Perception, and the Kuhlman-Finch Test I; or (c) concept-formation abilities, using the Illinois Test of Psycholinguistic Abilities (Kirk, McCarthy, and Kirk, 1961).

Although the results demonstrated no significant improvement for the experimental group in all three areas of ability, it should be noted that the two-month training period was a short one and that, though not significant, there were some trends in the positive direction. On the basis of this study alone, it would be premature to reject the usefulness of visual-perceptual training.

Studies Using Kephart's Program

In addition to Alley's negative findings with regard to the Frostig program, Alley and Carr (1968), using the experimental design described above, also found no positive effects of a program employing the recommended procedures of Kephart and some additional techniques of their own. Conclusions concerning Alley's earlier investigation with respect to the relative shortness of the training program (a total of twenty hours) hold for this study as well. While there was a lack of control for Hawthorne Effect in both of Alley's studies, however, the findings need not be discounted, since no significant differences favoring the experimental group were found in either experiment. If anything, this fact strengthens to some extent any conclusions we might draw about the lack of effectiveness of Frostig's and Kephart's techniques.

In a well-conceived and well-executed study, Edgar, Ball, McIntyre, and Shotwell (1969) compared an experimental group of eleven organically impaired, mentally retarded children who received sensory-motor training based upon the theory and techniques of Kephart with a control group whose participants received individual attention, but no sensory-motor training, in a structured setting. Both groups were equated for CA (3 to 8 years), MA (12 to 24 months), and general physical development.

Following a training period of fifteen to twenty minutes a day, three days a week, for eight months, it was found that the experimental group made significantly greater gains than did the control group on three out of four of the Gesell Developmental Schedules (Gesell and Armatruda, (1947): Motor, Language, and Personal-Social. Overall, experimental subjects also rated higher on the Full Scale. The only nonsignificant difference was found on the Adaptive Behavior Schedule. This highly controlled investigation thus offered supporting empirical evidence that Kephart's sensory-motor training techniques can improve mentally retarded children's performances in a number of areas, including those not specifically sensory-motor in nature.

Maloney, Ball, and Edgar (1970), also investigating the effects of techniques recommended by Kephart, claimed to improve upon the design of Edgar et al. (1969) by giving the control group as much social reinforcement as the experimental group received and by attempting to promote "attention" in this control group to a degree equal to that in the experimental group.

The sensory-motor training group (S-M), attention-comparison group (A-C), and no-treatment control group (N-T), equated for age (around 14 years) and IQ (around 42), exhibited a wide range of diagnostic categories. The S-M group was trained forty minutes a day, three days a week, for two months. Seen for the same period of time, the A-C subjects engaged in activities involving equal amounts of interpersonal interaction, physical contact with experimenters, and social reinforcement for attending to and/or succeeding at the activities. These tasks for the A-C group, in Maloney et al.'s judgment, required a minimum of sensory-motor skills. The following results were obtained on pre- and posttest measures:

1. On the Purdue Perceptual-Motor Survey (Roach and Kephart, 1966), both the S-M and A-C groups made significant gains, with significantly greater gains for the former.
2. On a modified version of the Eye, Hand, and Ear Test (Head, 1925), only the S-M group achieved a significant pre- versus posttest increase.
3. On a modification of the Personal Orientation Test (Weinstein, 1958), both S-M and A-C groups increased their scores markedly, with significantly greater gains for the S-M group.
4. On the Finger Localization Test (Benton, 1959b), no significant differences were found among the three groups.
5. After an additional 4 weeks of finger training, groups S-M and A-C did not improve their scores on the Finger Localization Test.
6. No significant differences in improvement were found on any of the measures when the S-M group was divided into organics, mongoloids, and functionally mentally retarded.

On the basis of results on the Eye, Hand, and Ear Test and the Personal Orientation Test, the authors supported Kephart's claim that sensory-motor training develops body image. This finding also led them to conclude that Kephart's approach affects more than motor skills of a very specific nature. But Kephart's position that fine motor generalizations necessarily follow gross motor generalizations was not supported by the data of Maloney et al., who concluded, "The present findings failed to support the hypothesis that generalization from sensory-motor training would occur in finger localization after a period of specific finger training" [p. 465].

In general, the design and methodology of the Maloney et al. study were sound enough to merit acceptance of their conclusions. Unlike the majority of studies discussed here, this one made a genuine attempt to provide systematic and well-controlled empirical investigation. By identifying and trying to eliminate major methodological weaknesses of other studies, the authors successfully skirted some of the many external factors invariably present when experiments cannot be performed in a laboratory setting. Recognizing the possibility that sensory-motor training encourages attention to the task as well as to sensory-motor training per se, Maloney et al. took a forward step in research on perceptual, motor, and perceptual-motor training. It should not be assumed, however, that they were completely successful in controlling for attention training. A pre- and posttest measure of attention for both the S-M and A-C groups would have ensured that attention training was equally successful in both groups.

In a follow-up of the previous work by Maloney et al. (1970), Maloney and Payne (1970) studied sixteen of the subjects who had received sensory-motor training and fourteen of the subjects in the no-treatment control group. After eight months, it was found that the experimental group maintained its superior performance over the control group on the Eye, Hand, and Ear Test and on the Personal Orientation Test. There is evidence, then, that sensory-motor training's effectiveness in promoting body image will remain stable for at least eight months after the initial training period. The N for the experimental group, though, reflected an attrition rate of 20 percent, while the N for the control group showed a loss of 26 percent. No explanation was reported for these substantial losses, but they require that the results be interpreted with some caution.

Painter (1968) reported on the effectiveness of a group sensory-motor program for a 6-year-old child named Bill, described as a slow learner. Bill was 1.5 years behind in school, with an IQ of 85. The remediation program, made up of twenty-one half-hour training sessions given over a two-month span, was based upon the theoretical constructs of Kephart and Barsch. In order to overcome Bill's withdrawn behavior, Painter also made a concerted effort to increase the youngster's social skills.

Pretest and posttest measures, nine months apart, the experimental treatment program being in effect the last two months, included the Stanford-Binet, the Peabody Picture Vocabulary Test, and the Illinois Test of Psycholinguistic Abilities. No gain was shown on the Stanford-Binet (from 85 to 86), but on the Peabody Picture Vocabulary Test, the student increased his IQ score from 104 to 120. Painter's data further showed that Bill increased substantially on all but two of the nine Illinois

Test of Psycholinguistic Abilities' subtests. Also provided was anecdotal information from the teachers, parents, and psychologist, suggesting that Bill improved both academically and socially.

Unfortunately, the number of inadequacies in the experimental design of this study render it almost worthless as a true evaluation of Barsch's and Kephart's approaches. As Painter readily admitted, the positive results possibly owed as much to Bill's behavior training and encouragement as to his sensory-motor training. In addition, there was no control group (or, in this case, no control subject), nor was Bill used as his own control except on a pretest versus posttest basis. Therefore, there was no way of controlling for any influential effects other than the stated program. The lack of a control group also left uncontrolled both the Hawthorne Effect and the possible effects of test practice. Furthermore, unsystematic, anecdotal reports of the teacher, parents, and psychologist may be considered highly suspect. These serious limitations make it impossible to draw any conclusions from these studies of the efficacy of Barsch's and Kephart's training rationale and procedures.

In a report on a larger group of children enrolled in the same program based upon Barsch's and Kephart's principles, Painter (1966) again claimed positive findings. Twenty children in the lower half of their kindergarten class, according to Goodenough MA scores, were divided into experimental and control groups of ten each. The subjects were equated on IQ, CA, MA, and sex.

After twenty-one half-hour sessions over a seven-week period, Painter used mean gain scores and sign tests of significance to support her claim that a number of areas of functioning were improved by the systematic program of rhythmic and sensory-motor activity. Looking at the Draw-a-Man test, she contended that ability to draw a human figure was improved; and because of improvement in the distortion score on the drawing of the human figure, she stated that distortion of body image concept was ameliorated. As measured by the Berry Geometric Form Reproduction Test, the experimental group also supposedly improved markedly over the control group in visual-motor integrity.

Administered only as posttests were the Illinois Test of Psycholinguistic Abilities and a sensory-motor performance test devised by Painter and a colleague. On two of the Illinois Test of Psycholinguistic Abilities' subtests—motor encoding and auditory vocal association—the experimental group performed significantly better. Painter thus stated that the program "will improve psycholinguistic abilities" [p. 115]. Significantly better performances by the experimental group on Painter's own test led her to the conclusion that the program improved sensory-motor spatial skills.

Although this study was certainly a more sound one than Painter's earlier experiment (Painter, 1968), it still suffers from some rather serious limitations. The author's claims of success must be viewed cautiously. The most obvious and limiting source of error was a failure to control for the Hawthorne Effect. Painter herself admitted to this flaw, as well as to the time and space limitations which prevented equal attention to the control group. Also questionable is the conclusion that lessened distortion in drawings of the human figure signifies an improvement of the body image concept. To imply that the ability to draw the human figure is directly correlated with the concept of body image is to regard the development of body image as a much more simplistic concept than, in fact, it is.

The use of Painter's homemade test for sensory-motor spatial performance, without comments and data on the reliability or validity of the instrument, was a serious methodological weakness. In addition, the results on the Illinois Test of Psycholinguistic Abilities were not positive enough to warrant Painter's generalization that the program affected improvement in psycholinguistic abilities. Only two of the nine subtests showed a significant difference in favor of the experimental group and the one, motor encoding, seems highly questionable as a task of *psycholinguistic* ability. Painter's results, then, are of doubtful merit and add limited knowledge about the effectiveness of Barsch's or Kephart's program.

A Study Using Strauss and Lehtinen's Program

After six weeks of instructing a teacher in the methods of Strauss and Lehtinen, Watkins (1957) set up a nondistracting classroom for fourteen institutionalized, mentally retarded children described by the staff as hyperactive and perseverative. The diagnostic breakdown, based upon case histories, revealed nine cases of brain injury, two of familial retardation, two mixed, one psychotic, and one child for whom information was incomplete. IQs ranged from 15 to 58, with a mean of 45. The perceptual-training activities, as recommended by Strauss and Lehtinen, were administered.

After ten months of perceptual training in the nondistracting classroom environment, Watkins reported improvement from several sources of information. Using progress notes, work samples, and the teacher's evaluation, Watkins categorized the variables of "behavior" and "perception" in terms of "degree of progress," using a three-category rating scale of "none," "some," and "very noticeable." In Watkins's opinion, nine of the children made very noticeable progress, and some progress was noted in all. In addition, the author claimed that the mean IQ increased from 39 to 43 after ten months and that, out of a total of forty-five admissions, sixteen children were discharged, with only two of these failing to show improvement.

Watkins mentioned at the beginning of his article that it had been "prepared as a report rather than as a scientific evaluation conforming to experimental design" [p. 455]. There is no need to refute this confession. The questions that arise concern the method and criteria used for inclusion in this special classroom, the criteria used for the diagnostic breakdown, the lack of a control group, and the validity, reliability, and objectivity of the methods used for evaluating the children's behaviors after the program. We also wonder about the age of the children or how well a teacher can learn the methods of Strauss and Lehtinen in a six-week training session based upon readings and instruction by other staff members.

Studies Using a Variety of Techniques

Unlike previous sections, which dealt with studies employing the programs and recommended training techniques of Frostig, Kephart, and Strauss and Lehtinen, this section discusses four studies that used a variety of techniques not specifically attributed to any one individual. Training techniques reported in these four studies are not necessarily different from those used by the above-mentioned practitioners, but the authors chose a variety of methods from the recommendations of different persons.

Lillie (1968) reported on the effectiveness of sixty-five motor-development lessons administered over a period of five months to a group of sixteen children of low socioeconomic status. Mean chronological age was 60.69 months, and mean IQ was 76.75. A kindergarten group, to control for the Hawthorne Effect, and a home control group were used for comparison.

Lillie adapted the Lincoln-Oseretsky Motor Development Scale (Sloan, 1955) into a gross motor and fine motor scale based on previous factor analytic studies (Fleishman and Ellison, 1962; Fleishman, Thomas, and Munroe, 1961; Guilford, 1958). Using these as pretest and posttest measures, he reported that on the fine motor score, the experimental group made significant gains over both control groups, and the kindergarten control group gained significantly more than the home control group. On the gross motor scale, no significant differences were found.

Unfortunately, the inclusion of a kindergarten group may not have controlled legitimately for Hawthorne Effect. No doubt it lessened the possibility of such error when compared to the home control group; but, since no attempt was made to change the traditional curriculum, and since there was no reported attempt to make the kindergarten group appear "experimental," it is uncertain whether results may be attributed to the Hawthorne Effect.

In addition, Lillie indicated that a language-development program was implemented concurrently with the motor-development program in the experimental classroom. Lillie rejected the possibility that this bias was operative since, using posttreatment IQ and Peabody Picture Vocabulary Test scores as well as pretreatment Lincoln-Oseretsky scores as covariates, there were still significant differences in the same direction among the groups. He concluded that there existed "little possibility that fine motor development was influenced by the same curriculum factors that influenced gains in language and IQ [since] differences in fine motor development are independent of development in language and IQ" [p. 807]. Although these results may rule out the specific effects of the language program, the Hawthorne Effect may still have been operating. The introduction of yet another structured program may have further differentiated the experimental group from the traditional nursery-school group and heightened the possibility of the Hawthorne Effect.

Ross (1969) randomly divided forty educable mentally retarded children of early elementary school age into an experimental and a control group. For twenty to twenty-five minutes, three times weekly, over a training period of six months, the experimental group was given motor training through basic games and sports. To the control group was administered a standard physical education program written for all special classes in California. The latter group also participated in another special project, which required that its subjects spend as much time out of the classroom as did the experimental group. During this time, the children were organized into groups not exceeding four in number.

Both the experimental and the control groups were given pre- and posttreatment with the Basic Skills Test, a measure of skills essential to games and sports, and eight items selected from the Brace Scale (Brace, 1927) for general motor ability. On pre- and posttest comparisons for the three groups, Ross found support for the training program's effectiveness. The experimental group made significant gains on both the Basic Skills Test and Basic Items Test, while the control group did not.

Although the author presented evidence for the high reliability of the Basic Skills Test and for the full administration of the Brace Items Test, there was no indication of the reliability or validity of the eight-item, shortened version of the latter. While the findings did at least confirm the hypothesis that the children would improve on the Basic Skills Test, it should be kept in mind that the skills purportedly improved were of a very specific nature. A posttest measure of the IQ scores used to equate the two groups would have provided data concerning the validity of generalizations about the training.

Chansky and Taylor (1964) studied the effects of training educable mentally retarded children (IQs ranging from 51 to 75) in the reproduction of block designs. The investigation centered upon three groups of thirteen subjects each, aged 8 to 11. For ten weeks, experimental group I received forty-five minutes to one hour a week of individualized instruction. Experimental group II differed only in that its children were trained in groups of an unspecified number. A third group, the control, received no special perceptual training. Pretest and posttest measures were taken for the Wechsler Intelligence Scale for Children, the Benton Visual Retention Test, and the California Achievement Test.

On the California Achievement Test, it was found that the two experimental groups consistently improved more than the control. Both experimental groups improved significantly in comparison with the control group on the subtests of Vocabulary and Reading, with experimental group II also improving significantly more than controls on Arithmetic Fundamentals and Spelling. There were no differences in improvement between experimental groups. On the Wechsler Intelligence Scale for Children, experimental group I improved significantly more than controls on Similarities, Vocabulary, Picture Arrangement, Block Design, Object Assembly, Verbal Scale, Performance Scale, and Full Scale. In a comparison of experimental group II and the controls the former gained significantly more on Similarities, Vocabulary, Verbal Scale, Performance Scale, and Full Scale. It was also found that experimental group I gained significantly more than did experimental group II on Block Design, Object Assembly, and the Performance Scale. On the Benton Visual Retention Test, each of the two experimental groups improved significantly over the controls but did not differ from one another.

The authors concluded that, due to an increase in organizational ability and discrimination in perceptual fields, the experimental subjects improved in achievement and intelligence test scores. They attributed differences between experimental groups on the Wechsler Intelligence Scale for Children to the greater amount of corrective feedback available to children receiving individualized instruction.

Aside from the limitations that Chansky and Taylor mentioned, i.e., lack of control for the nature of the retardation in the groups and curricula that differed for each of the groups, there was no attempt to control for the Hawthorne Effect. The positive results, therefore, may be attributable to the greater amount of attention that the experimental groups received.

To thirty-two institutionalized, profoundly retarded children Webb

(1970) administered a wide variety of activities devised to stimulate tactility, kinesthesia, vision, and audition. The seventeen males and fifteen females ranged from 2.5 to 17.5 years in age (median = 9 years, 11 months), and from 2 to 21 months (median = 8 months) on the Vineland Social Maturity Scale. Training for an hour a day, four days a week, ranged from five-and-a-half to ten-and-a-half months (median = 8 months).

Subjects were given pre- and posttests of the Vineland Social Maturity Scale and an index devised by the author to assess awareness, manipulation, movement, and posture. Webb reported consistent gains on both of those instruments. Although the author did not mention the computation of statistical tests of significance, she did state that there was a lack of statistical significance achieved on the two instruments. Webb blamed failure to find statistically significant improvement on a lack of refinement in the assessment instruments, but it was her clinical judgment that the children did show gains. The lack of a control group in this study left the possibility of Hawthorne Effect and did not control for the possibility that any gains shown may have been due to maturation. A median gain of two-and-a-half months on the Vineland Social Maturity Scale, for instance, could very likely be attributed to maturation.

Apart from the absence of a control group and other design limitations (e.g., no proven reliability or validity of the author's index, exceedingly wide age range for the subjects, and extremely wide maturity ranges as measured by the Vineland Social Maturity Scale), we must question Webb's conclusion that clinical improvement was shown. It remains to be told how she made this clinical judgment, which may well have been based upon the nonsignificant trends shown on the two measures that she herself called unrefined. If this is the case, then Webb was guilty first of discounting negative statistical evidence by blaming the measures used, then of using those very same instruments as bases for positive clinical judgments. Webb's study cannot be considered a valid evaluation of sensory-motor training. The statement that clinical analysis of behavior changes was more "meaningful" than statistical comparison demands proof.

STUDIES ON LEARNING DISABLED POPULATIONS

Studies Using Frostig's Program

In an experiment done by Lewis (1968), five second-grade youngsters were given the Frostig program in visual perception for three hours weekly over ten weeks. Pretests and posttests on the SRA reading test showed a gain significant at the .01 level, but pre- and posttests on the Developmental Test of Visual Perception showed a significant gain only on the subtest of eye-motor coordination.

A number of methodological weaknesses render unwarranted Lewis's opinion that the program helped to improve reading ability. First, it is unclear how eight children reading at the first-grade level on the SRA were reduced to five labelled "reading disabled" following administration of the Weschler Intelligence Scale for Children and the Frostig test. Lewis provided no information about cut-off scores used for inclusion. A second drawback in this study was the small sample size itself. Too, without the use of a control group, the experimenter could not control for the Hawthorne Effect, practice on test-taking, or other random treatments. Thus, it is impossible to assess effectiveness of the Frostig program on the basis of Lewis's study.

R. I. Cohen (1966) administered the Winterhaven Perceptual Forms Test and the Harsh-Soeberg Survey of Primary Reading Development to 818 first graders. She then divided the 145 low-scoring children (with a mean IQ of 98.1 on the Pintner-Cunningham Primary Test of Ability) into an experimental group which received Frostig training and a control group that received no treatment. Pre- and posttests of the above two measurements were given after ten weeks of twenty-minute-per-day training, and the subjects were retested after ten additional weeks of regular instruction. Cohen stated that both groups made large gains on the Winterhaven Perceptual Forms Test, but that greater gains were made by experimental subjects who, she asserted, also "maintained their lead over gains made by control subjects" [p. 62]. Although the control subjects scored significantly higher than the experimental group on the reading posttest, Cohen discounted the difference by noting that the control group scored almost significantly better than the experimental group on the pretest.

The manner in which Cohen analyzed data and reported her findings possibly allowed for serious error. For one thing, she listed no criteria for placement of subjects into the experimental or control group. Nor did she mention what kind of cut-off score, if any, was used to determine which subjects would be included and where. This nonreporting becomes crucial, since Cohen discounted differences between groups because of their great initial differences. How large were the initial differences? Should a covariance analysis have been used to control for pretest differences? Not only do these questions cast doubt on Cohen's findings of significant differences in perceptual improvement and nonsignificant differences in reading improvement, but the lack of control for Hawthorne Effect makes the former finding even more suspect.

A Study Using Getman's Program

Halgren (1961) reported on the effectiveness of a variety of visual-motor exercises, some recommended by Getman, given to an experimental group of ninth-grade boys five days a week for ten weeks. The control group received typical remedial reading instruction. Subjects in both groups were selected on the basis of a high school entrance examination on which they ranked at the bottom of their freshman class. The two groups were "homogeneously" formed by the assistant principal.

When unidentified IQ and reading tests were given as pre- and post-tests, it was found that the experimental group gained seven IQ points, whereas the control group gained none, and that the experimental group increased on the reading test from 6.1 to 7.5 years, whereas the control group gained only from 6.1 to 6.9 years.

Unfortunately, Halgren did not discuss any use of statistical procedures, so there is no way of knowing whether the differences in gain were significant. Missing information with respect to the assistant principal's equation of the two groups also leaves unanswered the extent to which they were equal before the experiment. Although it is known from the limited data reported that the two groups scored similarly on the reading test before treatment, it is not known how closely they were matched for IQ or age. In addition, the findings might appear more justified if the reader were told what specific IQ and reading tests were used. Finally, selection for participation on the basis of an entrance examination is a questionable procedure unless the instrument has proven reliability and validity. The author offered no data on this apparently homemade testing device. All these considerations obviously raise serious questions concerning the adequacy of the Halgren study.

A Study Using the Winter Haven Program

On the basis of the Bender Visual-Motor Gestalt Test (scored by the Koppitz System), Keim (1970) selected a group of seventy-four kindergarten children with visual-motor deficiencies. Half were then assigned to a group that received the Winter Haven Program (MacQuarrie, 1967) in addition to regular programming, while the other half formed a control group which received ordinary kindergarten training. A second control group consisted of children evidencing no visual-motor problems.

Pre- and posttest measures showed no significant differences between the groups on the Peabody Picture Vocabulary Test, the Stanford-Binet, or the Bender-Gestalt. In addition, on a posttest only (no pretest was mentioned), the group receiving the Winter Haven Program did not score significantly differently on any of the subtests of the Metropolitan Readiness Tests. Of possible significance, though, was Keim's report that teachers using the Winter Haven Program were dissatisfied with many of its aspects.

Although one may agree with Keim's conclusion that the Winter Haven Program did not produce anticipated results, methodological weaknesses and lack of information in his reporting indicate a need for caution in interpreting the findings. For example, Keim did not mention the basis for identification of the seventy-four children with supposed motor problems according to the Bender-Gestalt. Without cut-off scores, one would be unable to specify the extent of disability in those children. The range of Peabody Picture Vocabulary Test IQs for all subjects was reportedly between 80 and 130; but because no mean or median score was given on this measure, there was no clear description of the population studied.

Other flaws are also evident. Absent from this experiment was any control for the Hawthorne Effect. Though this is not so serious a problem when the experimental group does not show greater gains than the control groups, the omission of control for this source of error merits attention. With regard to the treatments given the groups, no mention was made of the program's length. Should one assume that the program went on for a whole school year, for half a year, or for a shorter period of time? Finally, use of the Bender-Gestalt test, even with the Koppitz adaptation for children, may be of questionable value for 5-year-old children. This study, then, adds no evidence for the positive effectiveness of visual-motor training; but, due to the numerous limitations noted above, neither does it necessarily provide negative evidence in a convincing manner.

Studies Using a Variety of Techniques

The effectiveness of various exercises designed to remediate visual-motor difficulties was discussed in an article by Khan (1968). During one summer, an optometrist administered numerous psychological measures to fifteen of the eighteen children admitted to a certain residential treatment center. (Two of the youngsters were excluded because they were psychotics, and the third was eliminated because of his age—5 years.) Of the fifteen children screened, eight were thought to have visual-motor problems. These eight, ranging in age from 7 to 11 years, possessed normal intelligence but exhibited severe emotional disturbances.

After ten weeks of training for one hour daily five days a week, pre- and posttest data were examined. The five subjects functioning at the first or early second-grade level (two to three years behind grade level) on the Durrell Analysis of Reading Difficulty pretest either did not improve or else gained less than half a grade. Three other children, only one to one-and-a-half years behind in reading according to the Stanford Achievement Test, raised their reading ability almost to the appropriate grade level. Khan also reported that in his clinical judgment there was a minimal amount of emotional improvement.

The small number of children studied, the lack of a control group, and the absence of any tests of statistical significance reflect major sources of error and severely limit any conclusions that might be drawn from this study. The author himself suggested that his experiment ought to be considered a pilot to more controlled investigations.

In another study, McCormick, Schnobrich, and Footlik (1969), assigned an entire first-grade population of an elementary school either to an experimental or to a control group, the two being equated for age, sex, IQ, and reading achievement as measured by the Metropolitan Achievement Tests, Primary I (Durost, 1959). The training program contained a number of exercises similar to those used by Barsch, Getman, Kephart, and others. Subjects were taught in groups of five for one hour daily, two days a week, over nine weeks.

When the children again took the Metropolitan Reading Test, there was no difference found between the experimental and control groups for the total first grade. However, a comparison of intellectually average children in the bottom 30 percent for initial reading achievement showed that subjects receiving the experimental program gained significantly more than did the control group. Because of these results, the authors concluded that their perceptual training program was beneficial for children below, though not at, grade level in reading.

As McCormick et al. admitted, because the control group received no treatment whatsoever, the "extra-attention factor" (Hawthorne Effect) was not controlled. In their estimation, this inequity posed no problem; they dismissed it by citing an earlier study (McCormick, Poetter, Schnobrich, and Footlik, 1968) which concluded that slight improvement in reading achievement was not significant for a control group receiving extra attention, whereas gain for the experimental group was significant. To discard operation of the Hawthorne Effect for this reason is not a sound research procedure. The Hawthorne Effect is an ambiguous and nebulous phenomenon, the exact nature of its process unsolved. It is precisely its vagueness that makes it so unpredictable, and supposed absence from one situation does not preclude its presence in another. While the effects of extra attention and/or low-pupil-teacher ratio may not always be present, they have been influencing factors in enough educational and psychological studies to demand control. In any investigation failing to control for the Hawthorne Effect, the conclusions always remain suspect.

STUDIES ON "DISADVANTAGED" POPULATIONS

A Study Using Frostig's Program

Following an eight-month training period, during which it was exposed for twenty-five minutes per school day to the sensory-motor and visual-perceptual training exercises of Frostig and Horne (1964), an experimental group of kindergarten children from an Office of Economic Opportunity target area scored significantly higher than did a control group on five of eight sections of the Metropolitan Reading Readiness Test (Hildreth, Griffiths, and McGauvran, 1965) and on the Eye Motor Coordination mean scaled score of Frostig's Developmental Test of Visual Perception.

Unfortunately, this study, done by Alley, Snider, Spencer, and Angell (1968), contained many sources of error. No mention was made of the basis for assignment to experimental- or control-group status. Compounding this problem was an apparent neglect to match the two groups on any variables, e.g., age or IQ. In fact, the limitations in a posttest-only design are accentuated even more because of this failure to equate the groups. In addition, since control-group activities were not described, it is unclear whether control subjects were given any amount of extra attention, or whether the Hawthorne Effect might have been operating. All these unanswered questions and limitations make it impossible to draw any conclusions regarding the Frostig program's effects on this population.

A Study Using Elkind's Program

Elkind and Deblinger (1969), applying Piaget's construct of decentration to the process of reading, investigated the effects of training in perceptual activity on the reading of second-grade, inner-city black children. The nonverbal exercises were designed to enable the youngsters "to explore, reorganize, schematize, transport, and anticipate perceptual configurations and arrays" [p. 13]. While the experimental subjects were involved with their exercises, a control group spent an equal amount of time on *The Bank Street Readers* (1966). Each group received its assigned training a half hour per day, three days a week, for fifteen weeks.

Pre- and postmeasures indicated that the experimental group increased significantly more than the control group on the Picture Integration Test of perceptual activity (Elkind, Koegler, and Go, 1964) and on the Word Recognition and Word Form sections of the California Achievement Tests (1957 ed., 1963 norms). The authors believed the results suggested that nonverbal training in perceptual activity increases certain aspects of reading achievement significantly more than does a traditional approach.

On account of some methodological limitations within this investigation, we must be cautious in interpreting its outcome. Elkind and Deblinger mentioned a greater discipline problem in the experimental group. This fact, coupled with a higher mortality rate in the experimental group (five experimental dropouts, as compared to one control dropout) due to "moves, illness, and incorrigibility," may mean that those children least likely to suceed, the "incorrigibles," were eliminated from the experimental group. In addition, it is important to note that the authors were the teachers for the groups, leaving open the possibility of experimenter bias. Elkind and Deblinger attempted to minimize the significance of this problem by stating that, since the experimental group did not do better than the control group on all the measured aspects of reading achievement, experimenter bias must not have been operating. The logic of this argument is indeed questionable. An experimenter need not bias *all* the measures in order to favor the experimental group or in order to eliminate significant differences that could have favored the control subjects.

Even if this study were fully sound from a methodological standpoint, it would still be presumptuous to conclude that perceptual training alone caused any differences. The experimental activities, while using the visual-perceptual modality, required a great deal of facility in dealing with conceptual and symbolic operations as well. They were of a different nature from the perceptual activities recommended by the advocates of Frostig, Getman, Kephart, and others.

STUDIES ON UNDIFFERENTIATED (NORMAL) POPULATIONS

Studies Using Kephart's Program

Ball and Edgar (1967), with thirty kindergarten children divided into an experimental group of fourteen and a control group of sixteen, carried out a well-controlled assessment of some of Kephart's suggested techniques

for developing laterality and body image. The experimental group received training approximately twenty minutes each day, five days a week,
for three-and-a-half months. Dependent variables, administered in a pretest versus posttest design, were a modification of Head's Eye, Hand, and
Ear Test (1925), Benton's test of right-left discrimination (1955), Benton's
test of finger localization ability (1959b), and a group intelligence test
(Pintner, Cunningham, and Durost, 1946). The first two tests measure
right-left discrimination ability, with Head's test requiring nonverbal responses only.

Results indicated that the application of some of Kephart's techniques
generalizes to right-left discrimination ability as measured by Head's
nonverbal test. Both groups gained to an essentially equal degree on the
finger localization test. No significant gains or differences between groups
were found for IQ or for the Benton test of right-left discrimination.

Although Ball and Edgar concluded that the results obtained on Head's
test "support the claim that generalization occurs from specific sensory-
motor training" [p. 391], it should be kept in mind that the ability measured by Head's test is nevertheless a very specific one. The fact that this
test is composed of imitative responses, and the fact that significant differences are lacking between the training and control groups on Benton's
verbal test of right-left discrimination, Benton's finger localization test,
and IQ, suggest the need for caution in interpreting these findings as
proof of highly generalized gains.

In another study (O'Connor, 1969), the entire first grade of an elementary school was divided into an experimental group which received
six months of training on Kephart-based techniques and a control group
which received physical education instruction. O'Connor assessed pretest
versus posttest performance on motor ability items from Carpenter (1942)
and Brace and Johnson, the Perceptual Forms Test, the Metropolitan
Readiness Test (pretest), the Metropolitan Achievement Test (posttest),
and posttest performance on lateral awareness and the Harris Test of
Lateral Dominance. He concluded that Kephart's techniques improve
physical motor performance and internal lateral awareness but do not
affect external lateral awareness, lateral preference, academic achievement, or the ability to draw geometric forms.

As O'Connor pointed out, the pupil-teacher ratios were vastly unequal
—ten to one for the experimental group and thirty to one for the control
group. Thus, there is no way of determining the extent to which significant or nonsignificant results were influenced by this difference. The
author also implied that experimental subjects received their training
from someone other than the regular classroom teacher, while the control
group engaged in its physical education program with the regular instructor. As so often happens, the Hawthorne Effect may not have been
controlled.

Studies Using a Variety of Techniques

Using kindergarten subjects, Jensen and King (1970) compared the effects on reading of three different kinds of visual-motor training: (a) tactile word tracing, (b) rearrangement of individual letters to form words, and (c) visual matching of word forms with one of four choices. Each subject was asked to read the words for which he had been trained during a training and testing period of about twenty-five minutes.

The authors found that tracing was significantly easier than matching, and matching was significantly easier than rearranging. On the reading task, they found no significant differences favoring either of the three types of training. Jensen and King therefore concluded that no one teaching method is best for all children and that instructional methods must be individually tailored for each child. They cautioned against accepting programs that claim superior results in reading achievement as the result of visual-motor training.

The lack of a control group deprived of visual-motor training makes it presumptuous to conclude from this study that visual-motor training does not improve reading performance. The authors' conclusion that individual training techniques should be adapted for children's particular learning styles is, for the most part, a valid one; but the fact that this conclusion was based upon a twenty-five-minute training and testing period weakens the argument. At any rate, the conclusion is logical in terms of developmental theory, particularly when we consider applying special teaching techniques to children with specific kinds of learning problems.

Another study (Gill, Herdtner, and Lough, 1968), using a population of 4.5-year-old children enrolled in a university laboratory school, assessed the effects of a program designed to establish body balance and spatial orientation via a variety of activities and equipment assigned for fifteen to twenty minutes per day. The nursery-school teacher randomly divided the children into an experimental group of fifteen subjects and a control group of thirteen, with general ability supposedly controlled. After an unspecified length of time, the authors concluded that the experimental group benefitted from its experimental treatment, as evidenced by scores on a modified version of Witkin's Rod-and-Frame Test (1962) and two of the five subtest scores on Frostig's Developmental Test of Visual Perception (Figure-Ground and Shape Constancy).

Gill et al., however, left uncontrolled so many sources of invalidity that their conclusion is untenable. Dictates of sound experimental research require that investigators assure the equality of experimental and control groups on relevant variables, especially when a posttest-only design is employed. Regarding this requirement, the only statement the reader can rely upon is that the teacher controlled for "general ability" while randomly assigning subjects. Not only did the experimenters have no control over the selection of the groups, but they also failed to mention what measures the teacher used in order assess general ability.

In addition, the report indicated no attempt at control for Hawthorne Effect. Upon request, control subjects, without instruction, were allowed to use the equipment available to the experimental group. Since such requests were rare, it must be concluded that the control group's treatment in no way equalled that of the experimental group in terms of extra attention.

From a statistical point of view, too, Gill et al. have drawn inappropriate conclusions. Analyzing the differences among the Nursery Experimental and Nursery Control (in addition to two other groups involved in another test not reported here), the experimenters, by means of analysis of variance, found four significant Fs out of six measures—the five subtests of Frostig's test and the modified Rod-and-Frame Test. Referring to a table showing the means of each of the four groups on the six measures, the authors pointed out that the experimental nursery group scored higher than did the other three groups on three of the four measures where Fs were significant.

Actually, the above analysis does not show the experimental group to be significantly better than the other three groups or, more importantly, than the nursery control group. Though the significant F in the analysis of variance indicates that all four groups significantly differed from one another in some way, it gives no clue as to which group or groups differed from which. Paired comparisons need to be performed as a further analysis in order to determine the sources and extent of differences. It is unwarranted to claim that the experimental program was a success by virtue of the fact that the experimental group had the highest mean score of the four groups compared. In fact, inclusion in the analysis of the two extra groups, totally irrelevant to the testing of the present hypothesis, may have been responsible for the significant Fs.

These methodological problems weaken the author's conclusion that "special directed experiences are clearly beneficial to perceptual development" [p. 1183].

RESEARCH NOT DEFINITIVE

Due to the faulty reporting and unsound methodological procedures of so many of the studies discussed in this chapter, the safest conclusion we can reach is that it is premature to draw any definitive conclusions regarding the efficacy of perceptual-motor training. It may aid the reader here to refer again to Tables 2 through 6 (pp. 181-87), which summarize each of the five sections presented in this chapter. Looking at the column for "Sources or Possible Sources of Error," it is apparent that, including the eleven studies criticized by Robbins and Glass (1969), only seven, or 17 percent of the forty-two studies were designed in such a manner that their findings can be taken seriously.[29] The other thirty-five studies either exhibited sources of error which invalidated the findings, or else contained so many flaws in reporting or handling the data that a very real possibility of sources of error was evident. The possible existence of sources of error may be considered every bit as serious as the real presence of error when the reader must decide whether to accept the findings and conclusions of a particular study. For example, when the experimental treatment group's progress may be owing to the fact that the Hawthorne Effect has been left uncontrolled, it is unwise to conclude that the experimental treatment has had a positive effect.

Without regard to possible or real sources of invalidity, the majority of the studies reported that experimental treatment was shown to be effective. As can be seen in the "Dependent Variables" column on Tables 3 through 6, which do not include the studies concerned with Delacato's program, thirty-nine of sixty-seven dependent variables under study, or 58 percent, were reported as being positively influenced. Reading only the authors' conclusions, one would probably decide that perceptual-motor training has a significant amount of empirical support. But, as previously mentioned, it must be remembered that only seven studies were so well designed that their findings need not be considered suspect.

Turning to these seven studies, it is obvious that even they do not provide satisfactory answers to questions about the value of perceptual-motor training. Two of the studies (O'Donnell and Eisenson, 1969; Robbins, 1966b) involved investigation of Delacato's procedures for neurological organization training. On the five dependent variables used in these two studies, no significant effects were evident due to the neurological training procedures. Variables under investigation ranged from specific skills such as creeping and crawling to more generalized, conceptual abilities measured by achievement tests. Although it is not ad-

---

[29] As noted earlier in this chapter, there is some evidence which could lead one to question the use of control for Hawthorne Effect as a criterion of sound experimental design (Cook, 1967). In order to allow for the possible nonexistence of the Hawthorne Effect, therefore, the thirty-five studies judged to be unsound were reassessed to determine how many were so judged solely on the basis of lack of control for Hawthorne Effect. This reassessment revealed that only three of the thirty-five (Lillie, 1968; McCormick et al., 1969; Talkington, 1968) would be considered sound if one were to ignore the variable of Hawthorne Effect. This only increased the total number of sound studies from seven to ten. Thus, not considering lack of control for Hawthorne Effect as a possible source of error, there were still only ten, or 24 percent, of the forty-two studies which could be considered well designed.

visable to refute the possible positive effects of the Delacato program on the basis of only two studies, we may conclude that to date Delacato's approach lacks supporting research evidence.

Four other methodologically sound studies, three using Kephart's approach and one assessing Frostig's program, dealt with mentally retarded populations. In contrast to the above two studies' negative conclusions about the Delacato method, these four investigative efforts reflected less agreement about the efficacy of perceptual-motor training. Exploring Kephart's techniques, one study (Alley and Carr, 1968), reported negative evidence on all five of the dependent variables: (a) motor abilities, (b) perceptual-motor abilities, (c) visual-motor retention, (d) visual-motor abilities, and (e) psycholinguistic abilities. On the other hand, two other studies (Edgar et al., 1969; Maloney et al., 1970) found positive effects, for the most part. Five dependent variables—motor development, language development, social development, perceptual-motor development, and body image—were improved by the Kephart program, while two others—adaptive behavior and finger localization—were not. The one study (Alley, 1968) concerned with Frostig's program found it to be ineffective in increasing scores on all five measures used.

The only other well-controlled experiment was that of Ball and Edgar (1967), who used Kephart's program with an unscreened kindergarten population. Kephart's program significantly increased the children's right-left discrimination ability, as evidenced by scores on a modified version of Head's nonverbal Eye, Hand, and Ear Test. No significant effects, however, were attributed to Kephart's program on Benton's more verbal right-left discrimination test (1955), Benton's test of finger localization ability (1959b), or a group intelligence test (Pintner et al., 1946).

Unfortunately, the above seven studies are the only ones that survive critical analysis. It is obvious that from these few studies little may be concluded concerning the effectiveness of perceptual-motor training, in general, let alone particular programs. The limited number of well-controlled studies prevents systematic and meaningful investigation of particular methods or populations.

Although the current state of research in perceptual-motor training is such that no conclusions or definitive statements can be made concerning its effects, a number of issues and thoughts do arise from the critical analysis of the forty-two studies in this chapter. If a discussion of these issues is presented, perhaps educators and psychologists presently involved in or contemplating future research may better conceptualize this field of study within a research framework.

Critics and advocates alike of perceptual-motor training have struggled with the problem of which dependent variable should be used to assess the effects of particular programs. Disagreement centers around the question of whether it is enough to show positive effects on specific motor or perceptual-motor abilities which may seem far removed from more academic and conceptual abilities, or whether achievement test scores or other measures of more conceptual skills need to be shown. Kephart, for instance, would opt for the former viewpoint, stating that certain non-academic abilities necessarily precede reading readiness. In this light, a study showing that perceptual-motor skills were increased by a particular method might provide sufficient evidence for its success and future use. Critics maintain, however, that perceptual-motor training programs, even if they were to improve perceptual-motor ability, would also need to show generalization or transfer of training to tasks involving higher thought processes.

Both points of view are valid as long as we keep in mind the element of time between training and measurement of the dependent variable or variables. Even if it is found in a particular study that perceptual-motor training has no effects on conceptual development, though it does increase perceptual-motor performance, the utility of such training procedures for advancing conceptual development should not be dismissed entirely. It may be that, given enough time, the subject who showed perceptual-motor improvement would then be primed to advance conceptually. The element of timing is an important, but heretofore neglected, consideration in the conduct and evaluation of studies. The child may be brought up to a level where he is perceptually ready, but this is no guarantee that he will automatically and immediately improve in academic achievement. He must further learn academic and more conceptual abilities if he is to improve in these areas also.

It is important not to discard perceptual-motor training as a teaching method if we find *immediately* after training that no improvement in conceptual abilities coincides with increased perceptual skills. The task of learning to read may be used as an example. Training in perceptual skills for a child who has never had them will not automatically increase reading skills. Once the child is perceptually ready, he may then learn to read. To expect progress in reading achievement to coincide with improvement in perceptual processing is not logical. The normal child must be maturationally ready before he takes on the task of reading. The non-reading child with a perceptual problem may, in addition, be even slower in learning to read and in building up concepts, since he may have to unlearn many false perceptions and any conceptions that he may already have constructed while living in an aberrant perceptual world.

Another aspect of timing, namely, the length of the experimental program, requires attention. In these studies, the amount of time devoted each day to the training program varied greatly, as did the duration of the program and the total amount of time invested. Tables 2–6 reveal that the total number of hours varied from .5 in one study (Jensen and King, 1970) to 290 in another (Kershner, 1968). Excluding from calculation these two extremes and the seven studies for which no total training time was given, the mean duration of experimental treatment for each of the remaining studies was about 31 hours. Since in one semester the average child will probably spend over 500 hours in school, 31 hours cannot be considered a very long period of time. It is therefore debatable whether a 31-hour training period for these studies allows for adequate assessment of the merits of any particular approach. Moreover, it is unlikely that those studies which lasted less than the mean number of hours have done justice to the perceptual-motor training techniques in question. The element of time must be more carefully considered in future investigations. The length of time spent in training should never be reported in such a way that it is not possible to calculate the total number of hours, as it was in seven of the thirty-one studies.

We must be careful in yet another way to give the experimental method a fair chance before we accept negative evidence. It is always possible that any particular individual's methods have been misused in a study. A hasty explanation resulting in a teacher's superficial knowledge of a particular approach could influence the accuracy with which she follows the special teaching method. In the studies of this chapter, the amount of or manner in which training was given to teachers was rarely reported. On the other hand, we should pragmatically consider the ease with which these special teaching techniques could be implemented in the public school. From this point of view, the teacher used in the experimental classroom should not be expected to have undergone an intensive course of study under Frostig, for instance, in order to use those techniques; but neither should she have only a superficial acquaintance with Frostig's approach gained through a cursory reading of the program manual.

Not only is there a need for better designed research, but also future researchers should be cautious with regard to the populations on which they test perceptual-motor training programs. Many studies have administered the experimental treatment to large numbers of children *en masse,* whether the youngsters were classified as normal, mentally retarded, reading disabled, or whatever. In research settings, scarcely any attempt has been made to apply perceptual-motor techniques to those children who are most likely to profit from them. If we accept a basic premise of learning disability theory—that children fail to learn for many different reasons—then approaches designed to ameliorate a specific area of deficit would not be appropriate for all children with learning disabilities. In other words, perceptual-motor exercises would probably be helpful for children who exhibit perceptual-motor deficits but not for youngsters who have difficulty learning for other reasons, e.g., slow language development.

It should also be mentioned that the efficacy studies in this chapter have usually failed to separate the effects of perceptual training from those of motor treatment, and studies on the effects of different kinds of perceptual or motor exercises are virtually nonexistent. Sometimes, for instance, authors claim to be training motor skills when, in fact, the lessons described also contain many visual exercises (e.g., Lillie, 1968; Ross, 1969). If positive results were found, it would be difficult to determine which factors influenced the outcome. Granted, in this youthful stage of perceptual-motor research, it may not be possible, or even fruitful, to separate precisely the various influences; but one should not ignore a perceptual- or motor-training component when it is conceivably a viable variable.

Structure is yet another factor which remains unanalyzed in most perceptual-motor training studies. When a perceptual-motor-based curriculum is introduced, hand in hand with it may go the variable of a structured school program. Still unsolved is the dilemma of how to keep separate the effects of perceptual-motor exercises per se from those of the structured, task-oriented classroom procedure. This methodological problem cannot always be resolved by the inclusion of a Hawthorne control group. The positive, or perhaps negative, contribution of the added structure which may be concomitant with a perceptual-motor program is at this point an unknown, though its possible influence should be watched for. Sometime in the future, when other more basic problems of the "does it work?" nature have been cleared up, the effects of structure can be sorted out.

At the beginning of this chapter, we stated that controlled research in perceptual-motor training has a very short history, compared to its long tradition of clinical support. Unhappily, the first attempts at experimental testing of these techniques have added little to our knowledge, owing to their multitude of methodological drawbacks. Nearly twenty-five years after clinically based, perceptual-motor exercises were presented by Strauss and Lehtinen, there is still a need for well-controlled, empirical evidence about these techniques. Perceptual-motor advocates must finally direct themselves to the challenges put to them by vociferous critics.

One recent example of perceptual-motor training criticism is a highly emotional attack launched by Mann (1970), who raised many serious questions and crucial issues to which theoreticians, researchers, and practitioners in the field must address themselves. Mann aptly remarked that perceptual training approaches are often based upon inadequate knowledge of what so-called perceptual tests really measure. Any number of perceptual, as well as nonperceptual, processes are required for response to items on these tests. It is also true that, *at this point in time,* investigators are unable to differentiate the perceptual process into its many components, contrary to what the labels of some subtests would have us believe (Olson, 1968). This does not necessarily mean, as Mann suggested, that researchers should abandon all hope of ever being able to identify perceptual process constituents. It merely reminds us that these tests are, for the most part, pioneering efforts which need to be considered as such by critics and advocates alike. Although there may be truth to Mann's contention that the perceptual-motor approach can easily become a fad, it is premature to accept his suggestions of returning to traditional methods of instruction in order to teach children with perceptual-motor problems. No evidence in the literature indicates that traditional methods have been successful in teaching children with these difficulties.

The article by Mann reflects growing concern over perceptual-motor training programs. In order to counter attack from their critics, the advocates of this approach must begin adequately controlled exploration of their methods. Pilot studies and studies purporting to be rigorous but containing questionable methodological procedures are useful only as hasty first attempts to supply practitioners with an indication of those methods that *may* be helpful. While on the surface such investigations may masquerade as research studies, they often hide their deficiencies under the aura of the term "research" and in many cases may be less trustworthy than well conceived "clinical" studies or case histories. The time has now come for highly controlled, systematic investigations concerning the effects of perceptual, motor, and perceptual-motor training.

Although no persuasive empirical evidence has been brought to the fore in support of perceptual-motor training, neither has there been solid negative evidence. Owing to the lack of satisfactory research studies with proper methodological controls, it is injudicious to decide wholeheartedly that perceptual-motor training deserves or does not deserve approval. The ultimate acceptance or rejection of these theorists and their procedures ought to depend upon systematic, empirical investigations yet to be done. This is not to imply the obsolescence of former theories or practices in perceptual-motor training. On the contrary, new experimentation may well find itself drawing upon, refining, and expanding ideas from the past. As Campbell and Stanley (1966) have stated:

> Experimentation . . . is not in itself viewed as a source of ideas necessarily contradictory to traditional wisdom. It is rather a refining process superimposed upon the probably valuable cumulations of wise practice. Advocacy of an experimental science of education thus does not imply adopting a position incompatible with traditional wisdom [p. 4].

CHAPTER 7

Attention
and
Motor Control

PATHOLOGICAL ATTENTION AND MOTOR CONTROL

Isolated instances of concern for the pathological aspects of attention may be found dating as far back as 1890 (Ribot, 1890), but it was not until the classic studies of Heinz Werner and Alfred A. Strauss in the late 1930s and early 1940s that a substantial effort in this area was evidenced in the literature. As noted in chapter 3, Werner and Strauss in their landmark studies lay the foundation from which the field of learning disabilities eventually evolved. The earlier chapter dealt with their ideas and concepts as a whole. This one emphasizes the significance of their work in the specific areas of attention and hyperactivity.

Studies on Attention by Werner and Strauss

In a series of experiments (Werner and Strauss, 1939b, 1940, 1941; Strauss and Werner, 1942), Werner and Strauss presented quasi-experimental evidence for the existence of problems of attention and distractibility in brain injured, mentally retarded children.

In the first study (Werner and Strauss, 1939b), mentally retarded children classified as exogenous (brain injured) or endogenous (nonbrain injured) were given the now-famous marble-board task in which each child was asked to copy the experimenter's pattern on his own board containing a 10-inch-square matrix of holes. The exogenous subjects constructed their copies in an incoherent manner contrasting to the endogenous children's global and systematic approach.

In the second study (Werner and Strauss, 1940), the above differences in performance between the two groups was investigated further, using a modified marble board on which the holes formed a definitely patterned background. In accordance with Werner and Strauss's expectations, 84 percent of the exogenous subjects' copying responses were to the background, while only 15 percent of the endogenous group's responses were so categorized. Evidently the brain injured subjects were unable to refrain from using the salient (patterned) background in their copies. Furthermore, on a test designed to assess the same ability in the visual modality (tachistoscopic presentation of cards containing a familiar object embedded in a clearly structured background), 75.5 percent of the responses of exogenous subjects were to the background alone, while only 13.9 percent of the endogenous children's responses were classified in this manner. In other words, when asked what they had just seen flashed before them for a brief period of time, the exogenous children were more likely to respond, "Wavy lines," rather than, "A cup." A decade later, Klapper and Werner (1950) used many psychological measurements, including the marble-board test and the visual figure-background test, to investigate the psychological characteristics of cerebral palsied children. Using a case-history approach with three sets of identical twins, each pair including one normal and one cerebral palsied child, Klapper and Werner presented further evidence that brain damage results in difficulties in differentiating figure from background in both the visual and tactual modalities.

Compared to endogenous children, brain injured subjects were overly responsive to the background on a multiple-choice variation of the aforementioned visual, tachistoscopic test in which the subject was required to choose from among three cards the one most like the test card (Werner and Strauss, 1941). In addition, identical results were obtained on a task for which the child first felt, but could not see, a geometric figure made of rounded thumbtacks raised above a background of flat thumbtacks and then drew what he thought he had just felt. Again, Werner and Strauss' exogenous children were more likely than endogenous subjects to generate responses reflecting an inability "to respond selectively to the appropriate elements of the field" [p. 248].

After noting the bizarre responses of brain injured children on tasks of concept formation, Strauss and Werner (1942) attributed these findings to the inability of such children to refrain from responding to inessential stimuli. To use Goldstein's (1939) term, they were displaying "forced responsiveness." Specifically, it was found that the exogenous children often formed groupings or categories on the basis of inessential or accidental details. More commonly than the endogenous child, the brain injured subject attended to insignificant details of the objects before him.

Critical Commentary on the Werner and Strauss Studies

With these germinal investigations and reports, Werner and Strauss were building a strong case for an attention deficit in the brain injured, mentally retarded child. Not until ten years after Werner and Strauss's presentation before the American Association on Mental Deficiency in 1939, did the first strongly negative criticism of their work reach print (Sarason, 1949). Sarason aptly pointed out the circularity of Werner and Strauss's criteria for including children in the exogenous group. If no positive neurological signs were apparent, a child was still considered brain damaged on the basis of behavioral characteristics and psychological tests results. In other words, if a child manifested a short attention span and was distractible and/or hyperactive, he was labeled exogenous. Any finding, then, that such a child differed from an endogenous child on the experimental variables testing the ability to attend to figure as opposed to background would not be proof of an attention deficit due to organicity.

The seriousness of this critique should not be taken lightly. Yet it should be noted that Sarason's criticism was directed at the possible misclassification of children as brain damaged and does not negate the fact that for Werner and Strauss there existed a group of children, truly brain injured or not, who did apparently manifest attention problems. Though agreeing with the criticisms forwarded by Sarason, we could not necessarily discount the possibility that damage to the central nervous system may in some cases result in attention deficits. As will soon be shown, the controversy still rages in current psychological and educational literature whether the presence of central nervous system damage can be used as an indicator of problems of attention and hyperactivity. The following section explores some of the more recent studies dealing with this argy-bargy.

Cruickshank's Figure-Background Studies

As mentioned in chapter 3, Cruickshank and collaborators used the studies of Werner and Strauss as a point of departure in order to assess abilities of attention with known brain damaged, cerebral palsied subjects whose IQs varied from retarded to above normal.

Based upon a series of studies in which Dolphin and Cruickshank replicated the results of Werner and Strauss with regard to visual figure-background ability (Dolphin and Cruickshank, 1951a), conceptual ability (Dolphin and Cruickshank, 1951b), visual-motor ability (Dolphin and Cruickshank, 1951c), and tactual motor ability (Dolphin and Cruickshank, 1952), Cruickshank, Bice, and Wallen (1957), and Cruickshank, Bice, Wallen, and Lynch (1965) conducted a lengthy and thorough investigation on a large number ($N = 325$) of cerebral palsied children matched with a group ($N = 111$) of nonhandicapped normal children. The cerebral palsied group was divided into subgroups of spastics ($N = 211$) and athetoids ($N = 114$).

Employing identical or modified versions of the tasks of Werner and Strauss, Cruickshank et al. (1965) found considerable evidence to indicate that cerebral palsied children, particularly those identified as spastics, have difficulties similar to those of Werner and Strauss's exogenous subjects in selectively distinguishing figure from background. When asked to draw on paper a design they had felt on a marble board, the spastics made significantly more reference to the background than did the normal controls. The athetoids did not differ significantly from the normals on this variable but did tend to be more distracted by the background than were the normal children.

On a modified version of the Werner and Strauss testing devices, which the authors called the Syracuse Visual Figure Background Test, Cruickshank et al. found that both groups of cerebral palsied children made significantly fewer correct identifications of tachistoscopic presentations of slides with figures embedded in a structured background than did the nonhandicapped children. Furthermore, the athetoids made significantly more correct choices than did the spastics. On this same test, the athetoids made significantly fewer background responses than did the spastic children. In this respect the former scored virtually the same as did the normals.

Thus, as noted in chapter 3, Cruickshank's contact with Werner and Strauss led him to investigate along the same lines as his former colleagues and to arrive at similar conclusions. With a population of children more definitely diagnosed for brain injury than the subjects of Werner and Strauss, Cruickshank et al. (1965) presented data that cerebral palsied children, especially spastics, manifest distractibility problems in both the tactual and visual modalities.

Other Figure-Ground Studies

Only a few other studies comparing brain injured and non-brain injured children have used tasks requiring the subject to separate figure from ground.

Presenting pictures containing hidden and nonhidden objects, Vegas and Frye (1963) compared a group of brain injured and a group of familial retardates matched for mental age. The children were tested on their abilities to name as many objects as possible in each picture. Although the number of responses was greater for familials, it was found that the brain injured children named a greater percentage of hidden objects than did the familial children. Apparently the children diagnosed as brain injured were more apt to be distracted by the background stimuli.

However, Rubin (1969) employed a paradigm quite similar to that of Werner and Strauss (1941) and found no evidence to support the latters' claim that mentally retarded, brain injured children manifest figure-background pathology. Her methodology significantly differed from that of Werner and Strauss in that her instructions to subjects primed them to give both a figure and a background response, since she had labeled both on a practice trial. In addition, on the basis of Rubin's data, we find that the only significant difference indicated by responses on the recognition test was that the brain damaged group chose more cards containing an incorrect figure and correct background. In spite of Rubin's disclaimer, this finding could be interpreted as giving at least partial support to the claims of Werner and Strauss.

Spivack (1963) presented a thoughtful and thorough critique of the figure-background studies performed by Werner and Strauss. He pointed out that on the typical figure-background slide, the background, due to the amount of space it takes up, is the dominant stimulus on the card. The brain damaged subject was asked to report what he saw after a brief tachistoscopic exposure. Even though he perceived the figure, he might be less sure of it than he was of the larger background; hence he might be disposed to report only the latter. Summarizing his own conclusions about figure-background research, Spivack referred to the above concern when he stated:

> Research in this area suggests that BI [brain injury] rather than retardation produces responses to background or intrusion of background in perception. The question remains open about whether such performance reflects a basic defect in BI Ss in the capacity to disregard background or the tendency for dominant aspects of complex stimuli to intrude upon or dampen out less dominant features, or whether the research techniques have allowed nonperceptual response characteristics to guide performance. It is of interest that Werner and Strauss (1941) raise the first two possibilities in the discussion of their series of experiments. The possibility of alternative explanations has not been pursued [p. 485].

The first two interpretations offered by Spivack and by Werner and Strauss, too, would be congruent with the hypothesis that brain injury tends to result in an attention deficit. Spivack's third alternative (that brain injured subjects may not respond when uncertain) poses a knotty problem which needs to be considered in future research. As noted above, it is not appropriate, as Rubin (1969) has done, to cue the subject that he is supposed to see a figure and a background, since this procedure may result in a heightened attention or set to see a figure. In other words, given the extra cue that a figure should be seen, the brain injured subject may attend more intently than he ordinarily would and thus would be able to perceive a figure that he could not see under other circumstances. Although this possibility, of course, is every bit as speculative as Spivack's third alternative, it should not be overlooked. An experiment that assesses for brain injured subjects the intercorrelations between figure-ground tasks and other tasks measuring attention would contribute to a solution of the dilemma. Highly positive correlations would lend credence to the interpretations of Werner and Strauss.

The work of the developmental psychologist, Kagan (1965a, 1965b, 1966), in fact, lends some support to the notion that the ability to attend to the figure rather than the ground is a correlate of the ability to attend in a more general way. Kagan developed a test, Matching Familiar Figures, to assess whether an individual's cognitive style was reflective or impulsive. When asked to match a test figure with the identical one from an array of stimuli, those who reflected before responding made fewer errors than did the fast responders, the impulsives. Kagan (1965a) not only found stable individual differences on this task but also discovered that impulsives responded more poorly than reflectives on tests of inductive reasoning (Kagan, Pearson, and Welch, 1966) and on a reading task (Kagan, 1965b).

In addition to administering the Matching Familiar Figures task, Kagan (1966) assessed the visual analysis skills of first-, second-, third-, and fourth-grade children by using a type of figure-ground test. Each child, after learning four nonsense syllables for four complex designs, was given a response-transfer task. On this second task, the experimenter presented the child with three illustrations, each one containing either the figure, background, or element component of the original complex designs. The child was then asked to supply the correct nonsense syllable for each of the cards. This transfer task consisted of two illustrations of each of the three components for each of the four designs, for a total of two dozen items. Kagan found that for the younger children the numbers of correct identifications of the figure and background components were nearly equal. As age increased, correct figure responses increased markedly, while correct background responses decreased. These data indicate that there may be a developmental increase in the amount of attention a child gives to figure as opposed to background.

Relevant to the discussion here are the intercorrelations that Kagan found between the above visual-analysis task and the Matching Familiar

Figures task for the third- and fourth-grade subjects. From the inter-correlation matrix, it can be seen that reflectivity correlated highly with figure responses and negatively with background responses. This was true for both boys and girls in grade three and for girls in grade four. The evidence gives partial support to the notion that the ability to attend (or not to respond impulsively) on one task is related to the ability to attend to figure rather than background on another task. It should be kept in mind that Kagan's subjects, coming from entire classroom populations, represented a normal distribution of attention abilities and that the visual-analysis task was different in nature from those employed by Werner and Strauss and Cruickshank. Kagan's data nevertheless offer suggestive evidence that a study of attention skills and figure-background skills in brain injured subjects may find a positive association between the two.

Until such a study is performed, however, one is obliged to consider experiments using dependent measures to assess attention with tasks not requiring figure-ground discrimination. Spivack's concern about the possible effects of dominant background or response characteristics cannot now be discounted; but if attention deficits could be demonstrated for brain injured children on non-figure-ground tasks, this would increase the likelihood that findings in the studies by Werner and Strauss (1939b, 1940, 1941), Dolphin and Cruickshank (1951a, 1951b, 1951c), Cruickshank, Bice, and Wallen (1957), and Cruickshank, Bice, Wallen, and Lynch (1965), and Vegas and Frye (1963) actually did demonstrate that brain injured children are unable to attend to the figure and are distracted by the background.

Studies of Attention in Brain Damaged Children

Using a variety of measures, the following studies have tested the original claim by Werner and Strauss that problems of attention and distractibility exist in neurologically impaired, mentally retarded children.

In one experiment, Rosvold (Rosvold et al., 1956) measured the sustained attention of brain damaged children and non-brain damaged controls. The test, called the Continuous Performance Test, is composed of two tasks, the first of which (the X Task) requires the child to press a response key every time an X appears among other letters presented every 0.92 seconds, and the second of which (the AX Task) asks the child to respond whenever an X appears after an A. Not only did the brain injured children make more errors on both tasks than did the controls, but the former also performed even more poorly on the complex AX Task requiring short-term memory.

Bensberg and Cantor (1957), with a format requiring a reaction-time response either to a simple task or to a discrimination task, found that a familial group responded faster on both measures than did a group of organic retardates. In addition, a significant interaction was found between etiology and task, the difference between the two groups being greater on the more complex discrimination task than on the simple task. Later in the experiment, the organic group was divided into a group with definite signs of brain injury and a group whose diagnoses were less certain. It was then found that the former subjects were slower than the familials on both tasks, with no evident interaction between etiology and task, while the latter group was not significantly different from the familials on either task, though the interaction effect was present. Bensberg and Cantor concluded that such curious findings denote the heterogeneity of the behavioral consequences of brain injury.

Cruse (1961) found similar results when he compared brain injured and familial retarded children matched for chronological and mental age on a reaction-time task under low and high distractible conditions. The latter condition consisted of a room with a mirror, balloons, and toys. Initially, no differences in reaction time were found between the two groups; but when Cruse divided the brain injured group into those with and those without a determinate brain injury diagnosis, he noted that brain injured children with definite etiologies were distracted more than either the group with less definite etiologies or the familials.

Schulman, Kaspar, and Throne (1965) conducted an extensive investigation of a number of variables as they related to brain damage in brain injured, mentally retarded children. Using cluster analyses of a number of behavioral and diagnostic measures, they concluded that distractibility was supported almost unequivocally as a correlate of neurological impairment. In addition, many different attention measures were intercorrelated. Before accepting these results, however, one should consider McGhie's (1969) contention that Schulman et al. used a questionable criterion in selecting their brain injured children: a low IQ was assumed to be indicative of brain injury and thus served as one of the criteria.

With the same measures of attention as those used by Schulman et al., along with those designed by Banta (1969), Fisher (1970) compared three groups of non-institutionalized brain damaged children with mental ages between 3 and 4.5 years to normal preschool children matched for mental age. The three groups of brain damaged children were (a) an educable group, (b) a trainable group with Down's Syndrome, and (c) a trainable group without Down's Syndrome. All three groups of brain inured subjects differed significantly from the normal preschoolers on a number of attention tasks, but no differences were found between the trainable children with and without Down's Syndrome. Yet Fisher did find evidence indicating that, with a decrease in IQ, the chance of an attention deficit increases. However, since Fisher stated without clarification that a child was classified as brain damaged if "there were reasonable indications of organic components present" [p. 504], it is difficult to gauge the significance of his findings. His reporting therefore leaves Fisher open to the same criticisms that have been directed at the work of Werner and Strauss.

Problems in the Diagnosis of Brain Injury

Criticisms of Fisher's and Schulman et al.'s criteria for determining brain injury point out major difficulties that are invariably at the heart of controversies concerning research attempts to determine whether any behavioral characteristics are a consequence of central nervous system damage. Disagreement prevails as to what criteria should be used in order to classify a subject as brain damaged. The possible inaccuracy of behavioral and physical measures and the crudeness of neurological tests themselves pose an ever-present threat to the validity of results in brain-behavior research. This controversy is no less prevalent in animal research, where the experimenter enjoys the freedom to inflict a lesion and to sacrifice his subjects in order to inspect the nature of the insult. The diagnosis of brain injury presents a problem to anyone who considers that the site of the lesion may be an important variable in terms of the consequent behavioral characteristics. Only the strictest anti-localizationist is free from this burden.

Except for those studies that have used the more explicit diagnostic category of cerebral palsy for the brain injured group, the experimenters have been stymied in their investigations because of a lack of refinement in their diagnostic instruments. Historically speaking, most of the problems that faced Werner and Strauss in 1940 with regard to the diagnosis of brain damage are still present today. Even though some progress has been made in brain localization, researchers who have continued to study and experiment in this area over the past three decades have encountered one pitfall after another in their attempted diagnosis of brain injury.

Attention in Non-Brain Injured Populations

Just as a shift from the terminology of "minimal brain damage" to "learning disabilities" occurred at least in part due to problems of diagnosing brain damage (chapters 3 and 4), so have these same difficulties within the field of mental retardation led to a shift in concern from equating problems of attention with the presence of brain injury. Many researchers and theoreticians coming to the fore in the study of attentional processes in the retarded either consciously or unconsciously have tended to ignore the variable of central nervous system damage. With little or no etiological consideration, the most recent research attributes attention deficits to retarded children. This may be the most healthy attitude to adopt at this point in time, owing to the difficulties in neurological diagnosis. Rather than wait for the refinement of neurological instruments, a more profitable strategy may be to proceed with the development of research and theories without considering the variable of brain injury. Retarded children, as a group, may evidence attention deficits which, doubtless, ought to be fully explored. However, it is an extremely important fact that a considerable body of evidence, dating back to the collaborative efforts of Werner and Strauss, indicates the existence of a certain subgroup (or perhaps subgroups) within mental retardation that manifests more attentional difficulties than does another subgroup. Whether this differentiation is based upon etiological factors such as brain injury, or even upon nonetiological factors, remains to be solved by further experimental exploration.

Research by Zeaman and House (House and Zeaman, 1959, 1960; Zeaman and House, 1963), currently perhaps the best known work in the field of attention in the mentally retarded, is a prime example of the disregard for such etiological factors as brain injury. The specific learning task used by Zeaman and House was a modification of the Wisconsin General Test Apparatus, originally designed by Harlow (1942) for use with monkeys. The task involves a simple two-choice, color-form discrimination. Comparing the backward learning curves of retarded and normal groups, the authors, in a series of studies, concluded that the two populations differed not in terms of the rate of learning but in terms of their abilities to attend to the relevant cues or dimensions. Specifically, the backward learning curves demonstrated that retarded children, over many trials, perform well below normals matched for mental age, but suddenly and rapidly rise from a chance level to one comparable to that evidenced by normals. This was interpreted as indicating that once the retarded subject has learned to attend to the variable or variables relevant for discrimination, he learns as rapidly as his normal counterpart. These findings led Zeaman and House to adopt the theoretical position that the ability to attend, rather than the ability to learn per se, is what characterizes the condition of retardation.

Strengthening the theory advanced by Zeaman and House is the work of other individuals (Follini, Sitkowski, and Stayton, 1969; Hagen and Huntsman, 1971; Sen and Clark, 1968a, 1968b), who have used a variety of tasks to demonstrate attention deficits in the retarded. In fact, Zeaman and House's conclusions about retardation come close to rivaling in popularity such statements as Ellis's (1963) theory that retardates have shorter and weaker reverberation of the neural circuits and Spitz's (1963) theory that retardates evidence a reduction in cortical satiation. One advantage of the Zeaman and House theory over these other two is that it does not attempt to attribute characteristics of retardation to faulty neurological mechanisms. Such a theory, built upon observable behavioral differences between retarded and normal subjects, lends itself more readily to refutation or confirmation than do those based upon unobservable or hypothesized cortical happenings.

As neurophysiological theory advances, it is safe to assume that all theorists such as Zeaman and House, who have based their positions upon behavioral evidence only, will have to recast their concepts to comply with neurological findings. When such findings are conclusive, the Zeaman and House theory, if it has not already been seriously threatened by negative evidence, will also have to be reconsidered in exploration of the distinct possibility that brain damaged retardates are more susceptible than familials and normals to attention deficits. Thus, while their theory probably never would have enjoyed its present popularity if Zeaman and House had had to struggle with the problems inherent in the consideration of neurological impairment, a reassessment of their research and conclusions will eventually be necessary.

Recent Theoretical Formulations Concerning Brain Injury

It would be unfair to leave the reader with the impression that since the time of Werner and Strauss no theoretical positions have developed with regard to attention deficits and brain damage; for in addition to the work done by those who have chosen not to deal with the issue of brain injury, some individuals have advanced theoretical constructs designed to link attention deficits to central nervous system insult. Both Eisenberg (1964) and Birch (Birch, Belmont, and Karp, 1965) borrowed the Pavlovian dichotomy of excitation-inhibition. The latter's formulations are more extensive than those of the former, and an attempt has been made to legitimize them through experimental efforts.

Birch et al. (1965) conducted a study in which brain injured adults were asked to estimate the loudness of two tones of equal intensity presented at a 3-second interval. Characteristically, brain damaged subjects underestimated the loudness of the second tone, while the non-brain injured controls either overestimated the second tone or judged the two tones to be equal. It is important to Birch's cortical-inhibition hypothesis that when the experimenters increased the interval between the two stimuli, the brain injured subjects' responses began to approximate those of the control group, until, at an interval of 9 seconds, the brain injured subjects were responding in the same manner as the normals did after the 3-second interval. Birch posited that at short intervals the first stimulus interfered with the brain injured subjects' responses to the second tone. The neural impulses that the second tone should have fired appeared to be inhibited by the neural impulses fired by the first. This prolonged inhibition in the brain damaged individual, Birch speculated, was the result either of defective recovery mechanisms in the reticulo-cortical system or of alterations in the rate of decay or spread of inhibition of local excitation. For Birch, therefore, the brain damaged organism's ability to attend was apparently impeded by prolonged cortical inhibition.

Attention in the Learning Disabled

With the exceptions of Eisenberg's and Birch's formulations, few theoretical advances with regard to brain injury and attention have been made since the early writings of Werner and Strauss. Since the field of learning disabilities grew out of the research and theoretical ideas concerned with the brain damaged, mentally retarded (chapter 3), it is not surprising that, as in the field of brain injury, there exists a paucity of research and theory in learning disabilities with regard to distractibility. To be sure, the psychological characteristics of distractibility and lack of attention attributed to mentally retarded, brain damaged children have also been ascribed to children identified as learning disabled. This transition no doubt was due to the fact that the first writings on children later to be described as learning disabled held firmly to the belief that such children evidenced definite neurological damage of some kind (hence, the term "minimally brain damaged"). No matter what the reason, however, the fact remains that while learning disabled children have been described as exceedingly distractible, very little research or theorization on the subject has been forthcoming.

The few experiments on attention include one by Campanelli (1970) that investigated the effects of brain damage in children of normal intelligence who, while they could not be strictly classified as minimally brain damaged or learning disabled, were epileptics. The Continuous Performance Test (Rosvold et al., 1956) was administered under two degrees of environmental illumination in order to vary the amount of stress on the subject. Involved in this experiment were three groups of subjects: (a) children with focal lesions in the cortex, (b) children with nonfocal lesions in the reticular formation, and (c) a normal control group. Under illumination of ten footcandles, both brain damaged groups performed comparably, and both made more errors than the normal group. With an illumination of zero footcandles, all three groups evidenced a decrement in performance, the children with damage to the reticular formation decreasing in level of performance much more than the other two groups. Campanelli concluded that brain damage results in attention problems and that if the site of the lesion is in the reticular formation system, the attention deficit will be even more drastic. As Campanelli noted, the findings of this experiment were in agreement with theoretical formulations concerning the role of the reticular formation in the regulation of attention (Hebb, 1955).

In another study Keogh and Donlon (1972) found boys with severe learning disabilities to be more impulsive on Kagan's cognitive tempo task than boys with moderate learning problems. The latter performed similarly to normals of other studies.

Without minimizing the importance of Campanelli's and Keogh and Donlon's studies, we must look at the work of the Soviet neuropsychologist, Luria (1961, 1966a, 1966b), in order to find any semblance of a systematic investigation of attention in the child who would be described as minimally brain injured or learning disabled. Luria presented such children (called cerebro-asthenic in the Soviet Union) with a task in which each child was asked to press a response key to a visual or auditory signal designated as positive, but not to press following the appearance of a stimulus designated as negative. In comparison to his normal peer, Luria's minimally brain damaged child became disorganized in his responses when the presentation rate was increased sufficiently. Either he did not respond at all, or else, unable to control his responses, he began to press the keys impulsively when neither the positive nor the negative stimulus was present. In the latter case, the accumulation of excitatory impulses became too great to inhibit. Luria thereby presented evidence that the child described as either minimally brain injured or learning disabled is distractible and has difficulty in inhibiting motor responses.

Studies of Hyperactivity

Luria's conclusions are relevant not only to a discussion of distractibility but also to the consideration of another behavioral characteristic attributed by Werner and Strauss to the exogenous mentally retarded child: hyperactivity. For Werner and Strauss, the implication was that lack of attention (distractibility) and an inordinate amount of motor activity or impulsiveness go hand in hand. Since the relationship between distractibility and hyperactivity had much apparent validity and clinical support, hyperactivity, like the other traits attributed to the brain injured, mentally retarded child by Werner and Strauss, came to be designated as a common characteristic of the child with learning disabilities. The posited association with an attention deficit points to its relevancy as a topic of concern here.

Using as a data base the classic studies of Werner and Strauss, Strauss and Lehtinen (1947) and Strauss and Kephart (1955) advanced the theory that a breakdown at any point or points in the organism's processing of a stimulus results in the release of an excess of energy when the organism reacts, yielding a hyperactive response. The authors claimed that since the brain injured child encounters many difficulties in the organization and processing of stimuli, he is highly susceptible to hyperactive behavior. While such a formulation neatly connected for Strauss and his colleagues the psychological characteristics of the brain injured child, this energy-reservoir concept has received much criticism from more current neurological thinking (Cromwell, Baumeister, and Hawkins, 1963).

Aside from criticisms concerning the theoretical rationale of Strauss and Werner with regard to hyperactivity, there is the more crucial consideration of whether brain injured children do, in fact, evidence an excess of motor activity. Since serious questions have arisen concerning the endogenous-exogenous dichotomy used by Werner and Strauss, the correlation of hyperactivity with brain injury must be scrutinized closely.

A series of studies (Cromwell and Foshee, 1960; Forehand and Baumeister, 1970; Gardner, Cromwell, and Foshee, 1959) have purported to offer negative evidence regarding the existence of hyperactivity in brain injured subjects. Using a ballistograph to record electronically the amplitude and frequency of movements, Gardner et al. (1959) found that organics and familials did not differ in activity level and that both groups decreased in activity as visual stimulation (trinkets and Christmas lights) was increased. This latter finding, the authors contended, ran counter to the prediction by Strauss that stimulation will result in hyperactivity in the brain injured child. Cromwell and Foshee (1960), with the same ballistograph apparatus, also found that visual stimulation did not increase activity or hinder performance on a card-sorting task, either for organics or for familials. Forehand and Baumeister (1970) presented evidence that severely retarded individuals from a variety of diagnostic categories decreased in activity under high auditory-visual stimulation, auditory stimulation alone, and visual stimulation alone. Only under reduced auditory-visual stimulation did the subjects increase in activity.

At first glance, the above studies appear to present convincing data contrary to that recorded by Strauss et al. It should be noted, though, that these studies included adult retardates in their populations, whereas the work of Strauss dealt with brain injured children. Even if this obvious and important discrepancy is ignored, findings in these studies may be interpreted as being consonant with Strauss's hypothesis. In all the studies, each subject was placed in a chamber or in a space enclosed on three sides by screens, so that he was tested in an environment quite similar to the cubicles which Strauss and Lehtinen (1947) and Cruickshank et al. (1961) recommended for reducing environmental stimulation. This experimental situation was no doubt more stimulus-free than the open wards to which subjects were accustomed. Following the rationale of Strauss, any increase in stimulation such as lights and trinkets should result in the subject's attention to these objects, and such attention should result in decreased motor activity. By using a relatively stimulus-free experimental environment, these studies placed the brain injured subject in a situation in which he was able to function as does a familial subject in attending to the stimuli presented. Thus, the studies do not categorically negate the concepts of Strauss and, in fact, may support them.

On the basis of the above considerations, it is impossible to judge the claim that brain damaged, mentally retarded children exhibit hyperactivity. Since the literature yields little in the way of systematic experimentation on this subject, there is a void of research data upon which to rely. As was the case with attention, conclusive experiments investigating the presence of hyperactivity in the mentally retarded, brain injured child remain to be done.

Survey studies using hyperactivity as the independent variable have not reached definite conclusions either. Numerous investigators (W. W. Anderson, 1963; Ingram, 1956; Laufer, Denhoff, and Solomons, 1957; Preston, 1956) have concluded, as did Pasamanick,Lilienfeld, and Rogers (1956) that a high incidence of prenatal and paranatal complications (possible causes of brain injury) is associated with hyperactivity in children. Owing to the lack of control groups, these studies have been criticized by Minde, Webb, and Sykes (1968), who cited numerous investigations which found no such relationship. Reporting upon their own study, Minde et al. said they found no evidence that hyperactivity in the child of normal intelligence was associated with complications of pregnancy or delivery. Complicating their data, though, was their experimental sample's exceedingly high drop-out rate of 41 percent. It is obvious that a chaotic state exists in the literature dealing with attempts to determine whether hyperactivity is the consequence of brain damage in children of retarded or normal intelligence. Again, as was true with the psychological characteristic of attention, at the crux of this dilemma is the diagnosis of brain injury.

In another study by Minde and his associates evidence was found contrary to the general notion that hyperactivity and its concomitant problems disappear with age (Minde, Lewin, Weiss, Lavigueur, Douglas, and Sykes, 1971). They found that children of normal intelligence who had been referred four years earlier were still behavior problems and academic failures at twelve years of age.

In addition to the confusion that surrounds the diagnosis of brain injury, the problem of measuring motor activity must be solved before any definitive conclusions can be reached. In an extensive review, Cromwell et al. (1963) highlighted this dilemma by noting from the results of a number of investigations that "activity level should not be viewed as a single or homogeneous phenomenon" [p. 639]. As the authors mentioned, there are different kinds of motor activity and an even greater number of possible methods for measuring them. The evidence collected so far indicates that many of these measures do not correlate very highly with one another. Certainly the prudent researcher and theoretician concerned with hyperactivity will have to be aware of this issue.

Relevant to the concern about methods of measurement are the findings of Pope (1970). In a study of 7- to 11-year-old children diagnosed as minimally brain injured, she found that the subjects did not differ from controls with regard to total motor activity measured by instruments attached to the wrist and arm but did engage in more locomotor activity as determined by the instrument attached to the leg. When asked to perform a difficult task, the experimental children also evidenced more total activity and locomotor activity than did the controls. Pope's study represented a step forward in research on hyperactivity because it assessed various aspects of motor activity instead of relying upon gross and undifferentiated measures. While the results of one study do not establish a firm base upon which conclusions may be built, Pope's well-conceived research does present evidence to support the notion that children who might be categorized as minimally brain injured or learning disabled exhibit an excess of certain kinds of motor activity in certain kinds of situations.

The Relationship Between Hyperactivity and Distractibility

Turning to the assumption by Strauss and his colleagues that hyperactivity and lack of attention are related, we find fewer investigations of this relationship than of either characteristic alone. Evidence for the association of the two comes from the work of Kagan and his colleagues (Kagan, 1966; Kagan and Moss, 1962; Kagan, Rosman, Day, Albert, and Phillips, 1964) who have worked primarily with normal rather than with pathological populations of children. Kagan (1966) reported that on a study of 7- to 10-year-old boys those who were more analytic (i.e., paused to consider alternative conceptual groupings on a conceptual style test), according to impressionistic observation, were "less likely to display task-irrelevant gross motor behavior on the playground or in a restrictive laboratory setting" [p. 500].

More objective evidence for the association between hyperactivity and lack of attention comes from the Fels longitudinal study's finding that hyperactive behavior in children from 3 to 6 years of age was inversely correlated with involvement in intellectual activity during adolescence and adulthood (Kagan and Moss, 1962). Kagan et al. (1964) also found that a boy rated as hyperactive between ages 4 and 8 is unlikely to use analytic concepts at age 10. Kagan noted, too, that Schaefer and Bayley's (1963) classic longitudinal study determined that hyperactive infants tested later at ages 5 and 6 were inattentive to intellectual problems. These developmental studies not only present evidence for the relationship of hyperactivity and attention deficit, but also strongly suggest that overactive behavior in infancy and early childhood is the forerunner of later problems in concentration and attention. In addition, Harrison and Nadelman (1972) found black preschoolers who were reflective on Kagan's task were also better able to inhibit motor movement than impulsives.

Concerning the relationship between inattention and hyperactivity and their presence in the brain injured child, we have already mentioned the theoretical formulations of Strauss and Luria. Using some of the same concepts Luria, Eisenberg, and Birch had developed, Dykman (Dykman, Walls, Suzuki, Ackerman, and Peters, 1970) advanced some constructs to deal with this relationship in learning disabled youngsters. Crucial to the formulations of Dykman is a consideration of the reticular formation, a system often thought to be involved in attention and inhibition (Lindsley, 1951; Samuels, 1959). Dykman speculated that damage to the brain may result in diffuse cortical arousal because of defective cortical inhibitory networks. The neural excitation essential to learning is diverged to other brain structures of low excitatory threshold, such as the extrapyramidal motor system. In other words, hyperactivity results. Dykman therefore posited a reciprocal relationship between motor restlessness and the neural arousal necessary for concentration and attention, with interference to reciprocal inhibition resulting in a failure to suppress irrelevant neural excitation. It was hypothesized that brain injury upsets the reciprocal inhibition capabilities of the damaged organism.

While the studies and writings of the above researchers and theoreticians with regard to hyperactivity are important and, in some cases, exciting for their ingenuity, the body of data they have generated remains disconnected and enigmatic. As is true for attention, knowledge regarding hyperactivity and its many facets has not been advanced much since the work of Werner and Strauss. The newer field of learning disabilities, in particular, is almost devoid of research studies. This circumstance is even more prevalent in the study of hyperactivity, which has tended to be ignored by psychologists, because it involves motoric responses. On the other hand, attention has received more regard, because it is thought to be more of a central process and to involve higher thought processes. In fact, whenever the two are considered together, hyperactivity is often subsumed under the definition of attention. Only rarely is attention to an object defined in motoric terms. In this respect, it will be interesting in the coming years to observe the impact of the Soviet psychologists and neuropsychologists (e.g., Konorski, 1967; Luria, 1961, 1966a, 1966b; Sokolov, 1963; Zeigarnick, 1965) who have been more interested than Western investigators in the study of motor behavior. Since the early 1960s, their work has been slowly integrated into the mainstream of American psychology (White, 1970); and the beginnings of its influence in the field of learning disabilities may be observed in the work of such people as Dykman et al. (1970), as discussed earlier.

Educational and Psychological Significance of Attention and Motor Control

With regard to the present status of knowledge concerning attention deficits and hyperactivity, while the exact psychological processes involved, the cause or causes of each, and the exact interrelationships between the two are still a mystery, the numbers of research studies and clinical observations reported to date leave little doubt about the existence of children who evidence a short attention span or hyperactivity. Whether these characteristics may interfere with the learning abilities of the child is a question which has received some attention.

A number of studies indicate that the ability to attend to the task at hand is necessary, or at least related, to various facets of the child's academic achievement. Noting in interviews that academically underachieving adolescent boys frequently complained of problems in concentration, Silverman, Davids, and Andrews (1963) decided to compare the boys' ability to withstand distraction to that of a group of academic achievers. The experimental test of attention was that devised by Stroop (1935), requiring the subject first to identify the colors of colored rectangles and then to name the colors in which color-name words were printed (e.g., "red" printed in blue). The second part of Stroop's test, involving the potential-distractor task, required the child to attend to the hue but not to the name. Silverman et al. found that the underachievers not only were slower on the first and second tasks, but also made more errors than did the achievers on the second task. When the differences in rate on the first task were controlled, the underachievers also evidenced more distraction on the second task by taking longer to respond.

Lahaderne (1968) conducted a study using four sixth-grade classrooms for examining whether attention is related to attitudes toward school and teachers, and/or to IQ and academic achievement. Over a three-month period, for a total of nine hours in each of four classrooms, attention was assessed by direct observation of pupils in the classroom, using a modified version of the Jackson-Hudgins Observation Schedule (Jackson and Hudgins, 1965). Attitudes toward school were determined by the Student Opinion Poll II (Jackson and Getzels, 1959). The Scott-Foresman Basic Reading Test and Stanford Achievement Test were used to calculate academic achievement, while the Kuhlman-Anderson Intelligence Test was used to measure IQ.

Although almost no relationship was found between student attitudes and attention ratings, significant correlations were found between attention and various aspects of achievement and between attention and IQ. A regression analysis resulted in evidence of a singular effect of attention on achievement rather than an effect of attention on achievement due to the strong association between attention and IQ. These results led to the important conclusion that attention in school is a cognitively based behavior, not dependent upon the child's attitudes toward the school situation. Because the data of Lahaderne are correlational, no causal relationships may be inferred; but the results lend some support to the notion that attention is a significant ability in terms of classroom functioning.

Also using correlational techniques, Maccoby, Dowley, Hagen, and Degerman (1965) investigated the relationship between activity level and inhibition of motor movement and IQ in normal preschoolers. Previous attempts to determine relationships between activity level and intelligence or cognitive ability have resulted in contradictory findings. Some experimenters (Murphy, 1962; Sontag, Baker, and Nelson, 1958; and Witkin, Dyk, Faterson, Goodenough, and Karp, 1962) have found a positive relationship, while others (Cromwell, Palk and Foshee 1961; Grinsted, 1939; and Kagan, Moss, and Sigel, 1963) have found a negative one. Referring to these contradictory results, Maccoby et al. stated that the relationship between activity and intellectual performance is a function both of the particular situation in which activity level is assessed and of the particular kind of activity being considered. They noted that those studies assessing activity level in a problem-solving situation resulted in negative associations between activity and IQ. Thus, in situations where it may be assumed that the restriction of activity is necessary for problem solving, there is evidence that those children who are hyperactive tend to have lower IQs. In accordance with the above conclusions, Maccoby et al. found that the ability to inhibit movement in structured tasks was positively associated with measures of intellectual ability, whereas general activity scores in a free-play environment were not.

While the above studies dealt with the relationship between attention and general indicators of achievement and intelligence, other research (Staats, 1968; Staats, Brewer, and Gross, 1970), analyzing the behavior of children in terms of stimulus-response mechanisms and learning principles, has explored the role of attention in the acquisition of specific reading skills. In a publication that culminated nearly a decade of research, Staats et al. concluded that attention is an important variable in the early stages of learning to read. One of their experiments is particularly relevant to this point. Within a behavior modification framework, preschool children were taught by reinforcement to learn to read the letters of the alphabet, starting with the letter A and proceeding to Z.

Plotting the learning curves of the children, Staats et al. found that, for those children who successfully completed the alphabet, the first letters required a greater number of learning trials than did the latter ones. Too, there was a gradual decrease in the number of learning trials needed for acquisition of a letter as the children progressed from A to Z. The crucial finding was that the difference in the learning rate of those children who learned to read and those who did not occurred primarily at the beginning letters, the latter children requiring many more learning trials for the initial letters. Staats, in a previous investigation (1968), had found that the attainment of an alphabet-reading repertoire in children is characterized by a learning-how-to-learn process. Referring to this finding and the above-mentioned difference between the fast and slow learners, Staats et al. concluded that attention is important in the early stages of alphabet learning. In other words, attention appeared to be an important factor accounting for the difference between those children who learned the alphabet and those who did not. The slow learners did not learn to direct their attention to the task at hand.

Although Staats et al. did not mention it, their data and conclusions were similar to those in the work of Zeaman and House (1963), cited previously. From backward learning curves, Zeaman and House determined that retarded children, when compared to normals, learned at a much slower rate in the first trials of a two-choice discrimination task but, once attending to the relevant cues, accelerated quickly to a level comparable to that achieved by normals.

The above studies have shown that attention is no doubt an important variable in the learning of academic subject matter and in scoring high on intelligence tests (a strong predictor of classroom achievement). Attention has also been considered an important factor by researchers and theoreticians interested in the conceptual development of children. For example, Wohlwill (1962) stated that while the ability to attend to relevant information is not fully developed at the early, perceptual stages of development, it represents a *sine qua non* of conceptual functions; the formation of conceptual classes clearly requires the systematic, selective abstraction of relevant . . . from irrelevant information. The same is true in the realm of logical inference, deductive reasoning, mathematical problem solving, and other such manifestations of symbolically mediated behavior [p. 86].

Wohlwill suggested further that the Piagetian task of conservation may also involve attentional processes, since the individual must ignore irrelevant changes in the stimulus and select one invariant element upon which to focus.

Whereas Wohlwill stressed the function of selective attention in conceptual development while minimizing its importance in perceptual development, numerous researchers and theoreticians have outlined a major role for attention in perceptual development. Gibson (1963, 1969; Gibson and Walk, 1960), for example, relied heavily upon attentional processes in her theory of perceptual development in infants and young children. Both in her classic "visual cliff" studies of depth perception in animals and infants and her studies concerned with the perception of letters, Gibson presented evidence indicating that in order to distinguish one object from another, one must be aware of its distinguishing features. With regard to the perceptual learning of letters, Gibson, like Staats, suggested that attention is a crucial ability. While Staats presented attention in the context of a learning theory approach to the discrimination of letters, and Gibson in her extensive theoretical formulations considered attention in the more specific process of the discrimination of distinctive features of letters, both emphasize the importance of the child's ability to focus his attention during the learning process.

Another major perceptual-development theorist, Fantz (1966), stressed the importance of selective attention in infancy to perceptual development and later intellectual pursuits. By selectively attending to certain visual patterns instead of others, the infant is forming the bases from which he can later come to recognize and differentiate objects. According to Fantz, by the third month of life the infant is capable of decreasing his attention to those patterns which are familiar, while increasing his attention to those which are novel. Fantz theorized that this change and others give "a means for perceptual learning and familiarization with the environment; they prepare the infant for more active exploration and manipulation of the environment" (p. 171).

The Training of Attention and Motor Control

The studies and theories considered in the previous section add empirical and theoretical support to the intuitive conclusion that attention and control of motor activity are exceedingly important for intellectual development. Numerous investigators, interested in both abnormal and normal development in children, have concluded that these attentional abilities are a necessary prerequisite for other kinds of learning. Theorists of child development have included attention as an integral part of human conceptualizations.

The overwhelming concern for the development of attention in the child leads to important educational considerations. If the educator and psychologist accept the position that attention and the control of motor activity are critical components of learning, then they must construct means for engendering attentional skills in the distractible and hyperactive child. One need not be concerned here with the causal factors involved in problems of attention and motor activity. Although etiological questions might be fruitful in future research, the educator and psychologist need right now to be able to deal with distractible and hyperactive children in an educational setting. The important point is that children of both retarded and normal intelligence evidence attention and motor-control problems that contribute to their learning deficits. Regardless of etiology, then, there are children in need of help with attentional and motor-control skills.

In an effort to make theory relevant to classroom procedure, Cruickshank and his associates (Cruickshank, Bentzen, Ratzeburg, and Tannhauser, 1961) from 1957 through 1959 conducted a demonstration-pilot study designed to explore, within a research framework, the educational procedures recommended by Strauss and Lehtinen (1947) for brain injured children. The four basic elements of this program were (a) reduced environmental stimuli, (b) reduced space, (c) a structured school program and life plan, and (d) an increase in the stimulus value of the teaching materials.

Cruickshank was acquainted through his own studies with cerebral palsied children of normal intelligence (Cruickshank et al., 1957) and was aware of the increasing concern for nonretarded children who were evidencing problems of distractibility and hyperactivity. For this study, he adapted the Strauss-Lehtinen method for children of normal and nearnormal intelligence. While many of the children manifested positive signs of brain injury, this did not become the criterion for inclusion in the study. Instead, hyperactive and distractible children, with or without the diagnosis of brain damage, were used as subjects. The employment of these criteria circumvented the problems associated with diagnosis of brain injury and insured that children included in the program were appropriate for the educational procedures.

At the end of a year, after comparing the experimental group receiving the structured program to the control group receiving the traditional special-class curriculum, Cruickshank et al. indicated that the former had made significant improvement on six of ten scoring categories of the Bender-Gestalt; on the number of correct figures of the Syracuse Visual Figure Background Test; and on the ability to withstand distraction from background stimuli on the latter test. However, no significant differences were found between the two groups with regard to IQ, as measured by the Stanford-Binet and the Goodenough Intelligence Test, or with regard to social development, as measured by the Vineland Scale of Social Maturity. It was not possible to evaluate academic achievement for the two groups, since a large number of the children were not able to perform on all or part of the achievement pretest due to a combination of reading and distractibility problems.

In 1959, a year after the demonstration program ended, a follow-up study was conducted. During the twelve-month interim between these studies, none of the children from either the experimental or control group was in a classroom with a physical environment similar to that of the experimental group in the original program. Nor was there any attempt by the teachers to continue the highly structured curriculum of the project. From the follow-up data, it was found that the experimental subjects had lost the advantages they gained during the demonstration project.

Thus, in this first pilot effort to test the Strauss and Lehtinen procedures recommended for reducing the distractibility and hyperactivity of children, the results indicated only moderate success. It should be kept in mind, however, that the reduction of gains made by the experimental subjects, once they returned to regular classroom conditions, is not an unusual finding. Similar results frequently have been reported in research on the effects of compensatory preschool programs. Loss of gains may merely indicate that, unless the experimental treatment is sustained over time (in this case, longer than a year), the child's return to an environment not designed to deal with his hyperactivity and distractibility will erase any progress he may have made. The diminution of gains after a year's return to a less structured classroom does not negate the possible benefits of the more structured, experimental environment and curriculum. Nor does the lack of control for Hawthorne Effect necessarily negate the positive findings, although it does discourage unqualified acceptance of the results.

We must remember, however, that the Cruickshank study, the first attempt to test the hypotheses of Strauss and Lehtinen, was designed as a demonstration-pilot project. The authors were well aware of the limitations of attempting to do research within a public school setting in which the restraints of an established structure and organization are present. In spite of these limitations on controlled research, it may still be concluded that Cruickshank et al. offered some suggestive evidence that the Strauss and Lehtinen principles of reduced environmental stimulation and a structured program are beneficial for hyperactive and brain injured children. Since the results of this study should be considered within the appropriate context of a demonstration-pilot study, any conclusions or generalizations must be formulated with caution.

Although a pilot study by nature, the Cruickshank et al. investigation is by far the most thorough assessment of the Strauss-Lehtinen-Cruickshank teaching procedures. The literature reveals that no other investigators have carried out such an extensive research project on this subject. Using Strauss-Lehtinen-Cruickshank procedures, Frey (1961) found significant differences in favor of the program but his study contained even more methodological problems than that of Cruickshank et al.

Attempting to delineate the differences in reading skills between brain injured and non-brain injured children of normal and near-normal intelligence, Frey compared a group of each, matching for chronological age and IQ on a number of reading tests. He found, surprisingly, that the brain injured group was significantly superior to the non-brain injured group on almost all of the many reading measures. In an effort to account for this finding, Frey mentioned the fact that while the non-brain injured subjects attended a regular class or a typical special-education class, the brain injured children were enrolled in a classroom using a program based on the methods of Strauss, Lehtinen, and Cruickshank. Because of its post hoc nature, however, this explanation is questionable. The experimental design was not constructed to allow for such a conclusion. Two factors cause us to question the conclusion that this study offered evidence in favor of the Strauss-Lehtinen-Cruickshank program: the lack of control for Hawthorne Effect and the assumption we would have to make that the two groups were equal on the reading measures before the start of the experimental program. Frey's data are only suggestive of success with the methods employed.

The use of cubicles, another recommendation in the procedures of Strauss, Lehtinen, and Cruickshank, has also been the object of isolated investigation (Rost and Charles, 1967; Shores and Haubrich, 1969). For one semester, Rost and Charles conducted a study with brain injured and hyperactive children. Using the Wechsler Intelligence Scale for Children and the Wide-Range Achievement Test on a pretest versus posttest basis, the experimenters found no significant differences between the experimental group using the cubicles and the control group not using them. As possible explanations for these findings, Rost and Charles mentioned: (a) the brevity of the study (one semester), (b) uncontrolled teacher attitudes, (c) pupil problems unrelated to the experiment, and (d) similar factors. While any one of these is a legitimate explanation, brevity would seem to be the most crucial. The others are inherent factors in practically all educational research of this nature. Additional investigations of the above findings over a longer treatment period are needed before we could conclude with assurance that cubicle use alone is not beneficial for the improvement of intelligence and academic achievement.

It is important to keep in mind the fact that the study by Rost and Charles was testing an hypothesis not even held by Strauss and Lehtinen or by Cruickshank. Using cubicles in order to aid a child's concentration does not assure that he will automatically and immediately improve on the more conceptual ability measures such as intelligence and achievement. The cubicles are only a part of a total program designed to allow the hyperactive child to attend to the task at hand. Although examining one variable at a time to determine just why a program works is an appropriate research strategy, merely placing children in cubicles "for silent reading and workbook assignments" (Rost and Charles, p. 125) and then noting the effects on intelligence and achievement tests does not afford a reasonable evaluation of the total Strauss-Lehtinen-Cruickshank program. Neither does it assess adequately the usefulness of the cubicles, since they were not an integral part of the curriculum. In other words, the cubicles may actually have been effective in promoting attention and concentration, but the rest of the academic program may not have been strong or long enough to improve achievement. The control of attention and hyperactivity, like the training of perceptual-motor skills (chapter 6), may take some time, which means that immediate academic improvement should not be expected. Once the child is able to attend, the effectiveness of presenting academic material to him may be assessed.

Partial evidence favoring the cubicle as an attention primer comes from an experiment performed by Shores and Haubrich (1969). Using a small group of hyperactive and distractible children with IQs in the 80s and 90s, Shores and Haubrich placed the subjects in and out of cubicles for short periods of time, while measuring reading rates, arithmetic rates, and attending behavior. It was discovered that during the children's placement in the cubicles, their attention increased significantly, but their reading and arithmetic rates did not. The former finding substantiates the position that cubicle use increases attention, while the latter one neither endorses nor rejects the notion that academic achievement can be increased once cubicles are used to promote concentration. In the first place, the rate at which a child reads or performs arithmetic operations is only one way of measuring achievement. Also, the amount of time spent in the cubicle, two hours daily for sixteen days, may be too short a period for significant changes in achievement.

In a more thorough study of various kinds of stimulus reduction in the classroom, Gorton (1972) found results supporting the technique of decreasing stimuli in the environment. Using subjects as their own controls, he found that both normal and cultural familial retarded children performed best on addition tasks under a visual seclusion condition. The brain injured group, on the other hand, performed best when in the condition of reduced auditory and visual input. Not only is this study important for its suggestion that all children may benefit from reduced extraneous stimuli, but it also investigates the differential effect of stimulus reduction through different senses.

Jenkins, Gorrafa, and Griffiths (1972) also obtained evidence for the beneficial effects of isolating educable mentally retarded children from extraneous stimulation. They found that isolation implemented within a token system resulted in the completion of more assigned reading.

Obviously, more research is needed to determine the particular benefits of the total Strauss-Lehtinen-Cruickshank program and the specific benefits of the use of cubicles and reduced environmental stimulation. Hopefully, many problems encountered in conducting well-controlled research in the public school setting (Cruickshank et al., 1961) will be overcome in the near future. Meanwhile, evidence does suggest that the Strauss-Lehtinen-Cruickshank procedures benefit the perceptual and perceptual-motor ability of hyperactive and distractible children (Cruickshank et al., 1961) and that reduction of stimuli through the use of cubicles results in better attending behaviors of these children (Shores and Haubrich, 1969) and increased academic performance (Gorton, 1972). Since the importance of attention in cognitive functioning has already been shown, this latter finding is significant.

Other investigators besides Cruickshank have more recently considered attention and impulse control to be important behaviors to train, and a variety of techniques and approaches have shown merit. For example, Luria (1961) advanced a theory (based upon the work of Vygotsky [1962]) in which he posited a developmental progression by which speech comes to be a regulator of motor behavior and eventually becomes internalized.

Using the suggestions of Luria, Meichenbaum and Goodman (1969) have offered empirical evidence that impulsive children may bring their impulsive motoric behavior under control through overt speech. When kindergarten children were merely told to push a foot pedal for one signal, a blue light, and not to push when a yellow light appeared, it was found that subjects who were determined to be impulsive pushed the foot pedal under the yellow light condition significantly more often than did those who were reflective. However, when both groups were instructed to say "push" or "don't push" aloud as the lights came on, the impulsive children decreased their motoric responses to the yellow light to a point where they were performing as well as their reflective peers.

In another study, Palkes, Stewart, and Kahana (1968) also assessed procedures based on the theory of Luria. Hyperactive boys from 8 to 10 years of age were divided into a control and an experimental group. The Porteus Maze Test (1942), said by the authors to require absence of distractibility for performance, was used on a pre- versus posttest basis. Between the pre- and posttests, both groups were asked to perform a number of complex tasks for which the experimental group only was instructed, via experimenter and visual reminder cards, to make self-directed overt oral commands. Although on the pretest and posttest none of the subjects was induced to use the commands, it was found that the experimental group receiving the training in self-directed commands improved significantly on the Porteus posttest, whereas the control group did not. In addition, the experimental group performed significantly better on the posttest than did the control group.

Though the above studies attest to the efficacy of using Luria's techniques with hyperactive and distractible children, it remains unclear whether the most important component of training is in the promotion of: (a) overt labeling, (b) reflection prior to action, or (c) a combination of these. While the study by Meichenbaum and Goodman produced results simply by instructing the child to verbalize, Palkes et al. found positive results by using instruction that encouraged both reflection and overt verbalization. Too, a study by Schwebel (1966) indicated that merely instructing the impulsive child to "stop and think" before responding helps him to improve on a number of tasks. The relative influence of instructing a child to verbalize or to stop and reflect before responding represents a problem that deserves more investigation. The theoretical ideas of Luria will provide a provocative basis for future research on educational approaches for hyperactive children.

Cratty and Martin (1969) have presented their own approach to training hyperactive youngsters. Employing the relaxation training methods of Jacobson (1938), they developed a program designed to increase the child's awareness and control of his body. While the methods of Cratty and Martin appear to be carefully thought out, there is as yet no research substantiating their effectiveness.

A research study by Yando and Kagan (1968) represents yet another approach to reducing impulsivity in the distractible and hyperactive child. Impulsive first-grade children, when placed for one school year with teachers manifesting a reflective teaching style, seemed to become more reflective and less impulsive. The experimenters suggested that the increase in the latency of response (i.e., the control of impulsiveness) may have been mediated through modeling effects (Bandura, 1962) and/or direct reinforcement. The latter possibility gains support from a study (Allen, Henke, Harris, Baer, and Reynolds, 1967) investigating the effects of social reinforcement on the attending behavior of a highly distractible and hyperactive 4.5-year-old child. By systematically setting up a contingency whereby the teacher paid attention to the child while he was concentrating on tasks but withdrew this social reinforcement when he was not, Allen et al. were able to show that the child's attention to the task at hand could be increased.

The above study by Yando and Kagan seems to have provided an impetus for a number of investigations of the effects of modeling on the alteration of cognitive style (Denny, 1972; Heider, 1972; Ridberg, Parke, and Hetherington, 1971). These studies have demonstrated that through the use of models and verbalized instructional strategies impulsive children can be made to slow down their quick responding and in some cases reduce their errors on Kagan's task. These research efforts hold much promise in terms of implications for the learning disabled child who is impulsive.

As another possible teaching technique, Staats et al. (1970) offered support for the notion that the hyperactive and distractible child should be given tasks of short duration, an opinion corroborating the recommendation of Cruickshank et al. (1961) that the length of every teaching assignment should coincide with the attention span of each particular child.

The use of medication is now beginning to be investigated systematically as a means of controlling distractibility and hyperactivity. For example, Hollis and St. Omer (1972) found Chlorpromazine to decrease motor behavior in retardates. Also, Sprague, Barnes, and Werry (1970) found Methylphenidate to result in correct responding on a recognition task, decreased response time, and less motor activity when given to hyperactive and distractible emotionally disturbed children. Increased attention and cooperative behavior was also induced in the classroom. While many poorly controlled studies have been conducted, hopefully the above two studies will serve as models for further research into the use of chemical agents for the hyperactive child.

Regarding the training of attention skills, then, research conducted to date indicates that any one of many different approaches may provide the basis for valid training procedures. The history of research in this area is short, but the findings have already generated useful suggestions for the education of the distractible child. Moreover, the possibility of integrating several different methods with each other and with techniques yet to be devised is a provocative one.

LEARNING DISABILITIES AND THE MAINSTREAM
OF PSYCHOLOGY: A NEED FOR INTEGRATION

Up to this point, the discussion in this chapter has considered attention and the control of motor activity primarily from a pathological point of view, with occasional reference to the theories and research of investigators interested in the process of attention in the normal individual. However, integration of work from the mainstream of psychology and developmental psychology has often proved fruitful in clarifying issues and building concepts regarding the child who is atypical in his ability to attend and to control his hyperactivity. To obtain a complete understanding of the learning disabled child who manifests such problems we must also become conversant with the work of psychologists who have generated theories of the development and role of attention in the normal individual. These theories are considered here in the hope that future formulations concerning the hyperactive and distractible child will evidence a closer relationship than has so far been advanced between the mainstream of psychological theory and the field of learning disabilities.

Attention as a topic of concern has a long history, first with philosophers (e.g., René Descartes) and then with psychologists. As McGhie (1969) points out, the founder of the first psychological laboratory, Wilhelm Wundt, judged attention to be so crucial to perception that he wrote (Wundt, 1897): "The state which accompanies the clear grasp of any psychical content and is characterized by a special feeling, we call *attention*" (p. 209). Yet attention has only been studied systematically and rigorously within the past two or three decades, since the introspective tradition of Wundt influenced investigations for many years. Though amenable to subjective analysis, the presence and measurement of attention were not explored via operationally objective methods.

With the quest of psychology to establish itself as a science, such a vague and ill-defined concept as attention was purposely avoided in the rigorous experimental laboratories that were evolving (McGhie, 1969). The historical development, or nondevelopment, of information concerning the process of attention was commented upon by Solley and Murphy (1960), who pointed out that major figures in psychology, starting with James in his classic, *Principles of psychology* (1890), and proceeding onward through the writings of Titchener (1924), Paschal (1941), Hebb (1949), and Berlyne (1951), have lamented the lack of interest in attention. While each possessed the wisdom to reproach psychology's neglect of attention, except for the work of the latter two they themselves were unable to add but speculation concerning it.

With the advent of psychology's interest in communication and the passage and processing of information, McGhie (1969) noted, we find an increased concern for attention. In investigating the manner in which man obtains and uses information, it was a logical step also to explore the processes man uses in attending to selected informational input. McGhie's contention is supported by the following facts: (a) Broadbent (1958), one of the first individuals to present a model of attention based upon systematic, empirical data, titled his major work, in which he formulated an attentional model, *Perception and communication;* (b) this book was immediately preceded by some of the early explorations in applying information theory to psychology (e.g., Miller, 1953); and (c) Broadbent's terminology reflected that of information theory. In addition, attempts to conceptualize models of psychological functioning using a computer-programming format (e.g., Newell, Shaw, and Simon, 1958) evolved in the same chronological period as did the writings of Broadbent and no doubt were as influential as the work of information theorists.

The model proposed by Broadbent conceives of selective attention as occurring through the process of a filtering mechanism. Certain stimuli are attended to, while others are ignored, in the following way. When information coming to the organism passes through the filters, items selected for further processing are stored in a limited-capacity decision channel connected to a long-term memory bank. Ignored information, not passing through the filters, fades from memory.

Following the theoretical model of Broadbent, Hagen and his colleagues (Druker and Hagen, 1969; Hagen, 1967; Hagen and Frisch, 1968; Hagen and Huntsman, 1971; Hagen and Sabo, 1967; Hagen and West, 1970; Maccoby and Hagen, 1965) have explored the development of selective attention. Based upon an earlier study by Maccoby and Hagen (1965), Hagen (1967) presented the first in a series of publications using several experimental tasks for selective attention. Stimulus cards, each containing the picture of an animal and a household object, were presented one at a time and then turned face down in front of the subject, who had been prompted to attend to the animals. Once a group of these cards had been presented, the experimenter gave the child a cue card showing one of the animals and asked him to point to the same animal in the face-down array. After a number of such trials, the child was then presented with a second task in which he was asked to match up the animals with the household objects which he had been instructed to ignore during the first task. Scores on the first task constituted a central task recall, and scores on the second provided a measure of incidental recall. In this developmental study, it was found that central recall improved with age, while incidental performance did not. Additionally, the correlation between central and incidental performance was positive for the younger children but negative for the older ones. The young children who were good central task performers were also attendant to the irrelevant incidental information; on the other hand, the older children who performed well on the central task tended to ignore the irrelevant information, as evidenced by their low incidental scores.

These findings, indicating that the child develops the ability to attend selectively to relevant information and to ignore the irrelevant, have been substantiated in subsequent studies which varied different aspects of the experimental paradigm. Essentially the same results have been found while (a) varying the order of testing (Hagen and Sabo, 1967), (b) varying the presentation (Hagen and Frisch, 1969), and (c) manipulating the stimulus arrangements (Druker and Hagen, 1969).

Hagen and Huntsman (1971) extended the work of Hagen to the testing of retarded children. They discovered that institutionalized retarded children showed an attention deficit when compared to retarded children living at home and normal children of comparable mental age. The latter two groups did not differ. Hagen noted that his results were similar to those of Zeaman and House, who posited an attention deficit for the institutionalized retarded children used as their experimental subjects. He further commented (Hagen, in press) that the factor of institutionalization may be important in influencing selective attention, since he found attention deficit to be greater for the institutionalized retardates than for the noninstitutionalized. This hypothesis deserves further exploration, since the deleterious effects of institutionalization have been found in a number of situations (Zigler, 1966).

With differential reinforcement procedures, Hagen and West (1970) found that retarded children may be trained to attend selectively on a task similar to the one used in the other studies by Hagen. This finding corroborates earlier conclusions that attention may be trained.

While Hagen used the model of Broadbent as a starting point for the generation of his studies, he has most recently (Hagen, 1971) begun to explore the applicability of the attention model advanced by Neisser (1967), whose view of attention was thought to be more cognitive than that proposed by Broadbent.

Noting the integral role that attention plays in all psychological functioning, particularly in the storage and recall of information, Neisser (1967) presented a stimulating discussion of his theoretical model, rooted in the nineteenth-century school of "act psychology" and closely related to the more contemporary approach of Bartlett (1932, 1958). For Neisser, cognition, "the processes by which a perceived, remembered, and thought-about world is brought into being from as unpromising a beginning as the retinal patterns" (p. 4), and attention, "a *special allocation of cognitive resources*" (p. 39), are both active and constructive products of the individual.

According to Neisser, this constructive participation in the act of attention is a two-stage process. The first stage, the preattentive level, contains those processes that control immediate motor movement and the act of attention itself. The more discriminating second stage, the focal attention level, includes the ability to exhibit a more exacting analysis and synthesis of the object attended to. The preattentive control processes enable the person to select from a mass of stimuli a global representation of a particular object for further refined focal attention at the next level. In Neisser's view, some responses are completely under the control of the preattentive process. If a quick, unrefined response is all that a situation requires, only the preattention process will come into play.

More sophisticated decisions concerning the object under question are taken up by focal attention. Once the particular object attended to has been globally and wholistically selected through preattention processes, the individual analyzes and constructs specific attributes of the object. To refer to this more specific and accurate activity, Neisser borrowed from the psychoanalyst Schachtel (1959) the term "focal attention." Through wholistic segmentation, the object is thereby prepared for a more careful analysis and synthesis.

Neisser's emphasis upon an active attention process, whereby he views the attender as activator, is a crucial aspect of his model in terms of comparison to the positions of other theorists. The concept of the individual as an active participant in the process of attending, for example, differentiates Neisser's construct from the filter model of Broadbent. Broadbent's model does not allow for constructive action on the part of the individual, but rather portrays the organism as possessing a sieve-like mechanism through which some information passes while the rest does not. For Broadbent, the individual is a passive attender, whereas for Niesser, he is an active participant.

The fact that Neisser presented a two-stage model of attention is yet another unique feature of his position. In some respects, one may think of Neisser's preattentive stage as being very similar to Broadbent's approach to attention. Both viewpoints are concerned with gross differentiation of stimuli. But the model of Neisser, by including a second stage, undertakes a more thorough explanation of attention to specific details.

Though the theoretical formulations of Neisser are based for the most part on adult populations, they do generate interesting questions in terms of the normal and abnormal development of attentional processes in the child. A productive area of study would be a comparison of the developmental rates of the two stages of attention. Does the child require preattentive processes before he is able to engage in focal attention, or do both abilities develop concurrently? Intuitively, one would expect an earlier development of preattentive processing, but systematic investigation needs to be directed toward this problem. Such a developmental perspective with regard to Neisser's model no doubt also would enable one to refine it, particularly with respect to the distinction between the two stages.

The two-stage approach of Neisser can also be applied to the study of the child who is manifesting difficulties in attention. Looking generally at the two levels of problems in attending, it is interesting and theoretically relevant to attempt to predict at which level the learning disabled child is more likely to have problems. Much convincing evidence emanating from the historical and classical work of the neuropsychologist Sherrington (1906) suggests that most problems would occur at the second stage, focal attention. Such a prediction is based upon the hypothesis that insult to the central nervous system is likely to interrupt or interfere with higher integrative processes before it affects lower ones.

The contemporary work of Deutsch and Schumer (1967) shares Sherrington's point of view. In a well-controlled study, they presented evidence showing that brain injured children manifest problems in intermodal or intersensory integration more often than in intramodal or intrasensory integration. If, as Neisser implies, preattentive processes are more primitive than focal attention processes, then children with attention problems, especially those which are neurologically based, can be expected to experience more difficulties in focal attention than in preattention. This possibility, however, remains to be fully investigated in a systematic manner.

Currently, there is no basis for a conclusion that problems would never be manifested in the preattentive phase. A reconsideration of the Werner and Strauss (1941) visual figure-background test, in terms of a two-stage theory of attention, reveals the possibility that some of the exogenous children of Werner and Strauss and some of the cerebral palsied children of Cruickshank et al. (1965) had problems at the preattentive level. Using the rationale of Neisser, a global recognition of figure from background requires operation of the preattentive stage. The findings that many of the above children made a large percentage of responses only to the background, while ignoring the figure, gives supportive evidence to an interpretation that their preattention abilities were impaired.

Since a major concern of learning disabilities' theorists is to isolate specifically where and in what ways a particular child is experiencing difficulties in learning, the ideas of Neisser, for one, stand out as possible sources of identifying such problems more accurately. The particularly appealing aspect of Neisser's work is that it provides a theory dealing with attention as more than a simple, singular phenomenon. The judicious application of such an approach offers the researcher and theoretician in learning disabilities at least the groundwork from which to build an accurate picture of the way or ways in which a particular child manifests attentional difficulties. However, we should not be satisfied, for instance, with the mere discovery that a child has a problem at the preattentive level; this is still a crude description, and Neisser's model must be further differentiated through exploration in developmental and adult psychology. Because of their concern for specific analysis of attention problems in children, learning disabilities' theorists are in a particularly advantageous position from which to contribute to the refinement of psychological theories like that of Neisser. Here, then, is a possible opportunity for the evolution of a reciprocal relationship between learning disabilities and the mainstream of psychology.

CHAPTER 8

Future Directions

We have considered the field of specific learning disabilities within a behavioral as well as a neurological framework. In so doing, we have meant to emphasize that any forthcoming remedies for the problems of the learning disabled will not spring from either one of these approaches alone. Like any other appropriately conceptualized group of behaviors, normal or abnormal, learning disabilities ultimately have a neurological base and thus could derive from neurological disorder. Psychologists and educators therefore must consider the problem from a neurological position if appropriate mechanisms with which to confront these problems are eventually to be developed. Until neurological measures are refined considerably, and until neurological findings are translated into recommendations for educational programming, however, the classroom teacher's wisest alternative is to base her prescriptions on the behavioral characteristics of the child, regardless of etiological basis.

As pointed out previously, most of what is known regarding nutritional and environmental deprivation points to their possible involvement as etiological factors in neurological dysfunction. Admittedly, research relating these two worldwide factors to neurological dysfunction or to learning problems in humans is equivocal. Research with animals is of sufficient quality to lend support to the little and poorly controlled human research and to point to explanations which now may be accepted only at the level of well-conceptualized but untested theory. It would appear, however, that the nutritional-environmental deprivation hypothesis could account for the "brain-injured-like" behavior observed with such frequency and classical symptomatology in many urban schoolchildren. Much more research must be undertaken before the problem is thoroughly understood.

In addition to discussing behavioral and neurological concerns, we have traced the significant elements in the short history of the field of specific learning disabilities from a psychoeducational perspective. The fields of psychology and education have received special consideration for two reasons. In the first place, these professions to date have had the greatest impact on learning disabilities. Second, it seems likely that these two disciplines are destined to assume leading roles in the conceptualization of appropriate postnatal remedies for learning disabled children. The emphasis on psychoeducational issues does not minimize the role of neurology. Rather it puts into perspective the fact that within the confines of a neurological disability, the psychoeducational—hence behavioral—development of the child is in the greatest sense the responsibility of education and psychology.

AN INTERDISCIPLINARY RESPONSIBILITY

No dichotomy should exist between neurology on the one hand and psychology and education on the other. A multitude of professions ought to share the responsibility for the alleviation of specific learning disorders. Considerably more interchange among various disciplines must be brought to bear upon the learning problems of children. A host of professions—especially education, psychology, and neuropsychology—must come together within both clinical and research frameworks before substantial progress can materialize.

Neuropsychology and Neurophysiology of Learning

The precise nature of neurological development and dysfunction is a long way from being understood. Neurologists no doubt will have to create new instrumentation to determine yet undiagnosable brain lesions. For instance, innovative thinking might lead to use of the newly developed techniques of holography to this end. Means of preventing neurological damage during the crucial growth period of the human organism, the prenatal and perinatal stages in particular, also must be devised.

Because neuropsychology is an extraordinarily young profession, too often it is still only one person—a psychologist with some neurological training or interests—who sees the child in a clinical setting. Neurologists and psychologists must team together as equals to examine further the

normal and abnormal relationships among neurological function, learning, cognition, and perception. What happens as the result of neurodys-
function is presently in large part a matter of conjecture. While educators
may move ahead to serve the child without a knowledge of specific neuro-
dysfunction, it would be helpful to know with certainty the nature of the
learning disorder.

The total problem of brain function, demonstrated neurologically by
Critchley (1953) and psychologically by Reitan (1955, 1964), demands
continued and broader investigation. Color perception, binocular action
and interaction, localization of sound stimuli, capacity to differentiate
visual and auditory sound figures from their natural backgrounds, lateral
inhibition, and many other significant issues to adjustment and learning
require research and study. Dominance, long a perplexing matter in
gross- and fine-motor learning, still defies conclusive analysis. The issue
of mid-line confusion insofar as single or dual hemispheric motor activity
is concerned also requires further delineation. The significance of dual
hemispheric motor activity, if important at all, needs to be studied in
relation to the acquisition of specific knowledge in such activities as
handwriting, reading, and number concepts.

Neuropsychologists and neurophysiologists have much to contribute
to an understanding of the relationship between the motor cortex output
and its afferent input. When greater understanding of this relationship
exists, a fuller conceptualization of educational methodology for children
may be possible. Closely related to this topic is the problem of the significance of motor systems in conditioned behavior. While this matter
can be investigated by developmental psychologists, the neuropsychologist and neurophysiologist working as a team can probably go farther in
understanding the uniqueness of this relationship in both normal and
brain injured children.

Another problem concerns the learning process and related events at
the synapse. Here neurology and neuropsychology must team up for definitive study of what actually happens at the synapse and how such neuro-
physical activity may be affected by disturbances in the neurological
system. Evidence and knowledge related to this complex problem, for
which instrumentation may yet need to be invented or developed, would
go far in assisting the formulation of theory and understanding related
to the learning processes, not only in normal individuals, but particularly
in perceptually handicapped children.

Developmental Psychology

It is unfortunate that such a wide gap exists between the disciplines of
developmental psychology and special education in all areas of excep-

tionality. Through the years, there has been a trend for those within special education to shun the work of those dealing with normal populations. There is an urgent need for teacher training and doctoral level programs in special education to include courses in developmental psychology. At the same time, developmentalists must relate their research results and theoretical conceptualizations to children who are outside the norms of development. It probably was no accident that one of the foremost conceptualizers of deviant behavior in children, Heinz Werner, was also at the cutting edge of research and theory in normal human genetic and comparative psychological development.

Specifically, developmental psychology needs to turn its attention to numerous issues surrounding the learning disabled child. Teaming with obstetricians, pediatricians, and pediatric neurologists, developmental psychologists need to aim the spotlight of research at very early infant learning and behavior, particularly with respect to those children in whom the indications of positive neurological signs are present or suspected. No aspect of early child development should be overlooked in an attempt to understand more fully the nature of the postnatal development of these children. Kagan's interest in the differential reactions of young children to stimuli of differing degrees is of importance when we consider the stimuli differentiation problems of learning disabled children at school age. Concomitantly, from a learning and educational point of view, we should know how early in their lives it is possible to "train" children known to have neurological disorders in the ability to differentiate between stimuli. In the normal child, the acquisition of this ability is assumed by some psychologists to be a matter of development; educators maintain its acquisition depends on "readiness." In the disordered child, we must learn when training can be undertaken and how it is best done at a very early age.

Visual alertness and visual fixation, as well as auditory alertness and fixation, are still other issues which developmental psychologists (together with ophthalmologists and audiologists) need to study. A normative base is required for comparison with the perceptually handicapped child.

Additionally the work of Kagan on cognitive styles should be of utmost concern within the field of learning disabilities. As Glaser (1972) pointed out in his presidential address to the American Educational Research Association, educators should be turning their attention to the way in which children go about learning. Because of the learning disabled child's disorganized mode of learning, the issue of cognitive style takes on added significance for him.

The relationship of prematurity to subsequent specific learning disorder is another matter which should be high on a list of priorities. Although exceedingly incomplete data are available on any aspect of this problem, one study with cerebral palsied children does indicate prematurity to be the chief etiological factor in 8.1 percent of a population of 1105 subjects (Hopkins, Bice, and Colton, 1954). The previously cited work of Pasamanick and Knoblock (1961) is also relevant here.

More and more, developmental psychologists are turning their attention to the maternal attachment behavior of infants and to subsequent child and mother separation behaviors. This area of study is unique and exceedingly important when physical or developmental disabilities of any nature are present or even suspected in the child. A new variable is inserted into what is, under normal circumstances, a very delicate relationship. The nature of the mother-child relationship when neurological or developmental problems are present has not been subject to critical investigation, nor has the relationship been studied between child and parent at the time it becomes obvious to the latter that a problem does, in fact, exist.

Relative to the problem of perception in learning disabled children, developmental and experimental psychologists have many and varied problems to investigate. Studies of form versus color, of form and color in two- or three-dimensional settings, and of perception of form versus color and dimension in terms of perceptual time all need careful research. The implications of findings from such studies for the educational scene are obvious. Studies of response set and contextual cues in relationship to perceptual judgment must be undertaken to ascertain if substitution mechanisms can be developed by certain children with learning disabilities when a specific sensory modality is impaired.

Developmental psychology may also help to enlighten us with respect to discrimination learning and transfer of learning in the learning disabled child. Children with specific learning disorders are characterized by uneven profiles insofar as the sensory modalities are concerned. A clear-cut example of this is seen in aphasic children, whose perceptual skills related to auditory input stimuli are very poor, but whose apprehension of visual or tactual input stimuli frequently is normal. The extent to which learning established through one sensory modality can be transferred to situations involving impaired sensory modalities in neurologically handicapped children must be explored. Findings related to this problem can have immediate application in the educational setting.

While we have stressed the importance of acquiring further information regarding perceptual development or motor development, future studies need to focus on the interaction of these two developmental systems and the differences between them at the time of interaction.

Other aspects of child development begging for investigation which are essential for a total understanding of the child with specific learning disabilities include all matters relative to selective attention and hyperactivity. Assumptions of how these two factors interrelate appear in literature, but experimental evidence of their interrelationship is lacking. Indeed, little is known, except through observation, of the nature of selective attention or of hyperactivity in learning disabled children.

The work of John Hagen, whose investigation of selective attention already has been discussed, contains much of significance and should be pursued further with perceptually handicapped children. Likewise, the ideas of Gardner (1966) concerning cognition and cognitive structure in brain injured children need to be explored further. Furthermore. the findings of this research must be put into such a form as to permit application in the educational programming for these children. Although Hagen is a developmental psychologist and Gardner a clinical psychologist, the neuropsychologists, too, must consider their work in order to ascertain what is taking place neurologically during human cognitive development.

It is unnecessary to catalogue the total spectrum of needs wherein research with learning disabled or perceptually handicapped children is required. Yet some issues emerge with such force as to demand specific attention here. Memory and related processes, for example, must be thoroughly investigated. Developmental implications of paired-associate learning must be pursued in both learning disabled and normal populations. Problem solving and thinking should be explored further. The developmental acquisition of language, too, merits thorough investigation by psychologists and speech and language pathologists.

Finally, the significance of operant conditioning in the adjustment and learning of learning disabled children requires much more attention. The important theoretical and applied work of Frank Hewitt and of Frank Taylor at the University of California at Los Angeles and in the Santa Monica Public Schools demonstrates possible directions which further work should take and hints at the kinds of payoffs which may be obtained for children and their families through similar efforts.

RESEARCH POLICY

The great need for investigation into many issues related to the problems of learning disorders is by now all too apparent. In order to reduce the enormity of undone research and simultaneously eliminate unnecessary and wasteful duplication of effort, more effective organization and direction must emerge at the federal level.

Following thorough study and consultation, the Bureau for the Education of the Handicapped of the U.S. Office of Education should adopt and publicize both a research policy in this field and a statement of research funding related to priorities. The priority statement must be complete and inclusive of all areas. On the basis of policy and priorities, research contracts should be solicited. Insofar as nonsolicited research proposals meet the priority and policy requirements, they should be accepted routinely from those generated by people in the field. For areas which appear not to be under current investigation, research proposals should be solicited on a sole-source basis.

Although the psychological and educational aspects of specific learning problems in children are closely intertwined, the practicalities of federal research funding usually have dictated that they be considered separately. In the future, however, interdisciplinary research should be encouraged, and the federal policy of single-bureau financing should encompass non-educational personnel and concepts.

While on other occasions the generation of research by those in the field without recognition of a total national need might have been acceptable, at this time in the history of special education, time does not permit a research program resulting only from self-stimulated interests of researchers. The pressure to understand the child with specific learning disabilities is too great and the needs too urgent. No longer can we wait for indefinite periods of time for the professions to fill in all the missing pieces of the mosaic.

Much needs to be done in this field besides educational research. Of all the professions, psychology and education have led the way in research with learning disabled children. Even this work, however, has been characterized by short-term efforts, relatively small populations of children, lack of adequate controls, and frequent failure to understand the nature of the concept of learning disorder. The need for national priorities in psychological research therefore is every bit as urgent as it is in the federal educational establishment. The National Institute of Mental Health, the National Institute for Child Health and Human Development, and the National Science Foundation, among others, should assume responsibility for national directions. Interagency sponsorship of research in this field of child development should be encouraged in order to bring the greatest number of resources to converge on a crisis situation at the earliest opportunity.

Research Priorities

Although numerous areas of investigation within the field of learning disabilities are in need of research, a few stand out as prime topics for disciplinary and interdisciplinary study on a "request for proposals" basis. That so many areas are deficient in extensive study is no doubt due to the fact that learning disabilities, as a new area of special education, has borrowed heavily from other fields and frequently has failed to update much of the theory and research from which it has drawn. A case in point is the consideration given in the last chapter to problems of attention.

Historically, while scattered instances of interest in problems of attention date at least as far back as the late nineteenth century (Ribot, 1890), the birth of extensive concern for this area did not occur until the late 1930s and early 1940s with the work of Werner and Strauss on brain injured, mentally retarded children. In spite of encountering numerous methodological problems, Werner and Strauss with the landmark efforts set the stage for investigation of children manifesting short attention spans and/or hyperactivity.

Approximately fifteen years passed before Cruickshank, together with collaborators, carried forth the Werner and Strauss concepts and research regarding attention to the investigation of neurologically impaired (cerebral palsied) children of near-normal, normal, and above-normal intelligence. Still later, with a more sophisticated research approach, Cruickshank et al. (1957, 1965) replicated for this group of children the findings of Werner and Strauss. These endeavors helped to prepare the way for investigation of attention problems in children with normal intelligence. In addition, they influenced consideration of the fact that many other psychological characteristics originally observed by Werner and Strauss in brain injured, mentally retarded children were manifest in children of normal intelligence (i.e., learning disabled).

There is little doubt that interest in attentional problems of children of normal intelligence was an outgrowth of and became a replacement for concern for such problems in mentally retarded, brain injured children. Yet, since the work of Cruickshank in the early and mid-1950s, this evolution has been a slow one, and little research or theory has been proffered to date with regard to the intellectually normal child who has problems of attention and/or hyperactivity. Without disdaining the importance of the work of Werner and Strauss, we can scarcely ignore the regretful fact that rudimentary concepts forwarded in the 1930s and 1940s with the brain injured, mentally retarded still prevail more than thirty years later in discussions of the learning disabled child with an attention deficit.

The dated nature of some learning disability concepts seems paradoxical when we realize that within the field of mental retardation itself there has occurred a shift in concern which tends to ignore the work of Werner and Strauss. Writings by House and Zeaman (1959 and 1960) and Zeaman and House (1963), for instance, have focused upon the global condition of mental retardation, regardless of etiology, as a determinant of attention deficit. The numerous problems and issues raised in the diagnosis of brain injury have no doubt contributed to the current movement toward disregard for etiology. We might say, therefore, that while learning disability theorists may have been guilty of unquestioningly accepting the work of Werner and Strauss without attempting to advance or modify it to any great extent, mental retardation theorists may have prematurely discarded the Werner and Strauss concepts. This is not to imply that either field, any more than the other, should totally reverse its present direction. In the study of specific learning disabilities, for example, it is not necessary that the Werner and Strauss concepts regarding attention and hyperactivity be consigned to antiquity. On the contrary, they should be employed as a springboard to future exploration of the child who is called learning disabled.

With regard to attention, the mainstream of psychology has followed a developmental course similar to that of the individuals whose interest lies in its maldevelopment. Sporadic concern for both the normal and abnormal facets of attention predates the arrival of the twentieth century; yet not until recently have there been concerted efforts to shed light on these issues. Even though investigators within both areas have begun almost simultaneously to explore attention and motor activity, little integration has been evidenced between the two. Only a few individuals have made attempts to bridge the fields. The years ahead should offer ample opportunity for a valuable interchange between the broad area of psychology and the specific study of learning disabilities, an opportunity which heretofore has been relatively ignored, not only with respect to distractibility and hyperactivity, but also with regard to research and theorization as a whole.

Among the numerous other aspects of psychological functioning in learning disabled children in need of investigation, language and auditory factors also merit high priority. The excellent work of Kirk, Bateman, McCarthy, and others to whom references already have been made have emphasized the role of language in the total disordered state of affairs in some children. These authors have appropriately placed upon audition and audio-motor development a stress which is undeniably important to consideration of growth and adjustment in learning disabled children. Too little is yet known regarding the auditory perceptive modality and specific learning disorders, although a few clues have been forthcoming. The result of the inability of the child to translate "input" auditory stimuli into "output" responses results in part in language disorders. It also results in the inability of the child to respond correctly to auditory stimuli which require gross motor responses, e.g., "kick the ball," "shut the door," "write your name," "hang up your coat," "eat your dinner." In each of these situations, as Kephart has observed, the auditory input stimuli must be matched by an appropriate motor activity. The implications of Kephart's observation are great in terms of interrelationships on theoretical, research, and applied bases among neurologists, speech and language pathologists, audiologists, psychologists, and educators. A search of the literature does not reveal research or evidence of practice commensurate with the magnitude or importance of the problem. Indeed, with the exception of doctoral studies by McKay (1952) and Norris (1958), not since the early study of Werner and Bowers (1941) has there occurred much investigation into audio-motor function with children characterized by specific learning disorders. Despite the significance of this area, we have yet to learn much about the nature of audio-motor impairments and their relationship both to classroom environments and to teaching methods and materials.

Although only a few specific areas of concern for research priority have been singled out here, this does not negate the fact that research is needed in every aspect of the perceptual-motor, cognitive, language, and social development of learning disabled children. A particularly useful methodological framework into which these studies could be placed is that of longitudinal research with carefully selected groups of children. Little is known of the life-span development of individuals exhibiting developmental disabilities.

The early work of Cruickshank et al. (1961) was to have constituted a relatively long-term study of the relationship between learning environment and pupil adjustment. This study, originally funded by the U.S. Office of Education for a five-year period, was terminated at the end of two years, when unanticipated advances in Russian space technology prompted the federal government to establish programs and to divert its available funds to studies for the gifted. No long-term study of the application of theory to teaching situations or teaching materials has been undertaken since that time, in spite of the vast increase in consumer interest in this phase of education.

Because of the dearth of research to establish their value, myriad untested teaching materials are on the market today. To fault the manufacturers or developers of these materials and programs for this regrettable situation would be somewhat unfair, since educators in their desperation have demanded specific materials for children who have failed to learn in traditional programs. Nevertheless, systematic evaluation of these materials would be most appropriate.

Clinical teaching programs also abound, each one directly or indirectly related to some particular point of view. Even more programs claim to be "eclectic," while still others seemingly have no observable point of view on which programmatic decisions are made. Concepts of responsibility and accountability would dictate that evaluations of effectiveness be undertaken before decisions regarding continuation of the programs and further financial investments are made. Such studies must include the control of such variables as homogeneity of population, teaching environment, method, teacher qualifications, teaching materials, and other significant factors. The studies must be supported by funds sufficient to promise extensive evaluation, and financing must be guaranteed over a specified period of child development and not be subject to changes in political priorities. Much of the data lacking today could be in the possession of the professions had the political significance of Sputnik been integrated more logically into a system of national priorities. At the national level, priorities must be set which will permit educators to serve children appropriately, and which will allow consumers to invest their faith in what educators do to their children. Both the professional educator and the consumer lack information and security.

In spite of the complexities of a multiplicity of variables, the creation of a longitudinal study in the area of psychoeducational development of children with specific learning disorders can be conceptualized and effectively programmed. It is probably too large a responsibility for a specific school system where service needs must predominate. A better alternative would be a university-centered program involving numerous service settings. This broad base of operations could give the field vital and effective direction.

Investigation of a long-term nature is required for numerous issues. One of these pertains to the educational environment. Cruickshank has posited that the learning environment must be a reflection of the psychopathology of the child. Except for the studies by Jenkins et al. (1972) and Gorton (1972) and much less comprehensive studies by Rost and Charles (1967) and Shores and Haubrich (1969), no investigations have assessed the value of the nonstimulating classroom or stimuli reduction as a teaching tool with learning disabled children. An abundance of clinical data does help us to generalize about the effectiveness of this type of teaching setting, but carefully accumulated experimental information regarding the learning characteristics of these children is not available.

The issue of the learning environment is but one example of the needs in the field. Practically every aspect of the total problem, from epidemiology and demography to teacher preparation and teaching materials, needs in-depth study and research. Only when a significant segment of total child growth and development has been well analyzed will the field be able to stand securely and be held accountable to the consumer.

THE EDUCATIONAL MATCH AND PROTOTYPE PROGRAMS

Observers for some time have recognized the desirability of adapting the learning situation to the characteristics of the individual child. Kephart (1960, 1971) has written of the importance of the perceptual and motor match. Approaching the issue from a slightly different point of view, Peter (1965) has referred to the concept of "prescriptive teaching."

Cruickshank (1967) beginning in 1952 also has discussed the necessity of conceptualizing the education of children with specific learning disorders, with two important steps in mind. First, there must be a complete diagnostic "blueprint" consisting of data received from the child and from others who know him well. Of singular importance is a description of how the child operates in terms of those aspects of perceptual and motor functions on which learning of all types is based. Such a description would include a detailed understanding of the capacity of the child to respond appropriately to auditory, visual, and tactual input stimuli and of his capacity to produce a socially acceptable output response to such stimuli. The blueprint also must include data regarding the child's attention span within different kinds of learning situations. Second, once the ability to ignore extraneous stimuli in the various sensory modalities is determined, the child's specific pathology in such matters as figure-ground discrimination, dissociation, perseveration, and related fundamental learning characteristics then will be known. The child's understanding of space, time, and self can be determined and understood in terms of the capacity of the teaching program to support deficiencies. This match, then, about which authors have written, implies that the educational programs for children with specific learning disorders must be *deficit oriented*. We must teach to the disability while simultaneously being aware of and drawing upon the child's strengths.

The justifications for a deficit-oriented rather than strength-oriented curriculum are many. First, as within the Peter conceptualization, the disability-oriented curriculum permits a "prescription" to be developed for each child, each week, and each day. It permits a constant focus on the deficit in need of correction. Without the detailed and often qualitatively determined understanding of deficits, the obtaining of a perceptual-motor match, as described by Kephart, will be possible only rarely. If achieved without analysis, it will have been accomplished by the teacher on a trial-and-error basis long after the time when she should have had the information and should have begun a program of true educational development for the child. For children with specific learning disabiilty, every learning activity, whether it be gross-motor or fine-motor in nature, or whether it be of a nature not usually seen as "motor," must be complementary to the psychomotor deficit or psychopathology observed in the child. Content in teaching is of a lower priority than are the efforts to bring the child to a level of relatively continuous and universal success experiences based on perceptual-motor activities basic to all learning. When learning has been accomplished through the perceptual-motor match or through a psychoeducational match, then progress for these children is rapid. Without this crucial matching, progress is slow, and both teacher and child remain unmotivated.

Group-based research on these matters is needed to supplement data already provided by clinicians. As was shown earlier, little comprehensive research on perceptual-motor training has been conducted. While it is generally recognized that perceptual-motor problems are correlated with academic failure, the causal link has not been identified with certainty. With specific regard to the efficacy of perceptual-motor training for academic achievement, conclusive studies have yet to prove its apparent validity.

Viewing the individual child in terms of his specific abilities and disabilities is also in accord with a current trend to use criterion-referenced evaluation of pupil performance. There is a strong movement to assess children by using absolute levels of performance on certain specific tasks rather than traditional norm-referenced tests (Bloom, Hastings, and Madaus, 1971; Drew, Freston, and Logan, 1972; Glaser, 1963; Popham, 1970). The concept of teaching to the disability of children, without ignoring strengths, seems particularly well suited for criterion-referenced evaluation.

Two programs at the preliminary stages of development in California are exemplary of an approach of educating and evaluating children under a philosophy of pinpointing their disabilities at a behavioral level. At the Camarillo State Hospital Children's Services in Camarillo, Medical Program Director Nobert Rieger and his colleagues have isolated and described the behavior of seriously emotionally disturbed children. Furthermore, they have grouped this behavior so that it may be conceptualized by the service staff which provides personal care (including toilet training, dressing, hygiene, eating, care of clothing, bed-wetting, care of living area, chores, and sleeping). The "school" here includes gross-motor functions, fine-motor and body-image factors, perceptual skills, readiness skills, academic skills, language, speech, industrial arts, home economics, arts and crafts, physical education, and music. Social interaction is assessed to include all those functions which are designed to facilitate meaningful interaction, self-control, and self-awareness. Behavioral analysis and the analysis of the child's needs from the point of view of medicine, nursing, environment, and a variety of other support services are made in detail. All areas of assessment are carefully described, with parameters designed for each item under assessment.

From the material secured on each child, the program is determined. Staff time devoted to each item and to each child; the number of children needing similar types of professional attention; frequency of educational periods; and, ultimately, the number of staff members required to develop the function to a higher level—all these considerations are derived both from an administrative planning mechanism and from a psychotherapeutic tool in this "program-functions" approach. Essentially, this technique exemplifies the programmatic prototype developed in the Michigan Department of Mental Health for evaluation of each child in a residential care facility for the mentally retarded and for that child's subsequent developmental programming.

An even more detailed and sophisticated attempt to identify behavioral characteristics, created by the Santa Cruz County Office of Education, is the *Behavioral Characteristics Progression*. Still in preliminary form, the program has been developed as an instrument for programs for the mentally and behaviorally exceptional to help fill

> the need for a two-way *accountability tool* which ensures that the focal point of all program decision-making is the pupil. Such a tool would best offer a means of recording pupil progress to justify the need for educational resources. The need for a *communication tool* which provides all those involved (teacher, parent, aide, support staff, etc.) in the educational program with a common jargon and format to use in discussions concerning the pupil. The need for an *assessment instrument* which reduces the constraints (e.g., ages, labels) often placed on the education of a pupil and enhances the use of diagnostic data. The need for an *instructional instrument* which aids the special classroom teacher in developing possible behavioral objectives for each pupil related to community and societal goals [Santa Cruz County Board of Education, undated, p. 1].

It is rare that a program is conceptualized from the four-way approach of accountability, communication, assessment, and instruction. Immediately, its usefulness both to consumers and to research becomes apparent. In their introduction, the authors of the preliminary document made some exceedingly cogent statements as a background to the program:

> In his attempts to make education more relevant and accountable, the special educator seeks methods through which accurate assessment of pupil benefit can be confidently assured. In doing so, he has turned to behavior as an observable, dynamic indicator of pupil attainment. The behavioral approach to education describes learning as a change in behavior resulting from experience, practice, or training. As a pupil moves along the continuum of characteristics beginning with the earliest behavior displayed by an infant and ending with the most developmentally complex and socially adaptive behavior shown by an adult, his progress is manifest in his changing behavior.
>
> As a reliable measuring stick for the educational process, the characteristics used to describe and distinguish a pupil are most meaningful if observable and objective; in other words, they must be *behavioral* characteristics (abbreviated BC's). A pupil's characteristics are not his capabilities or potentials since, as such, they would allow opportunities for individual interpretation or guesswork. Behavioral characteristics represent a description of the pupil's *demonstrated* abilities or observable behaviors. Because behavioral characteristics can be confirmed through observation, educators can determine whether they have or have not been successful in teaching what they attempted to teach.

In order that behavioral characteristics be useful as descriptors of pupil behavior, they should be specific enough to permit observation, yet at the same time be practical. For example, the handicapped child often exhibits a short attention span. Would a characteristic on the level of "exhibits normal length attention span" be helpful to a teacher attempting to describe a pupil to his parents? It seems unlikely, since such a characteristic would probably omit all the steps a pupil goes through to progress from a short attention span to a normal one. Also, the word "normal" should be replaced with a more objetcive description. To solve this latter problem a specified amount of time can be substituted for the word normal, thus resulting in a BC of "exhibits a fifteen-minute attention span." However, this still represents a very general behavior leaving the possibility of differing individual interpretation. What exactly is an attention span? Is it possible to define this BC in operational terms; in terms of observable behaviors? Replacing attention span with something more specific could result in "works at task individually with adult for fifteen minutes." This seems more useful than the original, general BC. However, how does one know when to stop this breaking down of behavior into increasingly specific increments? Couldn't the work "task" be further defined in terms of what in particular the pupil is working on? This might result in "draws shapes individually with adult for fifteen minutes." And then the types of shapes could be specified. One could proceed until he reaches the point of diminishing returns, when the usefulness of the specificity begins to decrease. The more specific the behavioral characteristic becomes, the more limited is its application. A tradeoff must be made between these two aspects: precision of behavioral description and limitation of behavioral description.

The behavioral characteristic is meant to be a behavioral description, neither mechanical nor inflexible. "Strikes with bat a ball thrown from five feet" is an adequately specific BC. This behavior need not be separated into all its component parts: holds bat in hands, plants feet, shifts weight, straightens elbows, twists wrists, and connects bat with ball. Such an analysis doesn't give a true representation of the way in which human beings develop. At a certain point in the breaking down of behaviors, the increments become mechanical rather than human.

Behavioral characteristics, if adequately precise and practical, can be a good means of communicating needs and accomplishments. They can strengthen communication by giving all people involved in the educational process a common scale upon which to base their discussion concerning the pupil. In a total system of educational communication, a common language becames a vital tool, the cornerstone of the system. If behavioral characteristics are to serve this function, a universal method for determining what a pupil's BS's are, and a format for the ordering of these BC's must be specified.

The Behavioral Characteristics Progression (abbreviated BCP) has been designed to provide teachers, administrators, legislators and parents with a practical assessment tool based upon behavioral characteristics. As such, it functions as a communication medium capable of collective application. The teacher can use the BCP to show the parent how the pupil's behavior has changed in terms that the parent can readily observe. The administrator can use the BCP and associated documented methodologies to illustrate to his board precisely how a budget change will affect the pupils. The legislator can use the BCP to show those in State government specific characteristics that handicapped pupils demonstrate, ensuring that laws passed will respond realistically to the needs of pupils. Thus, through use of the BCP, the pupil becomes and remains the focal point of all educational activities [Santa Cruz County Board of Education, p. 2-4].

The behavioral characteristics referred to in the Santa Cruz program are essentially the same as the characteristics of psychoeducational deficit mentioned earlier in this chapter. Irrespective of terminology, it is necessary to analyze the behavior and learning characteristics of children in such detail that it becomes obvious where instruction must begin. Cruickshank (1967) has written that analysis must make it possible to identify the most primitive level of performance where a success experience can be assured, so that the instructional program for that child may begin at that level. While intended for mentally retarded and behaviorally exceptional children, the Santa Cruz program could easily be extended to make it applicable to and appropriate for children with specific learning disorders. Because of the program's inherent characteristics of accountability, assessment, communication, and instruction, careful implementation would provide a quantitive basis for both short- and long-term educational research with children who have specific learning disorders. Programs of an applied nature which can be also the basis of research might do much to correct the paucity of current knowledge about specific learning disabilities.

Against the background which has been quoted above, the authors of the *Behavioral Characteristic Progression* have now isolated some twenty-five behavioral characteristics, examples of which include visual perception, auditory perception, language comprehension, listening, impulse control, personal relationships, and adaptive behaviors. For each behavioral characteristic, there has been identified developmentally a series of skill steps which the child must learn before the behavior is acquired at a mature level of social acceptance. Evaluation of the individual follows carefully developed steps whereby, through observation and diagnostic assessment, each pupil is assessed on each characteristic, and a level of skill acquisition is determined.

Figure 42 illustrates in preliminary form the behavioral analysis for a few of the characteristics which have been identified. Although the figure only indicates a possible seven degrees of skill acquisition, the program actually includes as many as forty steps for some characteristics. The child for whom this record was made on June 6, 1971, performed at a 1.0 level in "listening" skills and at a 3.0 level for attention span. From the assessment, the teacher obtained a profile indicating where the child was on that given date.

Referring again to the *listening* characteristic on Figure 42, the reader

		1.0	**2.0**	**3.0**	**4.0**	**5.0**	**6.0**	**7**
1	VISUAL PERCEPTION	Turns eyes to right.	Follows moving object with eyes. Eyes fix on object momentarily.	Horizontally tracks within 90° arc (no crossing midline.	Horizontally tracks past midline (greater than 90° arc).	Diagonally tracks past midline (greater than 90° arc).	Horizontally tracks within 180° arc, eyes and head.	Moves eyes ently of hea 180-degree
2	VISUAL MOTOR (SECONDARY)	Uses fingers past midline with fine (exact) pincer movement.	Builds tower of two blocks.	Turns pages 2-3 at a time.	Holds crayon and scribbles.	Turns pages one at a time.	Builds tower of 3-4 blocks.	Places roun in round ho
3	AUDITORY PERCEPTION	Startle-response to sudden loud sound.	Turns head toward source of loud sound.	Attends to dominant sound while other sounds present.	Momentarily stops activity when sound is made.	Reaches or turns toward noise made behind head.	Responds to single speaker by looking directly at him.	Reacts pos or negative soft or har toned soun
4	LANGUAGE COMPREHENSION (RECEPTIVE LANGUAGE)	Responds to spoken sounds.	Stops activity upon simple command.	Imitates phys. gesture when word or phrase paired with gesture is spoken.	Gestures approp. to simple verbal requests without physical model.	Responds to name, i.e., stops activity, looks up, or goes to speaker.	Points to familiar object when name of the object is spoken.	Points to fa object in re when its na spoken.
5	LANGUAGE DEVELOPMENT (EXPRESSIVE LANGUAGE)	Makes sounds to get attention and/or to converse.	Imitates sounds or words without association.	Uses simple gestures and sound to indicate needs.	Says name of object or person (possibly indistinct), first word.	Repeats symbol with visual clues (says ball when shown ball).	Repeats symbol without visual clues.	Identifies or persons names.
6	LISTENING	Looks in direction of speaker.	Looks directly at speaker.	Looks at face of speaker.	Looks at mouth of speaker.	Looks directly at speaker through duration of speech.	Maintains eye contact when spoken to or speaking.	Replies to sational o
7	SOCIAL SPEECH	Maintains appropriate social distance.	Responds to and makes verbal greetings and farewells.	Remains quiet when others are talking.	Asks for what is desired.	Says "thank you", "you're welcome" or "please" when reminded.	Says "thank you", "you're welcome" or "please" after some hesitation.	Says "thank compliment Says "pleas requests.
8	GROSS MOTOR DEVELOPMENT (SECONDARY)	Catches large ball thrown from 4-6 feet with hands and body.	Throws large ball from chest position with two hands.	Jumps 2-3 foot distance, feet together.	Stands on one foot for 5 seconds, no support.	Performs complete forward roll/ backward roll.	Maintains momentum on swing.	Rides tricy
9	ATTENTION SPAN	Attends to task less than 5 sec. when supervised.	Attends to task without supervision for less than 5 sec.	Attends to task for less than 10 sec. when supervised.	Attends to task without supervision for less than 10 seconds.	Attends to task for less than 15 sec. when supervised.	Attends to task without supervision for less than 15 seconds.	Attends to less than 1 onds when vised.
10	TASK COMPLETION	Starts task/assignment only with much reminding from teacher.	Starts task/ assignment before end of class period.	Starts task/ assignment with no prompting.	Completes 25% or less of task/ assignment.	Completes 25-50% of task/assignment	Completes 50-75% of task/assignment.	Completes of task/assi
11	READING	Points to object when its name is spoken.	Points to picture of object when its name is spoken.	Matches objects by color.	Matches objects by size.	Matches objects by shape.	Discriminates between grossly different written words.	Discrimina tween simi written wor cat and ha
12	SPELLING	Identifies first letters (approx. 1/3) of alphabet.	Identifies last letters (approx. 1/3) of alphabet.	Identifies middle letters (approx. 1/3) of alphabet.	Identifies alphabet in sequence.	Pairs consonant sounds to correct letter.	Pairs vowel sounds to correct vowel.	Pairs cons blend sound correct con letters.
13	WRITING	Makes marks with pencil/crayon (pencil can be held in fist).	Draws a vertical line, imitating adult.	Draws a horizontal line, imitating adult.	Performs push-pull strokes, imitating adult.	Holds pencil in fingers.	Traces lines.	Copies mo horizontal line.
14	MATH	Sorts according to color, shape, size.	Copies block designs/bead patterns, maintaining sequence/order.	Demonstrates concept of oneness (draws 1 circle, claps 1 time).	Demonstrates concept of twoness (e.g., draws 2 circles).	Differentiates/locates more, less, big, little, long, short, top, bottom.	Refers to distance in gross manner (near, far).	Refers to es/activiti gross time tions (bein
15	ORGANIZATION AND JUDGEMENT	Sorts blocks by color.	Sorts blocks by color and length.	Sorts blocks by size.	Sorts blocks by color and size.	Sorts blocks by shape (squares, circles, triangles).	Places obj. in up, down, above, below, under, in, out, next, before position.	Uses gener for object i of variety (e.g., poo
16	IMPULSE CONTROL	Sits quietly less than 1 min. when group is listening to stories, music.	Takes turn in game activity 25% of time or less.	Sits in seat, etc., w/out fidgeting, moving for 25% or less of activity.	Sits quietly less than 5 min. when group is listening to stories, music.	Changes activity w/out emotional outbursts when cue well defined.	Changes routine w/ out emotional outbursts when alternatives presented.	Sits quietly than 10 min group is lis to stories,

FIGURE 42   Analysis of a pupil's behavioral achievement. Shaded area shows skills accomplished at date indicated. Unshaded areas illustrate skills yet to be learned with a bar indicating for each the acquisition goal for future teaching for each skill. (Reproduced with permission Santa Cruz County Office of Education, California.)

will note that, after careful evaluation of the child and of the instructional opportunities for the child, the teacher set a level of 5.0 as the goal to be achieved next in this area. The items between the level of accomplishment and the established goal constitute the areas around which instruction is to be organized. Similar goals will be established for all other behavioral characteristics. Frequent reassessments keep the child, the instructional program, and the teacher in harmony with one another and permit a deficit-oriented program of learning to function as a success-based developmental experience for the child. Self-motivation and accountability are built in for both child and teacher.

While it does not represent the only way in which research in the education of children with specific learning disabilities may be developed, the Santa Cruz approach has a positive potential which should not be underestimated. Regardless of the research implications, the educators in this school system have seen the wisdom of analysis of learning deficits followed by the establishment of attainable goals and means of reaching them. Global goal setting, i.e., preparation for life and living, have no meaning except in the broadest terms for children with specific learning disorders. With this group of children, the emphasis must be on the specific. Specific disorders must be complemented with specific educational materials and techniques which are conceptualized to exploit the disorder to the child's own development, to minimize it, or to eliminate it entirely. The traditional and global goals of education will then begin to apply. When schools move to conceptualize the education of these children in the way the Santa Cruz system has endeavored to do, then results both in terms of child growth and in terms of collectable objective data will be forthcoming. Less structured approaches appear to violate the child's needs and to promise much more restricted returns for the child, for his family, and for the teacher.

TEACHER EVALUATION

In addition to the need for assessment of each child's progress in individual behaviors, there exists a need for an evaluation measure of teacher effectiveness. Kauffman, Hallahan, Payne, and Ball (in press), at the University of Virginia, are currently in the formative stages of developing a precise, quantitative, and functional schema for the evaluation of teaching and learning. This evaluation approach seems particularly applicable to educational environments (such as the Santa Cruz Project) that stress teaching children with specifically delineated learning problems.

Briefly, the evaluation model is composed of the following elements: (a) learner outcomes, (b) conditions for learning, and (c) rate of acquisition. Whenever an educational program posits instructional goals for a child, an objective test can be developed for assessing learning at any point in the teaching program. What an individual has acquired (A) may be expressed as the factor Bc minus Be, where Bc denotes behaviors currently in the child's repertoire, and Be represents behaviors of the child as he entered the program. Behaviors along an ontogenetic continuum, specific skill sequences, or a quantity of correct addition problems, among other behaviors, may represent A.

In terms of conditions for learning, in the simplest possible analysis, teaching consists of (a) presentation by the teacher of an antecedent event (Sa), (b) response (R) by the learner, and (c) presentation by the teacher of a subsequent event (Ss). In highly structured teaching situations, all three events occur. In less directive teaching, on the other hand, either the Sa or Ss component is omitted. The teacher thus may reinforce or correct emitted responses (R → Ss) or prompt responses which she neither corrects nor reinforces (Sa → R).

In this analysis, Sa and Ss are teacher-initiated and pupil-initiated acts respectively. The sum of teacher acts (ΣSa + ΣSs) constitutes teaching effort (C). Gump (1969) has shown that teacher acts can be defined and recorded as "the shortest meaningful bit of behavior directed toward students" (p. 216) and that teacher acts vary in kind and number depending on the type of classroom activity. Other research (Yamamoto, Jones, and Ross, 1972) indicates that the rate of teacher acts may be a primary factor distinguishing teacher-pupil interactions in classrooms differing in pupil achievement.

Working on the premise that the effective teacher accelerates the rate of learning, Kauffman, et al. also have included the dimension of time (T) with A and C. Time may be expressed in gross (e.g., weeks) or specific (e.g., seconds) units, as the teacher wishes.

A Teacher-Effectiveness Formula

Considering teacher effectiveness to be an inverse relationship both between behaviors acquired and time and between behaviors acquired and instructional effort, Kauffman et al. have quantified the product of the equations

$$E = \frac{A}{C} \text{ and } E = \frac{A}{T} \text{ as:}$$

$$E^2 = \frac{A^2}{TC} \text{ and } E = \frac{A}{\sqrt{TC}} = A\left(\frac{\sqrt{TC}}{TC}\right).$$

For ease of computation, the formula for deriving an effectiveness ratio may be rewritten:

$$E = \sqrt{\frac{A}{T\left(\frac{C}{A}\right)}}$$

As presented above, the formula is designed to measure the effectiveness of a teacher in teaching one set of behaviors to one learner. E is concept specific. That is, a teacher is not "effective" in some abstract sense of the word. Rather, he is effective in relation to teaching a specific skill. Naturally, he cannot teach a given skill to all children with the same effectiveness; but summing across children, we may find an average E ratio as follows:

$$E_{\overline{X}} = \frac{\left[A\left(\frac{\sqrt{TC}}{TC}\right)\right]_1 + \left[A\left(\frac{\sqrt{TC}}{TC}\right)\right]_2 + \cdots \left[A\left(\frac{\sqrt{TC}}{TC}\right)\right]_n}{N}$$

The beginning stages of development of this formula hopefully will provide the impetus for empirically researchable hypotheses related to teacher effectiveness. It is anticipated that the formula will give a framework for quantitative analyses of educational performance. A factorial analysis of teacher $\times$ method $\times$ child $\times$ task interactions is feasible and would allow assessment of conditions of maximum learning for the child on an empirical rather than a subjective basis. In a review of studies investigating interaction of treatment and aptitude, Reynolds and Balow (1972) found that, "In each of [the] studies, the interactions between pupil characteristics, teaching methods, and material suggest that the teacher would be more or less effective depending on the decisions he made to match the teaching system to the pupil" (p. 364).

The developers of the formula readily admit that the distribution of E ratios presently is a matter of speculation. Regardless of its distribution, however, it is safe to assume that $E_{\overline{X}}$ for a given teacher will become more stable and representative of his true effectiveness as the number of different children to whom he teaches a task increases. Furthermore, as teacher effectiveness and instructional methods become established, the relative influence of other variables impinging upon the learning process can be more easily assessed. Present formulations of learning ability (e.g., IQ) ignore variance contributed by the effectiveness of the teacher and instructional methods. As Reynolds and Balow (1972) have pointed out,

Precisely because general intelligence test results predict learning and performance in many situations, they are virtually useless for making choices among educational situations. Educational decisions require attention to variables that produce interaction effects with educational treatments, that is, variables that help educators to make a difference rather than a prediction [p. 359].

While such an evaluation procedure would aid all aspects of general and special education, it would be exceedingly beneficial in the education of learning disabled children whose intra-individual differences required modulation of instruction.

Kauffman et al. presently are working from a strictly theoretical basis; and they have only begun to collect data. It is their goal to refine this evaluation process in order that the teacher himself may be able to put it to use in the classroom. At this point, the formula does suggest fruitful areas of research. It is *not* suggested as a means of evaluating teachers for purposes of employment, advancement, or tenure. If the validity and reliability of the model is indicated by research, and if feasible methods of teacher self-evaluation are developed on an empirical basis, education will be served well.

SUMMARY

The field of learning disabilities cannot boast a long history. Its sudden emergence as a full-blown area within special education has resulted in a vacuum of essential knowledge regarding basic constructs. Numerous vectors for future directions in learning disabilities thus could be drawn.

A few areas of concern stand out as requiring immediate attention. Interdisciplinary efforts are desperately needed in all phases of research. At the federal government level, high priority areas need to be identified for funding on a "request for proposals" basis, and special attention should be given to proposals employing longitudinal methodologies. In addition, more prototype programs that concentrate on specifying the behavioral levels of each child and advancing the child in these specific areas must be created. Lastly, innovative evaluation paradigms are needed if the teacher is to be able to assess empirically his progress with individual children.

References

ABERCROMBIE, M. L. J., J. R. DAVIS, and B. SHACKEL. Pilot study of version movements of eyes in cerebral palsied and other children. *Vision Research,* 1963, *3,* 135-53.

ALBETRECCIA, S. I. Recognition and treatment of disturbance of body image. *Cerebral Palsy Bulletin,* 1958, *4,* 12-17.

ALLEN, K. E., L. B. HENKE, F. R. HARRIS, D. M. BAER, and N. J. REYNOLDS. Control of hyperactivity by social reinforcement of attending behavior. *Journal of Educational Psychology,* 1967, *58,* 231-37.

ALLEN, R. M., I. DYKMAN, and T. D. HAUPT. A pilot study of the immediate effectiveness of the Frostig-Horne training program for educable retardates. *Exceptional Children,* 1966, *33,* 41-42.

ALLEY, G. R. Perceptual-motor performances of mentally retarded children after systematic visual-perceptual training. *American Journal of Mental Deficiency,* 1968, *73,* 247-50.

ALLEY, G. R., and D. L. CARR. Effects of systematic sensory-motor training on sensory-motor, visual perception, and concept formation performance of mentally retarded children. *Perceptual and Motor Skills,* 1968, *27,* 451-56.

ALLEY, G. R., W. SNIDER, J. SPENCER, and R. ANGELL. Reading readiness and the Frostig training program. *Exceptional Children,* 1968, *35,* 68.

AMANTE, D., P. H. MARGULES, D. M. HARTMAN, D. B. STOREY, and L. F. WEBER. The epidemiological distribution of CNS dysfunction. *Journal of Social Issues,* 1970, *26,* 105-16.

AMERICAN ACADEMY FOR CEREBRAL PALSY. Statement of executive committee, February 15, 1965.

AMERICAN ACADEMY OF NEUROLOGY. Joint executive board statement—the Doman-Delacato treatment of neurologically handicapped children. *Neurology* (Minneapolis), 1967, *17*, 637.

AMERICAN ACADEMY OF PEDIATRICS. Executive board statement. *American Academy of Pediatrics Newsletter*, December 1, 1965.

AMERICAN ACADEMY OF PHYSICAL MEDICINE AND REHABILITATION. Statement on Doman-Delacato treatment of neurologically handicapped children, 1967.

ANASTASI, A. Heredity environment, and the question 'how?'. *Psychological Review*, 1958, *65*, 197-208.

ANDERSON, A. L. The effect of laterality localization of focal brain lesions on the Wechsler-Bellevue subtests. *Journal of Clinical Phychology*, 1951, *7*, 149-53.

ANDERSON, J. M. Review: Marianne Frostig developmental test of visual perception. In O. K. Buros (ed.), *The sixth mental measurements yearbook.* Highland Park, N.J.: Gryphon Press, 1965.

ANDERSON, W. W. The hyperkinetic child: A neurological appraisal. *Neurology* (Minneapolis), 1963, *13*, 968.

AUSUBEL, D. P. Teaching strategy for culturally deprived pupils: cognitive and motivational considerations. *Scholastic Review*, 1963, *71*, 454-63.

AYRES, A. J. Types of perceptual motor deficits in children with learning difficulties. Paper presented at the meeting of the Los Angeles County Guidance Association, April, 1964.

BAGDIKIAN, B. H. *In the midst of plenty: the poor in America.* New York: Beacon Press, 1964.

BALL, T. S. and C. L. EDGAR. The effectiveness of sensory-motor training in promoting generalized body image development. *Journal of Special Education,* 1967 *1*, 387-95.

BALOW, I. H. Lateral dominance characteristics and reading achievement in the first grade. *Journal fo Psychology*, 1963, *55*, 323-28.

BALOW, I. H. and B. BALOW. Lateral dominance and reading achievement in the second grade. *American Educational Research Journal*, 1964, *1*, 139-43.

BANDURA, A. Social learning through imitation. In M. R. Jones (ed.), *Nebraska symposium on motivation.* Lincoln: University of Nebraska Press, 1962. Pp. 211-69.

BANTA, T. J. Tests for the evaluation of early childhood education: The Cincinnati Autonomy Test Battery (CATB). In J. Hellmuth (ed.), *Cognitive studies.* Vol. 1. Seattle: Special Child Publications, 1969.

BARAITSER, M. E. The effect of undernutrition on brain-rhythm development. *South Africa Medical Journal*, 1959, *43*, 56.

BARNES, R. H. Experimental approaches to the study of early malnutrition and mental development. *Federation Proceedings,* 1967, *26*, 146. (b)

BARNES, R. H., S. R. CUNNOLD, and R. R. ZIMMERMAN. Influence of nutritional deprivations in early life on learning behavior of rats as measured by performance in a water maze. *Journal of Nutrition,* 1966, *89*, 399.

BARNES, R. H., A. U. MOORE, I. M. REID, and W. G. POND. Learning behavior following nutritional deprivations in early life. *Journal of the American Dietetic Association,* 1967, *51* 34. (a)

BARSCH, R. H. Counseling the parent of the brain-damaged child. *Journal of Rehabilitation,* 1961, *27* (3), 26-27.

BARSCH, R. H. The role of cognition in movement. Optometric Child Vision Care and Guidance, Optometric Extension Program Postgraduate Courses, 1964, Series 8, no. 4.

BARSCH, R. H. *A movigenic curriculum.* Madison, Wisconsin: Bureau for Handicapped Children, 1965. (a)

BARSCH, R. H. Six factors in learning. In J. Hellmuth (ed.), *Learning disorders.* Vol. 1. Seattle: Special Child Publications, 1965. Pp. 329-43. (b)

BARSCH, R. H. *Achieving perceptual-motor efficiency: A space-oriented approach to learning.* Seattle: Special Child Publications, 1967.

BARTLETT, F. C. *Remembering.* Cambridge: Cambridge University Press, 1932.

BARTLETT, F. C. *Thinking.* New York: Basic Books, 1958.

BATEMAN, B. *Interpretation of the 1961 Illinois Test of Psycholinguistic Abilities.* Seattle: Special Child Publications, 1968.

BECK, J. Unlocking the secrets of the brain. *Chicago Tribune Magazine,* 1964 (reprinted from articles on September 13 and 27, 1964).

BEERY, K. E. and N. A. BUKTENICA. *The developmental test of visual motor integration.* Chicago: Follett Publishing, 1967.

BÉHAR, M. Prevalence of malnutrition among preschool children of developing countries. In N. S. Scrimshaw and J. E. Gordon (eds.), *Malnutrition, learning and behavior.* Cambridge, Mass.: MIT Press, 1968.

BELL, R. W., C. E. MILLER, J. M. ORDY, and C. ROLSTEN. Effects of population density and living space upon neuroanatomy, neurochemistry, and behavior in the C57B1/10 mouse. *Journal of Comparative and Physiological Psychology,* 1971, *75,* 258-63.

BELMONT, L. and H. G. BIRCH. Lateral dominance, lateral awareness, and reading disability. *Child Development,* 1965, *36,* 57-71.

BENSBERG, G. J. and G. N. CANTOR. Reaction time in mental defectives with organic and familial aetiology. *American Journal of Mental Deficiency,* 1957, *62,* 534-37.

BENTON, A. L. Right-left discrimination and finger localization in defective children. *Archives of Neurology and Psychiatry,* 1955, *74,* 583-89.

BENTON, A. L. Significance of systematic reversal in right-left discrimination. *Acta Psychiatrica et Neurologica Scandinavia,* 1958, *33,* 129-37.

BENTON, A. L. Aphasia in children. *Education,* 1959, *79,* 1-5. (a)

BENTON, A. L. Finger localization and finger praxis. *The Quarterly Journal of Experimental Psychology,* 1959, *11,* 39-44. (b)

BENTON, A. L. *Right-left discrimination and finger localization: Development and pathology.* New York: Hoeber Medical Division, Harper and Row, 1959. (c)

BENTON, A. L. The fiction of the "Gerstmann syndrome." *Journal of Neurology, Neurosurgery, and Psychiatry,* 1961, *24,* 176-81.

BENTON, A. L. The visual retention test as a constructional praxis test. *Confina Neurologica,* 1962, *22,* 141-55.

BENTON, A. L. *The revised visual retention test: Clinical and experimental applications.* (3rd ed.) New York: Psychological Corporation, 1963.

BENTON, A. L. Constructional apraxia and the minor hemisphere. *Confina Neurologica,* 1967, *29* (1) . 1-16. (a)

BENTON, A. L. Problems of test construction in the field of aphasia. *Cortex,* 1967, *3,* 32-58. (b)

BENTON, A. L. Right-left discrimination. *Pediatric Clinics of North America,* 1968, *15,* 747-58.

BENTON, A. L. Development of a multilingual aphasia battery: progress and problems. *Journal of the Neurological Sciences,* 1969, *9,* 39-48. (a)

BENTON, A. L. Neuropsychological aspects of mental retardation. Paper presented at the Symposium on Developmental and Specific Handicaps, XIX International Congress of Psychology, London, July 1969. (b)

BENTON, A. L. and M. L. FOGEL. Three-dimensional construction praxis: A clinical test. *Archives of Neurology* (Chicago) , 1962, *7,* 347-54.

BENTON, A. L., J. C. GARFIELD, and J. C. CHIORINI. Motor impersistence in mental defectives. Paper presented at International Copenhagen Congress on the Scientific Study of Metal Retardation, Denmark, August 1964.

BENTON, A. L., J. F. HUTCHEON, and E. SEYMOUR. Arithmetic ability, finger localization capacity and right-left discrimination in normal and defective children. *The American Journal of Orthopsychiatry,* 1951, *21,* 756-66.

BENTON, A. L. and R. J. JOYNT. Reaction time in unilateral cerebral disease. *Confina Neurologica,* 1959, *19,* 247-56

BENTON, A. L. and F. L. MENEFEE. Handedness and right-left discrimination. *Child Development,* 1957, *28,* 237-42.

BENTON, A. L., S. SUTTON, J. A. KENNEDY, and J. R. BROKAW. The crossmodal retardation in reaction time of patients with cerebral disease. *Journal of Nervous and Mental Disease,* 1962, *135,* 413-18.

BENTON, C. D. Critique [of Cohen]. *Journal of Learning Disabilities,* 1969, *2,* 504-5.

BERLIN, I. N. Special learning problems of deprived children. *NEA Journal LV,* 1966, *23.*

BERLYNE, D. E. Attention, perception, and behavior theory. *Psychological Review,* 1951, *58,* 137-46.

BERNSTEIN, B. Social class and linguistic development: a theory of social learning. In A. H. Halsey, J. Floud, and C. A. Anderson (eds.) , *Education and society.* Glencoe, Illinois: Free Press, 1961.

BERRY, J. W. Matching of auditory and visual stimuli by average and retarded readers. *Child Development,* 1967, *38,* 827-33.

BETTMAN, J. W., JR., E. L. STERN, L. J. WHITSELL, and H. F. GOFMAN. Cerebral dominance in developmental dyslexia. *Archives of Ophthalmology,* 1967, *78,* 722-29.

BIRCH, H. G. Introducing the American Orthopsychiatric Association's President for 1964-1965, Arthur Benton, Ph.D. *American Journal of Orthopsychiatry,* 1964, *34,* 611-12.

BIRCH, H. G., I. BELMONT, and E. KARP. The prolongation of inhibition in brain-damaged patients. *Cortex,* 1965, *1,* 397-409.

BIRCH, H. G. and L. BELMONT. Auditory-visual integration in normal and retarded readers. *American Journal of Orthopsychiatry,* 1964, *34,* 852-61.

BIRCH, H. G. and L. BELMONT. Auditory-visual integration in brain-damaged and normal children. *Developmental Medicine and Child Neurology,* 1965, *7,* 135-44. (a)

BIRCH, H. G. and L. BELMONT. Auditory-visual integration, intelligence and reading ability in school children. *Perceptual and Motor Skills,* 1965, *20,* 295-305. (b)

BIRCH, H. G. and L. BELMONT. Reply to Sterritt and Rudnick. *Perceptual and Motor Skills,* 1966, *23,* 314.

BIRCH, H. G. and J. D. GUSSOW. *Disadvantaged children: health, nutrition, and school failure.* New York: Harcourt, Brace and World, 1970.

BIRCH, H. G. and A. LEFFORD. Intersensory development in children. *Monographs of the Society for Research in Child Development,* 1963, *28,* No. 5.

BIRCH, H. G. and A. LEFFORD. Two strategies for studying perception in "brain damaged" children. In H. G. Birch (ed.), *Brain damage in children: The biological and social aspects.* Baltimore: Williams and Wilkins, 1964. Pp. 46-60.

BIRD, J. When children can't learn. *Saturday Evening Post,* 1967, *240* (15), 27-31, 72-74.

BLOOM, B. I., J. T. HASTING, and G. F. MADAUS *Handbook on formative and summative evaluation of student learning.* New York: McGraw-Hill, 1971.

BOTHA-ANTOUN, E., S. BABAYAN, and J. K. HARFOUCHE. Intellectual development related to nutrition status. *Journal of Tropical Pediatrics,* 1968, *14,* 112.

BRACE, D. K. *Measuring motor ability: A scale of motor ability tests.* New York: Barnes, 1927.

BRATTGARD, I. O. The importance of adequate stimulation for the chemical composition of retinal ganglion cells during early postnatal development. *Acta Radiol.,* 1952, Suppl. 96.

BRAUN, J. S. Relation between concept formation ability and reading achievement at three developmental levels. *Child Development,* 1963, *34,* 675-82.

BROADBENT, D. E. *Perception and communication.* New York: Pergamon Press, 1958.

BRONFENBRENNER, U. Early deprivation: a cross-species analysis. In G. Newton, and S. Levine (eds.), *Early experience and behavior.* Springfield, Ill.: Charles C Thomas, 1968, 627-764. (a)

BRONFENBRENNER, U. When is infant stimulation effective? In D. C. Glass (ed.), *Environmental influences.* New York: Rockefeller University Press and Russell Sage Foundation, 1968, 251-57. (b)

BROWN, G. S. and D. P. CAMPBELL. *Principles of servomechanisms.* New York: John Wiley, 1948.

BROWN, R. I. The effect of visual distraction on perception in subjects of subnormal intelligence. *British Journal of Social and Clinical Psychology,* 1964, *2,* 20-28.

BRUNER, J. S. On perceptual readiness. *Psychological Review,* 1957, *64,* 123-52.

BRUNER, J. S., J. GOODNOW, and G. A. AUSTIN. *A study of thinking.* New York: John Wiley, 1956.

BRUNER, J. S., R. R. OLVER, and P. M. GREENFIELD. *Studies in cognitive growth.* New York: John Wiley, 1966.

BRYAN, Q. R. Relative importance of intelligence and visual perception in predicting reading achievement. *California Journal of Educational Research,* 1964, *15,* 44-48.

CABAK, V. and R. NAJDANVIE. Effect of undernutrition in early life on physical and mental development. *Archives of Disease in Childhood,* 1965, *40,* 532.

CAHILL, I. D. Child rearing in the culture of poverty. Presented to National League for Nursing, May 9, 1967.

CALDWELL, D. F. and J. A. CHURCHILL. Learning ability in the progeny of rats administered a protein deficient diet during the second half of gestation. *Neurology,* 1967, *17,* 95.

CAMPANELLI, P. A. Sustained attention in brain damaged children. *Exceptional Children,* 1970, *36,* 317-23.

CAMPBELL, D. T. Methodological suggestions from a comparative psychology of knowledge processes. *Inquiry,* 1959, *2,* 152-82.

CAMPBELL, D. T. and J. C. STANLEY Experimental and quasi-experimental designs in research on teaching. In N. L. Gage (ed.), *Handbook of research on teaching.* Chicago: Rand McNally, 1963.

CAMPBELL, D. T. and J. C. STANLEY. *Experimental and quasi-experimental designs for research.* Chicago: Rand McNally, 1966.

Canadian Association for Retarded Children. Institutes for the Achievement of Human Potential. *Mental Retardation* (Canada), 1965, Fall, 27-28.

CAPOBIANCO, R. J. Ocular-manual laterality and reading in adolescent retardates. *American Journal of Mental Deficiency,* 1966, *70,* 781-85.

CAPOBIANCO, R. J. Ocular-manual laterality and reading achievement in children with special learning difficulties. *American Educational Research Journal,* 1967, *4,* 133-38.

CARPENTER, A. The measurement of general motor capacity and general motor ability in the first three grades. *Research Quarterly*, 1942, *13*, 444-65.

CAWLEY, J. F. An assessment of intelligence, psycholinguistic abilities, and learning aptitudes among preschool children. Washington, D.C.: Project Head Start, ED-014-323, 1966.

CÉNAC, M. and H. HÉCAEN. Inversion systématique dans la designation droite-gauche chez certains enfants. *Annals Med.-Psychol.*, 1943, *101*, 415.

CHAMPAHAM, S., S. G. SRIKANTIA, and C. GOPALAN. Kwashiorkor and mental development. *American Journal of Clinical Nutrition*, 1968, *21*, 844.

CHANSKY, N. M. and M. TAYLOR. Perceptual training with young mental retardates. *American Journal of Mental Deficiency*, 1964, *68*, 460-68.

CHASE, H. R. and H. R. MARTIN. Undernutrition in child development. *New England Journal of Medicine*, 1970, *282* (17), 933-39.

CHILD, C. M. *Physiological foundations of behavior*. New York: Holt, 1924.

CHILDREN'S BUREAU PUBLICATION #46. The nation's youth. Washington, D.C., U.S. Government Printing Office, 1968.

CHOMSKY, N. *Aspects of the theory of syntax*. Cambridge, Mass.: MIT Press, 1965.

CLARK, K. B. *Dark ghetto*. New York: Harper & Row, 1965.

CLAWSON, A. Relationship of psychological tests to cerebral disorder in children. *Psychological Reports*, 1962, *10*, 187-90.

COHEN, R. I. Remedial training of first grade children with visual perceptual retardation. *Educational Horizons*, 1966, *45*, 60-63.

COHEN, S. A. Comments from Dr. Cohen. *Journal of Learning Disabilities*, 1969, *2*, 661. (a)

COHEN, S. A. Studies in visual perception and reading in disadvantaged children. *Journal of Learning Disabilities*, 1969, *2*, 498-507. (b)

COHEN, S. A. Cause versus treatment in reading achievement. *Journal of Learning Disabilities*, 1970, *3*, 163-66.

COLE, E. Book review: C. H. Delacato, The diagnosis and treatment of speech and reading problems. *Harvard Educational Review*, 1964, *34*, 351-54.

COLEMAN, H. M. Perceptual retardation in reading disability. *Perceptual and Motor Skills*, 1959, *9*, 117.

COLEMAN, H. M. Visual perception and reading dysfunction. *Journal of Learning Disabilities*, 1968, *1*, 116-23.

COLEMAN, J. S., E. Q. CAMBELL, C. J. HOBSON, J. McPORTLAND, A. M. MOOD, F. D. WEINFELD, and R. L. YORK. *Equality of educational opportunity*. Washington, D.C.: U.S. Office of Education, 1966.

COLEMAN, P. D. and A. H. RIESEN. Environmental effects on cortical dendritic fields, I., rearing in the dark. *Journal of Anatomy*, 1968, *102*, 363-74

COLEMAN, R. I. and C. P. DEUTSCH. Lateral dominance and right-left discrimination: A comparison of normal and retarded readers. *Perceptual and Motor Skills*, 1964, *19*, 43-50.

COLLIER, G. H. and R. I. SQUIBB. Malnutrition and the learning capacity of the chicken. In N. S. Scrimshaw and J. E. Gordon (eds.), *Malnutrition, learning and behavior*. Cambridge, Mass.: MIT Press, 1968.

COLLIS, W. R. F. and J. MARGARET. Multifactoral causation of malnutrition and retarded growth and development. In N. S. Scrimshaw and J. E. Gordon (eds.), *Malnutrition, learning and behavior*. Cambridge, Mass.: MIT Press, 1968.

COOK, D. L. The impact of the Hawthorne Effect in experimental designs in educational research. Report to Office of Education, Project No. 1757, Contract No. OE-3-10-041, 1967.

CORAH, N. L. and B. J. POWELL. A factor analytic study of the Frostig developmental test of visual perception. *Perceptual and Motor Skills*, 1963, *16*, 59-63.

COTTON, C. A. A study of the reactions of spastic children to certain test situations. *Journal of Genetic Psychology*, 1941, *52*, 27.

COURSIN, D. B. Effects of undernutrition on central nervous system function. *Nutrition Review*, 1965, *23*, 65-68.

COVINGTON, M. V. Stimulus deprivation as a function of social class membership. *Child Development*, 1967, *38*, 607.

COWLEY, J. J. and R. D. GRIESEL. The effect on growth and behavior of rehabilitating first and second generation low protein rats. *Animal Behavior*, 1966, *14*, 506.

CRAGG, B. G. Changes in visual cortex on first exposure of rats to light. *Nature*, 1967, *215*, 251-55.

CRATTY, B. J. and M. M. MARTIN. *Perceptual-motor efficiency in children*. Philadelphia: Lea and Feibiger, 1969.

CRAVIOTO, J. Nutrition and learning in children. In N. S. Springer (ed.), *Nutrition and mental retardation*. Ann Arbor, Michigan: Institute for the Study of Mental Retardation and Related Disabilities, 1972, 25-44.

CRAVIOTO, J. Protein metabolism in chronic infantile malnutrition (kwashiorkor). *American Journal of Clinical Nutrition*, 1958, *6*, 495.

CRAVIOTO, J., H. G. BIRCH, and C. E. GAONA. Early malnutrition and auditory-visual integration in school-age children. *Journal of Special Education*, 1967, *2*, 75.

GRAVIOTO, J. and E. R. DELICARDIE. Intersensory development of school-age children. In N. S. Scrimshaw and J. E. Gordon (eds.), *Malnutrition, learning and behavior*. Cambridge, Mass.: MIT Press, 1968.

GRAVIOTO, J., E. R. DeLICARDIE, and H. G. BIRCH. Nutrition, growth, and neurointegrative development: An experimental and ecologic study. *Pedriatics*, 1966, *38* (Suppl. 2), 319.

CRAVIOTO, J. and B. ROBLES. Evolution of adaptive and motor behavior during rehabilitation from kwashiorkor. *American Journal of Orthopsychiatry*, 1965, *35*, 449.

CRITCHEL, M. *The parietal lobes*. London: Edward Arnold Ltd., 1953.

CROMWELL, R. L., A. BAUMEISTER, and H. F. HAWKINS. Research in activity level.

In N. R. Ellis (ed.), *Handbook of mental deficiency.* New York: McGraw-Hill, 1963.

CROMWELL, R. L. and J. G. FOSHEE. Studies in activity level. IV. Effects of visual stimulation during task performance in mental defectives. *American Journal of Mental Deficiency,* 1960, *65,* 248-51.

CROMWELL, R. L., B. F. PALK, and J. G. FOSHEE. Studies in activity level. V. The relationship among eyelid conditioning, intelligence, activity level, and age. *American Journal of Mental Deficiency,* 1961, *65,* 744-48.

CRONHOLM, B. and D. SCHALLING. Effects of early brain injury on perceptual-constructive performances in adults. *Journal of Nervous and Mental Disease,* 1968, *147,* 547-52.

CRUICKSHANK, W. M. (ed.). *The teacher of brain-injured children.* Syracuse, N. Y.: Syracuse University Press, 1966.

CRUSCKSHANK, W. M. *The brain-injured child in home, school and community.* Syracuse, N. Y.: Syracuse University Press, 1967.

CRUICKSHANK, W. M. Lecture reported in Final Report, U.S.O.E. Contract, Advanced Institute for Leadership Personnel in Learning Disabilities, Department of Special Education, University of Arizona, 1971.

CRUICKSHANK, W. M., F. A. BENTZEN, F. H. RATZEBURG, and M. T. TANNHAUSSER. *A teaching method for brain-injured and hyperactive children.* Syracuse, N. Y.: Syracuse University Press, 1961.

CRUICKSHANK, W. M., H. V. BICE, and N. E. WALLEN. *Perception and cerebral palsy.* Syracuse, N.Y.: Syracuse University Press, 1957.

CRUICKSHANK, W. M., H. V. BICE, N. E. WALLEN, and K. S. LYNCH. *Perception and cerebral palsy.* (2nd ed.) Syracuse, N. Y.: Syracuse University Press, 1965.

CRUICKSHANK, W. M. and J. E. DOLPHIN. The educational implications of psychological studies of cerebral palsied children. *Exceptional Children,* 1951, *18,* 3-11.

CRUICKSHANK, W. M., E. MARSHALL, and M. A. HURLEY. *Foundations for mathematics.* Boston: Teaching Resources, 1971.

CRUICKSHANK, W. M. and J. L. PAUL. The psychological characteristics of brain-injured children. In W. M. Cruickshank (ed.), *Psychology of exceptional children and youth.* (3rd ed.) Englewood Cliffs, N. J.: Prentice-Hall, 1971.

CRUSE, D. B. Effects of distraction upon the performance of brain-injured and familial retarded children. *American Journal of Mental Deficiency,* 1961, *66,* 86-92.

DAVOL, I. H. and M. L. HASTINGS. Effects of sex, age, reading ability, SES, and display position on measures of spatial relations in children. *Perceptual and Motor Skills,* 1967, *24,* 375-87.

DAYTON, D. H. Early malnutrition and human development. *Children,* 1969, *16,* 216.

DE BEER, G. *Embryos and ancestors.* (3rd ed.) Oxford: Clarendon Press, 1958.

DEE, H. L., A. L. BENTON, and M. W. VAN ALLEN. Apraxia in relation to hemispheric locus of lesion and aphasia. *Transactions of the American Neurological Association,* 1970, *95,* 147-50.

DEHIRSCH, K. Specific dyslexia or strephosymbiolia. *Folia Phoniatrica,* 1952, *4,* 231-48.

DEHIRSCH, K. Gestalt psychology as applied to language disturbances. *Journal of Nervous and Mental Disease,* 1954, *120,* 257-61.

DEHIRSCH, K. Tests designed to discover potential reading difficulties at the six-year-old level. *American Journal of Orthopsychiatry,* 1957, *27,* 566-76.

DEHIRSCH, K. Concepts related to normal reading processes and their application to reading pathology. *Genetic Psychology,* 1963. (a)

DEHIRSCH, K. Two categories of learning difficulties in adolescents. *American Journal of Orthopsychiatry,* 1963, *33,* 87-91. (b)

DEHIRSCH, K. Differential diagnosis between aphasia and schizophrenic language in children. *Journal of Speech and Hearing Disorders,* 1967, *32,* 3-10.

DEHIRSCH, K. Clinical spectrum of reading disabilities: Diagnosis and treatment. *Bulletin of the New York Academy of Medicine,* 1968, *44,* 470-77.

DEHIRSCH, K. Stuttering and cluttering: developmental aspects of dysrhythmic speech. *Journal of Special Education,* 1969, *3,* 143-53.

DEHIRSCH, K. Preschool intervention. *Reading Forum,* NINDS Monograph No. II, 1971.

DEHIRSCH, K., J. JANSKY, and W. S. LANGFORD. Comparisons between prematurely and maturely born children at three age levels. *American Journal of Orthopsychiatry,* 1966, *36,* 616-28. (a)

DEHIRSCH, K., J. JANSKY, and W. S. LANGFORD. *Predicting reading failure.* New York: Harper & Row, 1966. (b)

DELACATO, C. H. *The treatment and prevention of reading problems: The neurological approach.* Springfield, Ill.: Charles C Thomas, 1959.

DELACATO, C. H. *The diagnosis and treatment of speech and reading problems.* Springfield, Ill.: Charles C. Thomas, 1963.

DELACATO, C. H. *Neurological organization and reading.* Springfield, Ill.: Charles C Thomas, 1966.

DENNIS, W. Causes of retardation among institutional children: Iran. *Journal of Genetic Psychology,* 1960, *96,* 47-59.

DENNY, D. R. Modeling effects upon conceptual style and cognitive tempo. *Child Development,* 1972, *43,* 105-20.

DEUTSCH, C. P. Environment and perception. In M. Deutsch, I. Katz, and A. Jensen. (eds.), *Social class, race, and psychological development.* New York: Holt, Rinehart, and Winston, 1968.

DEUTSCH, C. P. and F. SCHUMER. *Brain-damaged children: A modality-oriented exploration of performance.* Final Report to the Vocational Rehabilitation Administration, Department of Health, Education, and Welfare, Washington, D.C., 1967.

DEUTSCH, M. Minority group and class status as related to social and personality factors in scholastic achievement. *Monographs of the Society for Applied Anthropology*, 1962, 2.

DEUTSCH, M. The disadvantaged child and the learning process. In A. H. Passow (ed.), *Education in depressed areas*. New York: Teachers College Press, 1963.

DEUTSCH, M. Facilitating development in the preschool child: social and psychological perspectives. *Merrill-Palmer Quarterly*, 1964, *10*, 249-63.

DOBBING, J. Effects of experimental undernutrition on development of the nervous system. In N. S. Scrimshaw and J. E. Gordon (eds.), *Malnutrition, learning and behavior*. Cambridge, Mass.: MIT Press, 1968.

DOBBING, J. and E. M. WIDDOWSON. The effect of undernutrition and subsequent rehabilitation on myelination of rat brains as measured by its composition. *Brain*, 1965, *88*, 357.

DOLPHIN, J. E. A study of certain aspects of the psychopathology of children with cerebral palsy. Unpublished doctoral dissertation. Syracuse University, 1950.

DOLPHIN, J. E. and W. M. CRUICKSHANK. The figure-background relationship in children with cerebral palsy. *Journal of Clinical Psychology*, 1951, *7*, 228-31. (a)

DOLPHIN, J. E. and W. M. CRUICKSHANK. Pathology of concept formation in children with cerebral palsy. *American Journal of Mental Deficiency*, 1951, *56*, 386-92. (b)

DOLPHIN, J. E. and W. M. CRUICKSHANK. Visuo-motor perception of children with cerebral palsy. *Quarterly Journal of Child Behavior*, 1951, *3*, 198-209. (c)

DOLPHIN, J. E. and W. M. CRUICKSHANK. Tactual motor perception of children with cerebral palsy. *Journal of Personality*, 1952, *20*, 466-71.

DOMAN, G. and C. H. DELACATO. Train your baby to be a genius. *McCall's*, March, 1965, *65*, 169, 170, 172.

DOMAN, R. J., E. B. SPITZ, E. ZUCMAN, C. H. DELACATO, and G. DOMAN. Children with severe brain injuries: Neurological organizations in terms of mobility. *Journal of the American Medical Association*, 1960, *174*, 257-62.

DONNELLY, J. F., C. E. FLOWERS, R. N. CREADICK, H. B. WELLO, and G. B. GREENBERG. Maternal, fetal, and environmental factors in prematurity. *American Journal of Obstetrics and Gynecology*, 1964, *88*, 918-31.

DREW, C. J., C. W. FRESTON, and D. R. LOGAN. Criteria and reference in evaluation. *Focus on Exceptional Children*, 1972, *4*, 1-10.

DRUKER, J. F. and J. W. HAGEN. Developmental trends in the processing of task-relevant and task-irrelevant information. *Child Development*, 1969, *40*, 371-82.

DUNN, L. M. *Peabody picture vocabulary test manual*. Minneapolis: American Guidance Service, 1959.

DUROST, L. M. *Peabody picture vocabulary test manual*. Minneapolis: American Guidance Service, 1959.

Durost, W. N. *Metropolitan achievement tests, primary 1.* New York: Harcourt, Brace and World, 1959.

Dykman, R. A., R. C. Walls, T. Suzuki, P. T. Ackerman, and J. E. Peters. Children with learning disabilities: Conditioning differentiation and the effect of distraction. *American Journal of Mental Deficiency,* 1970, *40,* 766-82.

Edgar, C. L., T. S. Ball, R. B. McIntyre, and A. M. Shotwell. Effects of sensory-motor training on adaptive behavior. *American Journal of Mental Deficiency,* 1969, *73,* 713-20.

Eells, K., A. Davis, R. J. Havinghurst, V. E. Herriels, and R. W. Tyler. *Intelligence and cultural differences.* Chicago: University of Chicago Press, 1951.

Eichenwald, H. F. and P. C. Fry. Nutrition and learning. *Science,* 1969, *163,* 644.

Eisenberg, L. Behavioral manifestations of cerebral damage in childhood. In H. G. Birch (ed.), *Brain damage in children.* Baltimore: Williams and Wilkins, 1964. Pp. 61-73.

Elkind, D. and J. A. Deblinger. Perceptual training and reading achievement in disadvantaged children. *Child Development,* 1969, *40,* 11-19.

Elkind, D., R. R. Koegler, and E. Go. Studies in perceptual development. II. Part-whole perception. *Child Development,* 1964, *35,* 81-91.

Elkind, D., M. Larson, and W. VanDoorninck. Perceptual decentration in learning and performance in slow and average readers. *Journal of Education Psychology,* 1965, *56,* 50-56.

Ellis, N. R. The stimulus trace and behavioral inadequacy. In N. R. Ellis (ed.), *Handbook of mental deficiency.* New York: McGraw-Hill, 1963.

Erickson, R. C. Visual-haptic attitude: Effect on student achievement in reading. *Journal of Learning Disabilities,* 1969, *2,* 256-60.

Fantz, R. L. Pattern discrimination and selective attention as determinants of perceptual development in children. In A. H. Kidd and J. L. Riviore (eds.), *Perceptual development in children.* New York: International Universities Press, 1966. Pp. 143-73.

Fay, T. Twenty percent carbon dioxide inhalation in muscular rigidity. *Journal of the American Medical Association,* 1953, *152,* 1623.

Feld, S. C. and J. Lewis. The assessment of achievement anxieties in children. Mental Health Study Center, NIMH, 1967.

Fernald, G. M. *Remedial techniques in basic school subjects.* New York: McGraw-Hill, 1943.

Ferreira, A. J. *Prenatal environment.* Springfield, Ill.: Charles C Thomas, 1969.

Fisher, L. Attention deficit in brain damaged children. *American Journal of Mental Deficiency,* 1970, *74,* 502-8.

Fitzhugh, K. B., L. C. Fitzhugh, and R. M. Reitan. Wechsler-Bellevue comparisons in groups with "chronic" and "current" lateralized and diffuse brain lesions. *Journal of Consulting Psychology,* 1962, *26,* 306-10.

FLEISHMAN, E. A. Factor structure in relation to task difficulty in psychomotor performance. *Educational and Psychological Measurement,* 1957, *17,* 522-32.

FLEISHMAN, E. A. and G. D. ELLISON. A factor analysis of fine manipulative tests. *Journal of Applied Psychology,* 1962, *46,* 96-105.

FLEISHMAN, E. A., P. THOMAS, and P. MUNROE. The dimensions of physical fitness—a factor analysis of speed, flexibility, balance, and coordination tests. Technical report #3, Office of Naval Research, New Haven, Connecticut, September 1961.

FLESCHER, I. Ocular-manual laterality and perceptual rotation of literal symbols. *Genetic Psychology Monographs,* 1962, *66,* 3-48.

FOLLINI, P., C. A. SITKOWSKI, and S. E. STAYTON. The attention of retardates and normals in distraction and non-distraction conditions. *American Journal of Mental Deficiency,* 1969, *74,* 200-205.

FOREHAND, R. and A. A. BAUMEISTER. Effects of variations in auditory-visual stimulation on activity levels of severe mental retardates. *American Journal of Mental Deficiency,* 1970, *74,* 470-74.

FREEMAN, R. D. Controversy over "patterning" as a treatment for brain damage in children. *Journal of the American Medical Association,* 1967, *202,* 385-88. (a)

FREEMAN, R. D. Review of J. R. Kershener, An investigation of the Doman-Delacato theory of neuropsychology as it applies to trainable mentally retarded children in public schools. *Journal of Pediatrics,* 1967, *71,* 914-15. (b)

FREY, R. Reading behavior of public school brain injured and non-brain injured children of average and retarded mental development. Doctoral dissertation, University of Illinois, 1961.

FRISCH, R. E. Present status of the supposition that malnutrition causes permanent mental retardation. *American Journal of Clinical Nutrition,* 1970, *23,* 191.

FROSTIG, M. and D. HORNE. *The Frostig program for the development of visual perception: Teacher's guide.* Chicago: Follett, 1964.

FROSTIG, M., D. W. LEFEVER, and J. R. B. WHITTLESEY. A developmental test of visual perception for evaluating normal and neurologically handicapped children. *Perceptual and Motor Skills,* 1961, *12,* 383-94.

FROSTIG, M., D. W. LEFEVER, and J. R. B. WHITTLESEY. *The Marianne Frostig developmental test of visual perception.* Palo Alto: Consulting Psychology Press, 1964.

FROSTIG, M., and P. MASLOW. Reading, developmental abilities, and the problem of the match. *Journal of Learning Disabilities,* 1969, *2,* 571-74.

FROSTIG, M., P. MASLOW, D. W. LEFEVER, and J. R. B. WHITTLESEY. *The Marianne Frostig developmental test of visual perception, 1963 standardization.* Palo Alto: Consulting Psychology Press, 1964.

GADDES, W. H. A neuropsychological approach to learning disorders. *Journal of Learning Disabilities,* 1968, *1,* 523-34.

GARDNER, E. *Fundamentals of neurology.* (4th ed.) Philadelphia: W. B. Saunders, 1963.

GARDNER, R. W. The needs of teachers for specialized information on the development of cognitive structures. In W. M. Cruickshank (ed.) , *The teacher of brain injured children.* Syracuse, N. Y.: Syracuse University Press, 1966, chapter 9.

GARDNER, W. L., R. L. CROMWELL, and J. G. FOSHEE. Studies in activity level. II. Effects of distal visual stimulation in organics, familials, hyperactives, and hypoactives. *American Journal of Mental Deficiency,* 1959. *63,* 1028-33.

GARN, S. M. Malnutrition and skeletal development in the pre-school child. In pre-school child malnutrition: primary deterrent to human progress. *National Academy of Science-National Research Council Publication 1282.* Washington, D.C.: 1966, 43-62.

GERBER, M. and R. F. A. DEAN. The state of development of newborn African children. *The Lancet,* 1957, *1,* 1216.

GERSTMANN, J. Fingeragnoisie und isolierte agraphie—ein neues syndrom. *Zeitschraft fuer die Gesamte Neurologie and Psychiatrie,* 1928, *108,* 152-77.

GESCHWIND, N. The development of the brain and the evolution of language. *Monograph Series on Language and Linguistics,* 1964, No. 17.

GESELL, A. *The first five years of life.* New York: Harper, 1940.

GESELL, A. and K. ARMATRUDA. *Developmental diagnosis.* New York: Harper, 1947.

GESELL, A., F. ILG, G. BULLIS, G. GETMAN, and F. ILG. *Vision: Its development in infant and child.* New York: Hoeber, 1949.

GETMAN, G. N. Studies in perceptual development: How to provide intellectual care and guidance for children. Unpublished paper. Luverne, Minnesota, 1954. (a)

GETMAN, G. N. Studies in visual development: How to provide visual care and guidance for children. Unpublished paper. Luverne, Minnesota, 1954. (b)

GETMAN, G. N. View, review, and preview. Optometric child vision care and guidance. Optometric Extension Program, Post-Graduate Courses, 1963, Series 8, No. 1.

GETMAN, G. N. The visuomotor complex in the acquisition of learning skills. In J. Hellmuth (ed.), *Learning disorders.* Vol. 1. Seattle: Special Child Publications, 1965.

GETMAN, G. N. Vision, audition and problems of learning. A series of papers released by the Optometric Extension Program, Duncan, Oklahoma, to its membership, 1968-1969.

GETMAN, G. N. Critique [of Cohen]. *Journal of Learning Disabilities,* 1969, *2,* 503-4.

GETMAN, G. N., E. R. KANE, M. R. HALGREN, and G. W. MCKEE. *The physiol-*

ogy of readiness, an action program for the development of perception for children. Minneapolis: Programs to Accelerate School Success, 1964.

GETMAN, G. N. and N. C. KEPHART. *The perceptual development of retarded children.* Luverne, Minnesota. Mimeographed. Lafayette, Ind.: Purdue University, 1956.

GIBSON, E. J. Improvement in perceptual judgments as a function of controlled practice or training. *Psychological Bulletin,* 1953, *50,* 401-31.

GIBSON, E. J. Development of perception: Discrimination of depth compared with discrimination of graphic symbols. In J. C. Wright and J. Kagan (eds.), Basic cognitive processes in children. *Monographs of the Society for Research in Child Development,* 1963, 28, No. 2, Serial No. 86, 5-23.

GIBSON, E. J. *Principles of perceptual learning and development.* New York: Appleton-Century-Crofts, 1969.

GIBSON, E. J. and R. D. WALK. The "visual cliff." *Scientific American,* 1960, *202,* 2-9.

GIBSON, J. J. (ed.). Motion picture testing and research. *Army air foirces aviation psychology research program reports;* report 7. Washington, D.C.: U.S. Govenment Printing Office, 1947.

GIBSON, J. J. and E. J. GIBSON. Perceptual learning: Differentiation or enrichment? *Psychological Review,* 1955, *62,* 33-40.

GILL, N. T., T. J. HERDTNER, and L. LOUGH. Perceptual and socio-economic variables, instruction in body-orientation, and predicted academic success in young children. *Perceptual and Motor Skills,* 1968, *26,* 1175-84.

GLASER, G. H. *EEG and behavior.* New York: Basic Books, 1962.

GLASER, R. Instructional technology and the measurement of learning outcomes: some questions. *American Psychologist,* 1963, *18,* 519-21.

GLASER, R. Individuals and learning: adaptation or selection. Presidential address, American Educational Research Association Convention, Chicago, 1972.

GLASS, G. V. A critique of experiments on the role of neurological organization in reading performance. Unpublished paper. Urbana: University of Illinois College of Education, 1966.

GLOBUS, A. and A. B. SCHEIBEL. Synaptic loci on visual cortical neurons of the rabbit: the specific afferent radiation. *Experimental Neurology,* 1967, *18,* 116-31.

GOLDEN, N. E. and S. R. STEINER. Auditory and visual functions of good and poor readers. *Journal of Learning Disabilities,* 1969, *2,* 476-81.

GOLDSTEIN, K. *Die lokalisation in der grosshirnrinde. Handb. norm. pathol. physiologie.* Berlin: J. Springer, 1927.

GOLDSTEIN, K. The modifications of behavior consequent to cerebral lesions. *Psychiatric Quarterly,* 1936, *10,* 586-610.

GOLDSTEIN, K. *The organism.* New York: American Book, 1939.

GOLLIN, E. S. Developmental studies of visual recognition of incomplete objects. *Perceptual and Motor Skills,* 1960, *11,* 289-98.

GOLLIN, E. S. Further studies of visual recognition of incomplete objects. *Perceptual and Motor Skills,* 1961, *13,* 307-14.

GORDON, M. W. and G. C. DEANIN. Mitochondria and lysosomes: a proposal on the protein nutrition of the synapse. In N. S. Scrimshaw and J. E. Gordon (eds.), *Malnutrition, learning and behavior.* Cambridge, Mass.: MIT Press, 1968.

GORTON, C. E. The effects of various classroom environments on performance of a mental task by mentally retarded and normal children. *Education and Training of the Mentally Retarded,* 1972, 7, 32-38.

GOTTESMAN, I. I. Biogenetics of race and class. In M. Deutsch, I. Katz, and A. Jensen (eds.), *Social class, race, and psychological development.* New York: Holt, Rinehart, and Winston, 1968.

GREEN, L. J. Functional neurological performance in primitive cultures. *Human Potential,* 1967, *1,* 19-26.

GRINDER, R. E. *A history of genetic psychology.* New York: John Wiley, 1967.

GRINSTED, A. D. Studies in gross bodily movement. Unpublished doctoral dissertation, Louisiana State University, 1939.

GROTBERG, E. H. Neurological aspects of learning disabilities: a case for the disadvantaged. *Journal of Learning Disabilities,* 1970, *3 (6),* 25-31.

GUILFORD, J. P. The structure of intellect. *Psychological Bulletin,* 1956, *52,* 267-93.

GUILFORD, J. P. A system of psychomotor abilities. *American Journal of Psychology,* 1958, *71,* 146-47.

GUMP, P. V. Intra-setting analysis: the third grade classroom as a special but instructive case. In E. P. Willems and H. L. Raush (eds.), *Naturalistic viewpoints in psychological research.* New York: Holt, Rinehart, and Winston, 1969.

HAGEN, J. W. The effect of distraction on selective attention. *Child Development,* 1967, *38,* 685-94.

HAGEN, J. W. Strategies for remembering. Paper presented at Symposium, "Information Processing in Children," Carnegie-Mellon University, May 1971.

HAGEN, J. W. The effects of attention and mediation on children's memory. *Young Children,* in press.

HAGEN, J. W. and S. R. FRISCH. The effect of incidental cues on selective attention. Report No. 57, USPHS Grant HDO1368. Center for Human Growth and Development, University of Michigan, 1968.

HAGEN, J. W. and D. P. HALLAHAN. A language training program for preschool migrant children. *Exceptional Children,* 1971, *37,* 606-7.

HAGEN, J. W. and N. J. HUNTSMAN. Selective attention in mental retardates. *Developmental Psychology,* 1971, *5,* 151-60.

HAGEN, J. W. and R. A. SABO. A developmental study of selective attention. *Merrill-Palmer Quarterly,* 1967, *13,* 159-72.

HAGEN, J. W. and R. F. WEST. The effects of a pay-off matrix on selective attention. *Human Development,* 1970, *13,* 43-52.

HALGREN, A. Opus in see sharp. *Education,* 1961. *81,* 369-71.

HALLAHAN, D. P. Cognitive styles: Pre-school implications for the disadvantaged. *Journal of Learning Disabilities,* 1970, *3,* 4-9.

HALSTEAD, W. C. Preliminary analysis of grouping behavior of patients with cerebral injury by methods of equivalent and non-equivalent stimuli. *American Journal of Psychiatry,* 1940, *96,* 1263.

HALSTEAD, W. C. *Brain and intelligence: A quantitative study of the frontal lobes.* Chicago: University of Chicago Press, 1947.

HANAWALT, N. G. Review: Benton visual retention test, revised edition. In O. K. Buros (ed.), *The fifth mental measurements yearbook.* N. J.: Gryphon Press, 1959. Pp. 401-3.

HARDY, J. B. Perinatal factors and intelligence. In S. F. Osler and R. E. Cooke (eds.), *The biosocial basis of mental retardation.* Baltimore: Johns Hopkins Press, 1965.

HARING, N. G. and P. NOLEN. Special education programs and procedures for the disadvantaged with emphasis on children with learning disabilities. Paper presented at the Council for Exceptional Children Conference, Washington, D.C., May, 1967.

HARING, N. G. and E. L. PHILLIPS. *Analysis and modification of classroom behavior.* Englewood Cliffs, N. J.: Prentice-Hall, 1972.

HARING, N. G. and R. J. WHELAN. Experimental methods in education and management of emotionally disturbed children. In W. C. Morse (ed.), *Conflict in the classroom: The education of emotionally disturbed children.* Belmont, Calif.: Wadsworth, 1965.

HARLEM YOUTH OPPORTUNITIES UNLIMITED, INC. *Youth in the ghetto.* New York: Century, 1964.

HARLOW, H. F. Responses by rhesus monkeys to stimuli having multiple-sign values. In Q. McNemar and M. A. Merrill (eds.), *Studies in personality,* 1942. Pp. 105-23.

HARLOW, H. F. Learning theories. In W. Dennis (ed.), *Current trends in psychological theory.* Pittsburgh: University of Pittsburgh Press, 1951.

HARRIS, A. J. *Harris tests of lateral dominance: Manual of directions for administration and interpretation.* (3rd ed.) New York: Psychological Corporation, 1958.

HARRISON, A. and L. NADELMAN. Conceptual tempo and inhibition of movement in black preschool children. *Child Development,* 1972, *43,* 657-68.

HAVIGHURST, R. J. *The public schools of Chicago.* Chicago: The Board of Education of the City of Chicago, 1964.

HEAD, H. *Aphasia and kindred disorders of speech.* Vol. 1. Cambridge: Cambridge University Press, 1926. (a)

HEAD, H. *Aphasia and kindred disorders of speech.* Vol. 2. Cambridge: Cambridge University Press, 1926. (b)

HEBB, D. O. *The organization of behavior.* New York: John Wiley, 1949.

HEBB, D. O. Drives and the conceptual nervous system. *Psychological Review,* 1955, *62,* 243-53.

HÉCAEN, H. and J. AJURIAGUERRA. *Left handedness: Manual superiority and cerebral dominance.* New York: Grune and Stratton, 1964.

HÉCAEN, H., J. AJURIAGUERRA, and J. MASSONET. Les troubles visuoconstructives par lésion pariéto-occipitale droite. *Encepale,* 1951, *40,* 122-79.

HÉCAEN, H., W. PENFILD, C. BERTRAND, and R. MALMO. The syndrome of apractognosia due to lesions of the minor cerebral hemisphere. *Archives of Neurology* (Chicago) , 1956, *75,* 400-434.

HEIDER, E. R. Information processing and the modification of an "impulsive conceptual tempo." *Child Development,* 1972, *43,* 657-68.

HERRICK, C. J. *Neurological foundations of animal behavior.* New York: Holt, 1924.

HESS, R. D. Educability and rehabilitation: The future of the welfare class. *Journal of Marriage and Family,* 1964, *26,* 422-29.

HESS, R. D., V. SHIPMAN, and D. JACKSON. Early experience and the socialization of cognitive modes in children. *Child Development,* 1965, *36,* 869-86.

HIGGINS, C. and C. H. SIVERS. A comparison of Stanford-Binet and colored Raven's progressive matrices I. Q.s for children with low socio-economic status. *Journal of Consulting and Clinical Psychology,* 1958, *20,* 465-68.

HILDRETH, G. H., M. A. GRIFFITHS, and M. E. McGAUVRAN. *Metropolitan readiness tests, form A.* New York: Harcourt, Brace and World, 1965.

HILL, S. D., A. H. McCULLUM, and A. G. SCEAU. Relation of training in motor activity to development of right-left directionality in mentally retarded children: An exploratory study. *Perceptual and Motor Skills,* 1967, *24,* 363-66.

HILLERICH, R. L. Eye-hand dominance and reading achievement. *American Educational Research Journal,* 1964, *1,* 121-26.

HOLLINGSHEAD, A. B. and F. C. REDLICH. *Social class and mental illness.* New York: John Wiley, 1958.

HOLLIS, J. H. and V. V. ST. OMER. Direct measurement of psychopharmocologic response: effects of Chlorpromazine on motor behavior of retarded children. *American Journal of Mental Deficiency,* 1972, *76,* 397-407.

HOPKINS, T. W., H. V. BICE and K. C. COLTON. *Evaluation and education of the cerebral palsied child: New Jersey study.* Washington, D.C.: International Council for Exceptional Children, 1954.

HOUSE, B. J. and D. ZEAMAN. Position discrimination and reversals in low-grade retardates. *Journal of Comparative and Physiological Psychology,* 1959, *52,* 564-65.

HOUSE, B. J. and D. ZEAMAN. Visual discrimination learning and intelligence in defectives of low mental age. *American Journal of Mental Deficiency,* 1960, *65,* 51-58.

HOYT, C. Test reliability obtained by analysis of variance. *Psychometrika*, 1964, 153-60.

HUDSPETH, W. Delacato in review: The neurobehavioral implausibility of the Delacato theory. In M. Douglas (ed.), *Claremount reading conference: 28th yearbook*. California: Claremount Graduate School and Curriculum Laboratory, 1964. Pp. 126-31.

HUNT, J. McV. *Intelligence and experience*. New York: Ronald Press, 1961.

HUNT, J. McV. Intrinsic motivation and its role in psychological development. In D. Levine (ed.), *Nebraska symposium on motivation*. Vol. 13, Lincoln, Neb.: University of Nebraska Press, 1965.

HURLEY, R. *Poverty and mental retardation: A causal relationship*. New York: Vintage, 1969.

INGRAM, T. T. S. A characteristic form of overactive behavior in brain-damaged children. *Journal of Mental Science*, 1956, *102*, 550.

INHELDER, B. and J. PIAGET. *The early growth of logic in the child*. New York: Harper & Row, 1964.

Institutes for the Achievement of Human Potential. *Instruction sheets:* The Romper, 1963; The Harness, 1964.

Institutes for the Achievement of Human Potential. *A summary of concepts, procedures, and organizations*. 1964.

Institutes for the Achievement of Human Potential. *The Doman-Delacato profile and the Doman-Moran graphic summary*. 1963 (revised 1965).

Institutes for the Achievement of Human Potential. *Bulletin*, 1967, *12*, 57-58. (a)

Institutes for the Achievement of Human Potential. *Human Potential*, 1967, *1*. (b)

Institutes for the Achievement of Human Potential. *Statement of objectives*, undated.

IRETON, H., E. THWING, and H. GRAVEM. Infant mental development and neurological status, family socioeconomic status, and intelligence at age four. *Child Development*, 1970, *41*, 937-45.

JACKSON, C. M. and C. A. STEWART. The effects of nutrition in the young upon the ultimate size of the body and of the various organs in the albino rat. *Journal of Experimental Zoology*, 1920, *30*, 97

JACKSON, P. W. and J. W. GETZELS. Psychological health and classroom functioning: A study of dissatisfaction with school among adolescents. *Journal of Educational Psychology*, 1959, *50*, 295-300.

JACKSON, P. W. and B. HUDGINS. Observation schedule for recording pupil attention. Unpublished manuscript, 1965.

JACOBSON, E. *Progressive relaxation*. Chicago: University of Chicago Press, 1938.

JAMES, W. *Principles of psychology*. Vol. 1, New York: Holt, 1890.

JENKINS, J. R., S. GORROFA, and S. GRIFFETHS. Another look at isolation effects. *American Journal of Mental Deficiency*, 1972, *76*, 591-93.

JENSEN, A. Social class, race, and genetics: implications for education. *American Education Research,* 1968, *5,* 1-42.

JENSEN, N. J. and E. M. KING. Effects of different kinds of visual-motor discrimination training on learning to read words. *Journal of Educational Psychology,* 1970, *61,* 90-96.

JOHN, V. P. The intellectual development of slum children: some preliminary findings. *American Journal of Orthopsychiatry,* 1963, *33,* 813-22.

JOHN, V. P. and L. S. GOLDSTEIN. The social context of language acquisition. *Merrill-Palmer Quarterly,* 1964, *10,* 265-75.

JOHNSON, H. W. Society, nutrition, and research. In N. S. Scrimshaw and J. E. Gordon (eds.), *Malnutrition, learning and behavior.* Cambridge, Mass.: MIT Press, 1968.

JOHNSON, O. and H. R. MYKLEBUST. *Learning disabilities: Educational principles and practices.* New York: Grune & Stratton, 1967.

KAGAN, J. Impulsive and reflective children: Significance of conceptual tempo. In J. D. Krumbolz (ed.), *Learning and the educational process.* Chicago: Rand McNally, 1965. Pp. 133-61. (a)

KAGAN, J. Reflection-impulsivity and reading ability in primary grade children. *Child Development,* 1965, *36,* 609-28. (b)

KAGAN, J. Developmental studies in reflection and analysis. In A. H. Kidd and J. H. Rivoire (eds.), *Perceptual development in children.* New York: International Universities Press, 1966. Pp. 487-522.

KAGAN, J. On cultural deprivation. In D. C. Glass (ed.), *Environmental influences.* New York: Rockefeller University Press and Russell Sage Foundation, 1968.

KAGAN, J. and H. A. Moss. *Birth to maturity: A study in psychological development.* New York: John Wiley, 1962.

KAGAN, J., H. Moss, and I. SIGEL. Psychological significance of styles of conceptualization. *Monographs of the Society for Research in Child Development,* 1963, 28, No. 2 (Serial No. 86).

KAGAN, J., L. PEARSON, and L. WELCH. Conceptual impulsivity and inductive reasoning. *Child Development,* 1966, *37,* 583-94.

KAGAN, J., B. ROSMAN, D. DAY, J. ALBERT, and W. PHILLIPS. Information processing in the child: Significance of analytic and reflective attitudes. *Psychological Monographs,* 1964, *78* (1, Whole No. 578).

KAMII, C. K. Socioeconomic class differences in the preschool socialization practices of Negro mothers. Unpublished doctoral dissertation, University of Michigan, 1965.

KAPPELMAN, M. M., E. KAPLAN, and R. L. GANTER. A study of learning disorders among disadvantaged children. *Journal of Learning Disabilities,* 1969, *2,* 262-68.

KATZ, P. A. and M. DEUTSCH. Relation of auditory-visual shifting to reading achievement. *Perceptual and Motor Skills,* 1963, *17,* 327-32.

KAUFFMAN, J. M., D. P. HALLAHAN, J. S. PAYNE, and D. W. BALL, Teaching/

learning: Quantitative and functional analysis of educational performance. *The Journal of Special Education* (in press).

KEIM, R. P. Visual-motor training, readiness, and intelligence of kindergarten children. *Journal of Learning Disabilities,* 1970, *3,* 256-59.

KENDLER, H. H. and T. S. KENDLER. Vertical and horizontal processes in problem solving. *Psychological Review,* 1962, *69,* 1-16.

KENDLER, T. S. and H. H. KENDLER. Reversal and nonreversal shifts in kindergarten children. *Journal of Experimental Psychology,* 1959, *58,* 56-60.

KENNEDY, W. A., V. VAN DE RIET, and J. C. WHITE. A normative sample of intelligence and achievement of Negro elementary school children in the southeastern United States. *Monographs of the Society Research in Child Development,* 1963, *28* (6) .

KEOGH, B. and G. McDONLON. Field dependence, impulsivity and learning disabilities. *Journal of Learning Disabilities,* 1972, *5,* 331-36.

KEOGH, B. F. and C. E. SMITH. Visual-motor ability and school prediction: A seven year study. *Perceptual and Motor Skills,* 1967, *25,* 101-10.

KEPHART, N. C. *The slow learner in the classroom.* Columbus, Ohio: Charles E. Merrill, 1960.

KEPHART, N. C. *The slow learner in the classroom.* (2nd Ed.) Columbus, Ohio: Charles E. Merrill, 1971.

KEPHART, N. C. and A. A. STRAUSS. A clinical factor influencing variations in IQ. *American Journal of Orthopsychiatry,* 1940, *10,* 343-50.

KERSHNER, J. R. Doman-Delacato's theory of neurological organization applied with retarded children. *Exceptional Children,* 1968, *34,* 441-56.

KERSHNER, K., R. DUSEWICZ, and J. KERSHNER. The KDK adaptation of the Vineland Oseretsky motor development tests. In J. Kershner, An investigation of the Doman-Delacato theory of neuropsychology as it applies to trainable mentally retarded children in public school. Unpublished master's thesis, Bucknell University, 1967.

KEYO, A., J. BROZEK, A. HENSCHEL, O. MICKELSEN, and H. L. TAYLOR. *The biology of human starvation.* Minneapolis: University of Minnesota Press, 1950.

KHAN, A. U. Effect of training for visual motor difficulties in severely disturbed children. *Perceptual and Motor Skills,* 1968, *26,* 744.

KINCAID, J. C. Social pathology of foetal and infant loss. *British Medical Journal,* 1965, *1,* 1057-60.

KIRK, S. A. Behavioral diagnosis and remediation of learning disabilities. In Proceedings of the Conference on Exploration into the Problems of the Perceptually Handicapped Child, First Annual Meeting, Vol. 1, Chicago, April 6, 1963.

KIRK, S. A. *The diagnosis and remediation of psycholinguistic disabilities.* Urbana: University of Illinois Press, 1966.

KIRK, S. A. Illinois test of psycholinguistic abilities: its origins and implications. In J. Hellmuth (ed.) , *Learning disorders,* Vol. 3. Seattle: Special Child Publications, 1968.

KIRK, S. A. Lecture appearing in Final Report, U.S.O.E. Contract, Advanced

Institute for Leadership Personnel in Learning Disabilities, sponsored by Department of Special Education, University of Arizona, 1970.

KIRK, S. A., J. J. MCCARTHY, and W. D. KIRK. *Illinois test of psycholinguistic abilities,* experimental edition. Urbana: University of Illinois Press, 1961.

KIRK, S. A., J. J. MCCARTHY, and W. D. KIRK. *Illinois test of psycholinguistic abilities,* revised edition. Urbana: University of Illinois Press, 1968.

KLAPPER, Z. S. and H. WERNER. Developmental deviations in brain-injured (cerebral palsied) members of pairs of identical twins. *Quarterly Journal of Child Behavior,* 1950, *2,* 288-313.

KLAUS, R. A. and S. W. GRAY. The early training project for disadvantaged children: a report after five years. *Monographs of the Society Research in Child Development,* 1968, *33* (4).

KLEIST, K. *Gehirnpathologie.* Leipzig: Barth, 1934.

KLINEBERG, O. *Negro intelligence and selective migration.* New York: Columbia University Press, 1935.

KLØVE, H. and R. M. REITAN. The effect of dysphasia and spatial distortion on Wechsler-Bellevue results. *Archives of Neurological Psychiatry,* 1958, *80,* 708-13.

KOCH, R., B. GRALIKER, W. BRONSTON, and K. FISHER. Mental retardation in early childhood. *American Journal of Diseases of Childhood,* 1965, *109,* 243-51.

KONORSKI, J. *Integrative activity of the brain.* Chicago: University of Chicago Press, 1967.

KRAUS, B. *The basis of human evolution.* New York: Harper & Row, 1964.

KRECH, D., M. R. ROSENWEIG, and E. L. BENNETT. Environmental impoverishment, social isolation, and changes in brain chemistry and anatomy. *Physiological Behavior,* 1966, *1,* 99-104.

KUDER, G. F. and M. W. RICHARDSON. The theory of estimation of test reliability. *Psychometrika,* 1937, *2,* 151-66.

KUGELMASS, I. N., L. E. POULL, and E. L. SAMUEL. Nutritional improvement of child mentality. *American Journal of Medical Science,* 1944, *208,* 631.

LABOV, W. *The study of nonstandard English.* Champaign, Ill.: National Council of Teachers of English, 1970.

LAHADERNE, H. M. Attitudinal and intellectual correlates of attention: A study of four sixth-grade classrooms. *Journal of Educational Psychology,* 1968, *59,* 320-24.

LANGER, J. Werner's theory of development. In P. H. Mussen (ed.), *Carmichael's manual of child psychology.* (3rd ed.) New York: John Wiley, 1970. Pp. 733-72.

LARSEN, E. J. A neurologic-etiologic study on 1000 mental defectives. *Acta Psychiat. et Neurol.,* 1931, *6,* 37-54.

LASHLEY, K. S. *Brain mechanisms and intelligence: A quantitative study of injuries to the brain.* Chicago: University of Chicago Press, 1929.

LAT, J., E. M. WIDDOWSON, and R. A. McCANCE. Some effects of accelerating growth III, behavior and nervous activity. *Proceedings Royal Society,* London, 1961, *153,* 347.

LAUFER, M. W., E. DENHOFF, and G. SOLOMONS. Hyperkinetic impulse disorder in children's behavioral problems. *Psychosomatic Medicine,* 1957, *19,* 38.

LEE, J. M. and W. W. CLARK. *Lee-Clark reading readiness test.* (Rev. ed.) Monterey: California Test Bureau, 1962.

LETON, D. A. Visual-motor capacities and ocular efficiency in reading. *Perceptual and Motor Skills,* 1962, *15,* 406-32.

LEVINE, M. and G. SPIVACK. Rate of reversal of Necker Cube in diffuse brain injury. *Journal of Clinical Psychology,* 1962, *18,* 122-24.

LEWINN, E. B., G. DOMAN, R. J. DOMAN, C. H. DELACATO, E. B. SPITZ, and E. W. THOMAS. Neurological organization: The basis for learning. In J. Hellmuth (ed.), *Learning disorders.* Vol. 2. Seattle: Special Child Publications, 1966. Pp. 48-93.

LEWIS, J. N. The improvement of reading ability through a developmental program in visual perception. *Journal of Learning Disabilities,* 1968, *1,* 652-53.

LEWIS, O. The culture of poverty. *Scientific American,* 1966, *215,* 21.

LILLIE, D. L. The effects of motor development lessons on mentally retarded children. *American Journal of Mental Deficiency,* 1968, *72,* 803-8.

LINDSLEY, D. Emotion. In S. S. Stevens (ed.), *Handbook of experimental psychology.* New York: John Wiley, 1951. Pp. 473-516.

LINTON, T. S. A parent's guide to patterning and floor activity. Media, Pa.: Neurosurgical Institute and Neurosurgical Clinic for Children, undated.

LOWDER, R. G. *Perceptual ability and school achievement.* Winter Haven, Fla.: Winter Haven Lion's Club, 1956.

LOWRY, R. S., W. G. POND, R. H. BARNES, L. KROOK, and J. K. LOOSLI. Influence of caloric level and protein quality on the manifestations of protein deficiency in the young pig. *Journal of Nutrition,* 1962, *78,* 245.

LURIA, A. R. *The role of speech in the regulation of normal and abnormal behavior.* New York: Liveright, 1961.

LURIA, A. R. *Higher cortical functions in man.* New York: Basic Books, 1966. (a)

LURIA, A. R. *Human brain and psychological processes.* New York: Harper & Row, 1966. (b)

LYLE, J. G. Reading retardation and reversal tendency: A factorial study. *Child Development,* 1968, *40,* 833-43.

MACCOBY, E. E., E. M. DOWLEY, J. W. HAGEN, and R. DEGERMAN. Activity level and intellectual functioning in normal preschool children. *Child Development,* 1965, *36,* 761-70.

MACCOBY, E. E. and J. HAGEN. Effects of distraction upon centeral versus incidental recall: Developmental trends. *Journal of Experimental Child Psychology,* 1965, *2,* 280-89.

MacQuarrie, C. W. *A perceptual testing and training guide for kindergarten teachers.* Winter Haven, Fla.: Lions Research Foundation, 1967.

Maisel, A. Q. Hope for brain-injured children. *Readers Digest,* October 1964, 135-40.

Maloney, M. P., T. S. Ball, and C. L. Edgar. Analysis of the generalizability of sensory-motor training. *American Journal of Mental Deficiency,* 1970, *74,* 458-69.

Maloney, M. P. and L. E. Payne. Note on the stability of changes in body image due to sensory-motor training. *American Journal of Mental Deficiency,* 1970, *74,* 708.

Mann, L. Perceptual training: Misdirections and redirections. *American Journal of Orthopsychiatry,* 1970, *40,* 30-38.

Masland, R. L. Unproven methods of treatment. *Pediatrics,* 1966, *37,* 713-14.

Masland, R. L., S. B. Sarason, and T. Gladwin. *Mental subnormality: biological, psychological, and cultural factors.* New York: Basic Books, 1958.

Maslow, P., M. Frostig, D. W. Lefever, and J. R. B. Whittlesey. The Marianne Frostig developmental test of visual perception: 1963 standardization. *Perceptual and Motor Skills,* 1964, *19,* 463-99.

Matthews, C. G. and R. M. Reitan. Correlations of Wechsler-Bellevue rank orders of subtest means in lateralized and non-lateralized brain-damaged groups. *Perceptual and Motor Skills,* 1964, 19, 391-99.

Mayer, S. A. Maternal and infant care project in Newark: a progress report. *Public Health News,* 1965, *48.*

McArdle, M. T. Auditory discrimination in preschool children. Unpublished master's thesis, University of Tennessee, 1965.

McCarthy, J. J. Qualitative and quantitative differences in the language abilities of young cerebral palsied. Unpublished doctoral dissertation, University of Illinois, 1957.

McCarthy, J. J. and S. A. Kirk. *Illinois test of psycholinguistic abilities: Experimental edition.* Urbana: University of Illinois, 1961.

McCarthy, J. J. and J. F. McCarthy. *Learning disabilities.* Boston: Allyn and Bacon, 1969.

McCarthy, J. J. and J. L. Olson. *Validity studies on the Illinois test of psycholinguistic abilities.* Urbana: University of Illinois Press, 1964.

McConnell, O. L. Perceptual versus verbal mediation in the concept learning of children. *Child Development,* 1964, *35,* 1373-83.

McCormick, C. C., B. Poetter, J. N. Schnobrich, and W. S. Footlik. Improvement in reading achievement through perceptual-motor training. *Research Quarterly,* 1968, *39,* 627-33.

McCormick, C. C., J. N. Schnobrich, and S. W. Footlik. The effect of perceptual motor training on reading achievement. *Academic Therapy,* 1969, *4,* 171-76.

McFie, J., M. F. Piercy, and O. L. Zangwill. Visual spatial agnosia associated with lesions of the right hemisphere. *Brain,* 1950, *73,* 167-90.

McGhie, A. *Pathology of attention.* Baltimore: Penguin Books, 1969.

McKay, E. An exploratory study of the psychological effect of a severe hearing impairment. Unpublished doctoral dissertation, Syracuse University, 1952.

McNeill, D. The development of language. In P. H. Mussen (ed.), *Carmichael's manual of child psychology.* (3rd ed.) New York: John Wiley, 1970. Pp. 1051-69.

Meichenbaum, D. and J. Goodman. Reflection-impulsivity and verbal control of motor behavior. *Child Development,* 1969, *40,* 27-34.

Miller, D. Y. A comparative study of exogenous and endogenous mentally retarded boys on some aspects of the reading process. Unpublished doctoral dissertation, Syracuse University, 1958.

Miller, G. A. What is information measurement? *American Psychologist,* 1953, *8,* 3-11.

Miller, S. M., F. Riessman, and A. A. Seagull. Poverty and self indulgence: a critique of the non-deferred gratification pattern. In L. A. Ferman, J. L. Kornbluh, and A. Haber (eds.), *Poverty in America.* Ann Arbor: University of Michigan Press, 1965.

Minde, K., D. Lewin, G. Weiss, H. Lavigueur, V. Douglas, and R. Sykes. The hyperactive child in elementary school: A 5 year, controlled, follow-up. *Exceptional Children,* 1971, *38,* 215-21.

Minde, K., G. Webb, and D. Sykes. Studies on the hyperactive child. IV. Prenatal and paranatal factors associated with hyperactivity. *Developmental Medicine and Child Neurology,* 1968, 10, 355-63.

Mönckeberg, F. Effect of early marasmic malnutrition on subsequent physical and psychological development. In N. S. Scrimshaw and J. E. Gordon (eds.), *Malnutrition, learning and behavior.* Cambridge, Mass.: MIT Press, 1968.

Money, J. Dyslexia: A postconference review. In J. Money (ed.), *Reading disability: Progress and research needs in dyslexia.* Baltimore: Johns Hopkins Press, 1962. Pp. 9-33.

Money, J. Reading disorders in children. In J. Brenneman (ed.), *Kelley practice of pediatrics.* Vol. 4. Hagerstown, Md.: Hoeber, 1967. Pp. 1-14.

Moody, P. *Introduction to evolution.* (2nd ed.) New York: Harper & Row, 1962.

Murphy, L. *The widening world of childhood.* New York: Basic Books, 1962.

Myers, P. I. and D. D. Hammill. *Methods for learning disorders.* New York: John Wiley, 1969.

Myklebust, H. R., *The psychology of deafness.* New York: Grune and Stratton, 1960.

Myklebust, H. R. *The psychology of deafness; sensory deprivation, learning, and adjustment.* (2nd ed.) New York: Grune and Stratton, 1964, xii, 423.

Myklebust, H. R. Learning disabilities: Definition and overview. In H. R. Myklebust (ed.), *Progress in learning disabilities.* New York: Grune and Stratton, 1968.

Myklebust, H. R. Lecture given in Final Report, U.S.O.E. Contract, Advanced

Institute for Leadership Personnel in Learning Disabilities, sponsored by Department of Special Education, University of Arizona, 1970.

NAEYE, R. L. Undernutrition, growth, and development. *New England Journal of Medicine,* 1970, *282,* 975-76.

NEELY, J. E. A study of the relationship of figure background difficulty and school achievement in cerebral palsied children. Unpublished doctoral dissertation. Syracuse University, 1958.

NEISSER, U. *Cognitive psychology.* New York: Appleton-Century-Crofts, 1967.

NEWELL, A., J. C. SHAW, and H. A. SIMON. Elements of a theory of human problem solving. *Psychological Review,* 1958. *65,* 151-66.

NIELSEN, H. H. Social vulnerability and adjustment of cerebral palsied children. *Scandinavian Journal of Psychology,* 1964, *5,* 26-32.

NOLEN, P. A., H. P. KUNZELMANN, and N. G. HARING. Behavioral modification in a junior high learning disabilities classroom. *Exceptional Children,* 1967, *34,* 163-68.

NORRIS, H. J. An exploration of the relation of certain theoretical constructs to a behavioral syndrome of brain pathology. Unpublished doctoral dissertation, Syracuse University, 1958.

NOVAKOVA, V., J. FALTIN, V. FLANDERA, P. HAHN, and O. KOLDOVSKY. Effect of early and late weaning on learning in adult rats. *Nature,* 1962, *193,* 280.

O'CONNOR, C. Effects of selected physical activities upon motor performance, perceptual performance, and academic achievement of first graders. *Perceptual and Motor Skills,* 1969, *29,* 703-9.

O'DONNELL, P. A. and J. EISENSON. Delacato training for reading achievement and visual-motor integration. *Journal of Learning Disabilities,* 1969, *2,* 441-46.

OLSON, A. The Frostig developmental test of visual perception as a predictor of specific reading abilities with second grade children. *Elementary English,* 1966, *43,* 869-72, (a)

OLSON, A. Relation of achievement test scores and specific reading abilities to the Frostig test of visual perception. *Optometric Weekly,* 1966, *33.* (b)

OLSON, A. School achievement, reading ability, and specific visual perceptual skills in third grade. *Reading Teacher,* 1966, *19,* 490-92. (c)

OLSON, A. Factor analytic studies of the Frostig developmental test of visual perception. *Journal of Special Education,* 1968, *2,* 429-33.

ORTON, S. *Reading, writing and speech problems in children.* New York: Norton, 1937.

OSGOOD, C. E. A behavioristic analysis of perception and language as cognitive phenomena. In J. S. Bruner (ed.), *Contemporary approaches to cognition.* Cambridge, Mass: Harvard University Press, 1957. Pp. 75-118. (a)

OSGOOD, C. E. Motivational dynamics of language. In M. R. Jones (ed.), *Nebraska symposium on motivation.* Lincoln: University of Nebraska Press, 1957. Pp. 348-424. (b)

PAINTER, G. The effect of a rhythmic and sensory-motor activity program on perceptual motor spatial abilities of kindergarten children. *Exceptional Children,* 1966, *33,* 113-16.

PAINTER, G. Remediation of maladaptive behavior and psycholinguistic deficits in a group sensory-motor activity program. *Academic Therapy Quarterly,* 1968, *3,* 233-45.

PALKES, H., M. STEWART, and B. KAHANA. Porteus maze performance of hyperactive boys after training in self-directed verbal commands. *Child Development,* 1968, *39,* 817-26.

PARASKEVOPOULOS, J. N. and S. A. KIRK. *The development and psychometric characteristics of the revised Illinois test of psycholinguistic abilities.* Urbana: University of Illinois Press, 1969.

PASAMANICK, B. and H. KNOBLOCK. Epidemiologic studies on the complications of pregnancy and the birth process. In G. Caplan (ed.), *Prevention of mental disorders in children.* New York: Basic Books, 1961.

PASAMANICK, B., A. M. LILIENFELD, and M. E. ROGERS. Pregnancy experience and the development of behavior disorders in children. *American Journal of Psychiatry,* 1956, *112,* 613.

PASCHAL, F. C. The trend in theories of attention. *Psychological Review,* 1941, *48,* 383-403.

PATERSON, A. and O. L. ZANGWILL. Disorders of visual space perception associated with lesions of the right hemisphere. *Brain,* 1944, *67,* 331-58.

PAVENSTEDT, E. A comparison of the child-rearing environment of upper-lower and very low-lower class families. *American Journal of Orthopsychiatry,* 1965, *35,* 89-98.

PEARSON, P. B. Scientific and technical aims. In N. S. Scrimshaw and J. E. Gordon (eds.), *Malnutrition, learning and behavior.* Cambridge, Mass.: MIT Press, 1968.

PENFIELD, W. and L. ROBERTS. *Speech and brain-mechanisms.* Princeton: Princeton University Press, 1959.

PETER, L. J. *Prescriptive teaching.* New York: McGraw-Hill, 1965, *10,* 246.

PETTIGREW, T. F. *Profile of the Negro American.* Princeton: Van Nostrand Reinhold, 1964.

PIAGET, J. and B. INHELDER. *The child's conception of space.* London: Routledge and Kegan Paul, 1966.

PIAGET, J. and A. MORPH. Les isomorphismes partiels entre les structures logiques et les structures perceptives. In J. S. Bruner et al., (ed.), *Logique et perception.* (Etudes d'epistemologie genetique, 6). Paris: Presses Universitaires de France, 1958. Pp. 49-116.

PINTNER, R. D., B. V. CUNNINGHAM, and W. N. DUROST. *Pintner-Cunningham primary test.* Cleveland: World, 1946.

PLATT, B. S., C. R. C. HEARD, and R. J. C. STEWARD. Experimental protein calorie deficiency. In H. N. Munro and J. B. Alison (eds.), Vol. I., *Mammalian protein metabolism.* New York: Academic Press, 1964.

Pope, L. Motor activity in brain-injured children. *American Journal of Ortho-psychiatry*, 1970, *40*, 783-94.

Popham, J. *Criterion-referenced instruction: an introduction.* (Audio Tape) Los Angeles: Vimcet Associates, 1970.

Poppelreuter, W. *Die psychischen schadigung durch kopfschuss im kriege, 1914-1917.* 1918.

Porteus, S. E. *Qualitative performance in the maze test.* Vineland, N.J.: Smith, 1942.

Potter, M. C. Perception of symbol orientation and early reading process, *Contributions to education*, No. 939, 1949. Teachers College, Columbia University.

Prescott, J. Psychology of maternal social deprivation and the etiology of violent aggressive behavior: a special case of sensory deprivation. Unpublished manuscript presented at McGill University, 1967.

Preston, M. I. Late behavioral aspects found in cases of prenatal, natal, and postnatal anoxia. *Journal of Pediatrics,* 1956, *26,* 353.

Pribram, K. H. A review of theory in physiological psychology. *Annual Review of Psychology,* 1960, *11,* 1-40.

Rabinovitch, M. S. Syntax and retention in good and poor readers. *Canadian Psychologist,* 1968, *9,* 142-53.

Rajalakshmi, R. The psychological status of under-privileged children reared at home and in an orphanage in south India. *Indian Journal of Mental Retardation,* 1968, *1,* 53.

Rajalakshmi, R., K. Govindarajan, and C. Ramakrishnan. Effects of dietary protein content on visual discrimination, learning and brain biochemistry in the albino rat. *Journal of Neurochemistry,* 1965, *12,* 261.

Rappaport, S. R. (ed.) . *Childhood aphasia and brain damage: A definition.* Narbreth, Pa.: Livingston, 1964.

Rappaport, S. R. *Childhood aphasia and brain damage.* Vol. II. *Differential diagnosis.* Narbreth, Pa.: Livingston, 1965.

Rappaport, S. R. *Public education for children with brain dysfunction.* Syracuse: Syracuse University Press, 1969.

Read, M. S. Malnutrition and learning. *American Education,* 1969, *5,* 14.

Reed, H. C. and R. M. Reitan. Intelligence test performance of brain damaged subjects with lateralized motor deficits. *Journal of Consulting Psychology,* 1963, *27,* 102-6.

Reed, H. C. Lateralized finger agnosia and reading achievement at ages 6 and 10. *Child Development,* 1967, *38,* 213-20.

Reitan, R. M. Certain differential effects of left and right cerebral lesions in human adults. *Journal of Comparative and Physiological Psychology,* 1955, *48,* 474-77.

Reitan, R. M. Relationships between neurological and psychological variables and their implications for reading instruction. Mimeo. Elaboration upon an abbreviated paper entitled: Relationships between neurological and psychological variables and their implications for reading instruction. In H. A. Robinson (ed.), *Meeting individual differences in reading.* Chicago: University of Chicago Press, 1964. Pp. 100-110.

REYNOLDS, M. C. and B. BALOW. Categories and variables in special education. *Exceptional Children,* 1972, *38,* 357-66.

RIBOT, T. *The psychology of attention.* London: Longmans, Green, 1890.

RIDBERG, E. H., R. D. PARKE, and E. M. HETHERINGTON. Modification of impulsive and reflective cognitive styles through observation of film-mediated models. *Developmental Psychology,* 1971, *5,* 369-77.

RIDER, R. V., M. TABACK, and H. KNOBLOCH. Associations between premature birth and socio-economic status. *American Journal of Public Health,* 1955, *45,* 1022-28.

RIESEN, A. H. The development of visual perception in man and chimpanzee. *Science,* 1947, *106,* 107-8.

RIESEN, A. H. Relations between sensory deprivation and development of the nervous system. In U.S. Department of Health, Education, and Welfare, *Perspectives on human deprivation: biological, psychological, and sociological.* Washington, D.C., 1968, 293-97.

RIESSMAN, F. *The culturally deprived child.* New York: Harper & Row, 1962.

ROACH, E. F. and N. C. KEPHART. *The Purdue perceptual-motor survey.* Columbus, O.: Charles E. Merrill, 1966.

ROBAYE-GEELEN, F. Une analyse des fonctions perceptivo-intellectuelles chez les enfants atteints de troubles moteurs d'origine cerebrale. *Archivio Italiano di Pediatria E. Puericatura,* 1967, *25,* 67-76.

ROBAYE-GEELEN, F. *The brain damaged child.* Brussels: Charles Dessart, 1969.

ROBBINS, M. The Delacato interpretation of neurological organization: An empirical study. Unpublished doctoral dissertation, University of Chicago, 1965. (a)

ROBBINS, M. Influence of special programs on the development of mental age and reading. Report of Project No. S-349. Washington, D.C.: Cooperative Research Branch, Office of Education, Department of Health, Education, and Welfare, 1965. (b)

ROBBINS, M. Creeping, laterality and reading. *Academic Therapy Quarterly,* 1966, *1,* 200-206. (a)

ROBBINS, M. A study of the validity of Delacato's theory of neurological organization. *Exceptional Children,* 1966, *32,* 517-23. (b)

ROBBINS, M. Test of the Doman-Delacato rationale with retarded readers. *Journal of the American Medical Association,* 1967, *202,* 389-93.

ROBBINS, M. and G. V. GLASS. The Doman-Delacato rationale: A critical analysis. In J. Hellmuth (ed.), *Educational therapy.* Vol. II. Seattle: Special Child Publications, 1969.

ROBINOW, M. Field measurement of growth and development. In N. S. Scrimshaw and J. E. Gordon (eds.), *Malnutrition, learning and behavior.* Cambridge, Mass.: MIT Press, 1968.

ROBINSON, H. M., M. C. LETTON, L. MOZZI, and A. A. ROSENBLOOM. An evaluation of the children's visual achievement forms at Grade 1. *American Journal of Optometry,* 1958, *35,* 515-25.

ROHMANN, C. G., S. M. GARN, M. A. GUZMAN, M. FLURES, M. BÉHAR, and E. PAO. Osseous development of Guatemalan children on low protein diets. *Federation Proceedings,* 1964, *23,* 338.

ROSENGREN, W. R. Social class becoming "ill." In A. B. Shostak and W. G. Gomberg (eds.), *Blue collar world.* Englewood Cliffs, N.J.: Prentice-Hall, 1964.

ROSENZWEIG, M. R. Environmental complexity, cerebral change, and behavior. *American Psychologist,* 1966, *21,* 321-32.

ROSNER, B. S. Final report on planning grant: Treatment of brain-injured children. Vocational Rehabilitation Administration, National Association for Retarded Children, Gwen Foundation, 1967. (a)

ROSNER, B. S. Outcomes of treatment of brain-damaged children: Are controlled studies possible? Unpublished manuscript, 1967. (b)

ROSS, R. A. Some important factors in perinatal mortality statistics in a rural state. *American Journal of Obstetrics and Gynecology,* 1964, *88,* 342-48.

ROSS, S. A. Effects of an intensive motor skills training program on young educable mentally retarded children. *American Journal of Mental Deficiency,* 1969, *73,* 920-26.

ROST, K. J. and D. C. CHARLES. Academic achievement of brain injured and hyperactive children in isolation. *Exceptional Children,* 1967, *34,* 125-26.

ROSVOLD, H. E., A. F. MIRKSY, I. SARASON, E. D. BRANSOME, and L. H. BECK. A continuous performance test of brain change. *Journal of Consulting Psychology,* 1956, *20,* 343-52.

ROTH, F. A. The treatment of the sick. In F. Kosa, A. Antonousky, and I. K. Zola (eds.), *Poverty and health.* Cambridge, Mass.: Harvard University Press, 1969.

RUBIN, S. S. A reevaluation of figure-ground pathology in brain damaged children. *American Journal of Mental Deficiency,* 1969, *74,* 111-15.

RUDNICK, M., G. M. STERRITT, and M. FLAX. Auditory and visual perception and reading ability. *Child Development,* 1967, *38,* 581-87.

RYCKMAN, D. B. and R. WIEGERINK. The factors of the Illinois test of psycholinguistic abilities: A comparison of 18 factor analyses. *Exceptional Children,* 1969, *36,* 107-13.

SAMUELS, I. Reticular mechanisms and behavior. *Psychological Bulletin,* 1959, *56,* 1-25.

SARASON, S. B. *Psychological problems in mental deficiency.* New York: Harper, 1949.

SCHACHTEL, E. G. *Metamorphosis.* New York: Basic Books, 1959.

SCHAEFER, E. A. and N. BAYLEY. Maternal behavior, child behavior, and their intercorrelations from infancy through adolescence. *Monographs of the Society for Research in Child Development,* 1963, *28,* No. 3.

SCHIFFMAN, G. B. Critique [of Cohen]. *Journal of Learning Disabilities,* 1969, *2,* 505-6.

SCHULMAN, J. L., J. C. KASPAR, and F. M. THRONE. *Brain damage and behavior —A clinical experimental study.* Springfield, Ill.: Charles C Thomas, 1965.

SCHWEBEL, A. I. Effects of impulsivity on performance of verbal tasks in middle and lower class children. *American Journal of Orthopsychiatry,* 1966, *36,* 13-21.

SCRIMSHAW, N. S. Malnutrition, learning, and behavior. *American Journal of Clinical Nutrition,* 1967, *20,* 495.

SCRIMSHAW, N. S. and J. E. GORDON (eds.). *Malnutrition, learning, and behavior.* Cambridge, Mass.: MIT Press, 1968.

SEMMEL, M. I. and M. W. MUELLER. A factor analysis of the Illinois test of psycholinguistic abilities with mentally retarded children. Unpublished manuscript, George Peabody College, 1962.

SEN, A. and A. M. CLARKE. The effect of distraction during and after learning a serial recall task. *American Journal of Mental Deficiency,* 1968, *73,* 46-49. (a)

SEN, A. and A. M. CLARKE. Some factors affecting distractibility in the mental retardate. *American Journal of Mental Deficiency,* 1968, *73,* 50-60. (b)

SHAW, M. A study of some aspects of perception and conceptual thinking in ideopathic epileptic children. Unpublished doctoral dissertation, Syracuse University, 1955.

SHAW, M. C. and W. M. CRUICKSHANK. The use of the Bender Gestalt test with epileptic children. *Journal of Clinical Psychology,* 1956, *12,* 192-93. (a)

SHAW, M. C. and W. M. CRUICKSHANK. The use of the marbleboard test to measure psychopathology in epileptics. *American Journal of Mental Deficiency,* 1956, *60,* 813-87. (b)

SHERRINGTON, C. S. *The integrative action of the nervous system.* New York: Scribners, 1906.

SHERRINGTON, C. S. *Man on his nature.* (2nd ed.) Cambridge: Cambridge University Press, 1951.

SHORES, R. E. and P. A. HAUBRICH. Effect of cubicles in educating emotionally disturbed children. *Exceptional Children,* 1969, *36,* 21-26.

SHUEY, A. M. *The testing of Negro intelligence.* Lynchburg, Va.: J. P. Bell, 1958.

SHURE, G. and W. HALSTEAD. Cerebral localization of intellectual process. *Psychological Monographs: General and Applied,* 1958, *72,* No. 12.

SIEVERS, D. J. Development and standardization of a test of psycholinguistic growth in preschool children. Unpublished doctoral dissertation, University of Illinois, 1955.

SIGEL, I. E. Some thoughts on directions for research in cognitive development. In United States Department of Health, Education, and Welfare, *Perspectives on human deprivation biological, psychological, and sociological.* Washington, D.C.: 1968.

SIGEL, I. E. and P. P. OLMSTED. Styles of categorization among lower-class kindergarten children. Paper presented at the American Educational Research Association Annual Meeting. New York, 1967.

SILBERMAN, C. *Crisis in black and white.* New York: Random House, 1964.

SILVER, A. Diagnostic value of three drawing tests for children. *Journal of Pediatrics,* 1950, *37,* 129-43.

SILVER, A. and R. HAGIN. Specific reading disability: A delineation of the syndrome and relationship to cerebral dominance. *Comprehensive Psychiatry,* 1960, *1,* 126-34.

SILVERMAN, M., A. DAVIDS, and J. M. ANDREWS. Powers of attention and academic achievement. *Perceptual and Motor Skills,* 1963, *17,* 243-49.

SILVERSTEIN, A. B. Variance components in the developmental tests of visual perception. *Perceptual and Motor Skills,* 1965, *20,* 973-76.

SIMONSON, M., R. W. SHERWIN, H. H. HANSON, and B. F. CHOW. Maze performance of offspring of underfed mother rats. *Federation Proceedings,* 1968, *27,* 727.

SINGER, J. L. Psychosocial deprivation and the development of imaginative capacity in children and adults. In United States Department of Health, Education, and Welfare, *Perspectives on human deprivation biological, psychological, and sociological.* Washington, D.C.: 1968.

SINGER, R. N. and J. W. BRUNK. Relation of perceptual-motor ability and intellectual ability in elementary school children. *Perceptual and Motor Skills,* 1967, *24,* 967-70.

SKEELS, H. M. and H. B. DYE. A study of the effects of differential stimulation on mentally retarded children. *Proceedings of the American Association on Mental Deficiency,* 1939, *44,* 114-36.

SKEELS, H. M. and M. SKODAK. Adult status of individuals who experienced early intervention. Paper presented at the 90th annual meeting of the American Association on Mental Deficiency, Chicago, Ill., May 10-14, 1966.

SKEFFINGTON, A. M. Papers and lectures. Duncan, Okla.: Optometric Extension Program, 1926-1965.

SKUBIC, V. and M. ANDERSON. The interrelationship of perceptual-motor achievement, academic achievement, and intelligence of fourth-grade children. *Journal of Learning Disabilities,* 1970, *3,* 413-20.

SLOAN, W. The Lincoln-Oseretsky motor development scale. *Genetic Psychology Monographs,* 1955, 51, 183-252.

SMALL, V. H. Ocular pursuit abilities and readiness for reading. Unpublished doctoral dissertation, Purdue University, 1958.

SNYDER, R. T. and S. L. FREUD. Reading readiness and its relation to maturational unreadiness as measured by the spiral aftereffect and visual-perceptual techniques. *Perceptual and Motor Skills,* 1967, *25,* 841-54.

SOKOLOV, Y. N. *Perception and the conditioned reflex.* New York: Macmillan, 1963.

SOLAN, T. A. Visual perception and reading deficits. *Journal of Learning Disabilities,* 1969, *2,* 661-62.

SOLLEY, C. M. and G. Murphy. *Development of the perceptual world.* New York: Basic Books, 1960.

SONTAG, L. W., C. T. BAKER, and V. L. NELSON. Mental growth and personality development: A longitudinal study. *Monographs of the Society for Research in Child Development,* 1958, *23,* No. 2.

SPEARMAN, C. "General intelligence," objectively determined and measured. *American Journal of Psychology,* 1904, *15,* 201-93.

SPEARMAN, C. *The abilities of man.* London: Macmillan, 1927.

SPERLING, G. A model for visual memory tasks. *Human Factors,* 1963, *5,* 19-31.

SPITZ, H. H. Field theory in mental deficiency. In N. R. Ellis (ed.), *Handbook of mental deficiency.* New York: McGraw-Hill, 1963.

SPITZER, R. L., R. RABKIN, and Y. KRAMER. The relationship between "mixed dominance" and reading disabilities. *Journal of Pediatrics,* 1959, *54,* 76-80.

SPIVACK, G. Perceptual processes. In N. R. Ellis (ed.), *Handbook of mental deficiency.* New York: McGraw-Hill, 1963.

SPIVACK, G. and M. LEVINE. The spiral aftereffect and reversible figures as measures of brain damage and memory. *Journal of Personality,* 1957, *25,* 1-11.

SPRAGUE, R. H. Learning difficulties for first grade children diagnosed by the Frostig visual perceptual tests. *Dissertation Abstracts,* 1964, *25,* 4006-7.

SPRAGUE, R. L., K. R. BARNES, and J. S. WERRY. Methylphenidate and Thioridazine: learning, reaction time, activity, and classroom behavior in disturbed children. *American Journal of Orthopsychiatry,* 1970, *40,* 615-28.

STAATS, A. W. *Learning, language, and cognition.* New York: Holt, Rinehart and Winston, 1968.

STAATS, A. W., B. A. BREWER, and M. C. GROSS. Learning and cognitive development: Representative samples, cumulative-hierarchical learning, and experimental-longitudinal methods. *Monographs of the Society for Research in Child Development,* 1970, *35,* No. 8 (Serial No. 141).

STEPHENS, W. E., E. S. CUNNINGHAM, and B. J. STIGLER. Reading readiness and eye-hand preference patterns in first grade children. *Exceptional Children,* 1967, *33,* 481-88.

STERRITT, G. M. and M. RUDNICK. Auditory and visual rhythm perception in relation to reading ability in fourth-grade boys. *Perceptual and Motor Skills,* 1966, *22,* 859-64. (a)

STERRITT, G. M. and M. RUDNICK. Reply to Birch and Belmont. *Perceptual and Motor Skills,* 1966, *22,* 662 (b).

STOCH, M. B. and P. M. SMYTHE. The effect of undernutrition during infancy on subsequent brain growth and intellectual development. *South Africa Medical Journal,* 1967, *41,* 1027.

STOCH, M. B. and P. M. SMYTHE. Undernutrition during infancy and subsequent brain growth and intellectual development. In N. S. Scrimshaw and J. E. Gordan (eds.), *Malnutrition, learning and behavior.* Cambridge, Mass.: MIT Press, 1968.

STONE, M. and N. L. PIELSTICK. Effectiveness of Delacato treatment with kindergarten children. *Psychology in the Schools,* 1969, *6,* 63-68.

STRAUSS, A. A. Beitrage zur enisteilung, entstehung und klinik der schwersten schwachsinnsforme. *Arch. of Psych. u. Nerv.*, 1933, *9*, 693.

STRAUSS, A. A. Diagnosis and education of the cripple-brained, deficient child. *Journal of Exceptional Children*, 1943, *9*, 163-68.

STRAUSS, A. A. and N. C. KEPHART. Rate of mental growth in a constant environment among higher grade moron and borderline children. Paper presented at American Association on Mental Deficiency, 1939.

STRAUSS, A. A. and N. C. KEPHART. Behavior differences in mentally retarded children as measured by a new behavior rating scale. *American Journal of Psychiatry*, 1940, *96*, 1117-23.

STRAUSS, A. A. and N. C. KEPHART. *Psychopathology and education of the brain-injured child*. Vol. II. *Progress in theory and clinic*. New York: Grune and Stratton, 1955.

STRAUSS, A. A. and L. E. LEHTINEN. *Psychopathological education of the brain-injured child*. New York: Grune and Stratton, 1947.

STRAUSS, A. A. and H. WERNER. Deficiency in the finger schema in relation to arithmetic disability (finger agnosia and acalculia). *American Journal of Orthopsychiatry*, 1938, *8*, 719-25.

STRAUSS, A. A. and H. WERNER. Disorders of conceptual thinking in the brain-injured child. *Journal of Nervous and Mental Disease*, 1942, *96*, 153-72.

STRAUSS, H. Uber konstruktive apraxie. *Mschr. Psychiat.*, 1924, *56*, 65-124.

STROLE, L., T. S. LANGER, S. T. MICHAEL, M. K. OPLER, and T. A. C. RENNIE. *Mental health in the metropolis: the midtown Manhattan study*. New York: McGraw-Hill, 1962.

STROOP, J. R. Studies in interference in serial verbal reactions. *Journal of Experimental Psychology*, 1935, *18*, 643-61.

SUTTON, S., G. HAKEREM, J. ZUBIN, and M. PORTNOY. The effect of shift of sensory modality on serial reaction time: a comparison of schizophrenics and normals. *American Journal of Psychology*, 1961, *74*, 224-32.

TABA, H. Cultural deprivation as a factor in school learning. *Merrill-Palmer Quarterly*, 1964, *10*, 147-59.

TALKINGTON, L. W. Frostig visual perceptual training with low-ability level retarded. *Perceptual and Motor Skills*, 1968, *27*, 505-6.

TEUBER, H. L. and R. S. LIEBERT. Specific and general effects of brain injury in man: Evidence of both from a single task. *Archives of Neurology and Psychiatry*, 1958, *80*, 403-7.

TEUBER, H. L. and S. WEINSTEIN. Performance on a formboard task after penetrating brain injury. *Journal of Psychology*, 1954, *38*, 177-90.

THOMSON, A. M. Historical perspectives of nutrition, reproduction, and growth. In N. S. Scrimshaw and J. E. Gordon (eds.), *Malnutrition, learning and behavior*. Cambridge: Massachusetts Institute of Technology, 1968.

THOMPSON, J. D. The quality of human reproduction. In *Proceedings, the White House conference on mental retardation*. Washington: U.S. Government Printing Office, 1963.

THURSTONE, L. L. Primary mental abilities. Psychometric Monographs, 1938, *1*, 1-121.

TIEGS, E. and W. W. CLARK. *Manual: California achievement tests—complete battery.* Los Angeles: California Test Bureau, 1957.

TITCHENER, E. B. *The psychology of feeling and attention.* New York: Macmillan, 1924.

TRIPPE, M. J. A study of the relationship between visual-perceptual ability and selected personality variables in a group of cerebral palsied children. Unpublished doctoral dissertation, Syracuse University, 1958.

TYLER, L. E. *The psychology of human differences.* New York: Appleton-Century-Crofts, 1965.

UDENFRIEND, S. Factors in amino acid metabolism which can influence the central nervous system. *American Journal of Clinical Nutrition,* 1963, *12,* 287.

United Cerebral Palsy Association of Texas. The Doman-Delacato treatment of neurologically handicapped children. *Information Bulletin,* undated.

United States Department of Health, Education, and Welfare. *Perspectives on human deprivation biological, psychological, and sociological.* Washington, D.C.: 1968.

United States Department of Health, Education, and Welfare. Ten-state nutrition survey in the United States 1968-1970. Preliminary report to the Congress, April 1971.

UZGIRIS, I. C. Sociocultural factors in cognitive development. In H. C. Haywood (ed.), *Social-cultural aspects of mental retardation.* New York: Appleton-Century-Crofts, 1970.

VALVERDE, F. Apical dendrite spines of the visual cortex and light deprivation in the mouse. *Experimental Brain Research,* 1967, *3,* 337-52.

VEGAS, O. V. and R. L. FRYE. Effects of brain damage on perceptual performance. *Perceptual and Motor Skills,* 1963, *17,* 662.

VERNON, P. E. The structure of human abilities. New York: John Wiley, 1950.

VON SENDEN, M. *Raum und gestaltauffassung bei operierten blindgeborenen vor und nach der operation.* Leipzig: Barth, 1932.

VYGOTSKY, L. S. *Thought and language.* New York: John Wiley, 1962.

WACHS, T. D. Environmental stimulation and early intellectual development: a broader look at a one-sided problem. Paper presented to Indiana Psychological Association, West Lafayette, 1967.

WADA, J. and T. RASMUSSEN. Intracarotid injection of sodium amytal for the lateralization of cerebral speech dominance: Experimental and clinical observations. *Journal of Neurosurgery,* 1960, *17,* 266-82.

WATERLOW, J. C. and C. B. MENDES. Composition of muscle in malnourished human infants. *Nature,* 1957, *180,* 1361.

WATKINS, H. L. Visual perceptual training for the moderately retarded child. *American Journal of Mental Deficiency,* 1957, *61,* 455-60.

WEBB, R. C. Sensory-motor training of the profoundly retarded. *American Journal of Mental Deficiency*, 1970, *74*, 283-95.

WECHSLER, D. *Wechsler intelligence scale for children.* New York: Psychological Corporation, 1949.

WEDELL, K. The visual perception of cerebral palsied children. *Child Psychology and Psychiatry.* 1960, *1*, 215-27.

WEENER, P., L. S. BARRITT, and M. I. SEMMEL. A critical evaluation of the Illinois test of psycholinguistic abilities. *Exceptional Children,* 1967, *36*, 373-80.

WEINER, M. and S. FELDMANN. Validation studies of a reading prognosis test for children of lower and middle socioeconomic status. *Educational and Psychological Measurement,* 1963.

WEINSTEIN, S. Body image and brain damage. Paper presented at American Psychological Association, Washington, D.C., September 1958.

WEPMAN, J. M. *Auditory discrimination test.* Language Research Associates, 1958.

WERNER, H. Process and achievement: A basic problem of education and developmental psychology. *Harvard Educational Review,* 1937, May.

WERNER, H. *Comparative psychology of mental development.* New York: International Universities Press, 1948.

WERNER, H. The concept of development from a comparative and organismic point of view. In D. B. Harris (ed.), *The concept of development.* Minneapolis: University of Minnesota Press, 1957. Pp. 125-48.

WERNER, H. and M. BOWERS. Auditory-motor organization in two clinical types of mentally deficient children. *Journal of Genetic Psychology,* 1941, *59*, 85-99.

WERNER, H. and A. A. STRAUSS. Problems and methods of functional analysis in mentally deficient children. *Journal of Abnormal and Social Psychology,* 1939, *34,* 37-62. (a)

WERNER, H. and A. A. STRAUSS. Types of visuo-motor activity in their relation to low and high performance ages. *Proceedings of the American Association on Mental Deficiency,* 1939, *44*, 163-68. (b)

WERNER, H. and A. A. STRAUSS. Causal factors in low performance. *American Journal of Mental Deficiency,* 1940, *45*, 213-18.

WERNER, H. and A. A. STRAUSS. Pathology of figure-background relation in the child. *Journal of Abnormal and Social Psychology,* 1941, *36*, 236-48.

WERNER, H. and B. D. THUMA. Critical flicker frequency in children with brain injury. *American Journal of Psychology,* 1942, *55*, 394-99. (a)

WERNER, H. and B. D. THUMA. A deficiency in the perception of apparent motion in children with brain injury. *American Journal of Psychology,* 1942, *55*, 58-67. (b)

WHIPPLE, C. I. and F. A. KODMAN. A study of discrimination and perceptual learning with retarded readers. *Journal of Educational Psychology,* 1969, *60*, 1-5.

WHITE, S. The learning theory approach. In P. H. Mussen (ed.), *Carmichael's manual of child psychology.* Vol. L. New York: John Wiley, 1970. Pp. 657-701.

WIDDOWSON, E. M. Nutritional deprivation in psychobiological development: studies in animals. Washington, D.C., Pan American Health Organization, *Scientific Bulletin of WHO,* 1966, *134,* 27-38.

WIDDOWSON, E. M. and R. A. McCANCE. Some effects of accelerating growth I, general somatic development. *Proceedings Royal Society, London, Series B,* 1960, *152,* 188.

WILLIAMS, H. L., C. F. GIESEKING, and A. LUBIN. Interaction of brain injury with peripheral vision and set. *Journal of Consulting Psychology,* 1961, *25,* 543-48.

WINICK, M. Malnutrition and brain development. *Journal of Pediatrics,* 1969, *74,* 667.

WINICK, M. and A. NOBLE. Cellular response in rat during malnutrition at various ages. *Journal of Nutrition,* 1966, *89,* 300.

WINICK, M. and P. ROSSO. The effect of severe early malnutrition on cellular growth of the human brain. *Pediatric Research,* 1969, *3,* 181.

WITKIN, H. A., R. B. DYK, H. F. FATERSON, D. R. GOODENOUGH, and S. A. KARP. *Psychological differentiation: Studies of development.* New York: John Wiley, 1962.

WOHLWILL, J. F. From perception to inference: A dimension of cognitive development. In W. Kessen and C. Kuhlman (eds.), *Thought in the young child.* Chicago: Society for Research in Child Development, University of Chicago Press, 1962.

WOLF, J. *Temple Fay, M.D.—Progenitor of the Doman-Delacato treatment procedures.* Springfield, Ill.: Charles C Thomas, 1968.

WORTIS, H., J. L. BARDACH, R. CUTLER, R. RUE, and A. FREEDMAN. Childrearing practices in a low-socio-economic group. *Pediatrics,* 1963, *32,* 298-307.

WORTIS, J. Poverty and retardation: bio-social factors. In J. Wortis (ed.), *Mental retardation: an annual review, I.* New York: Grune and Stratton, 1970.

WORTIS, J. (ed.). *Mental retardation: an annual review, III.* New York: Grune and Stratton, 1971.

WUNDT, W. *Outlines of psychology.* C. H. Judd (trans.), Leipzig: Wilhelm Engelmann, 1897.

YAMAMOTO, K., J. P. JONES, and M. B. ROSS. A note on the processing of classroom observation records. *American Education Research Journal,* 1972, *9,* 29-44.

YANDO, R. M. and J. KAGAN. The effect of teacher tempo on the child. *Child Development,* 1968, *39,* 27-34.

ZANGWILL, O. *Cerebral dominance and its relation to psychological function.* Edinburgh: Oliver and Boyd, 1960.

ZEAMAN, D., and B. J. HOUSE. The role of attention in retardate discrimination learning. In N. R. Ellis (ed.), *Handbook of mental deficiency*. New York: McGraw-Hill, 1963.

ZEIGARNICK, B. V. *The pathology of thinking*. New York: Consultants Bureau, 1965:

ZIGLER, E. Mental retardation: Current issues and approaches. In L. Hoffman and M. Hoffman (eds.), *Review of child development research*. Vol. 2. New York: Russell Sage Foundation, 1966. Pp. 107-68.

Index